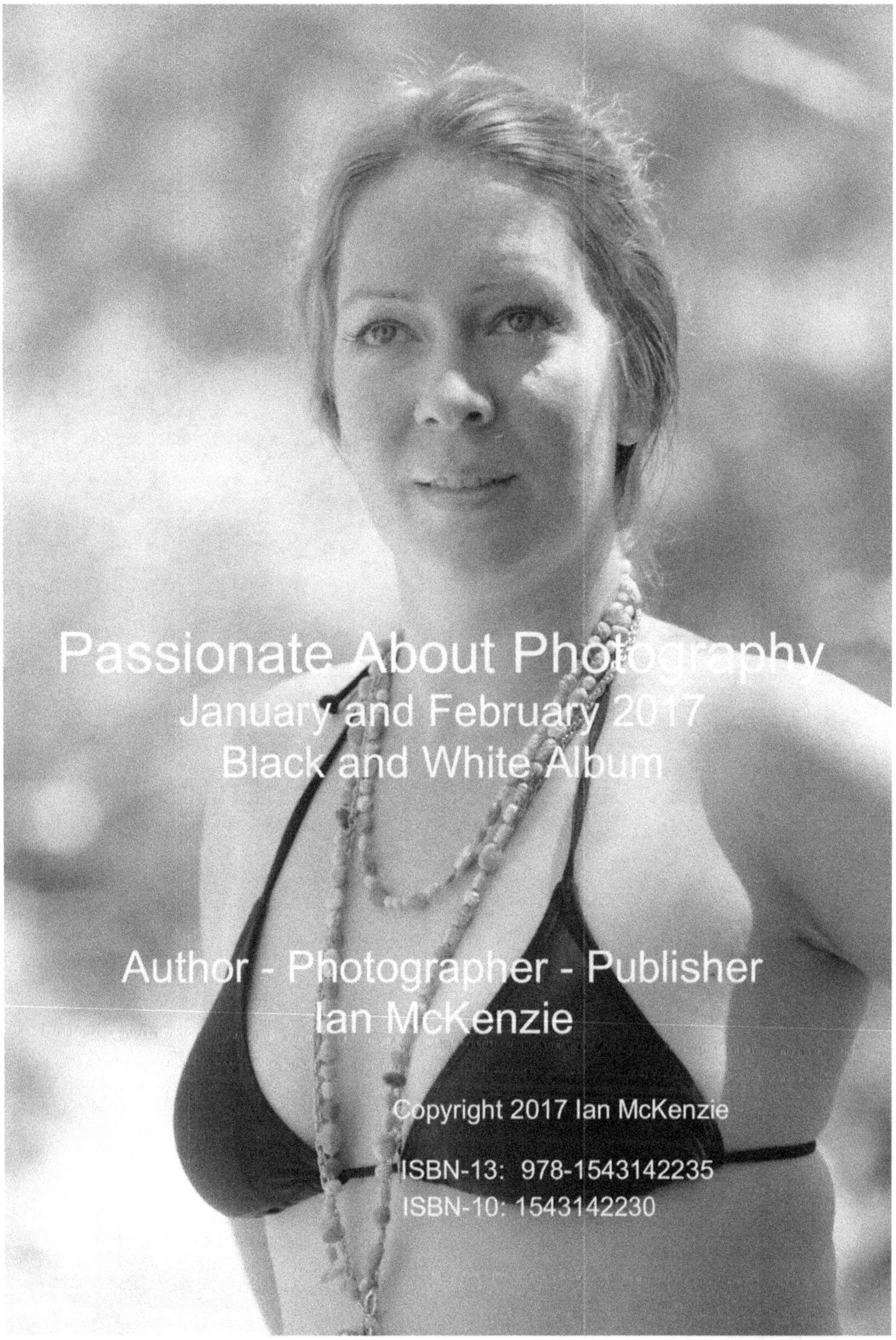

Passionate About Photography
January and February 2017
Black and White Album

Author - Photographer - Publisher
Ian McKenzie

ISBN-13: 978-1543142235
ISBN-10: 1543142230

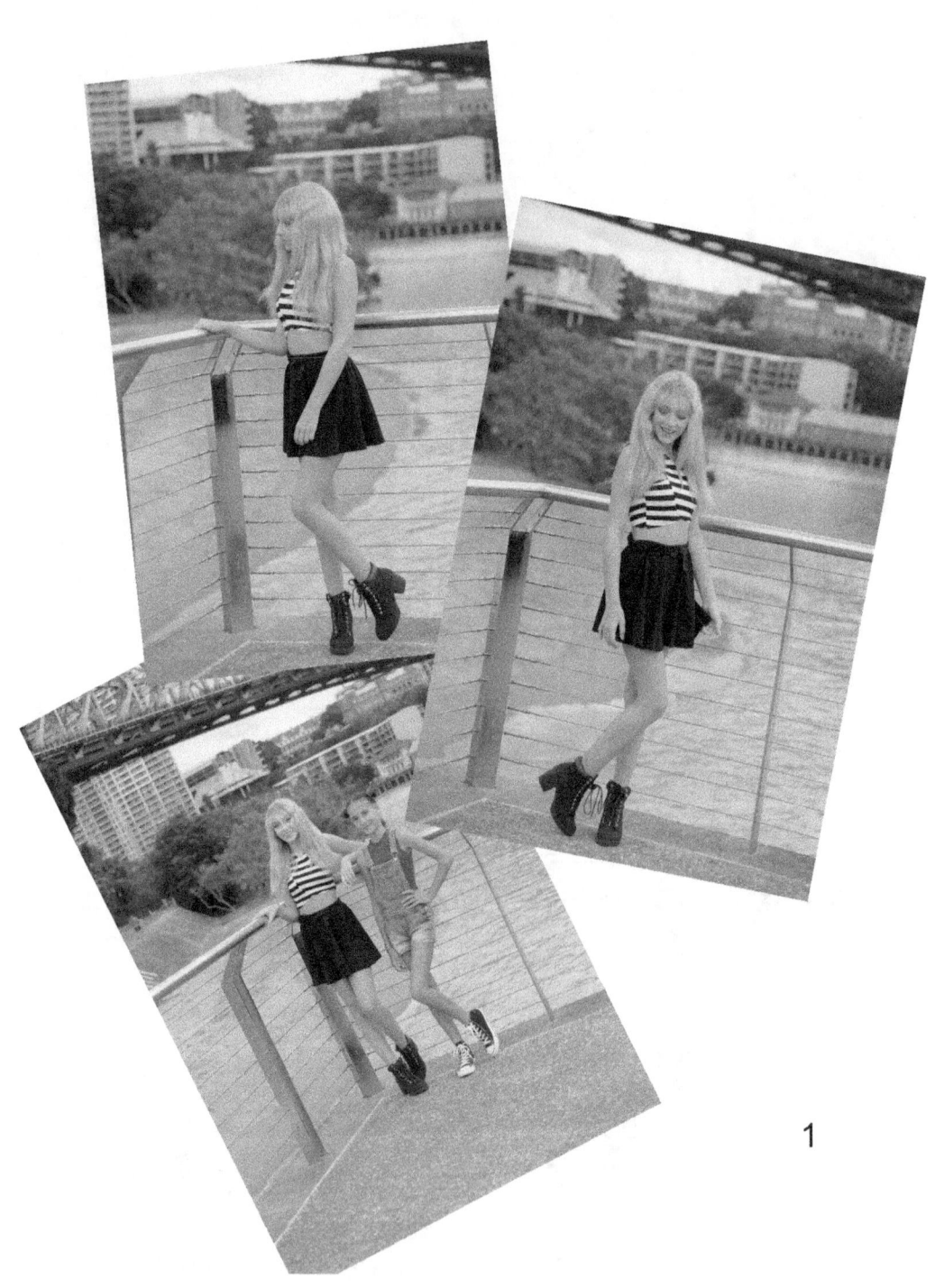

1

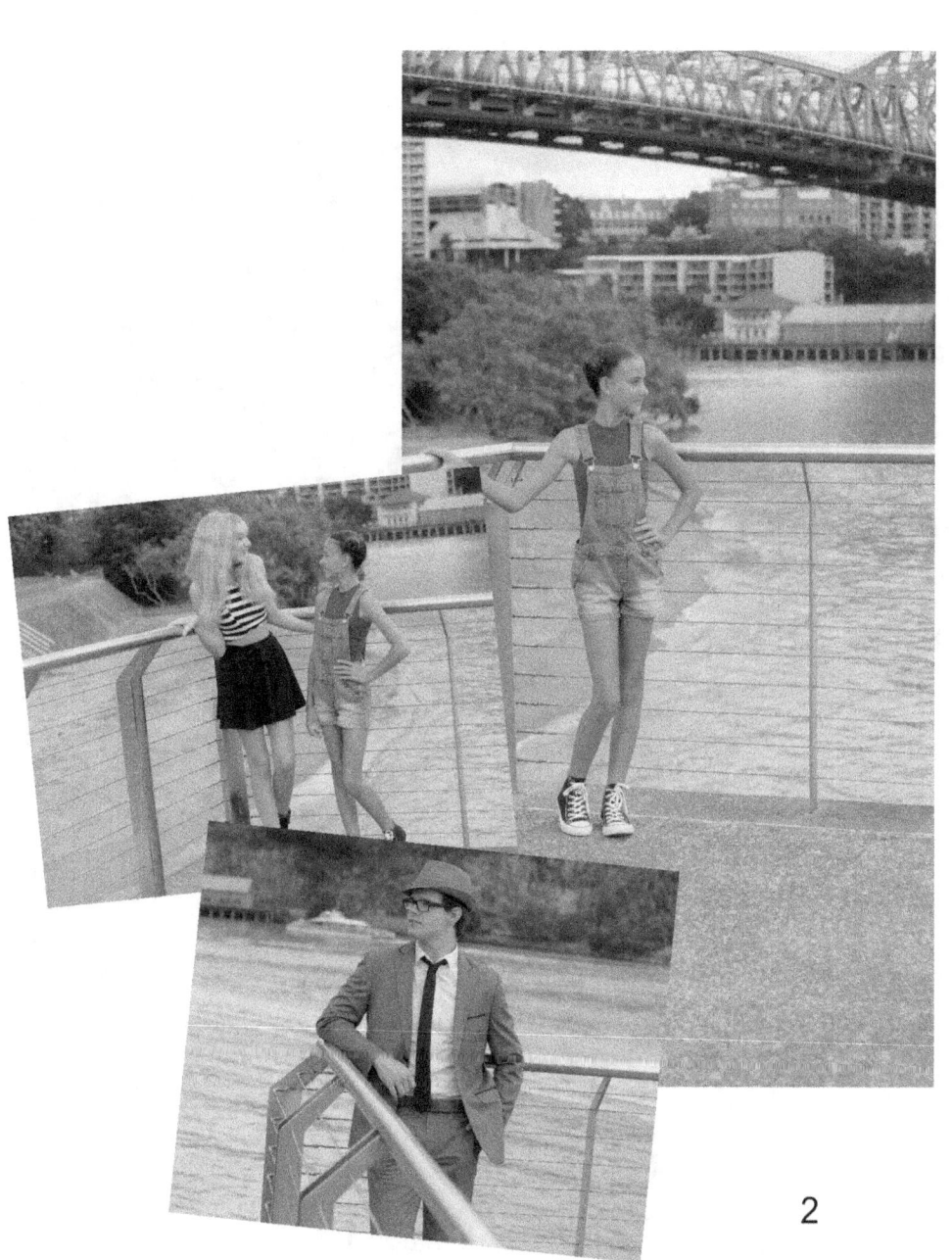

2

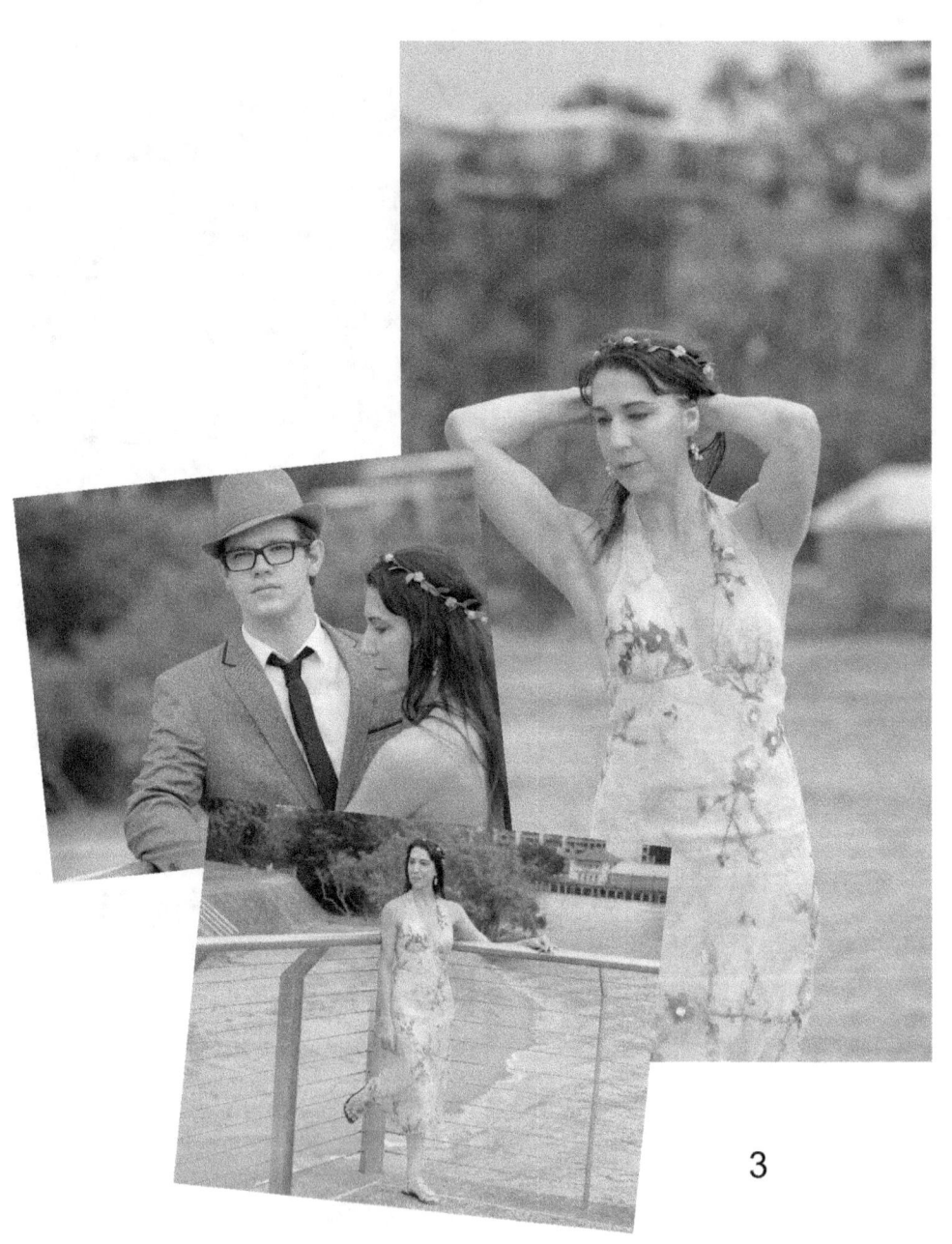

3

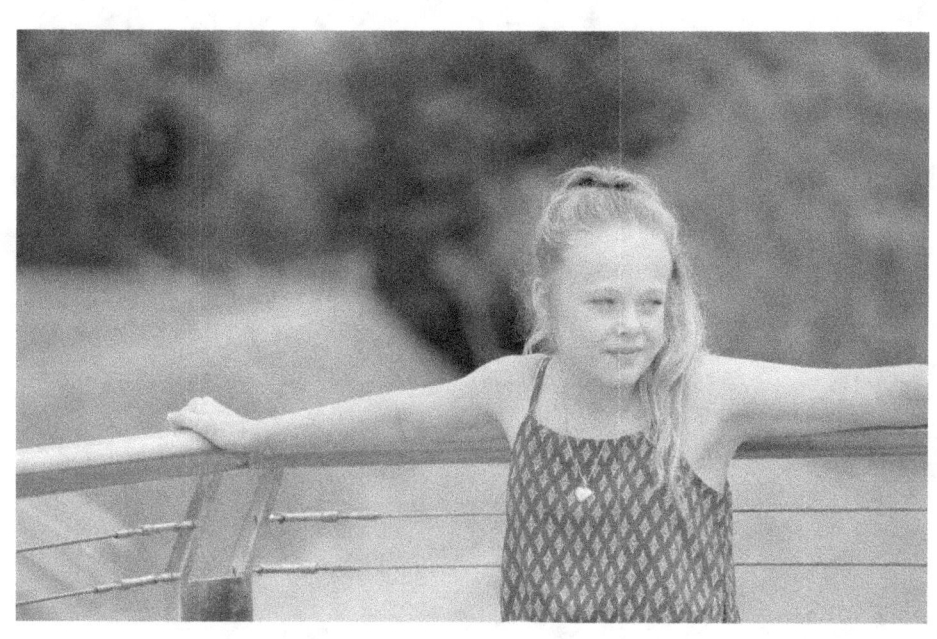

4

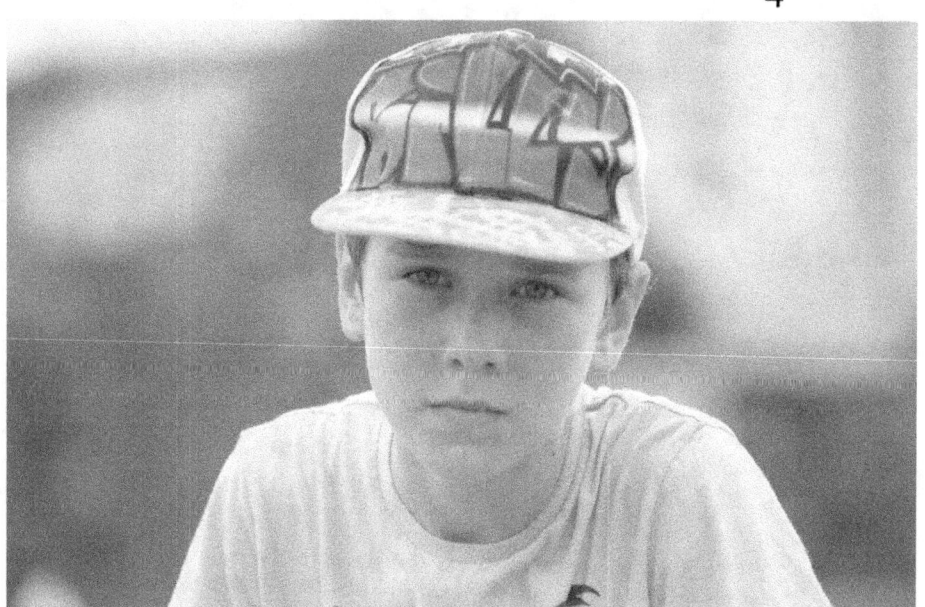

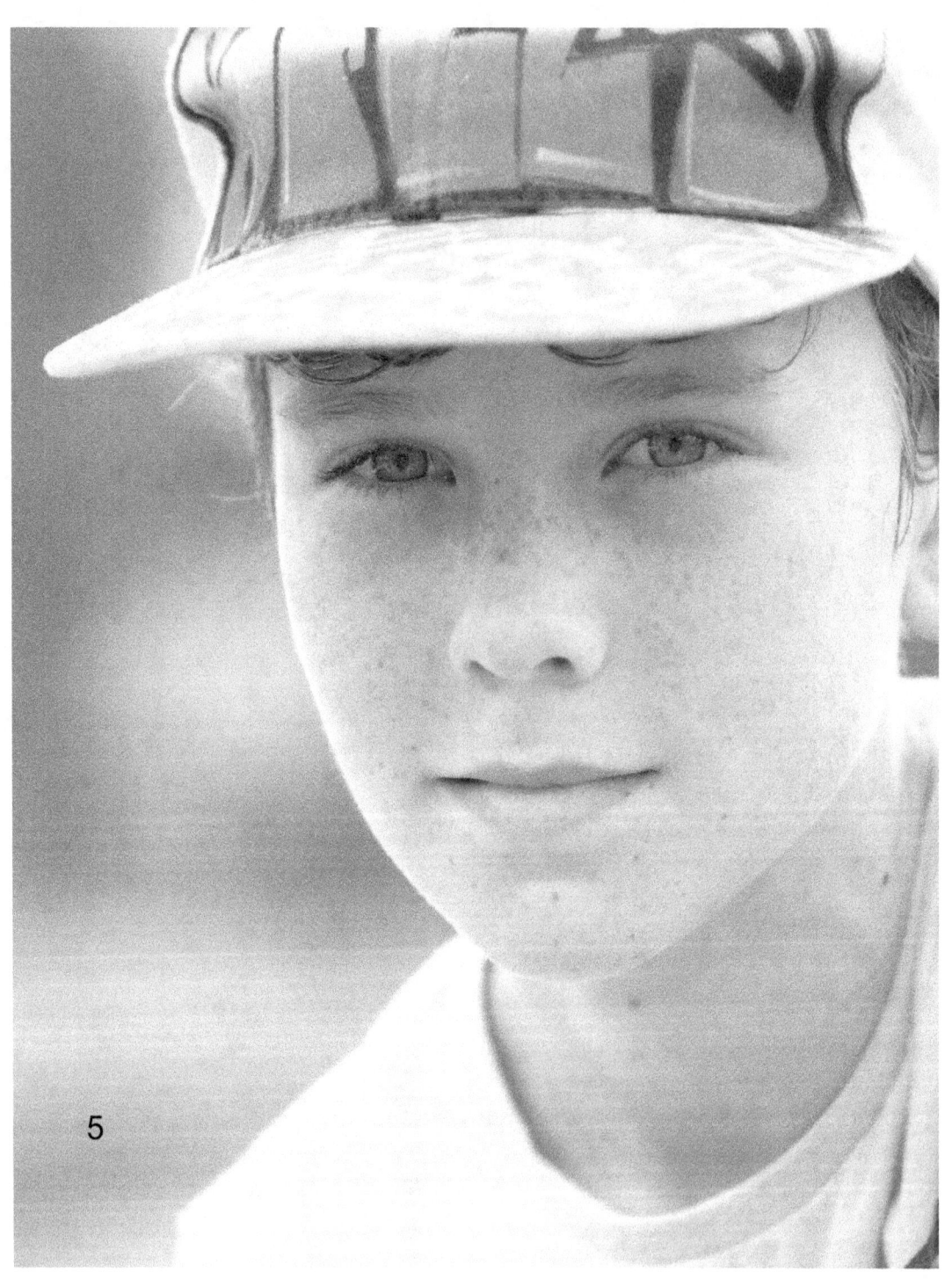

5

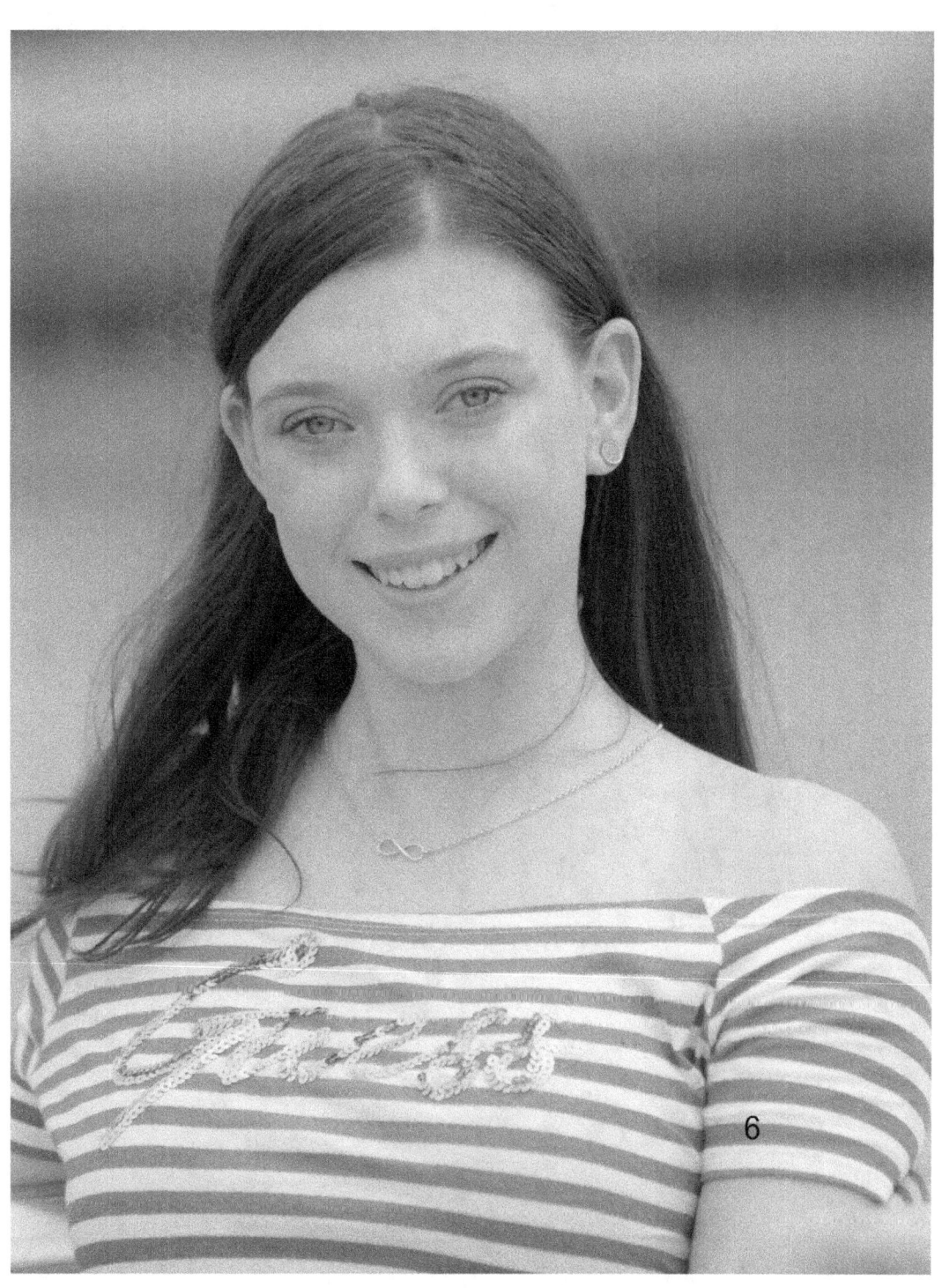

6

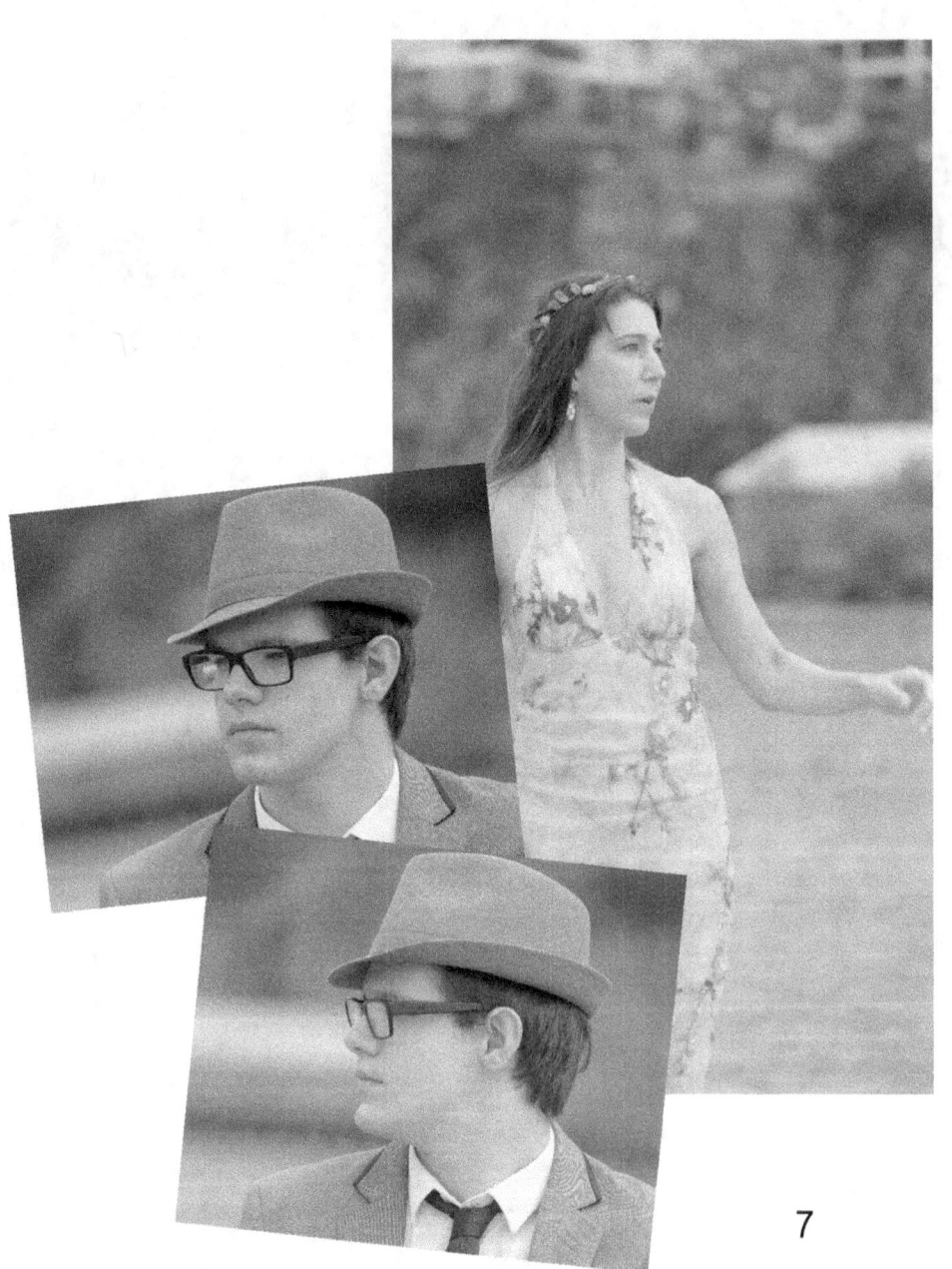

7

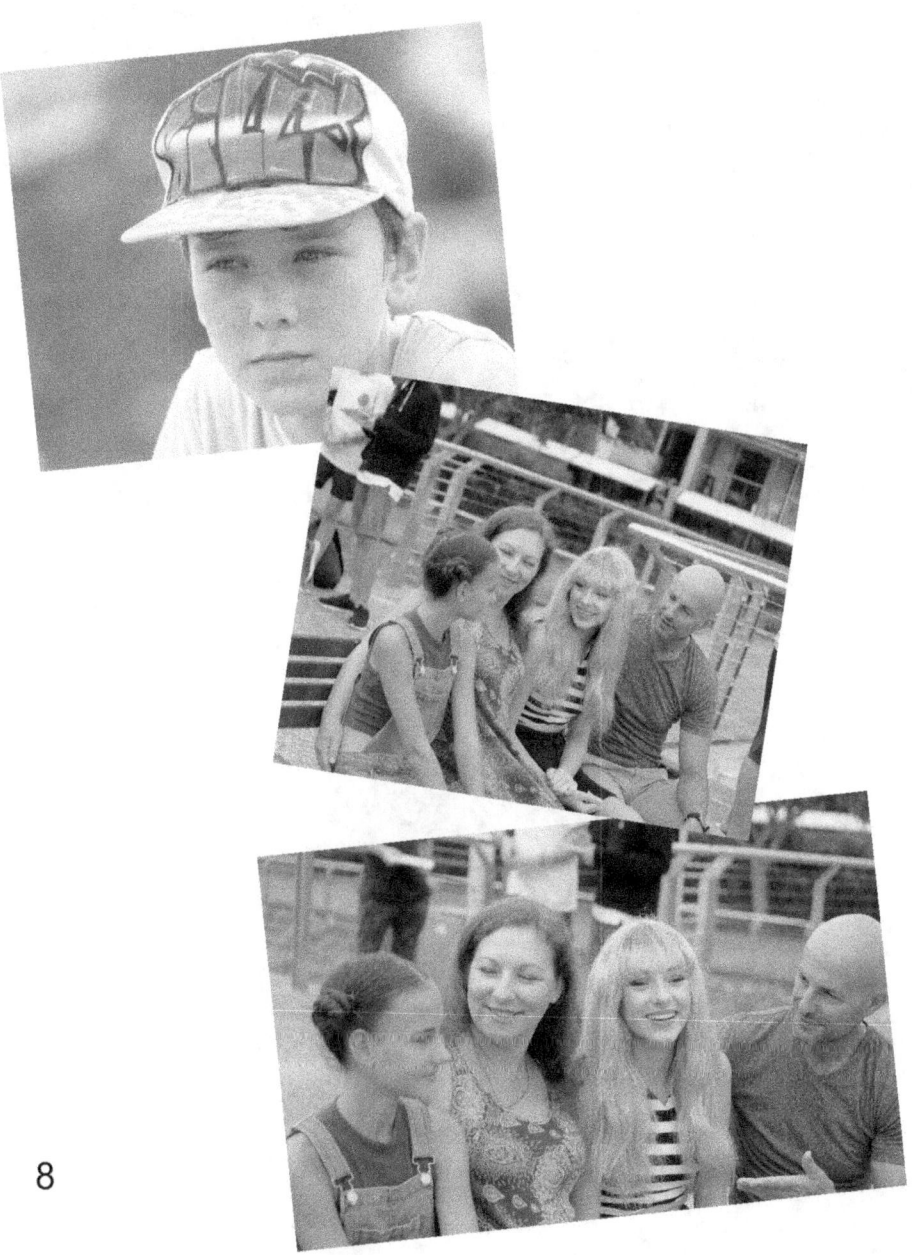

8

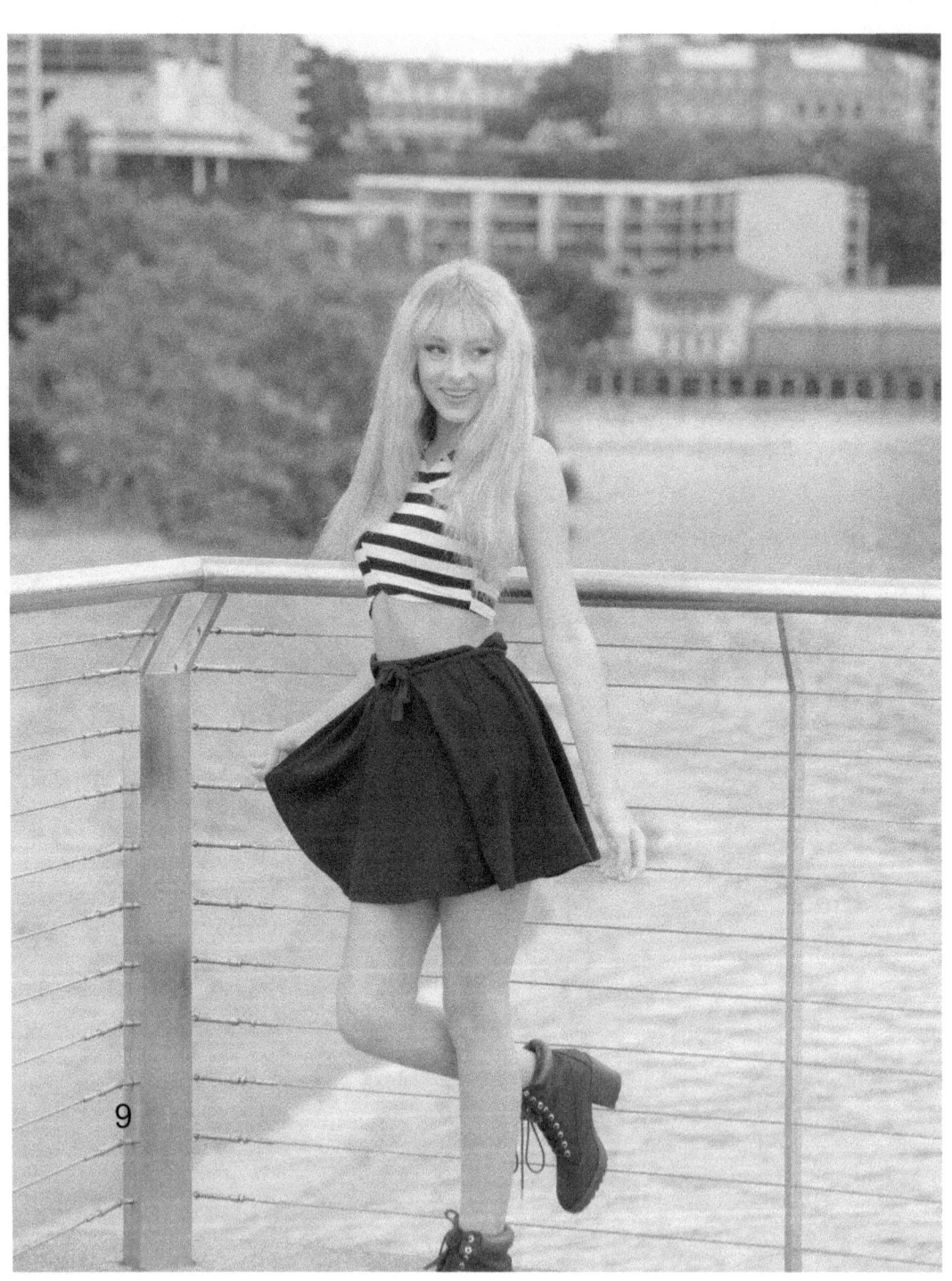

9

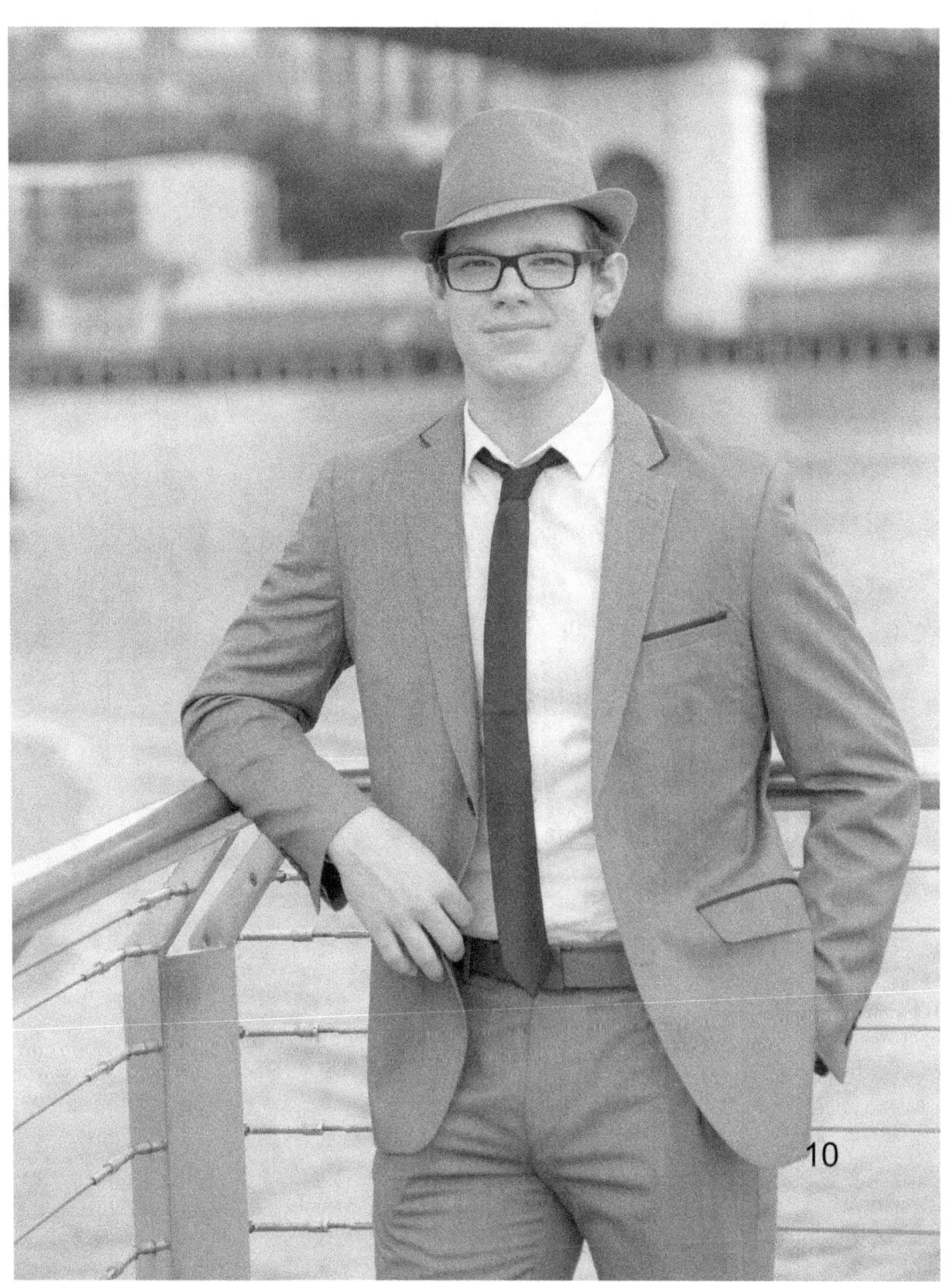

10

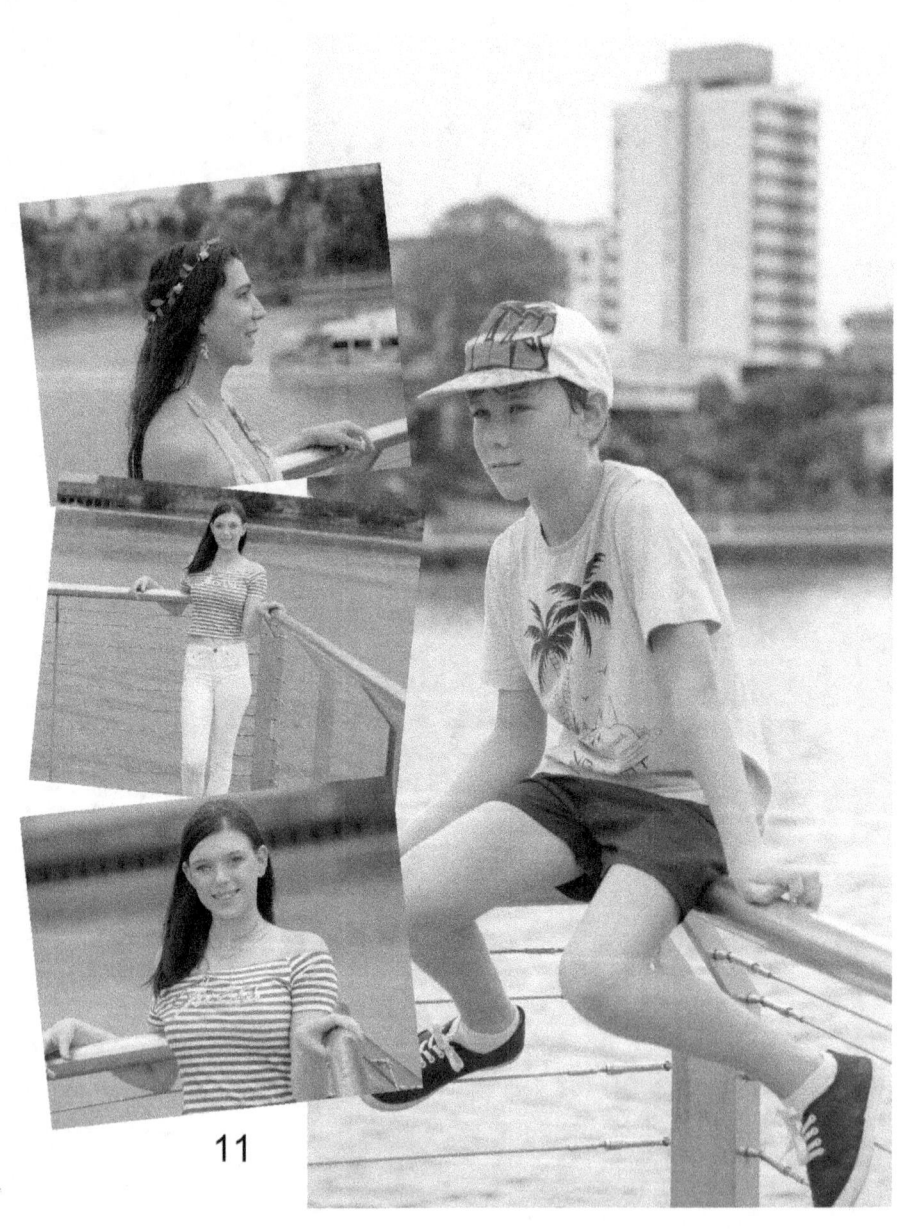

11

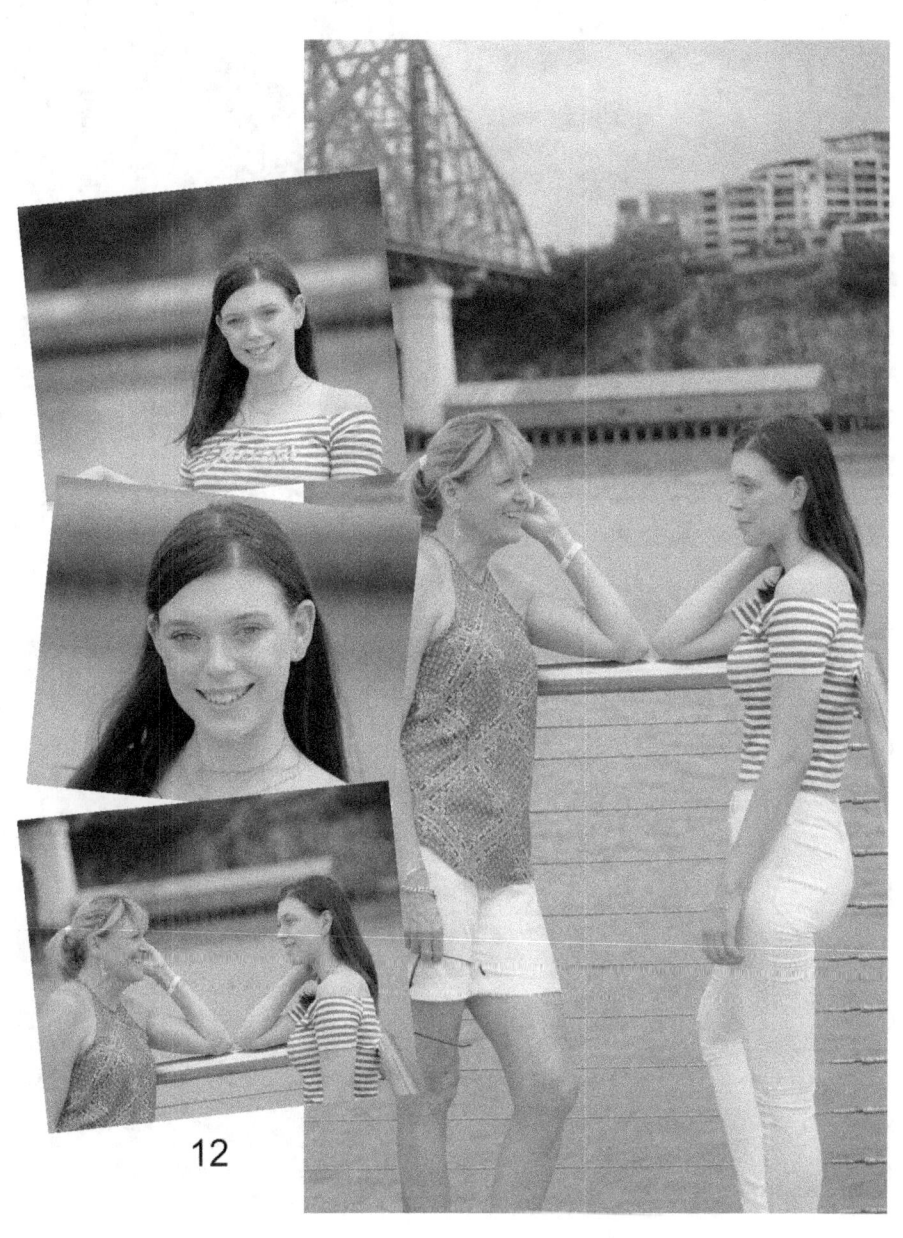

12

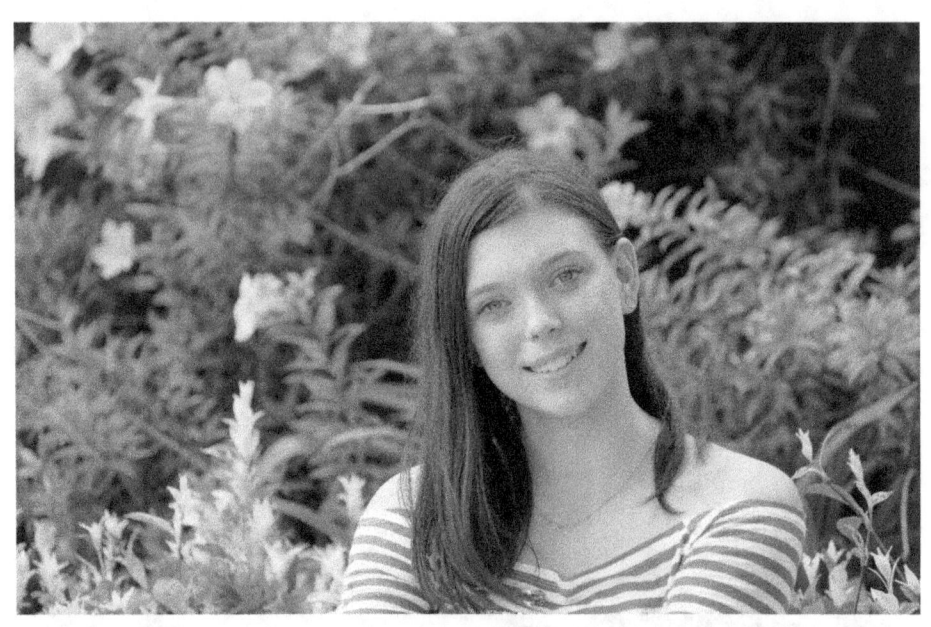

13

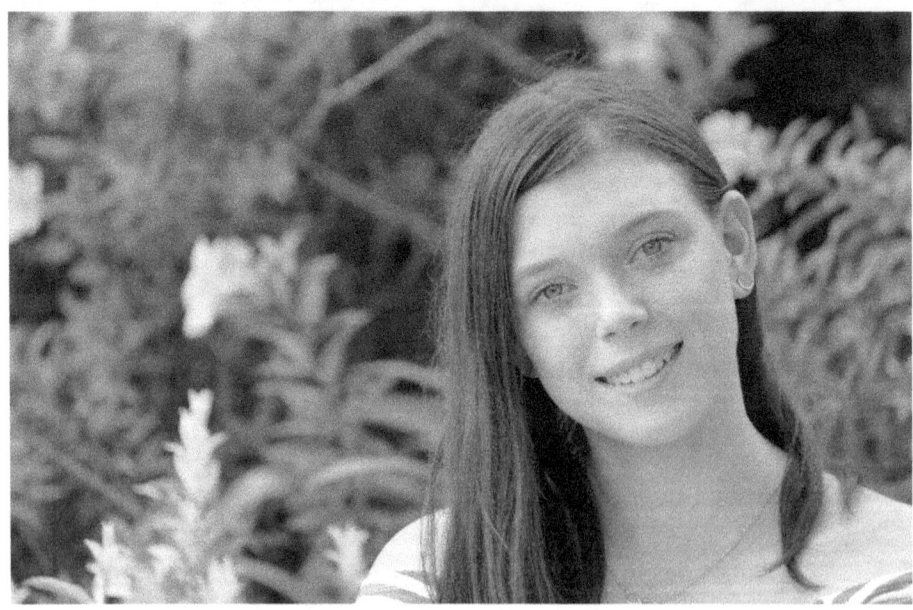

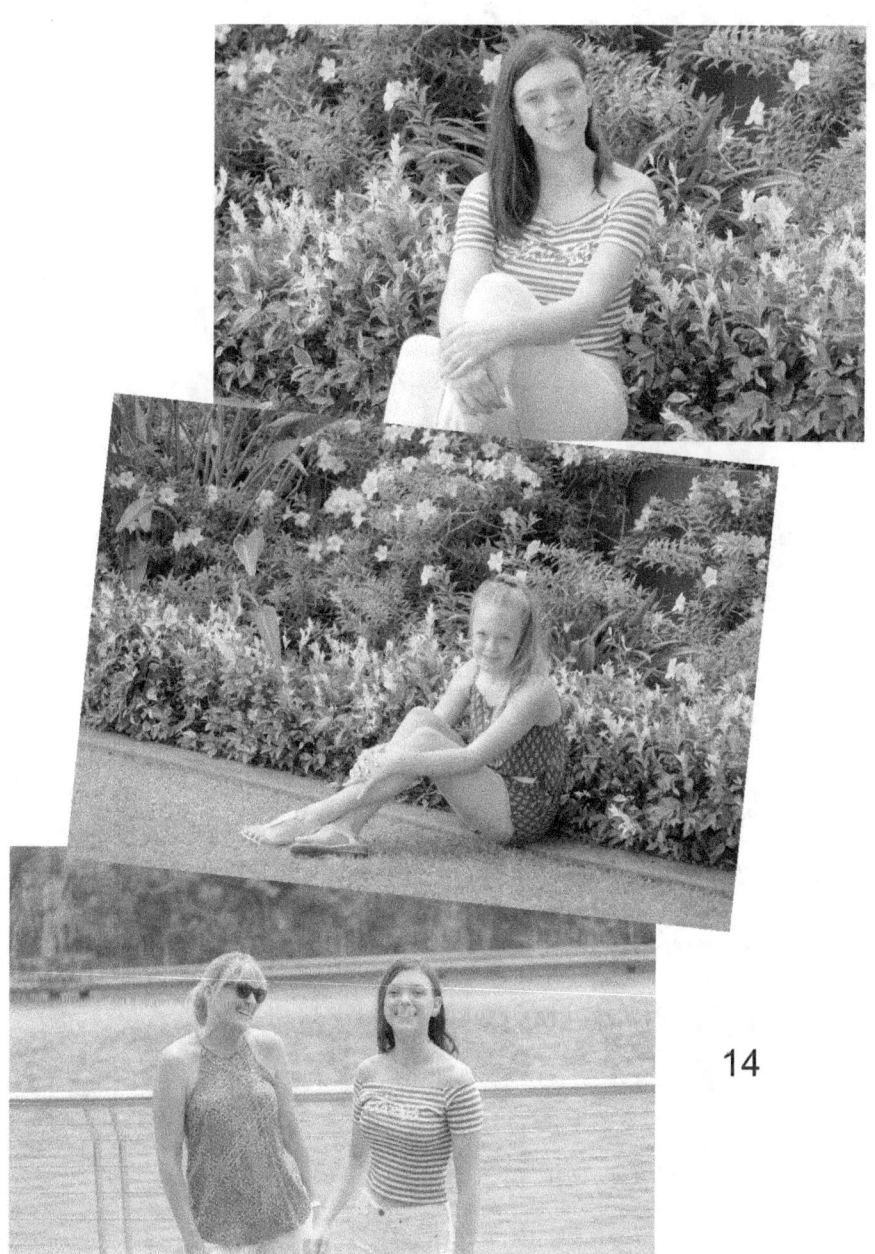

14

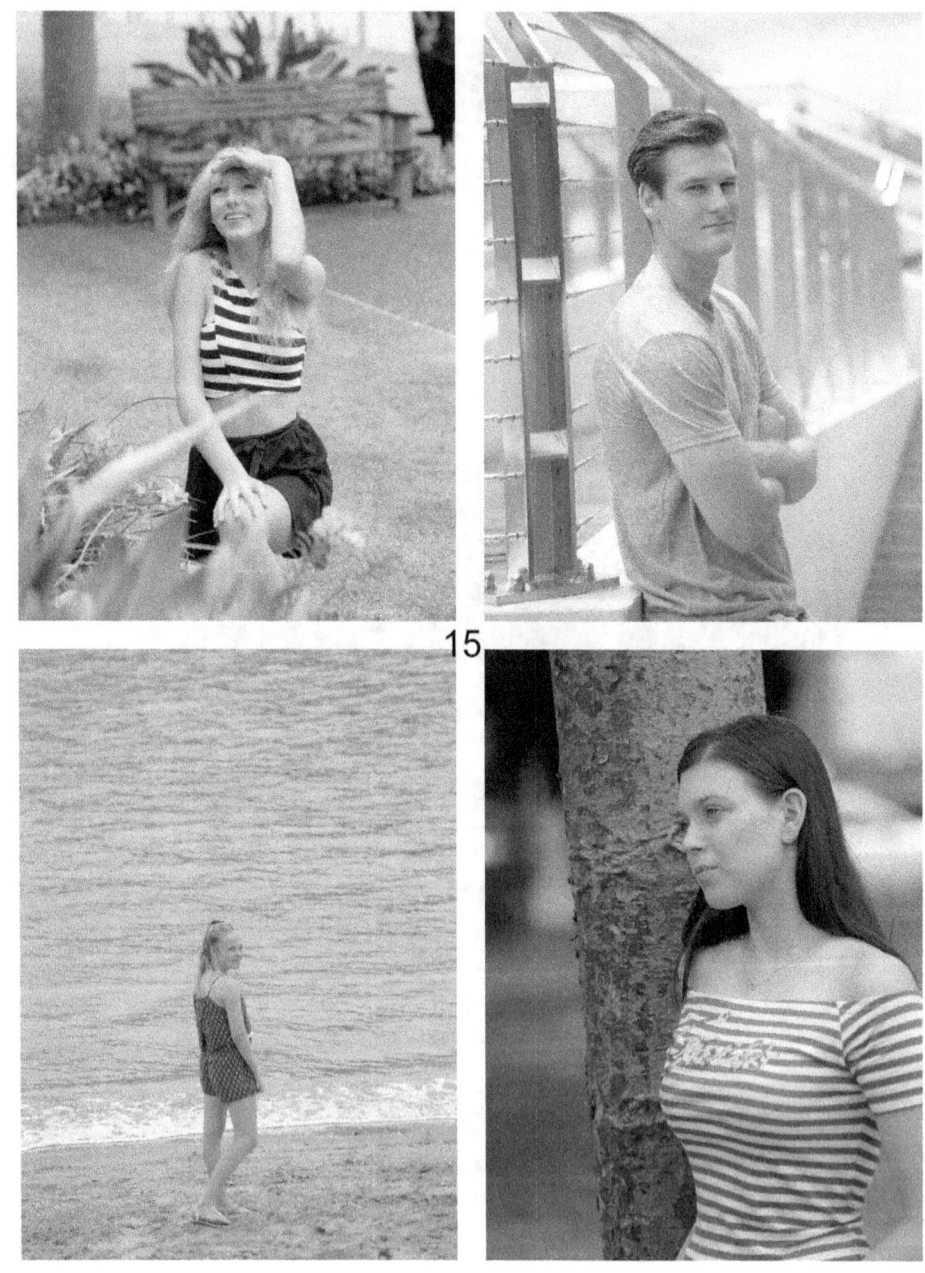

15

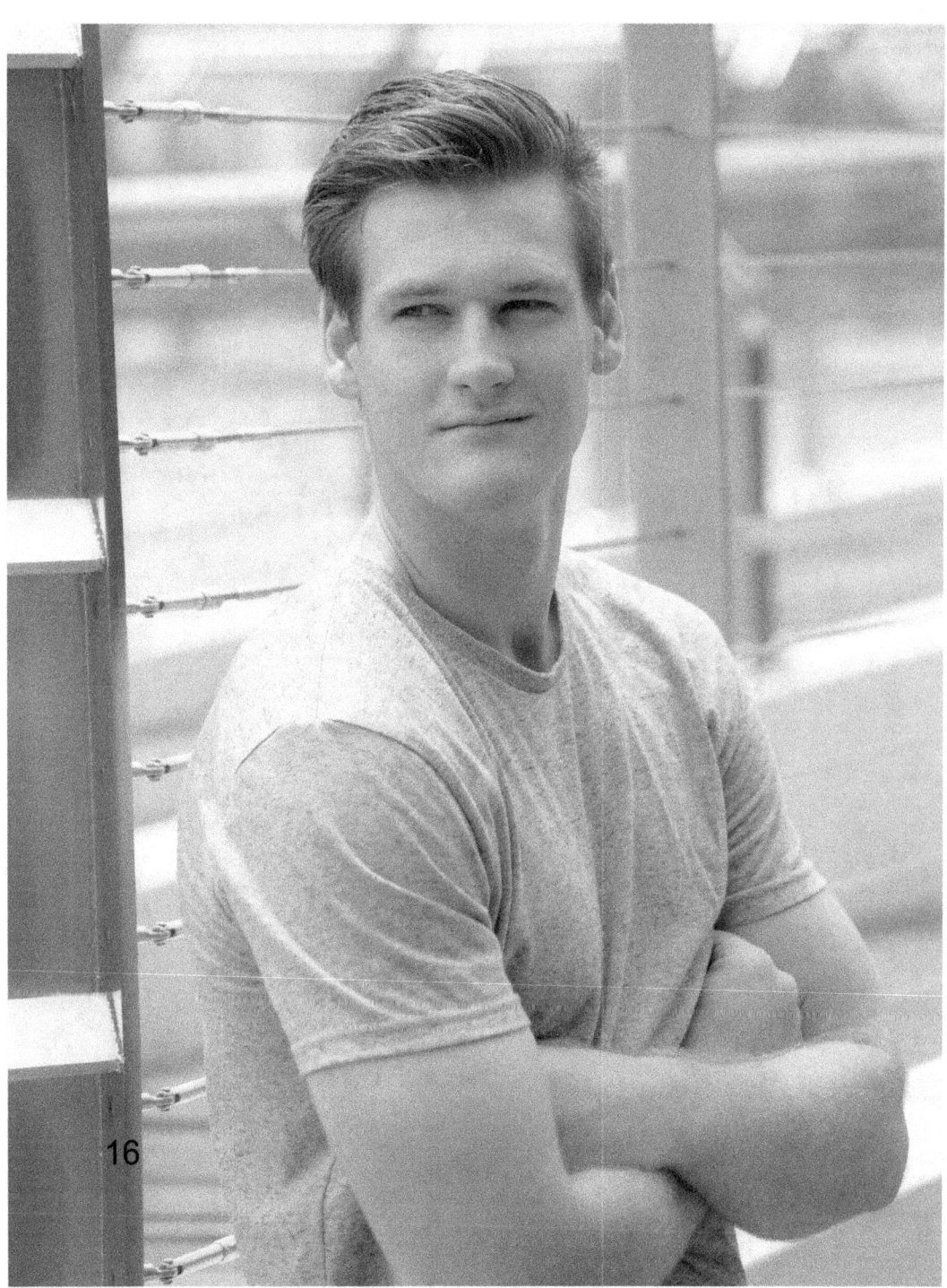

16

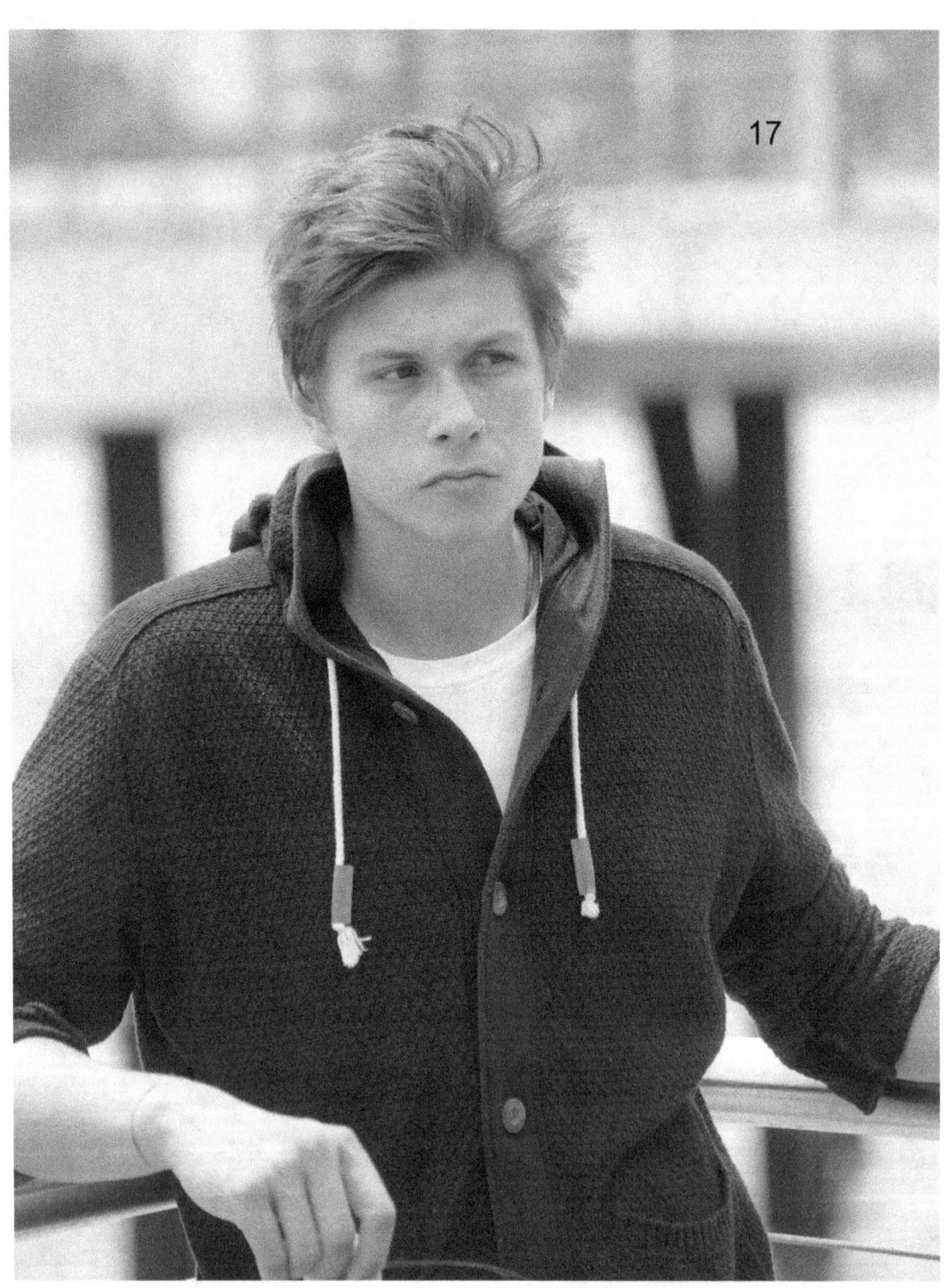

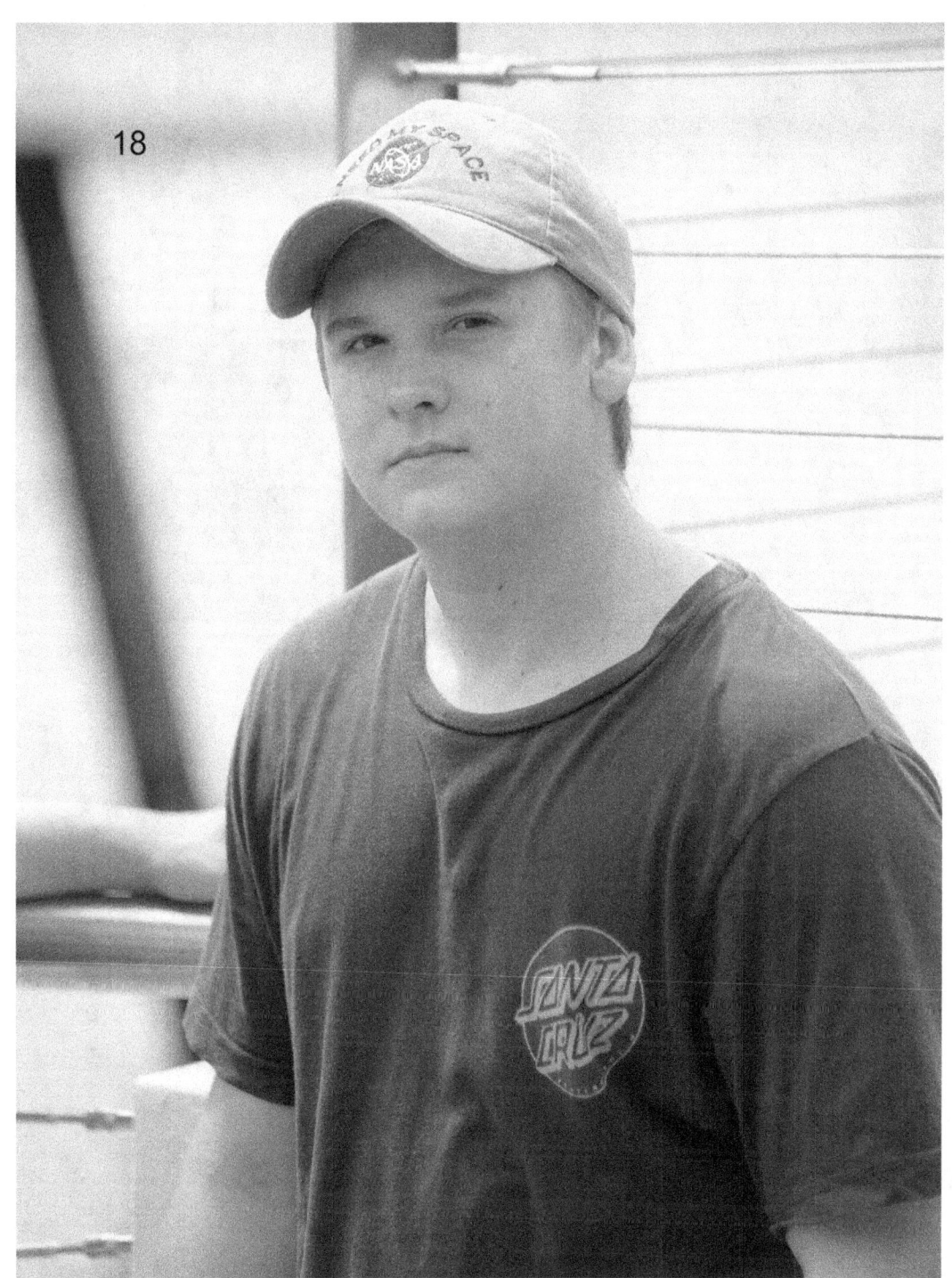

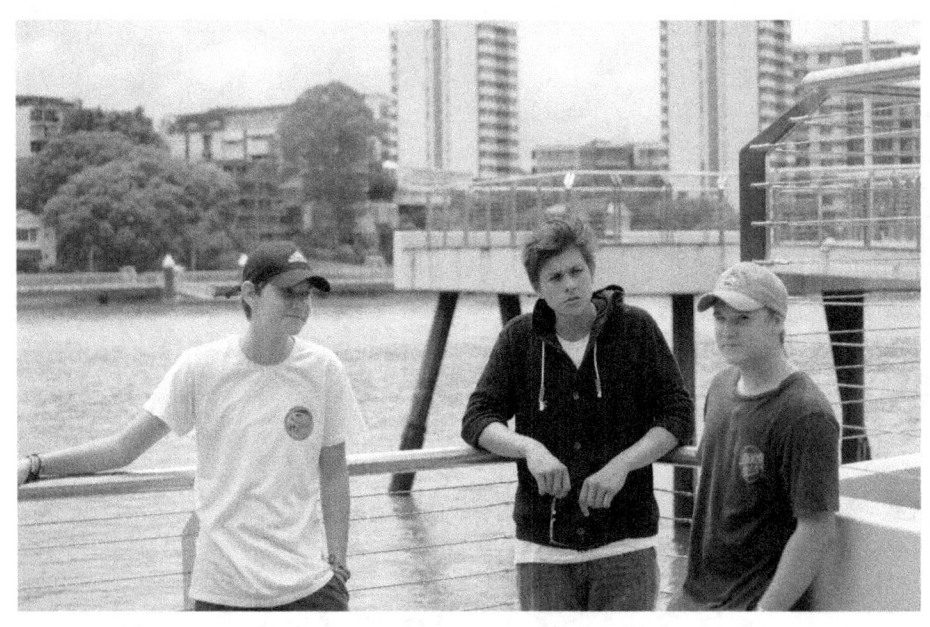

19

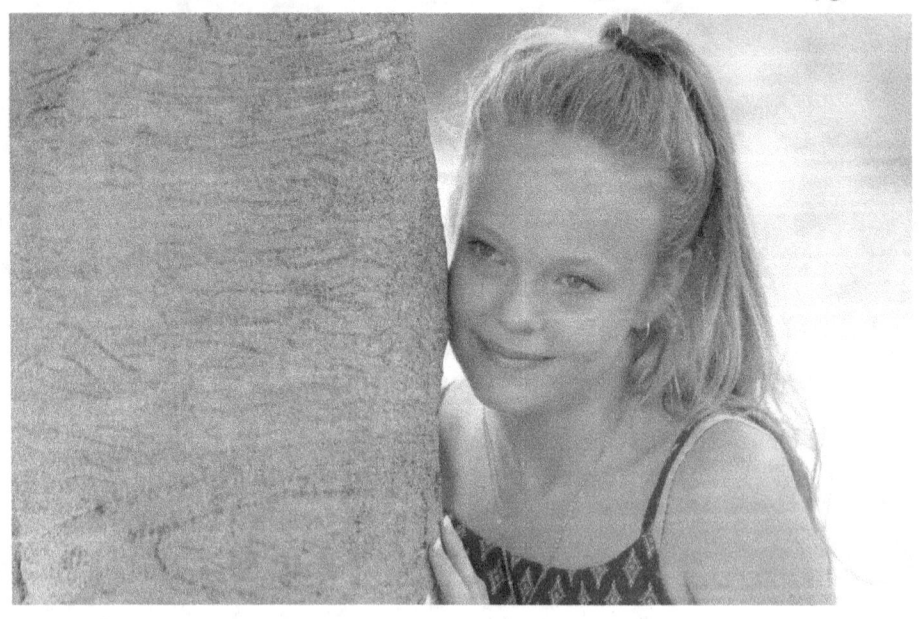

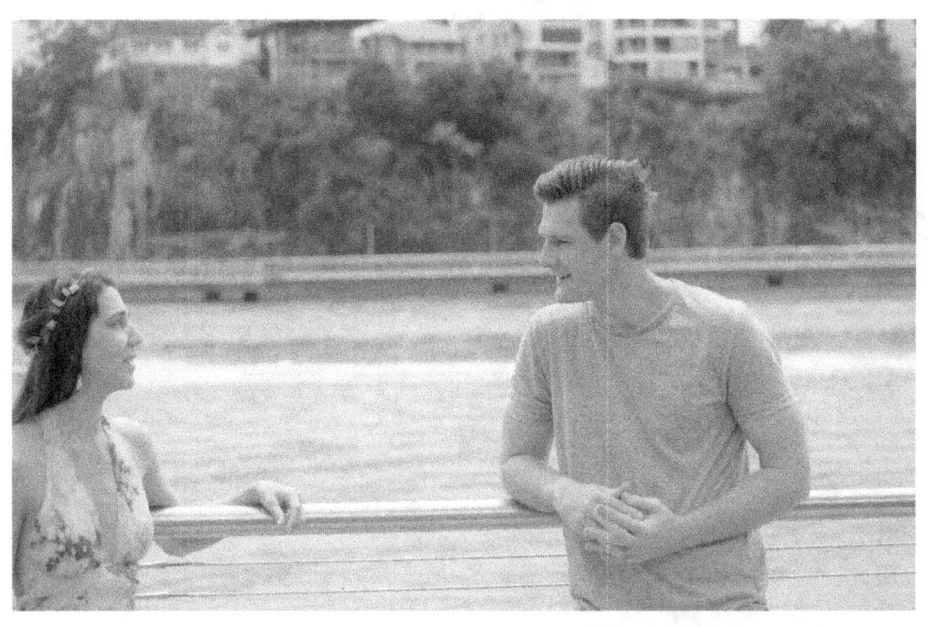

20

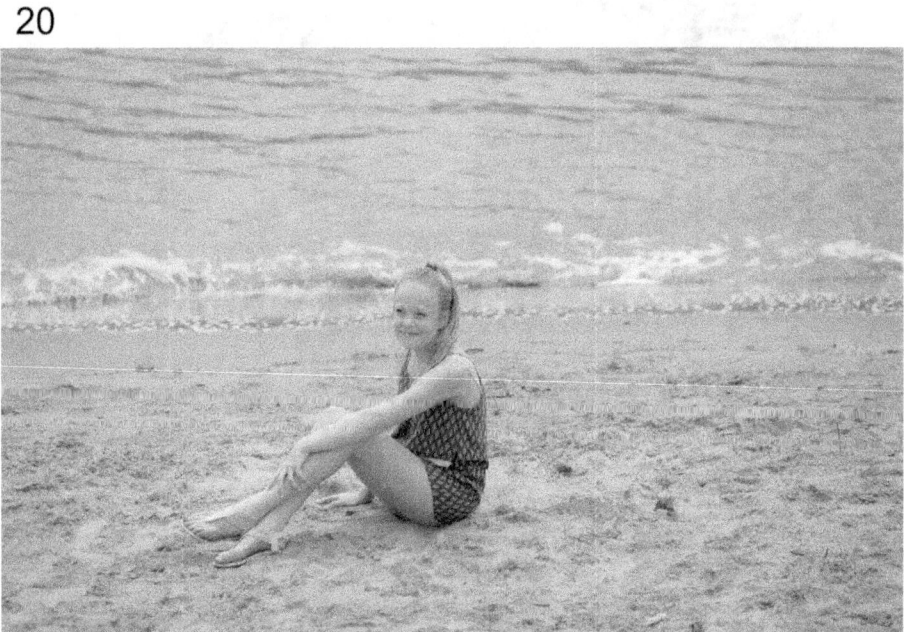

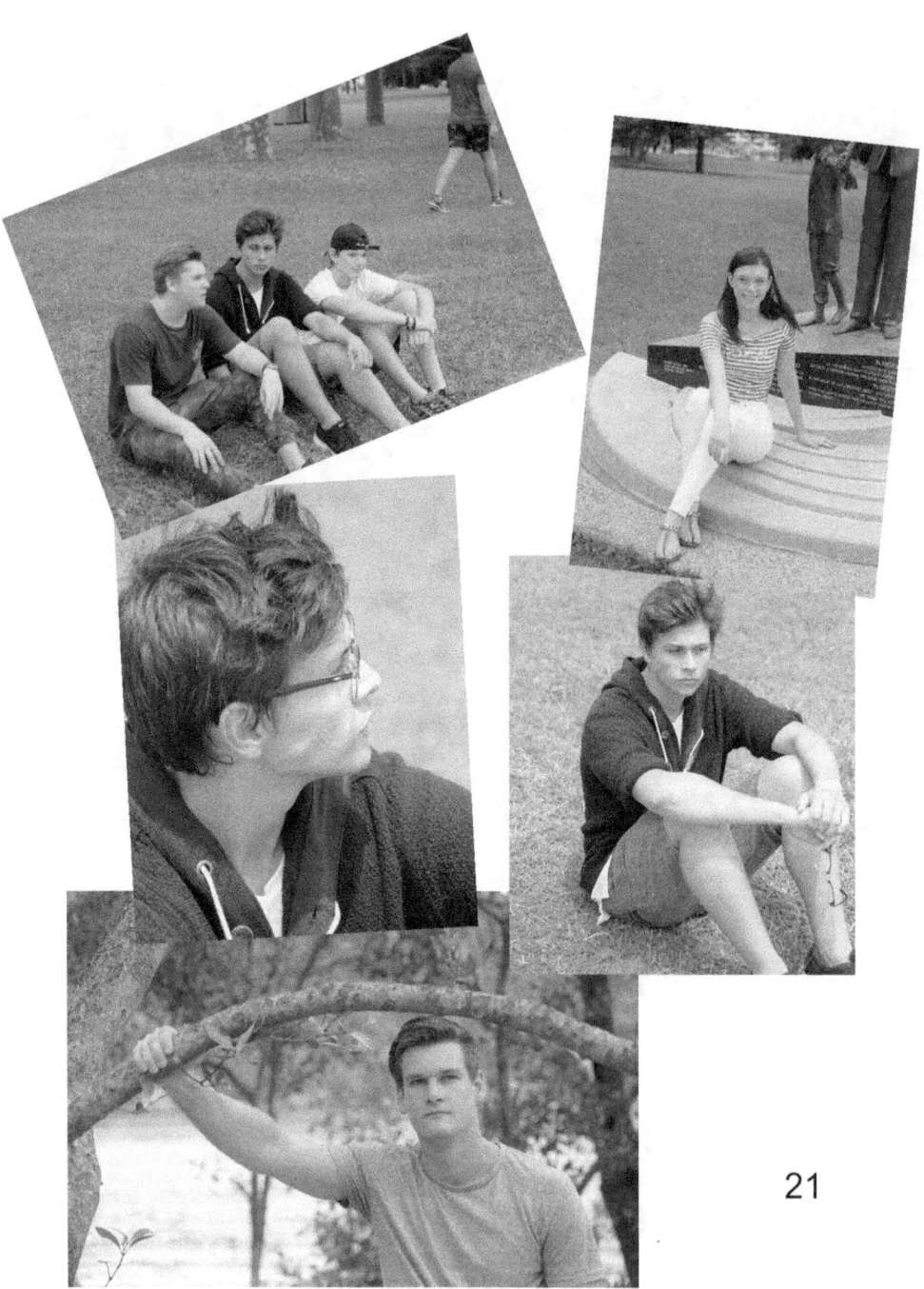

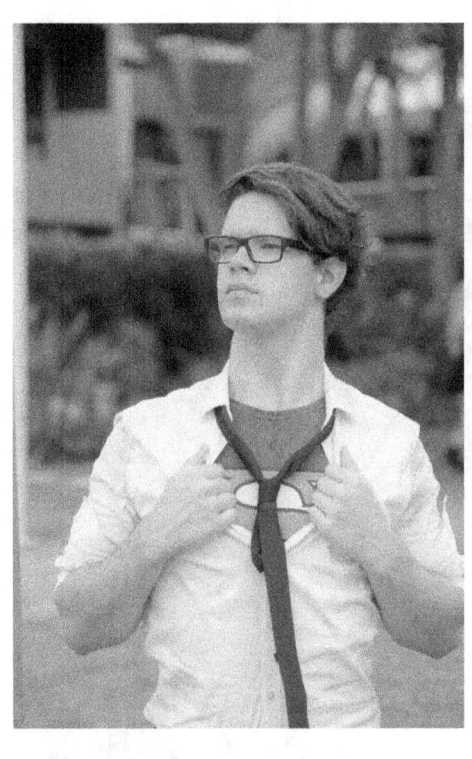 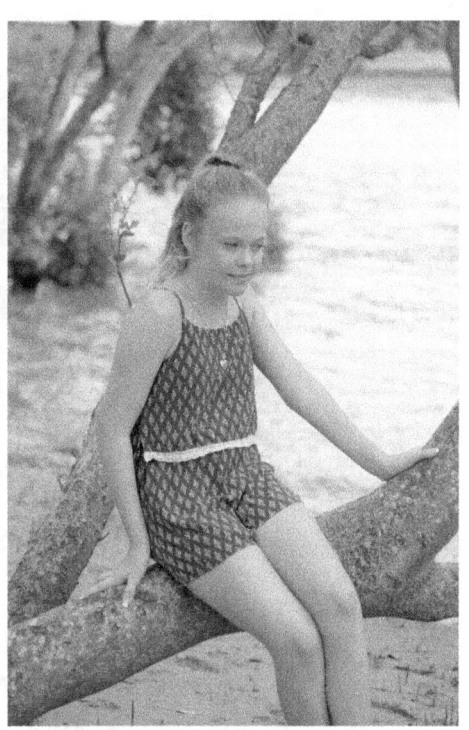

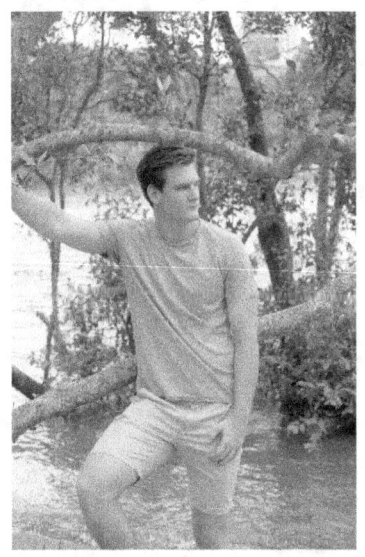 22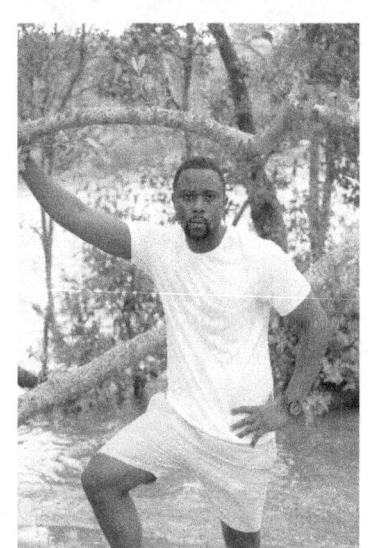

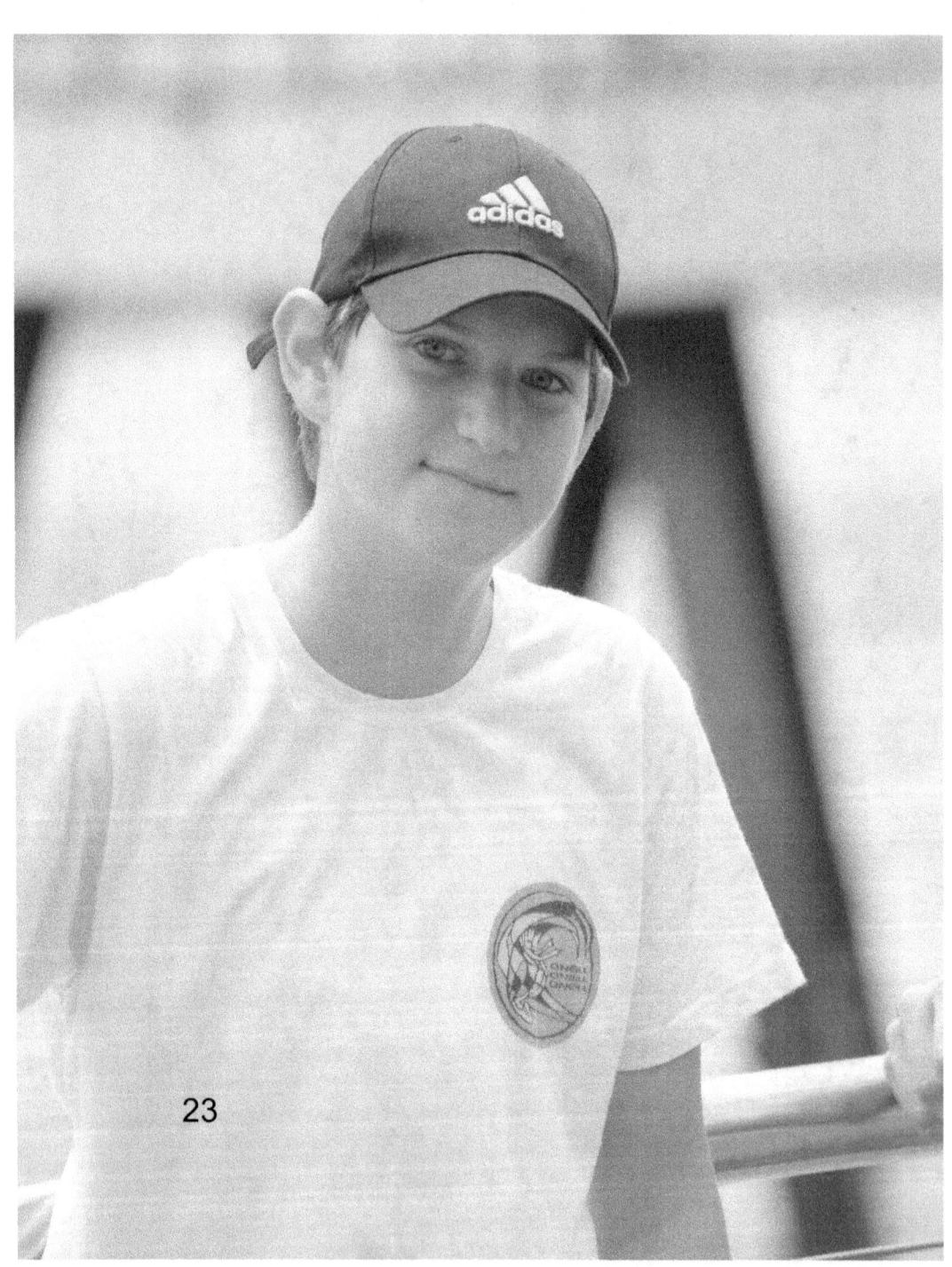

23

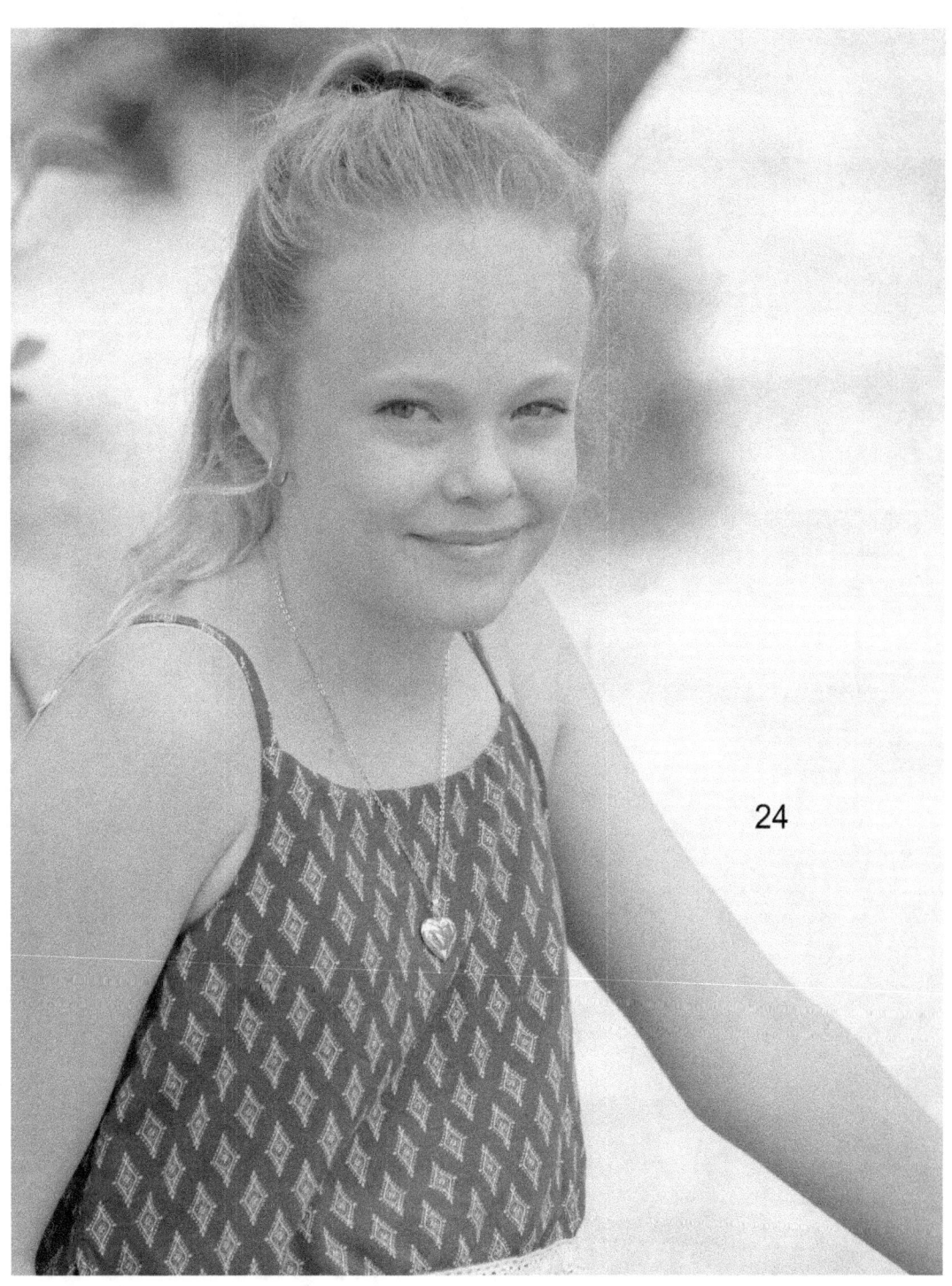

24

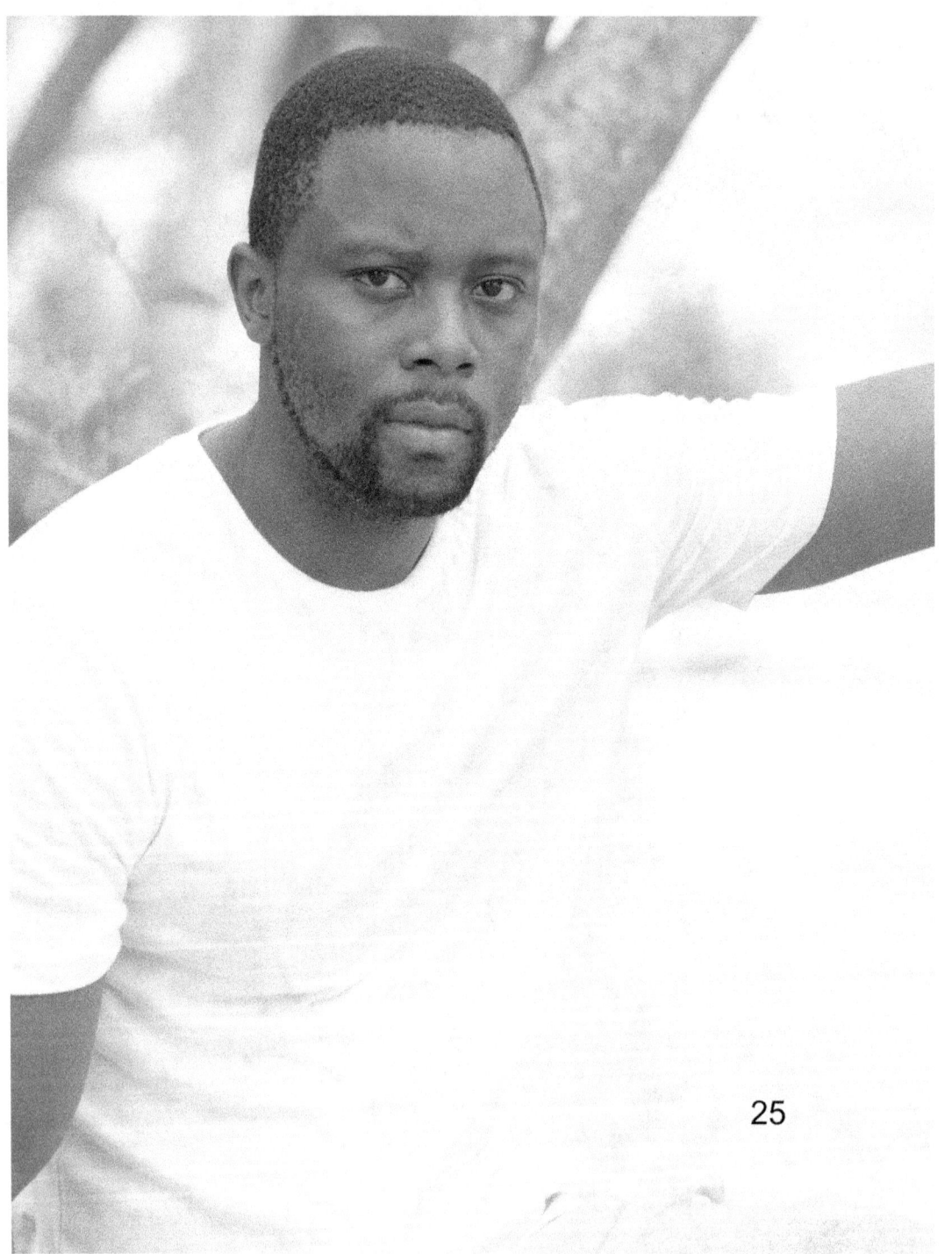

25

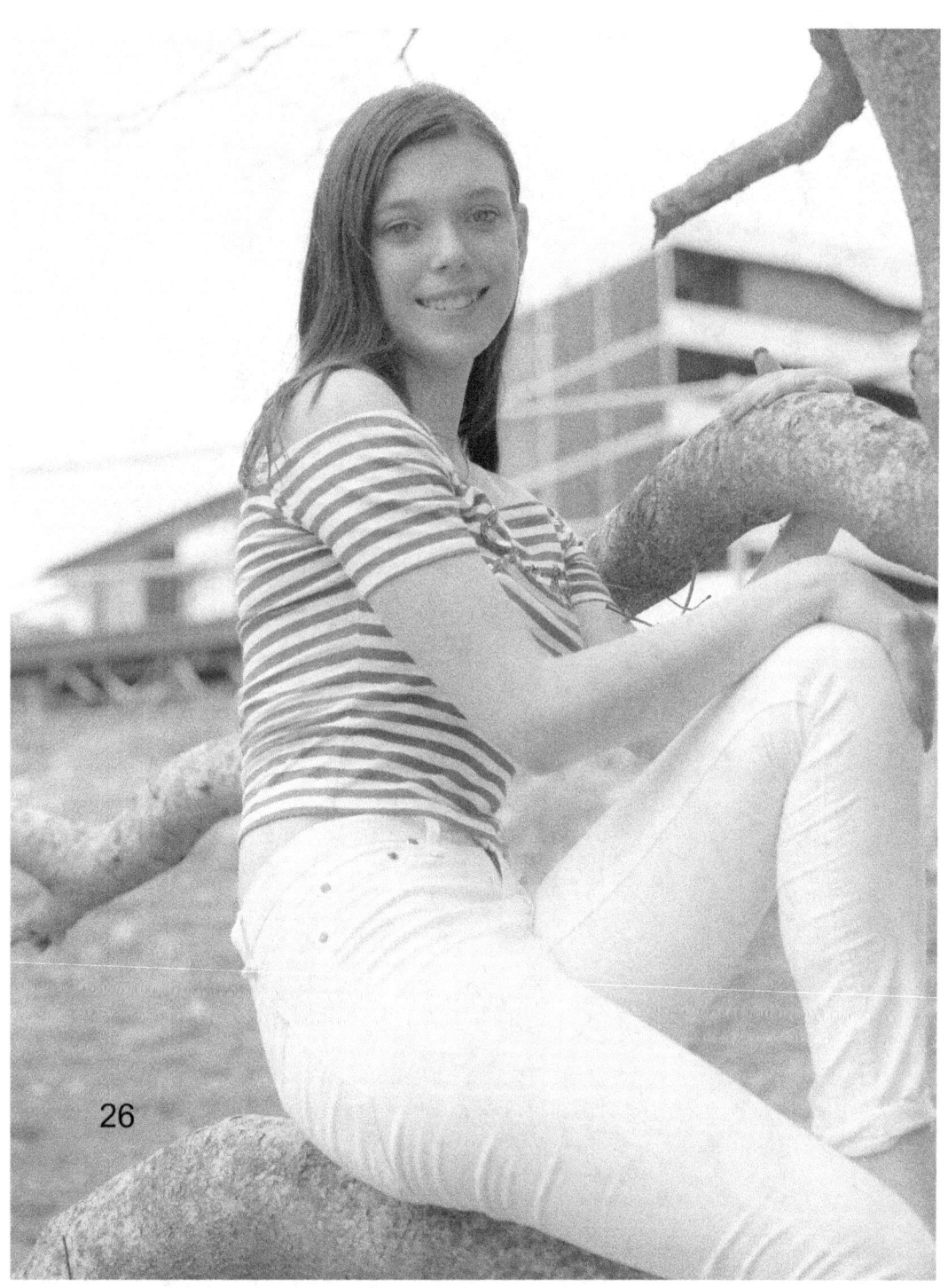

26

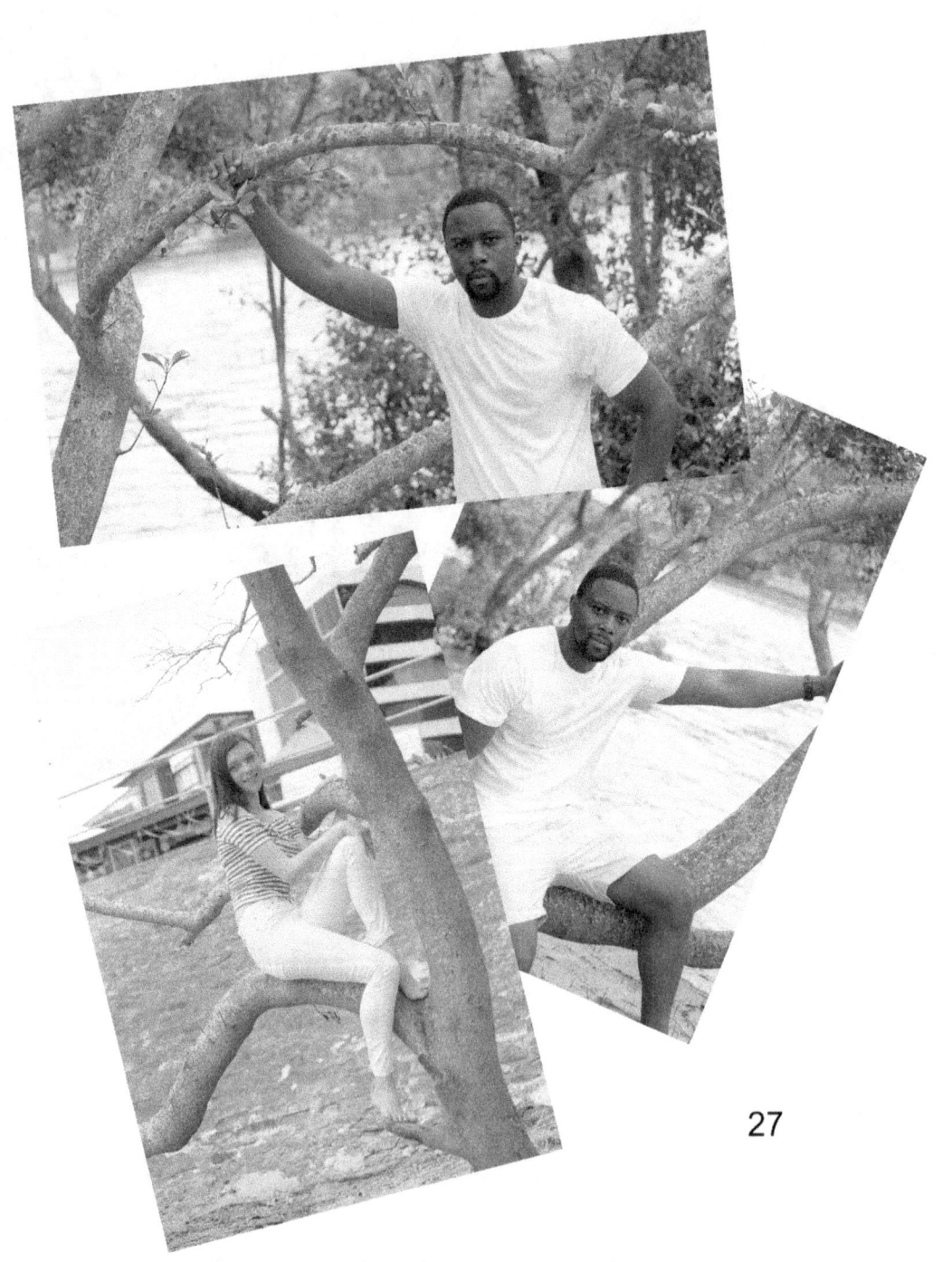

27

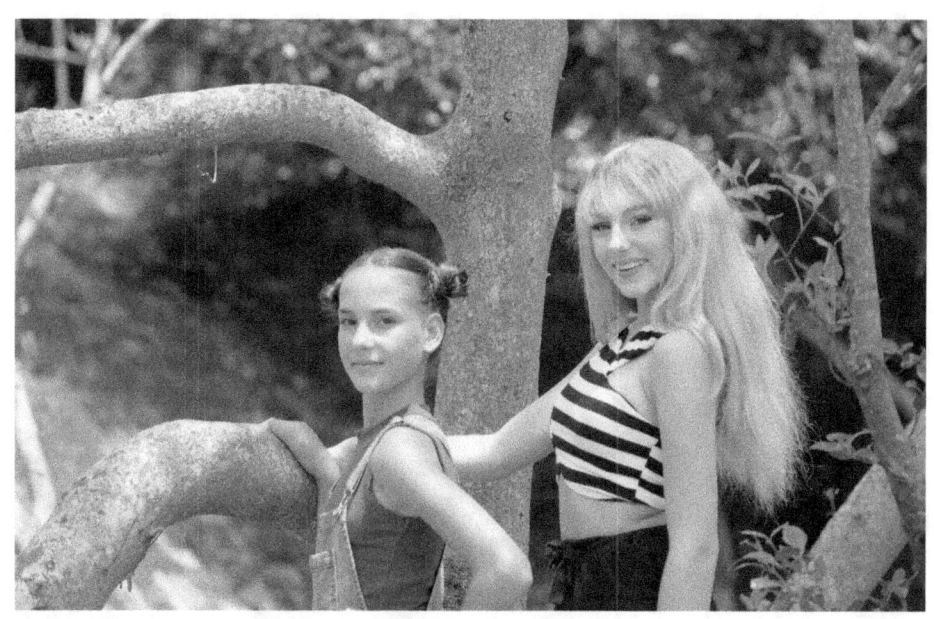

28

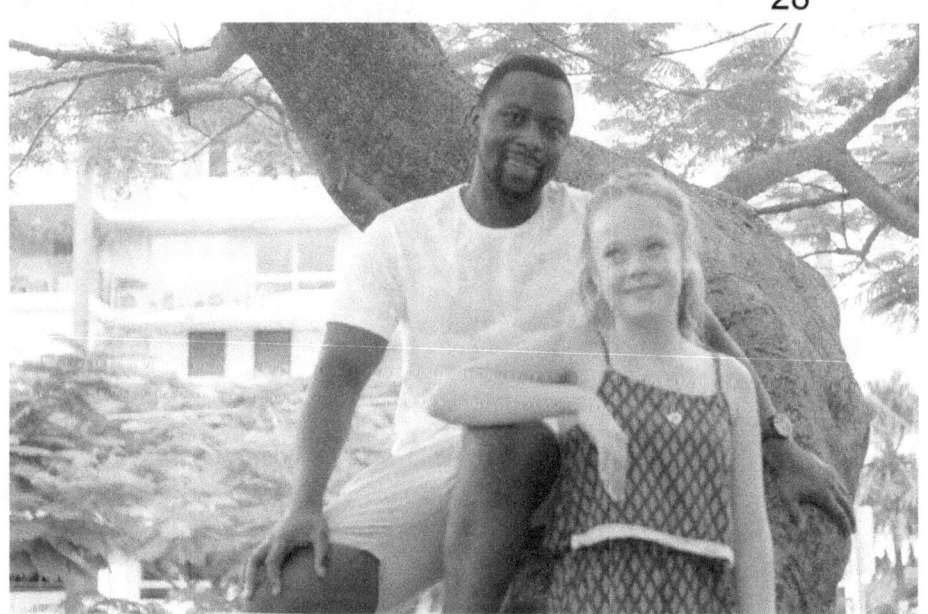

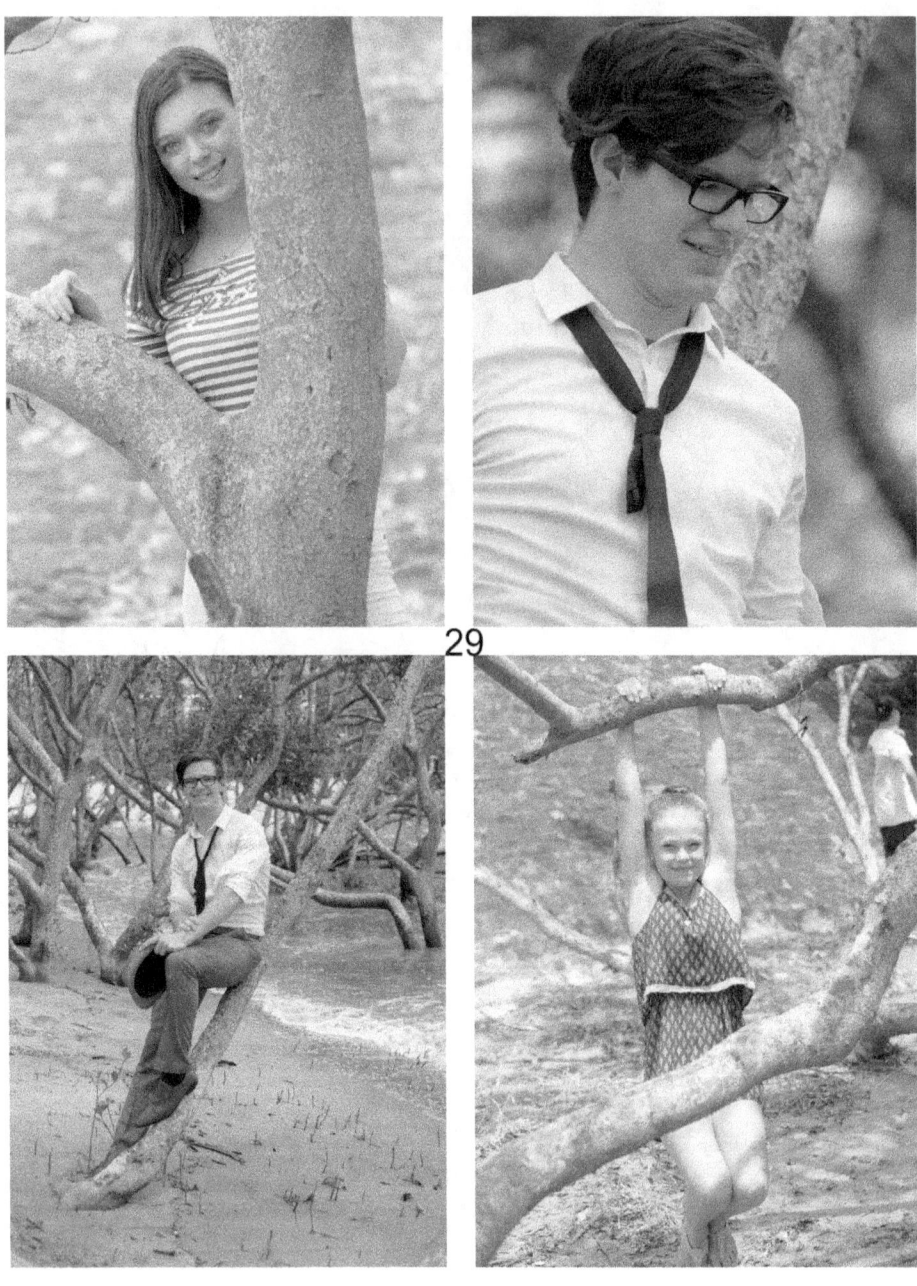

29

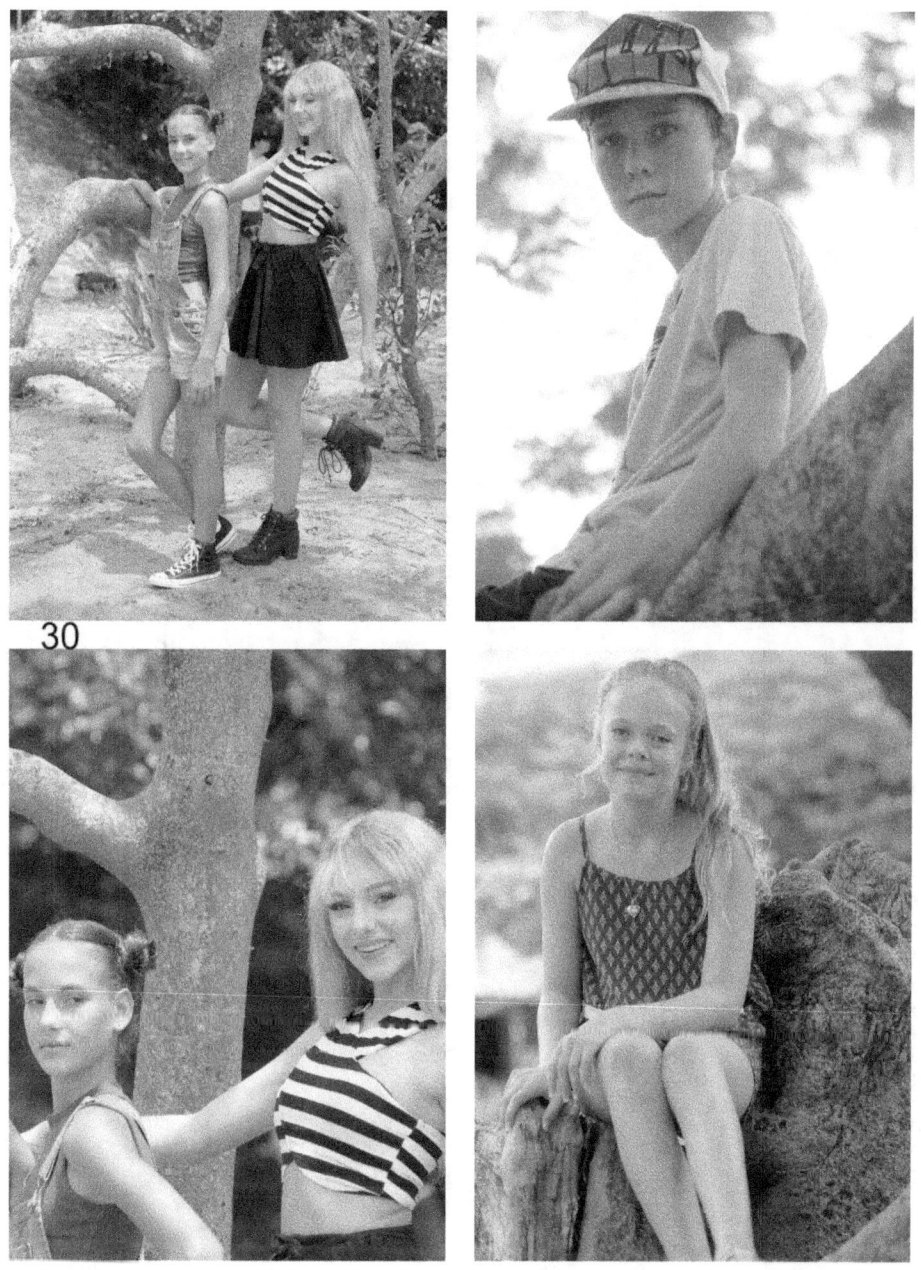

30

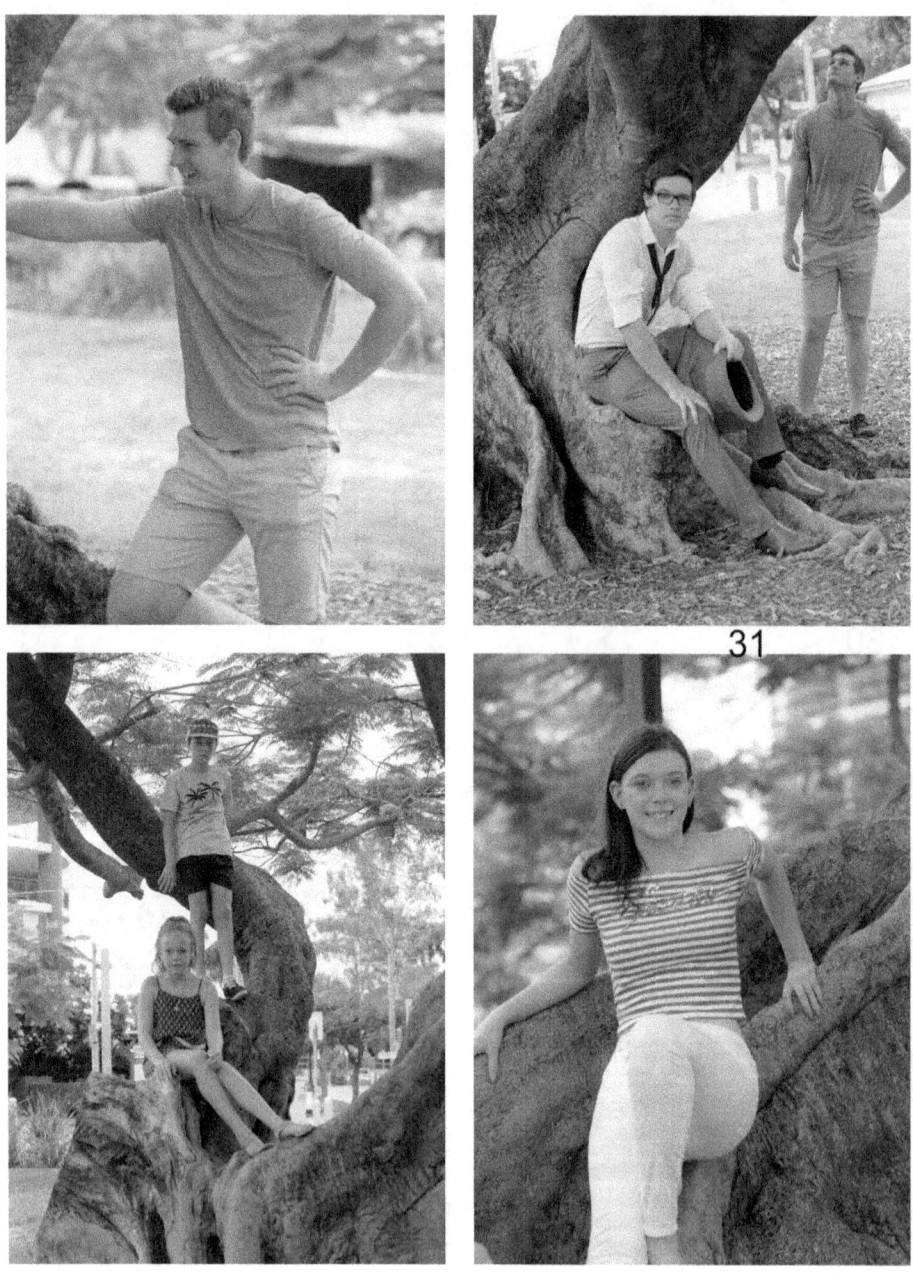

31

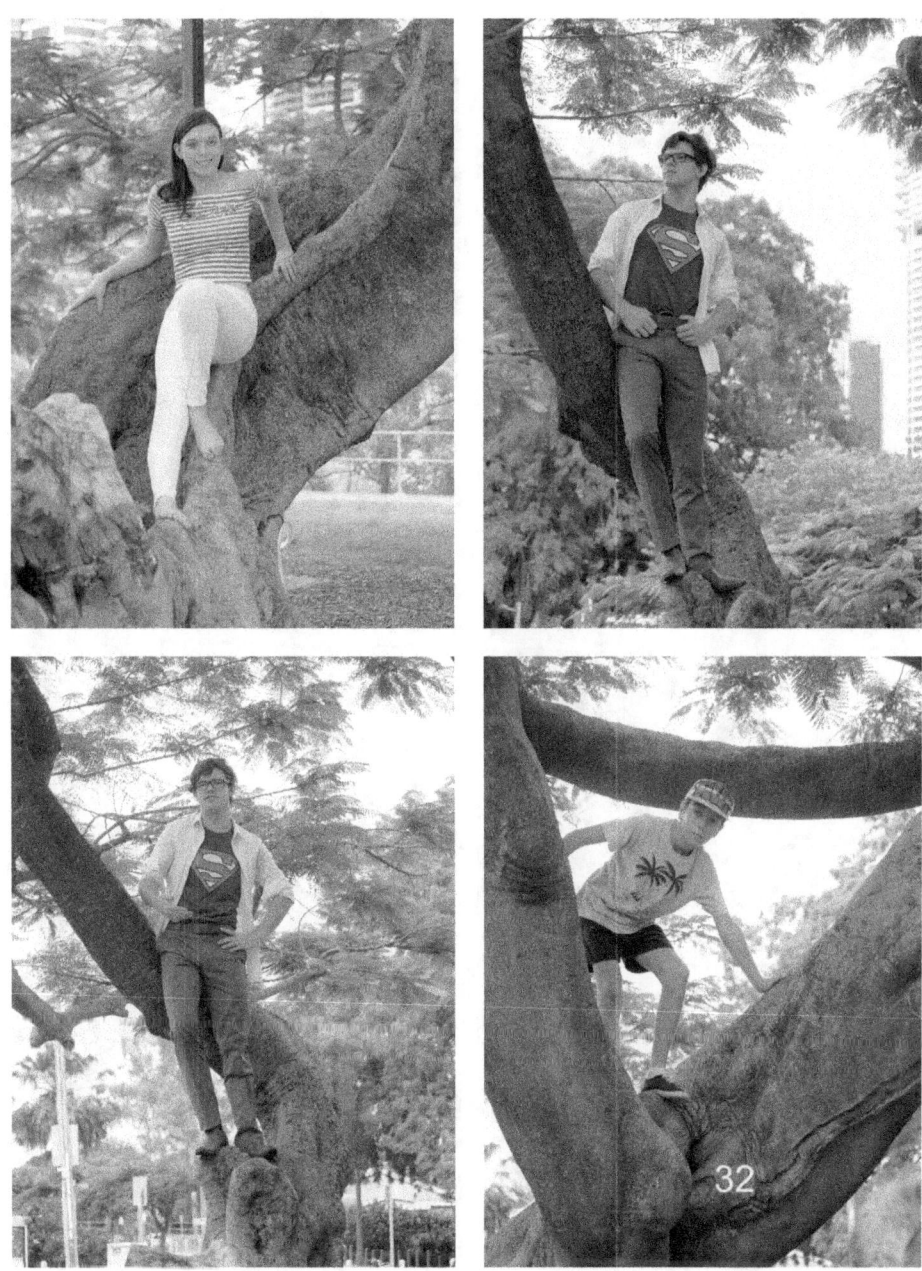

32

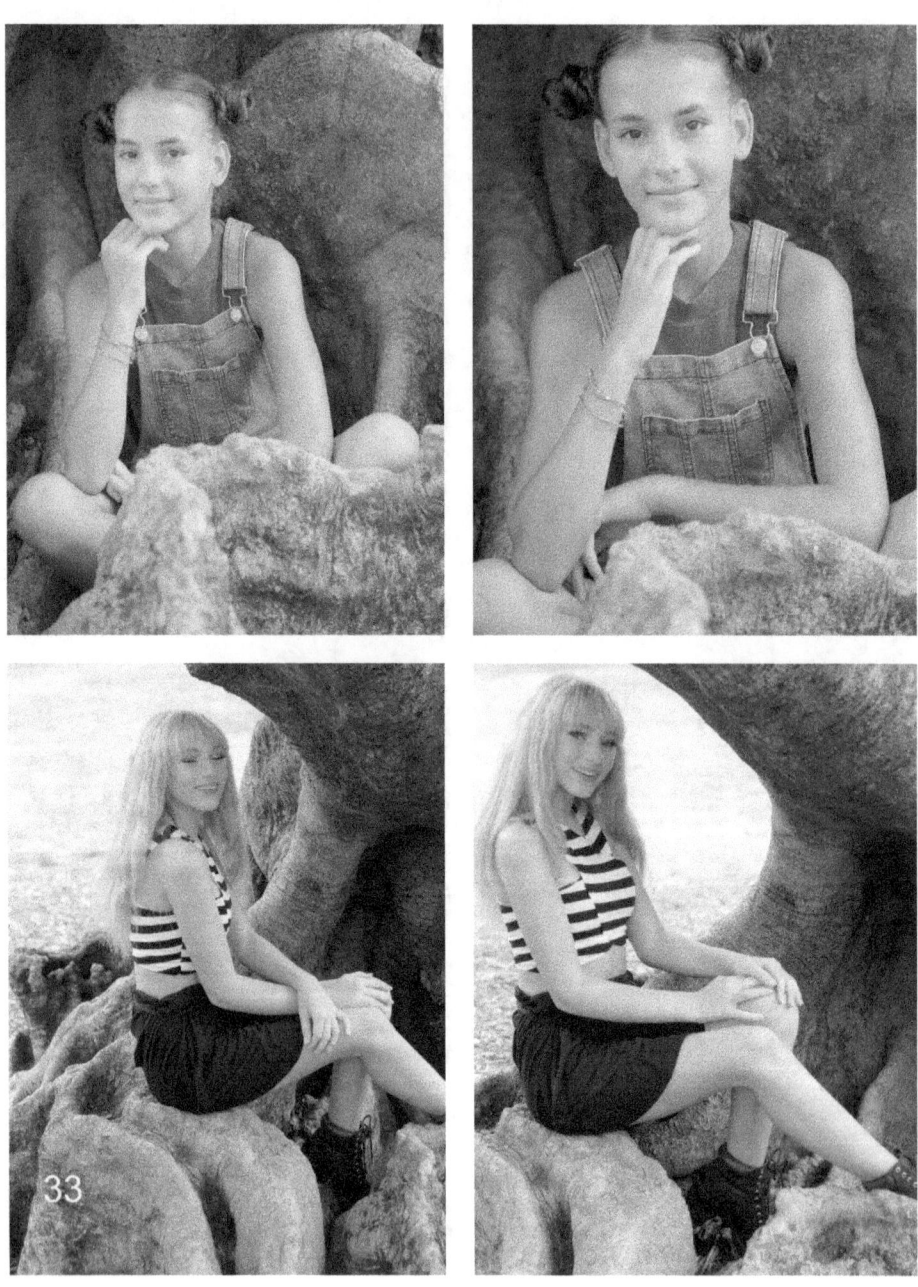

33

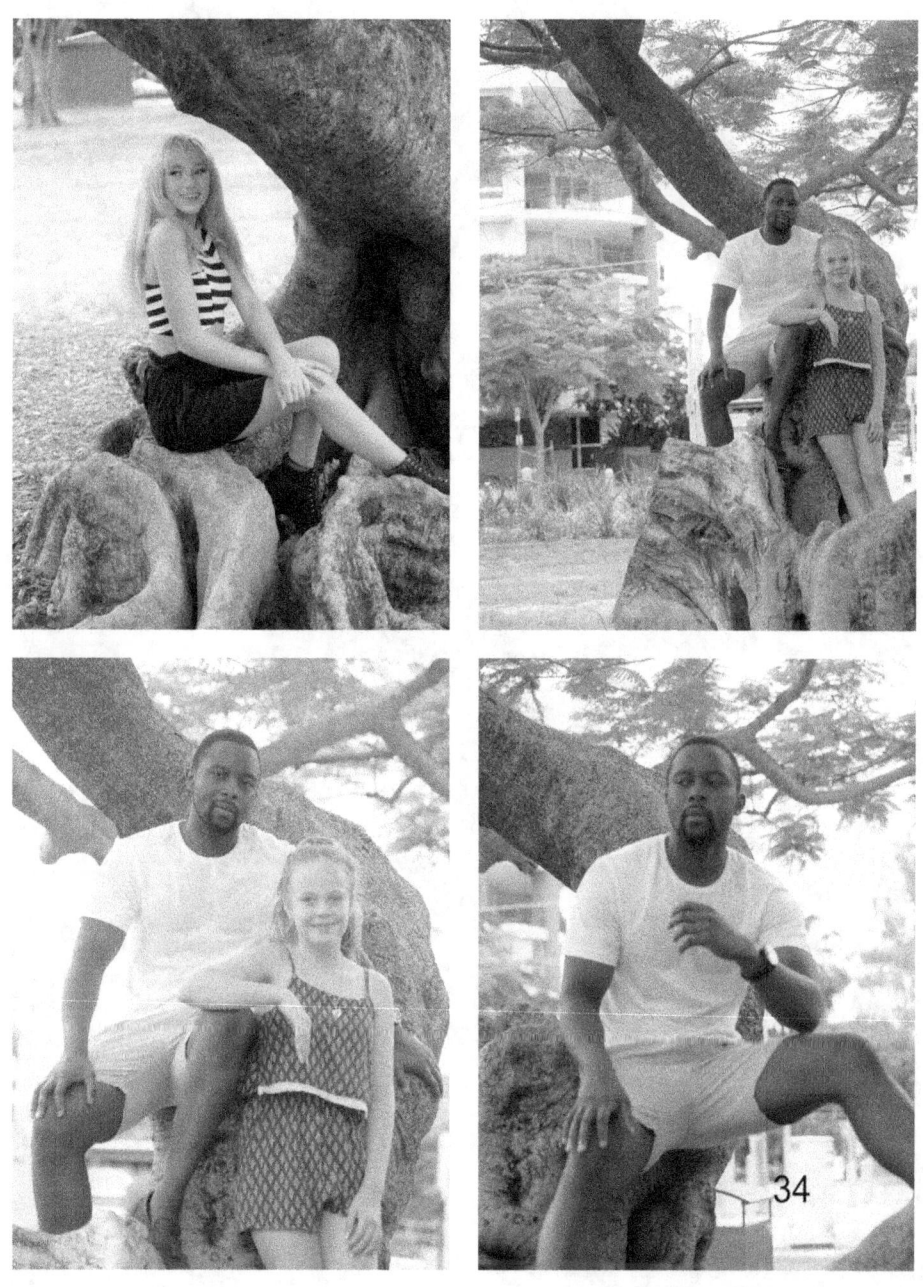

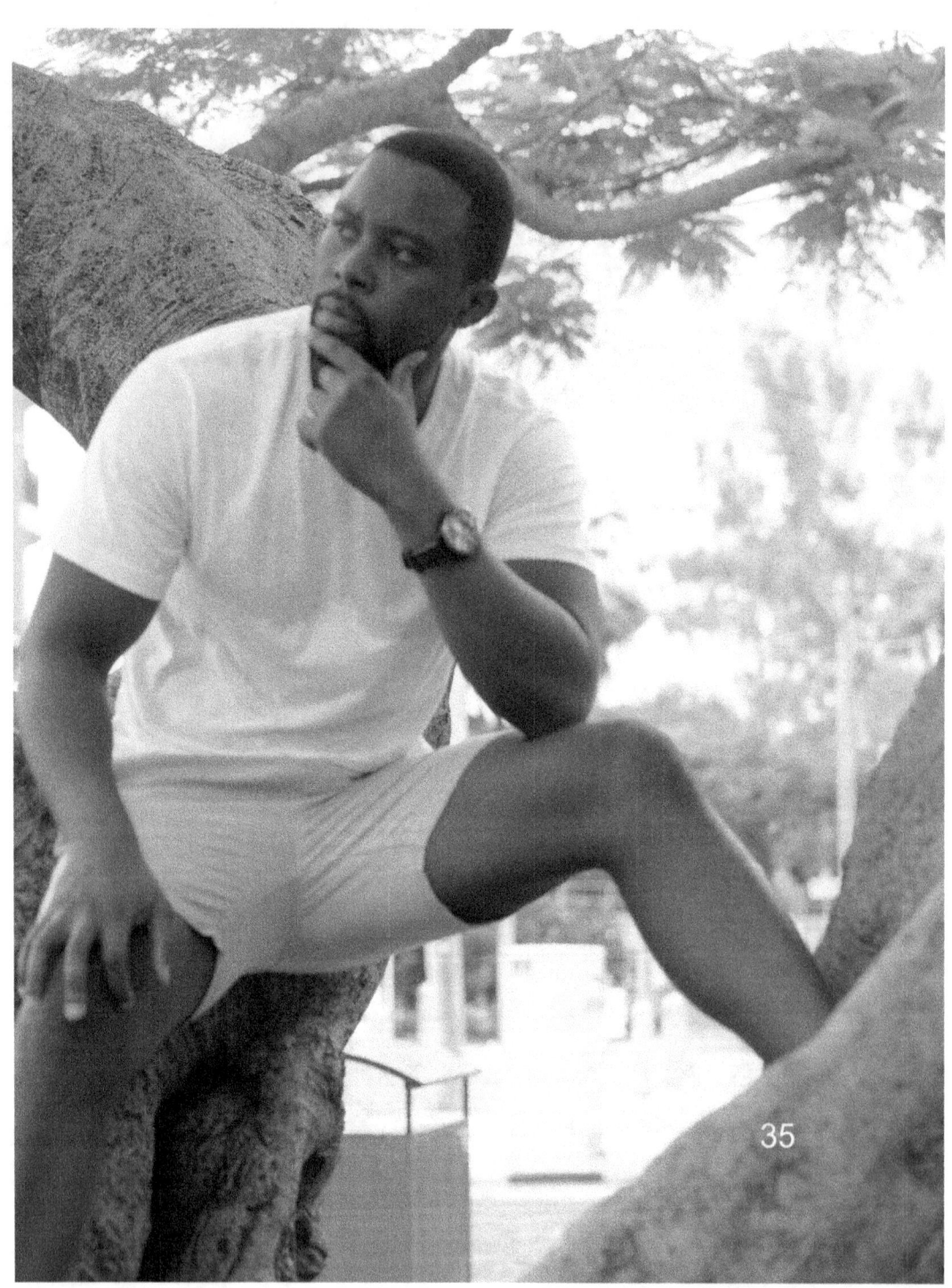

35

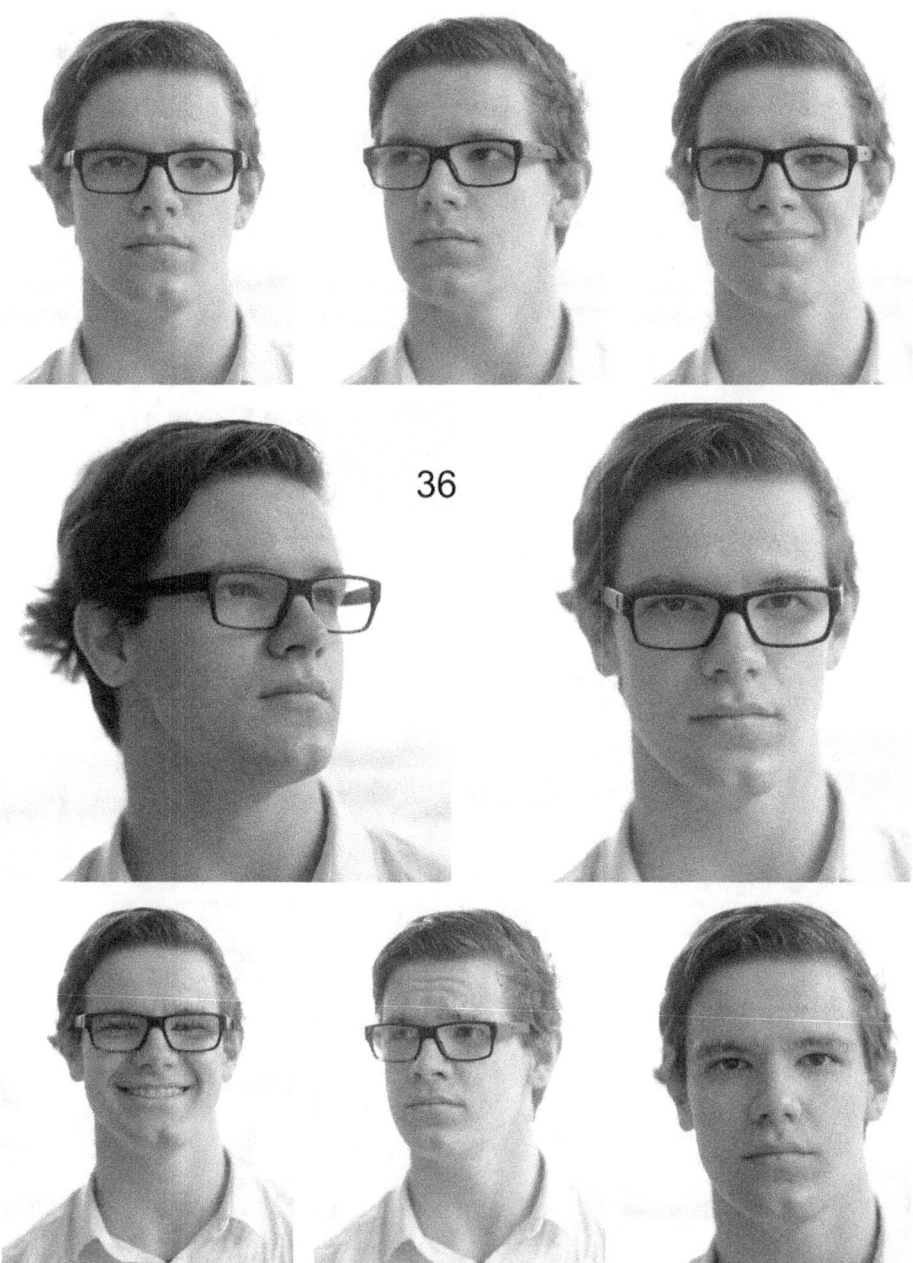

36

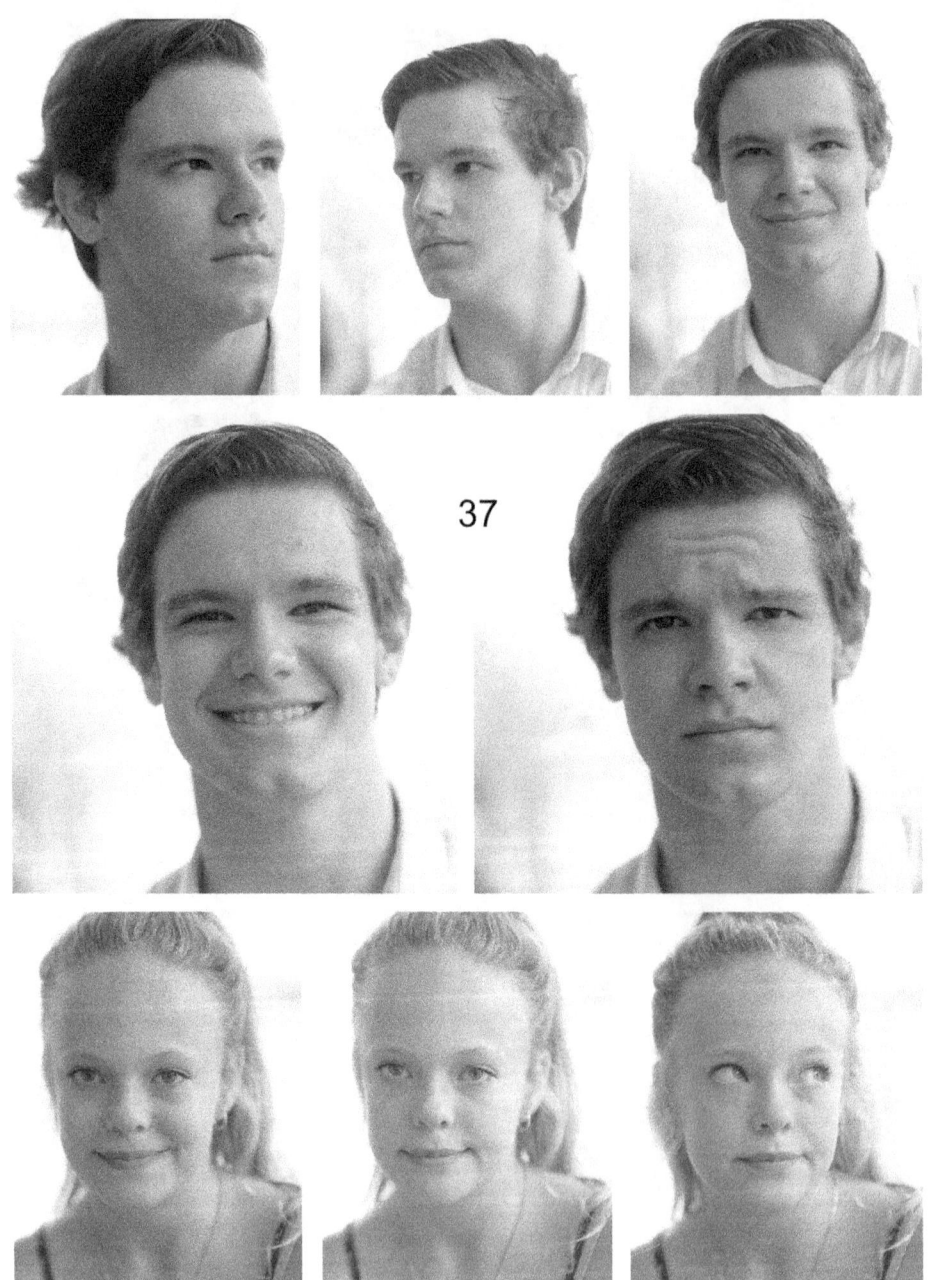

37

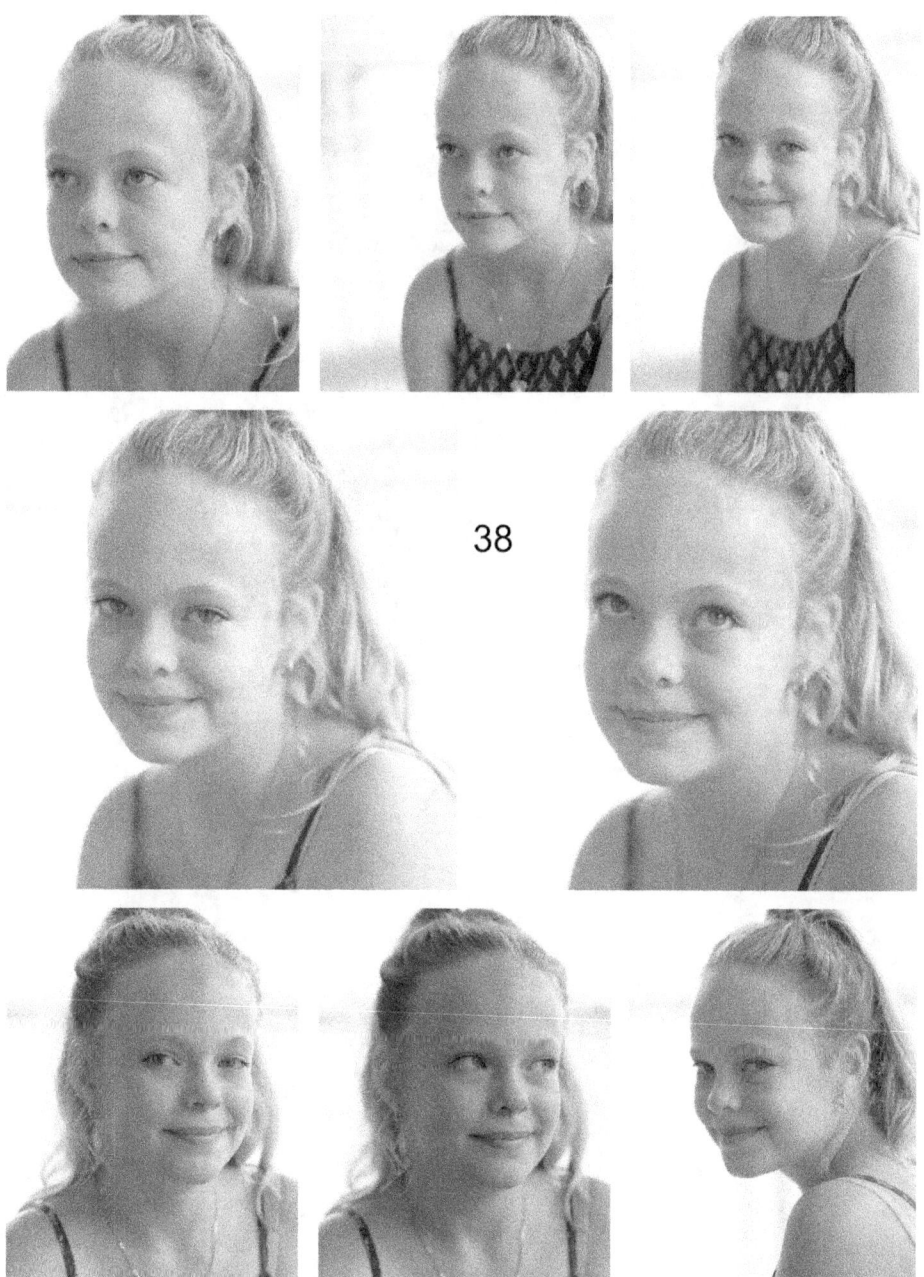

38

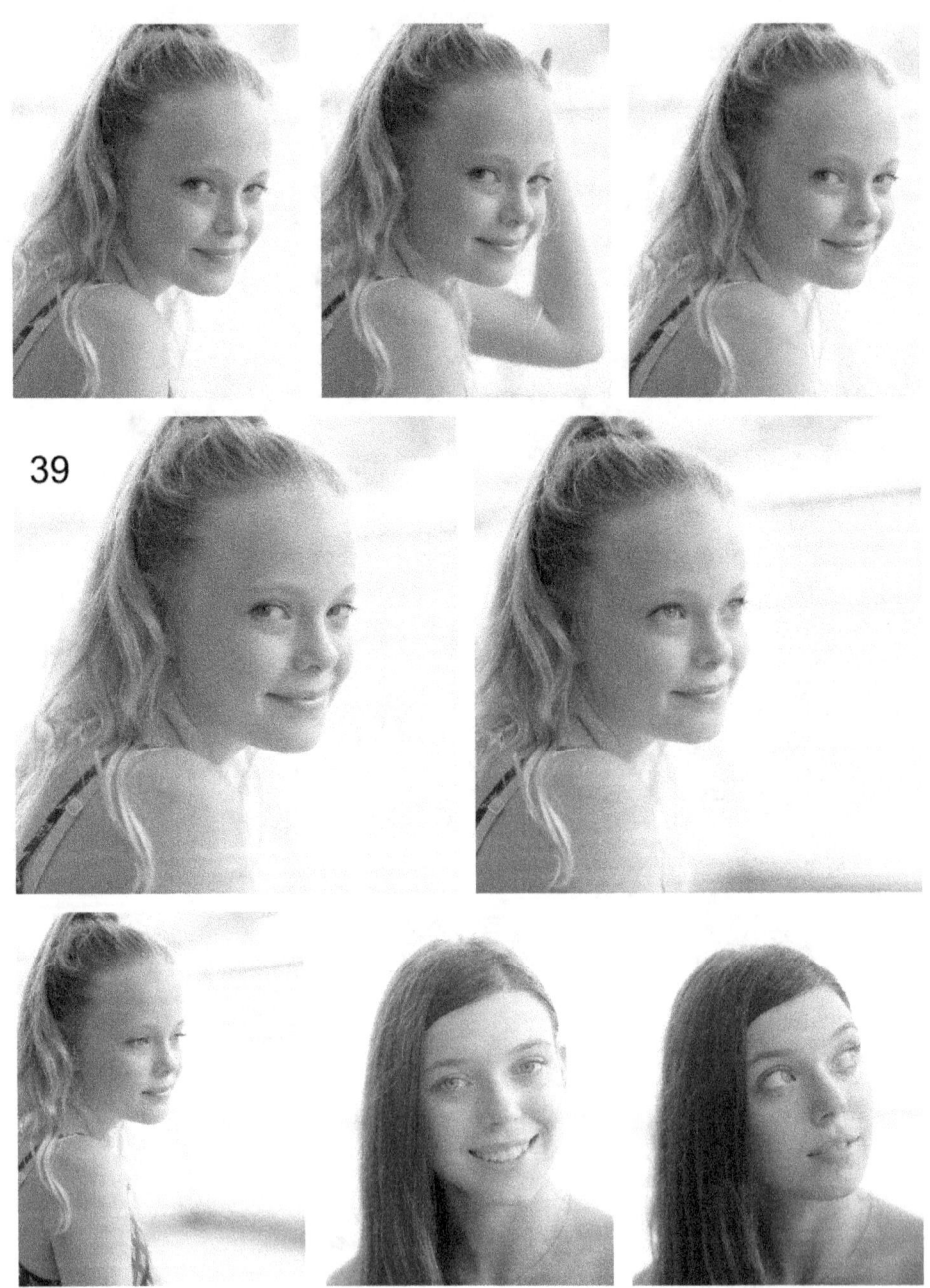

39

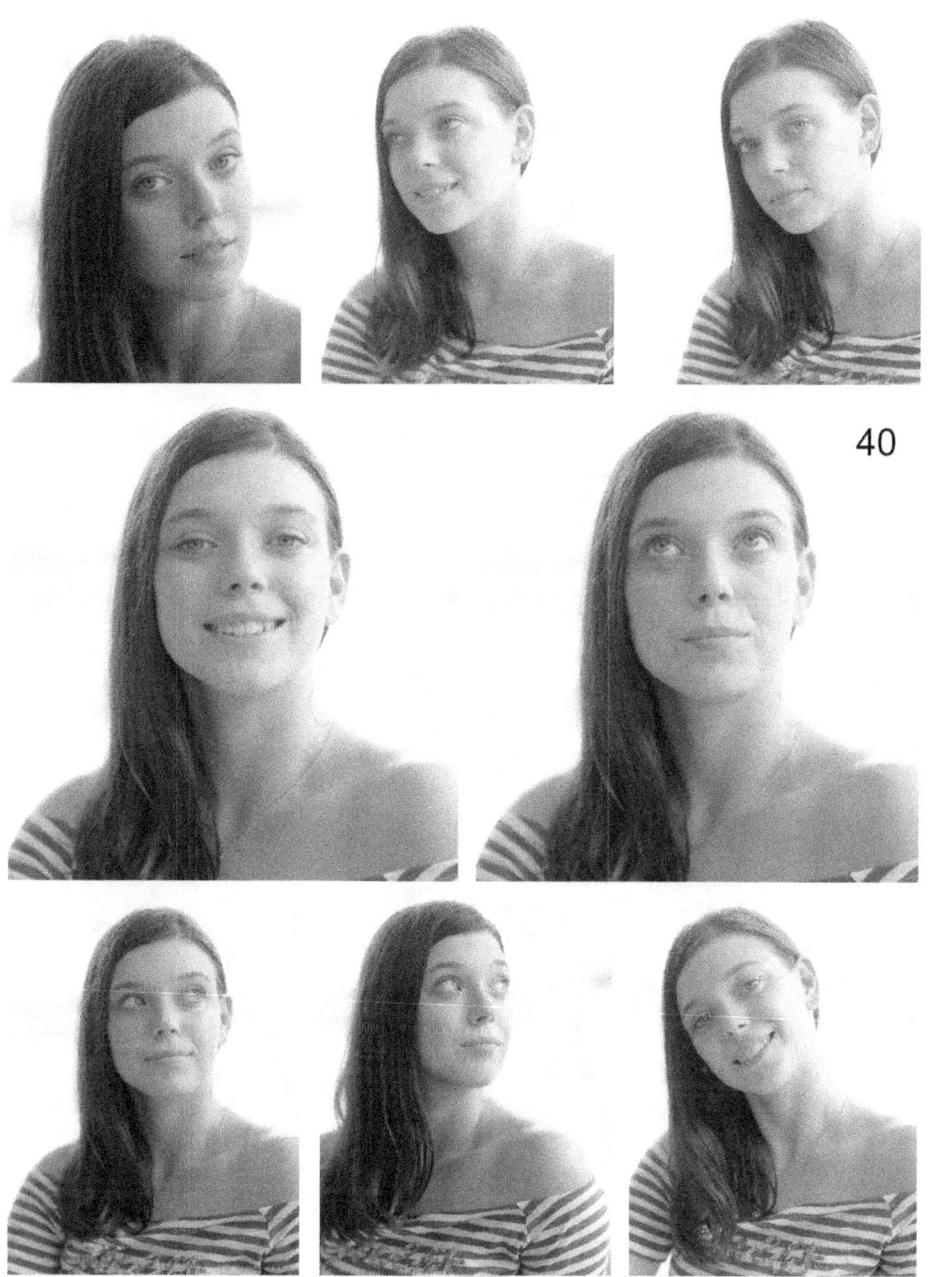

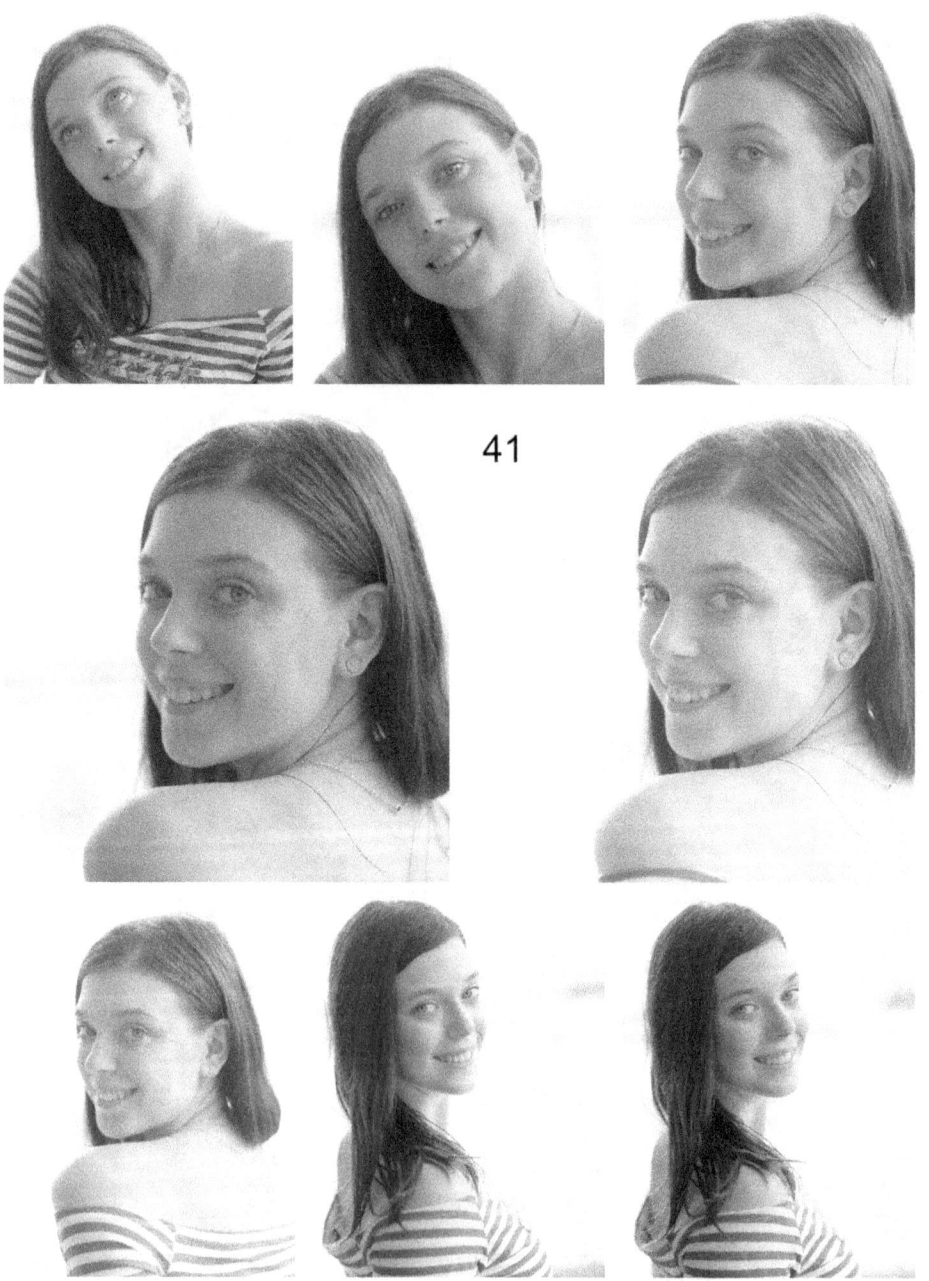

41

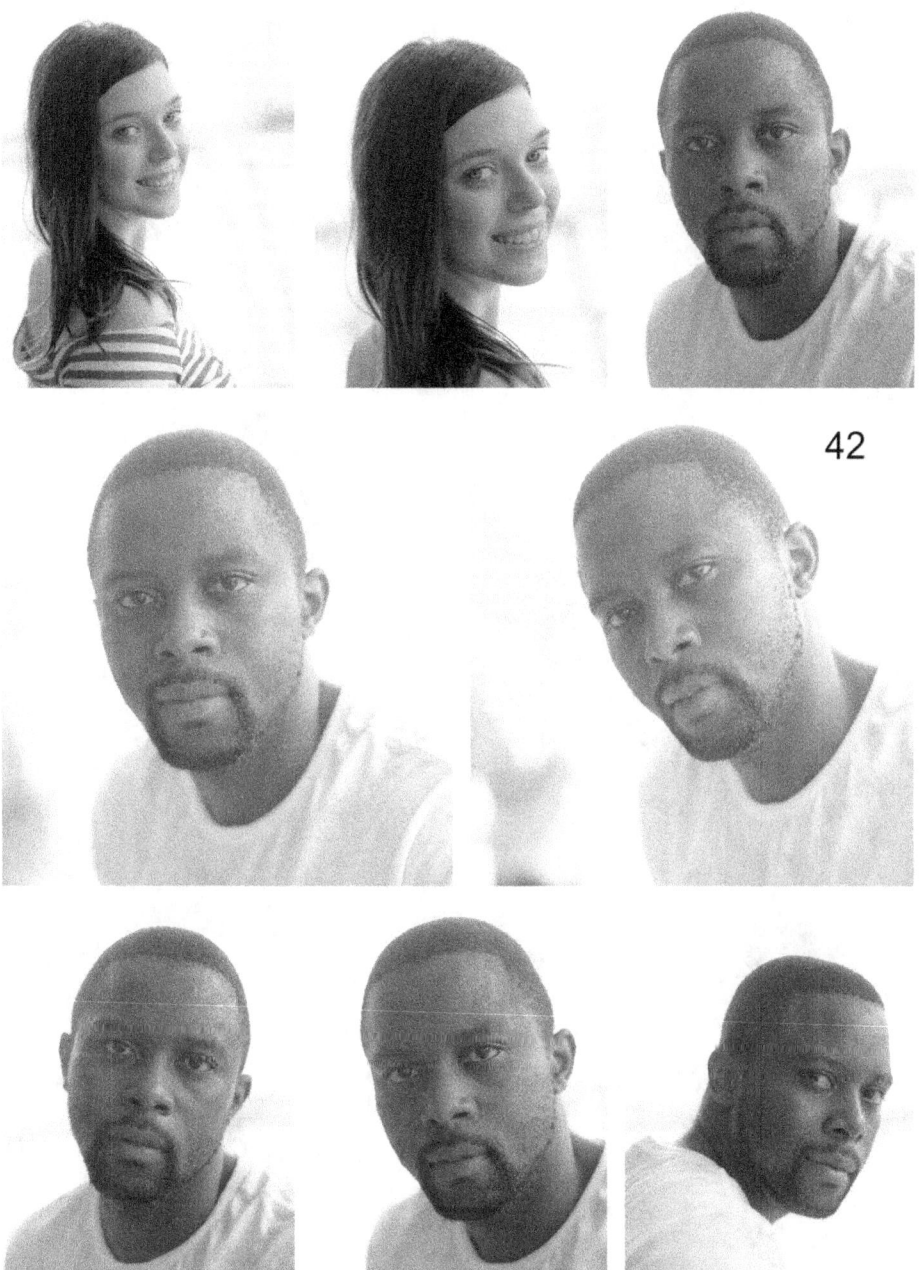

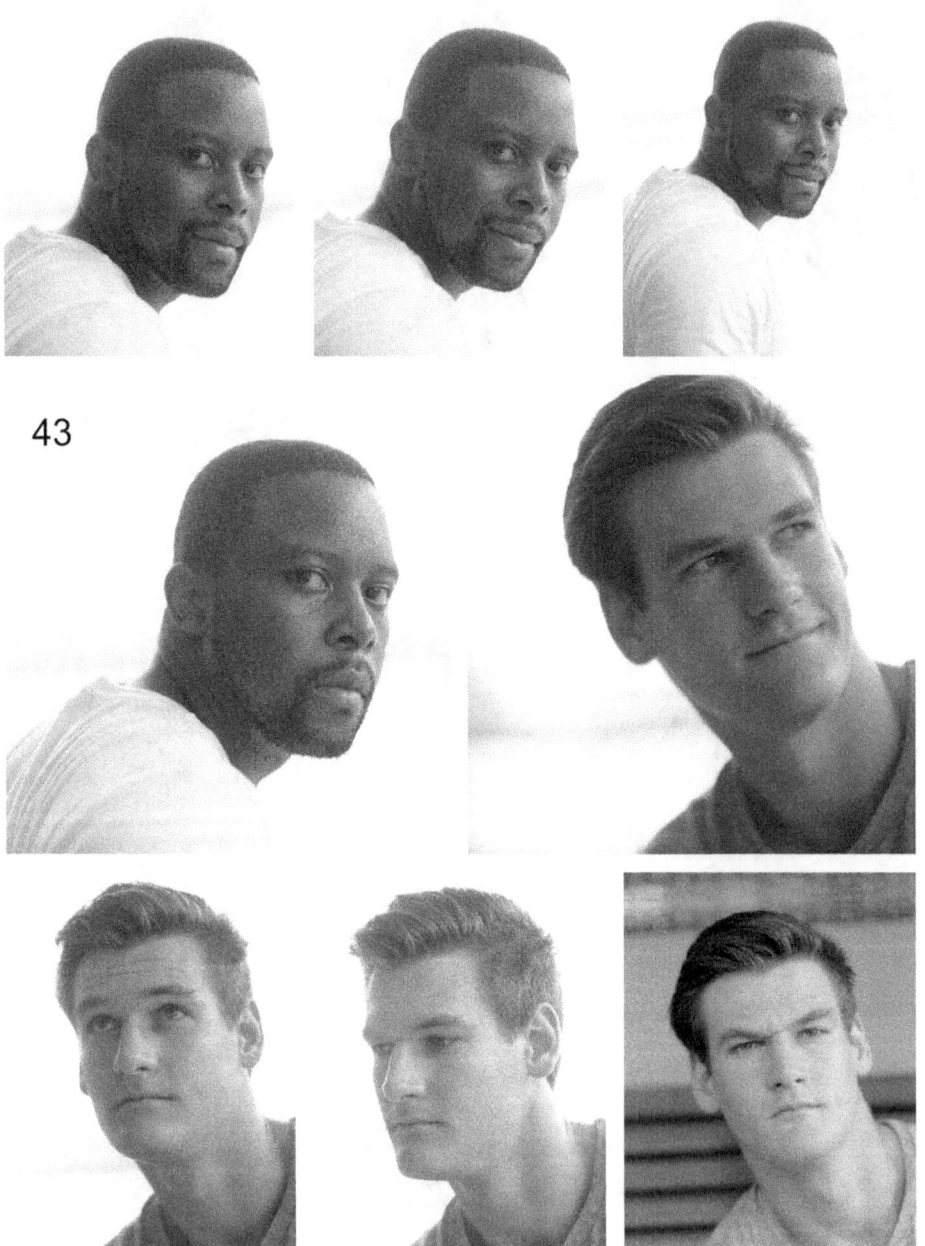

43

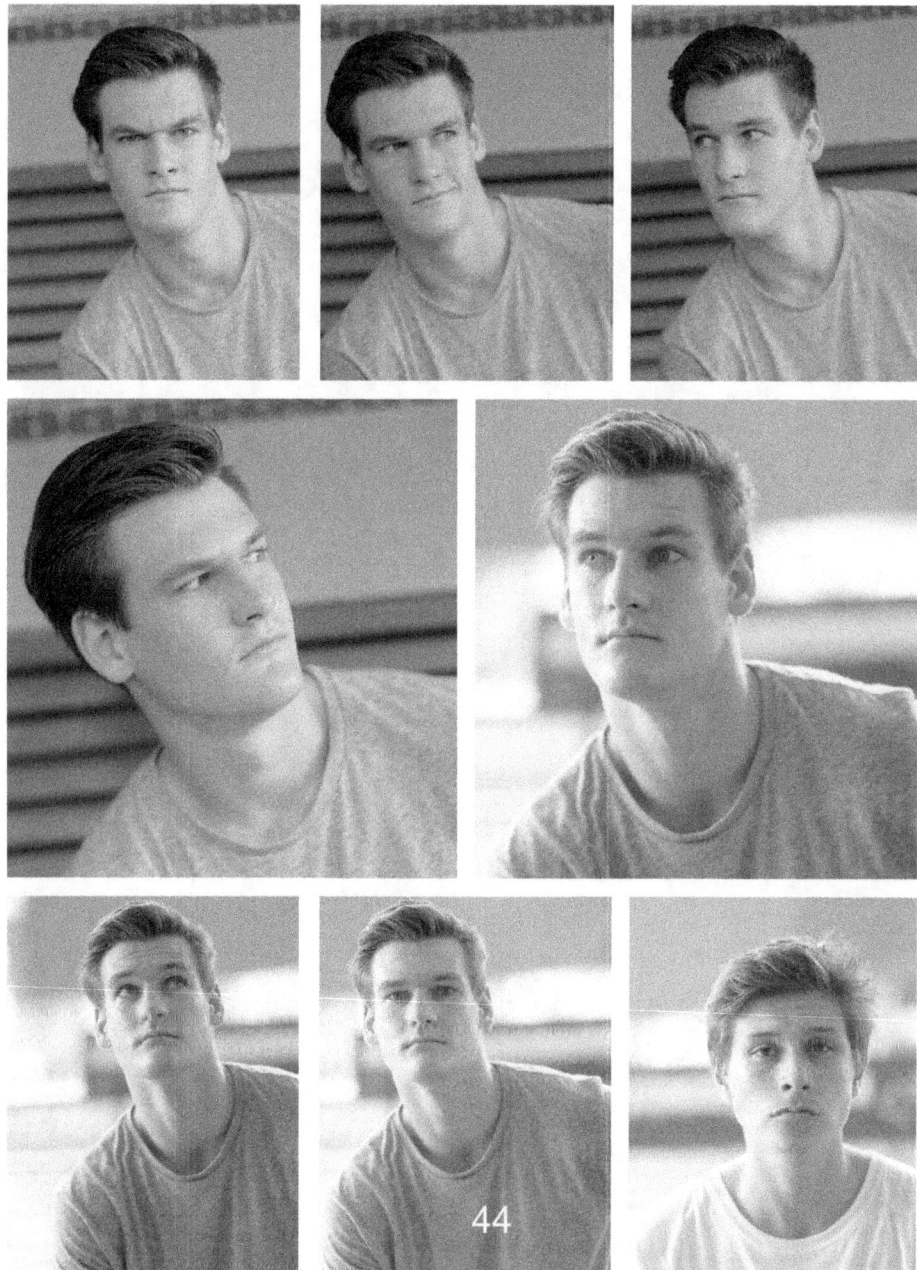

44

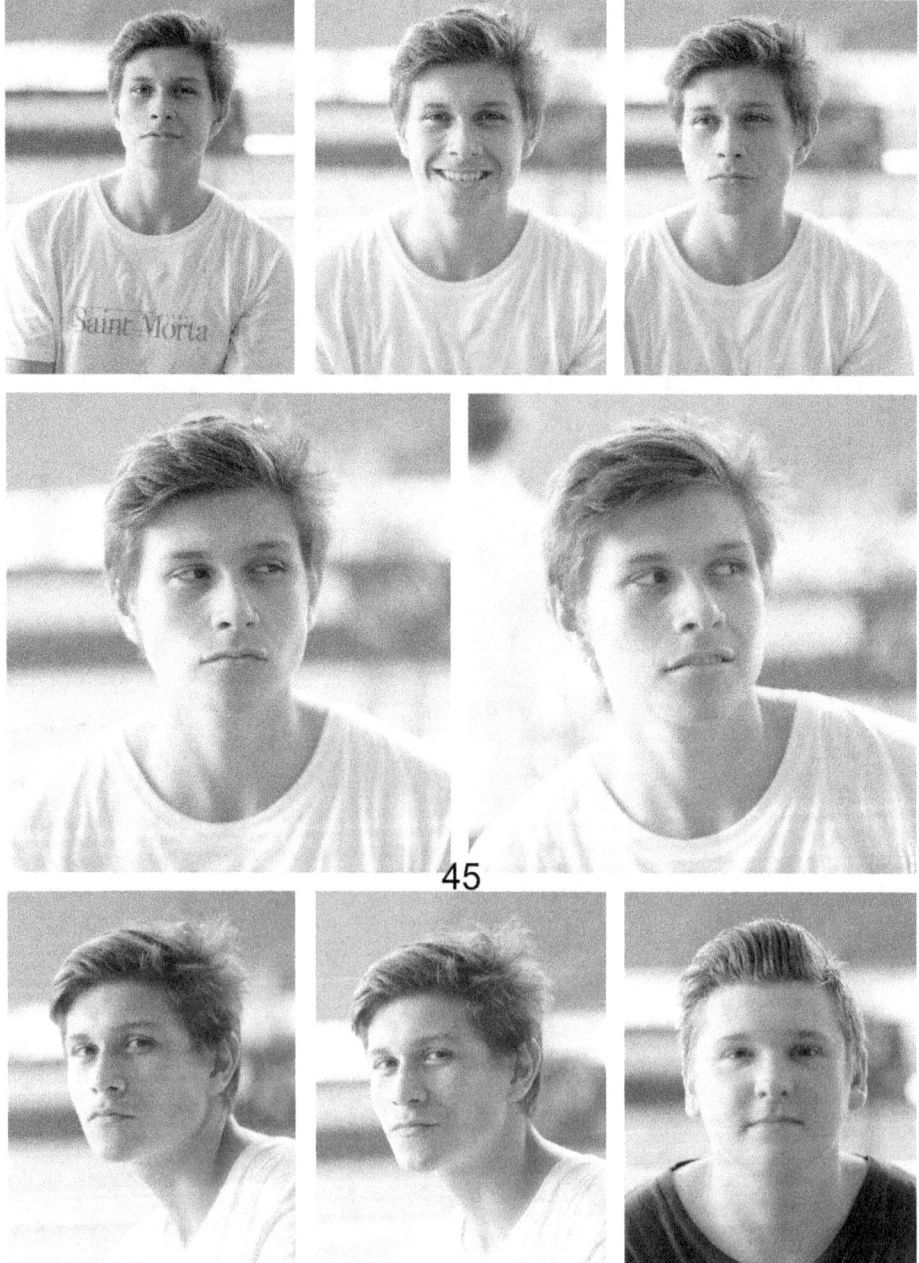

45

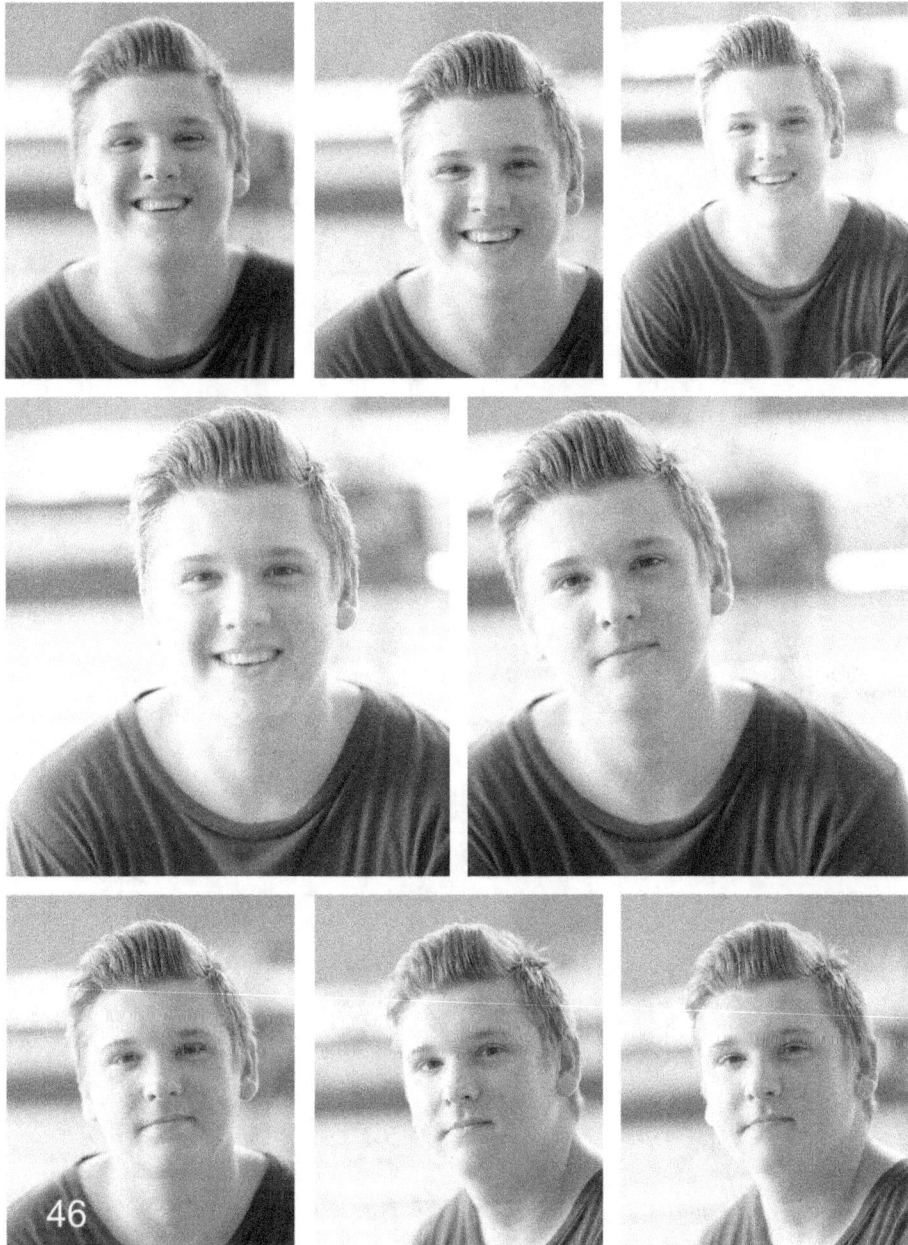

46

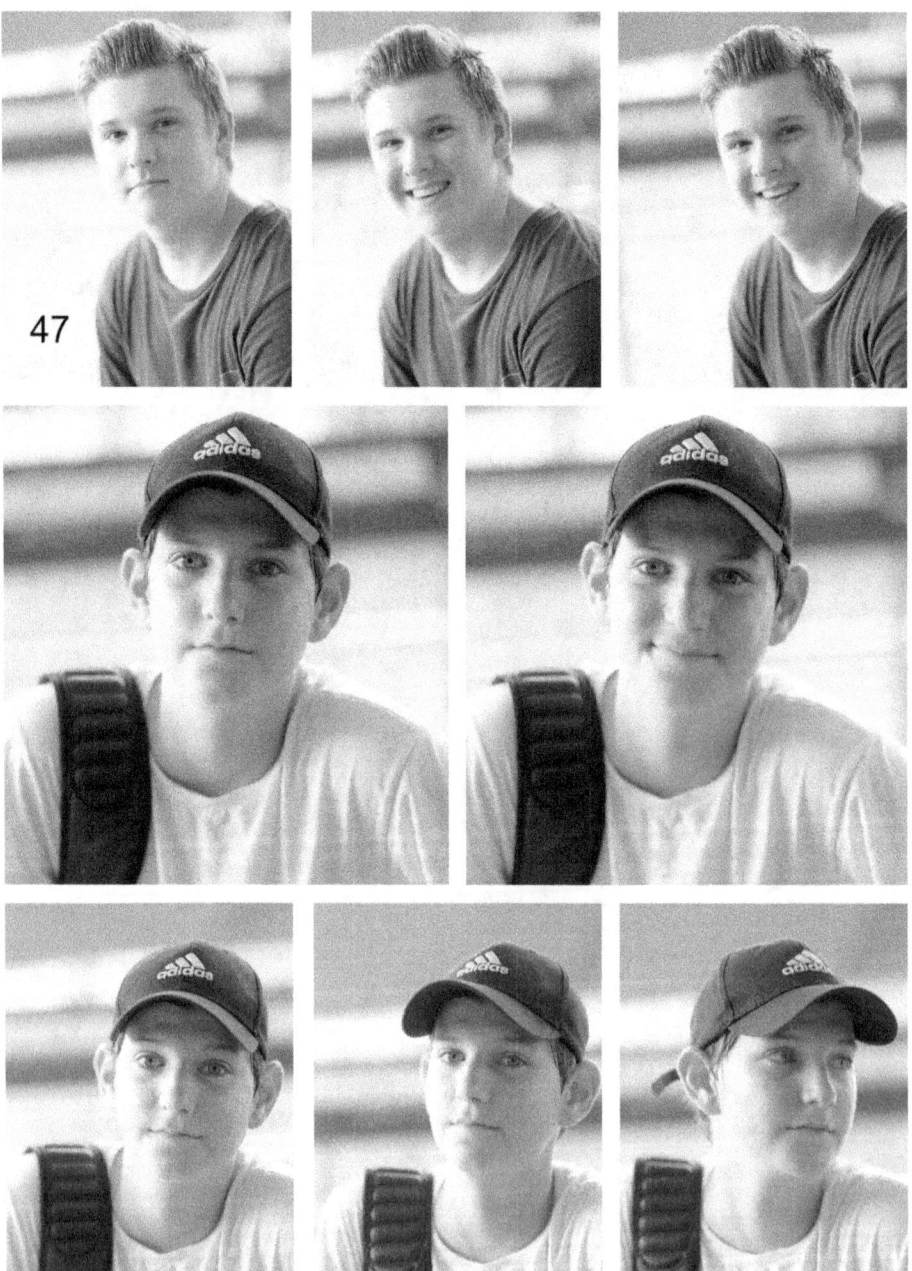

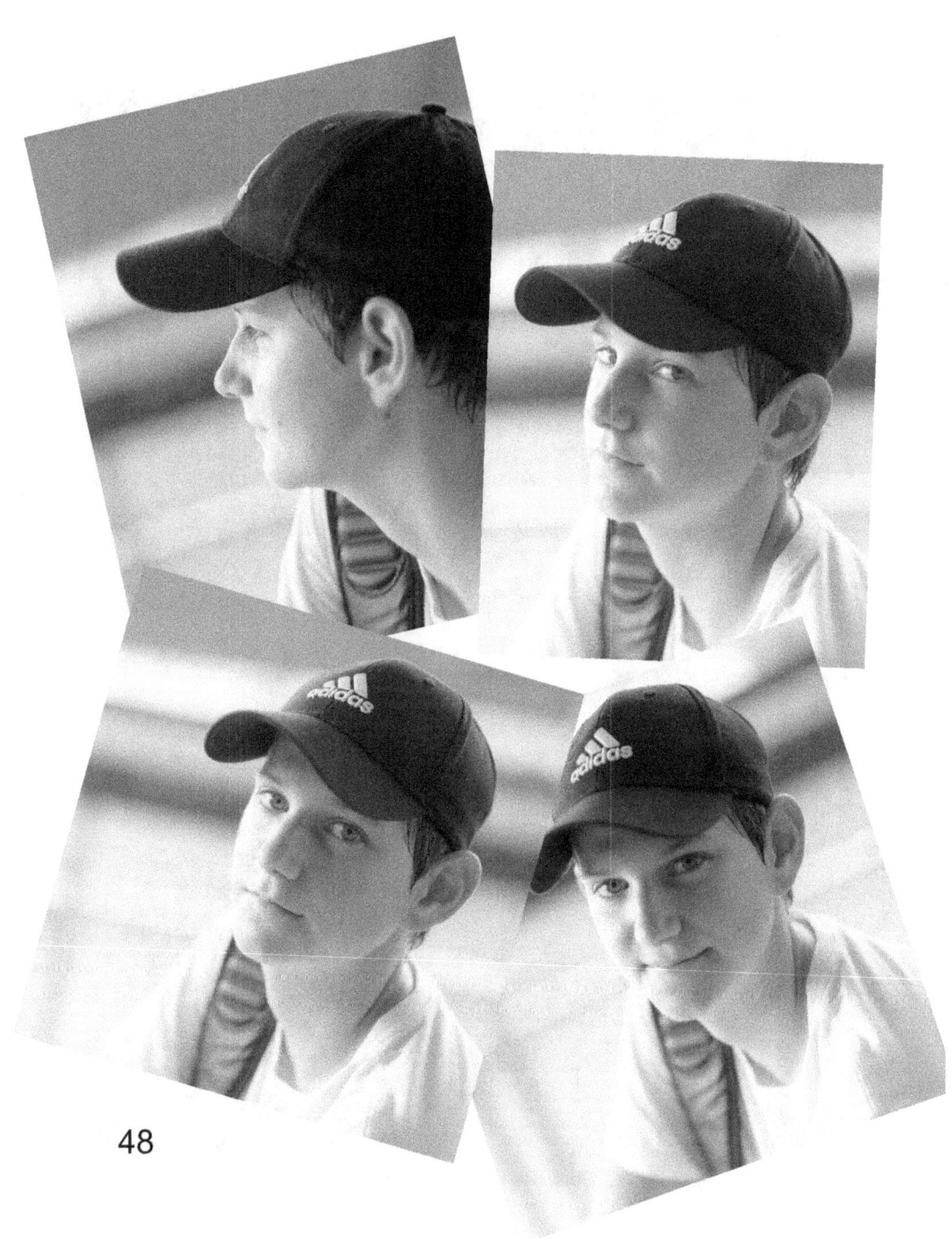

48

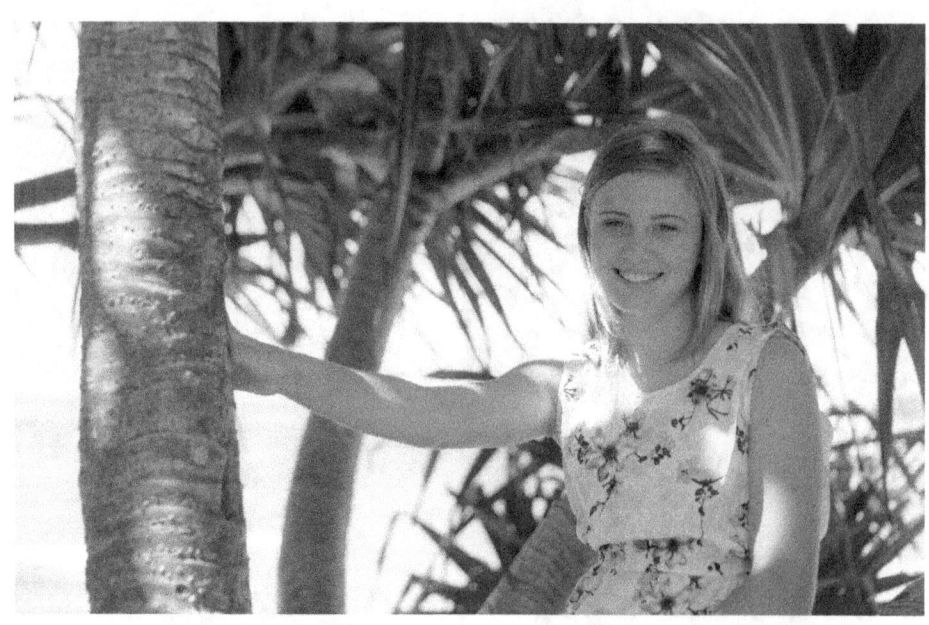

49

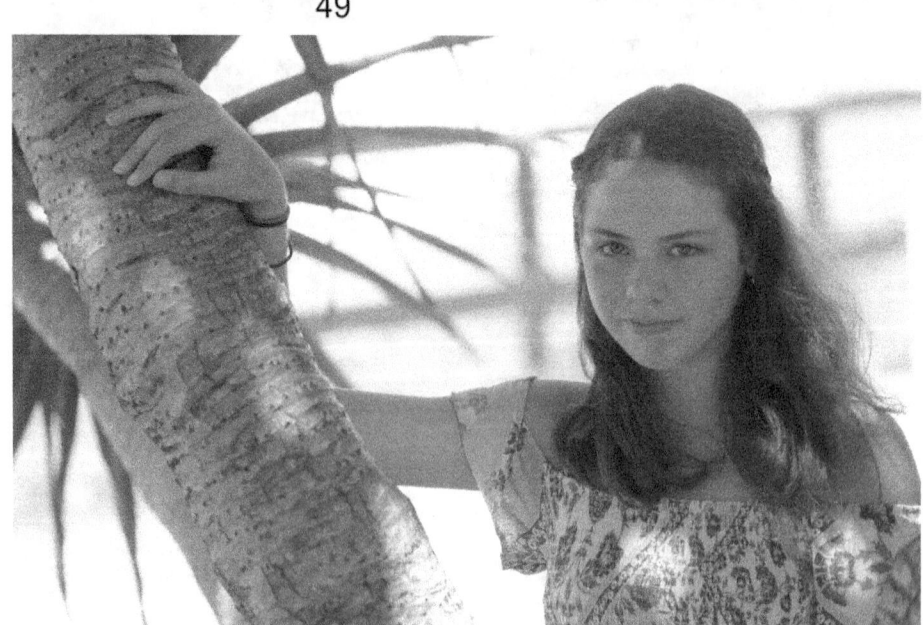

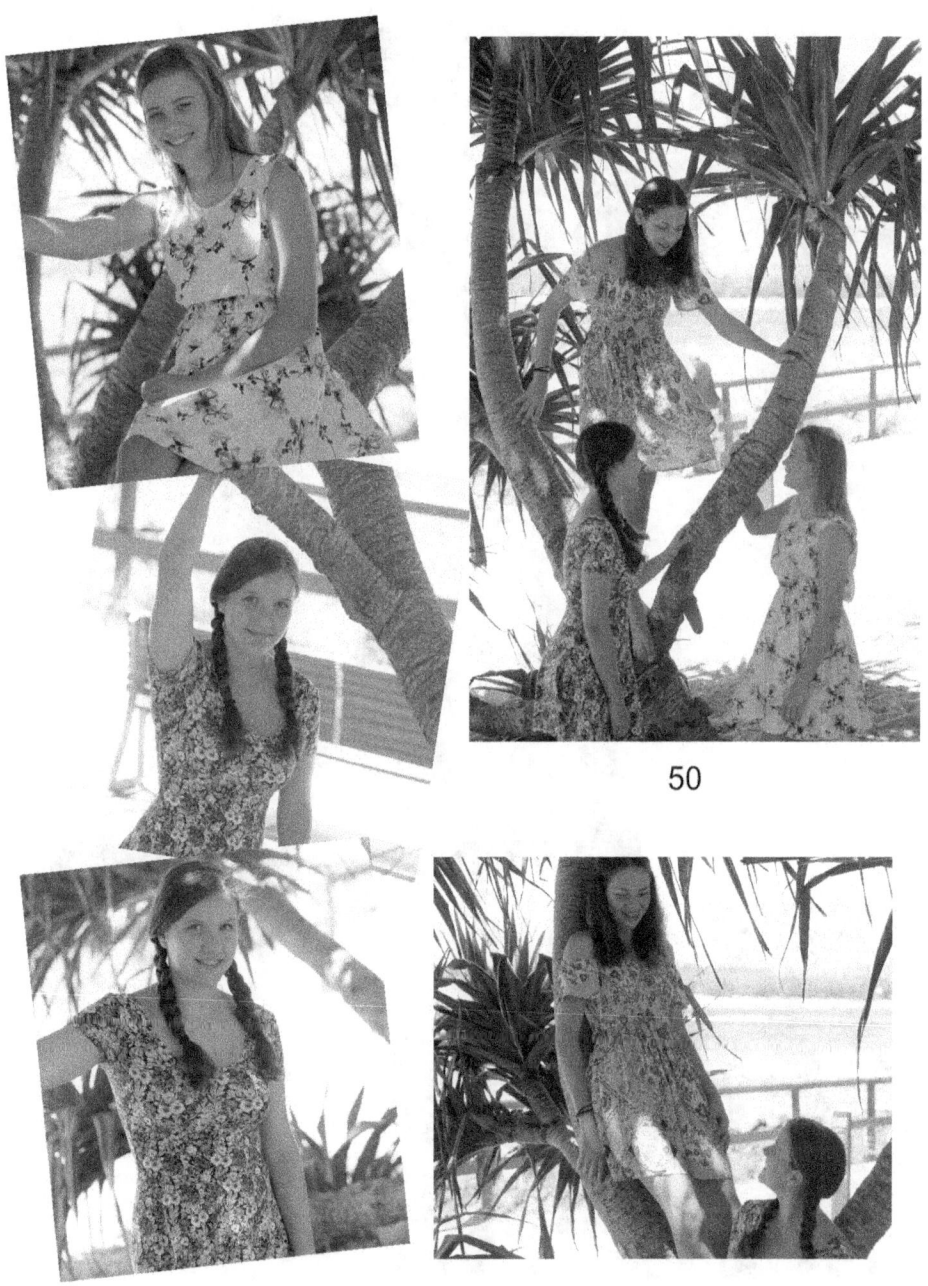

50

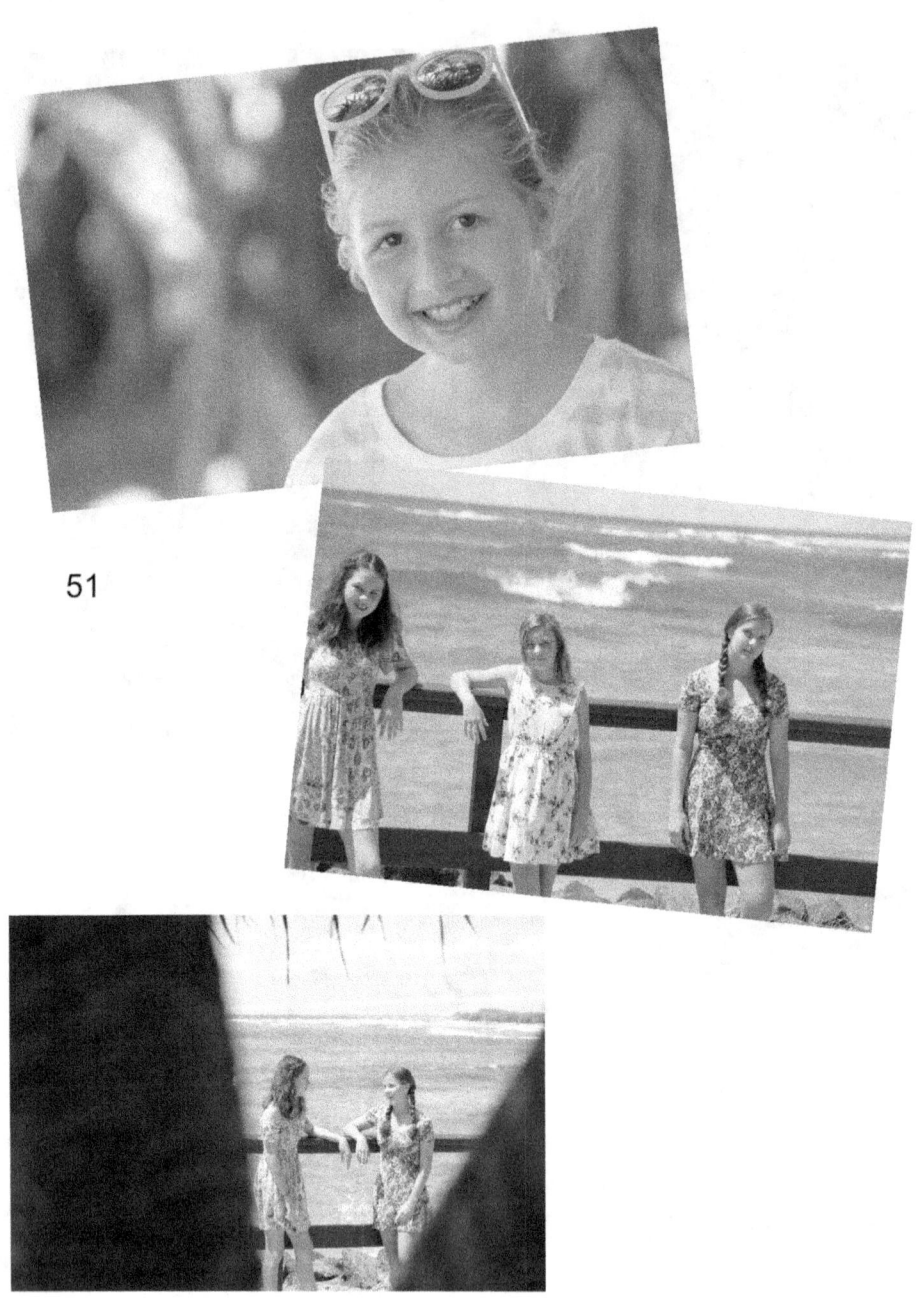

51

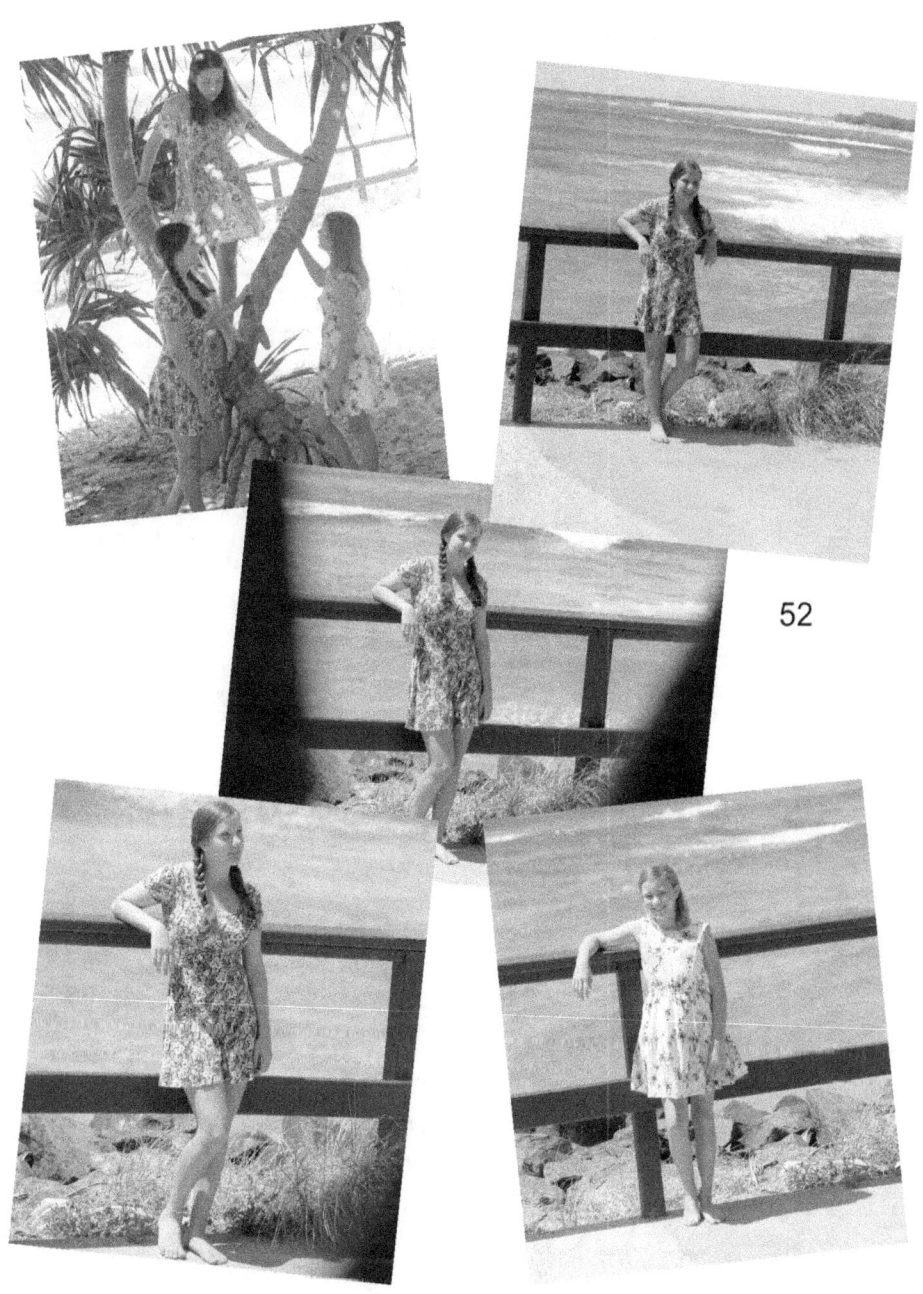

52

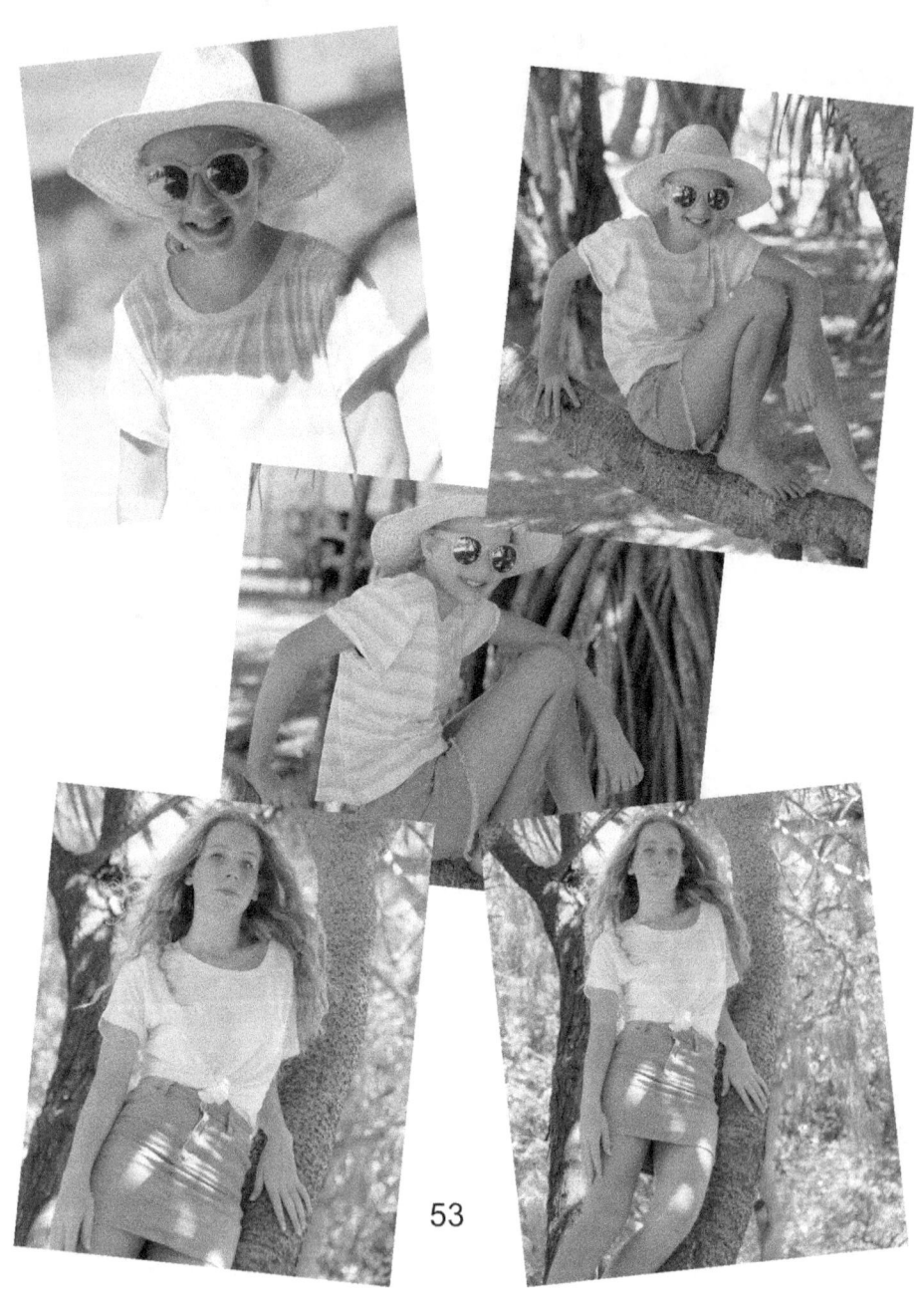

53

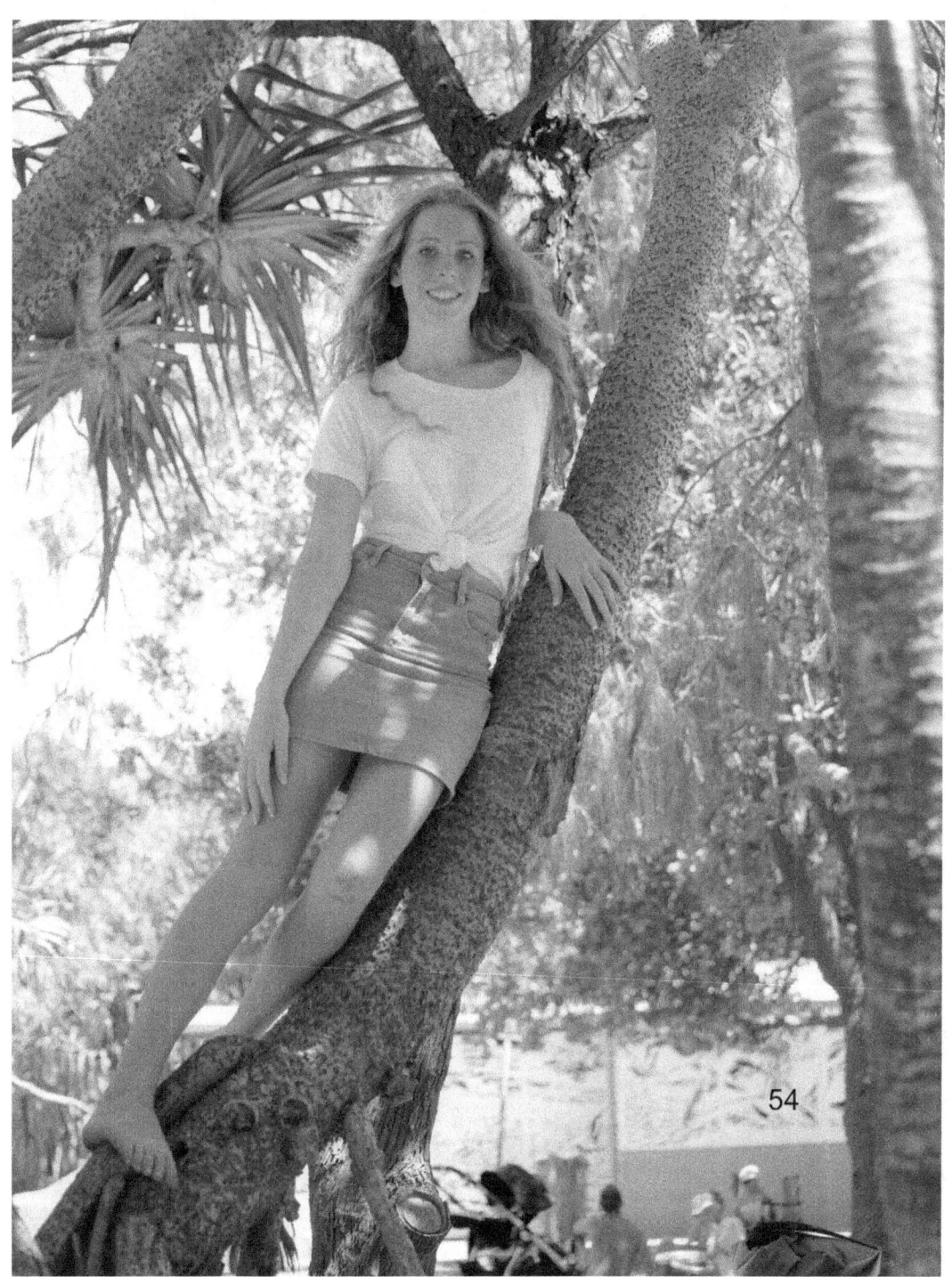

54

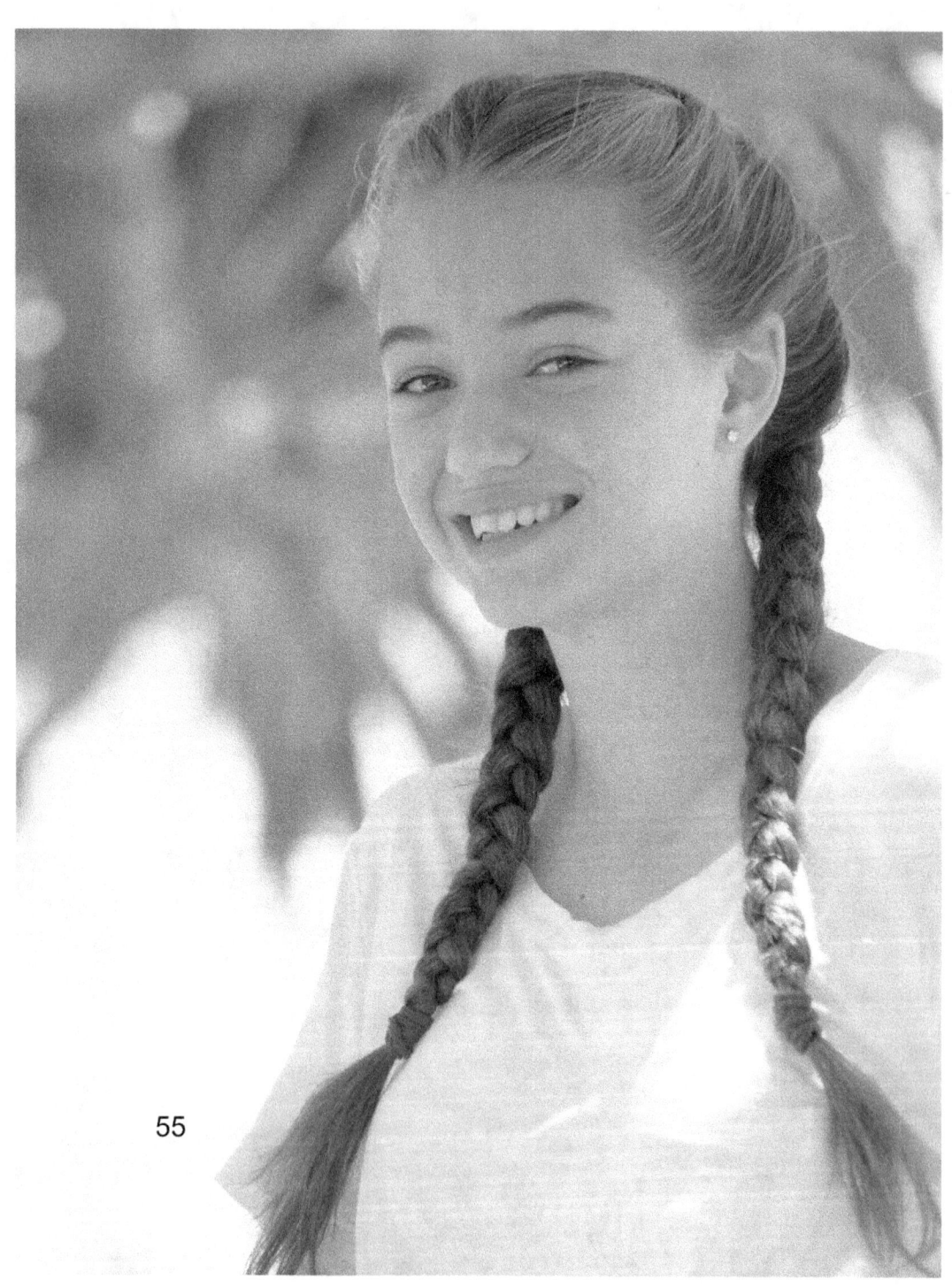

55

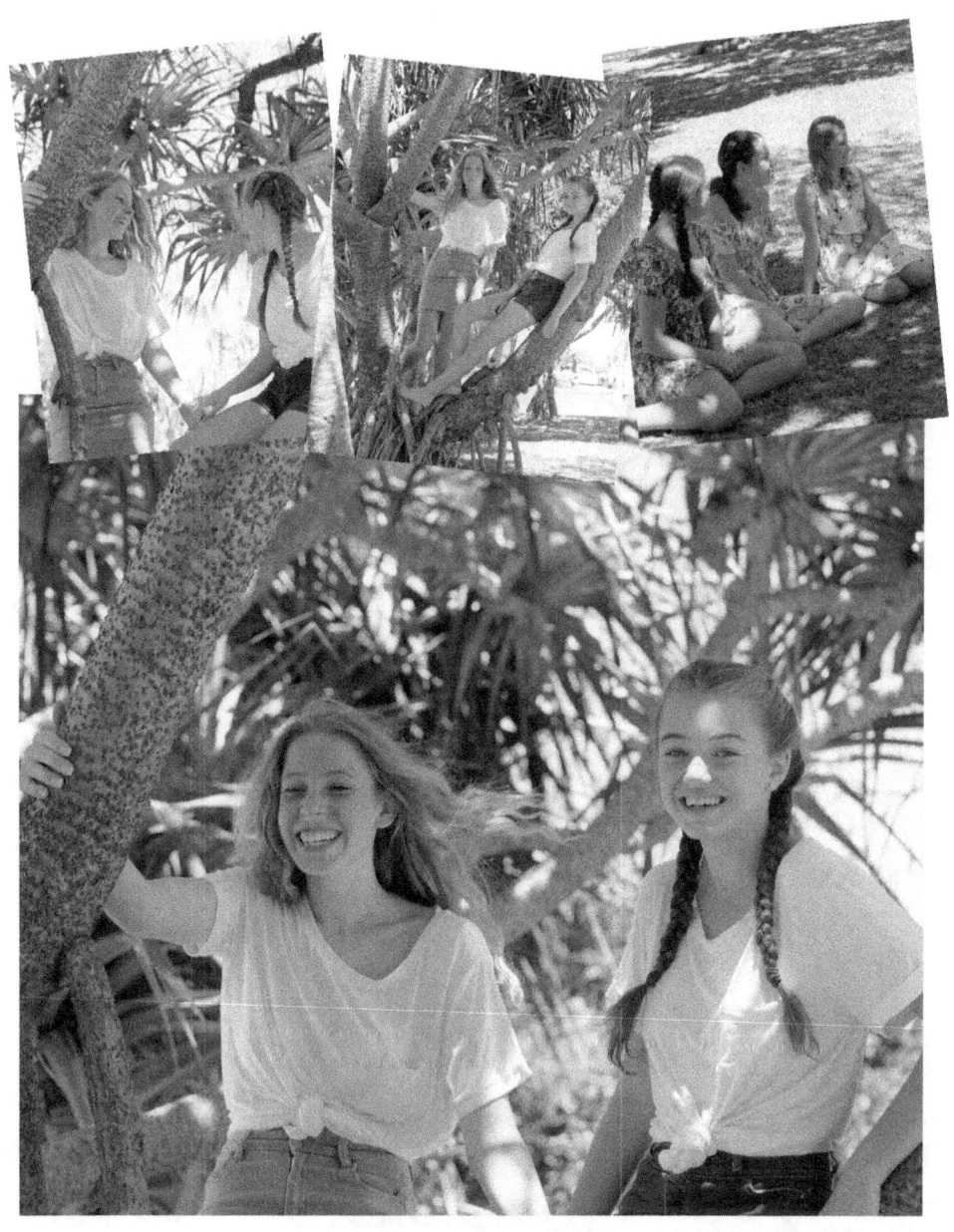

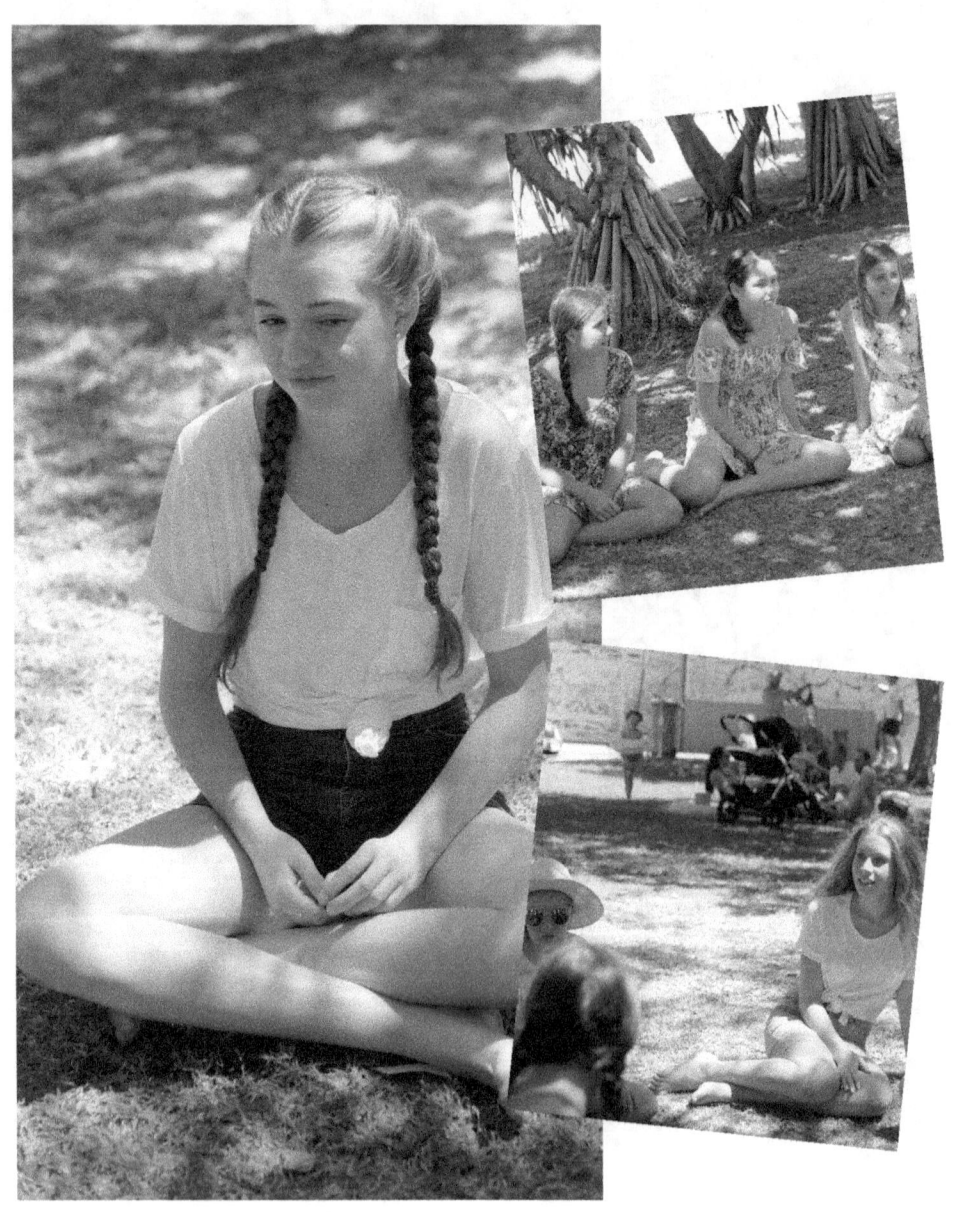

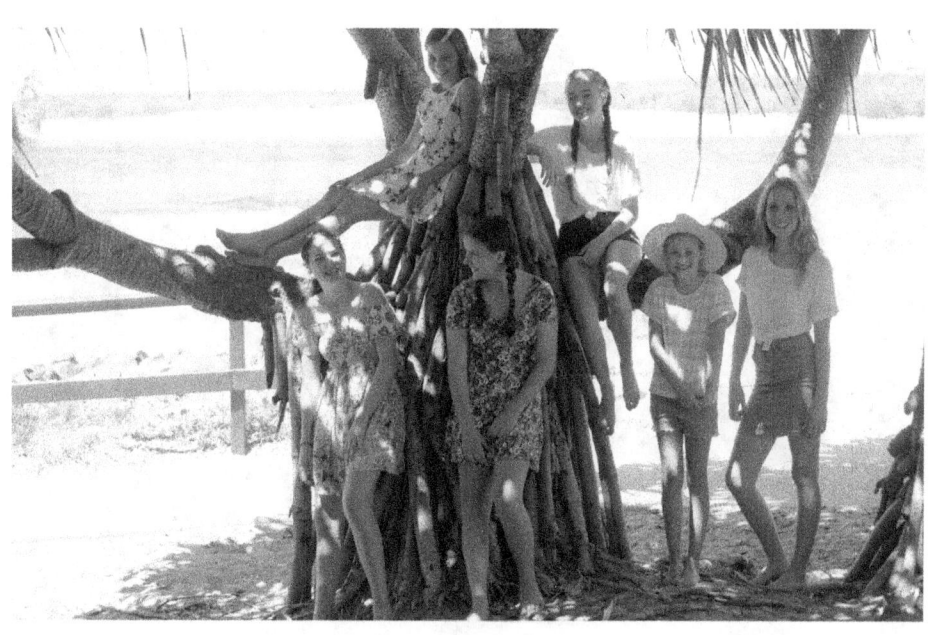

58

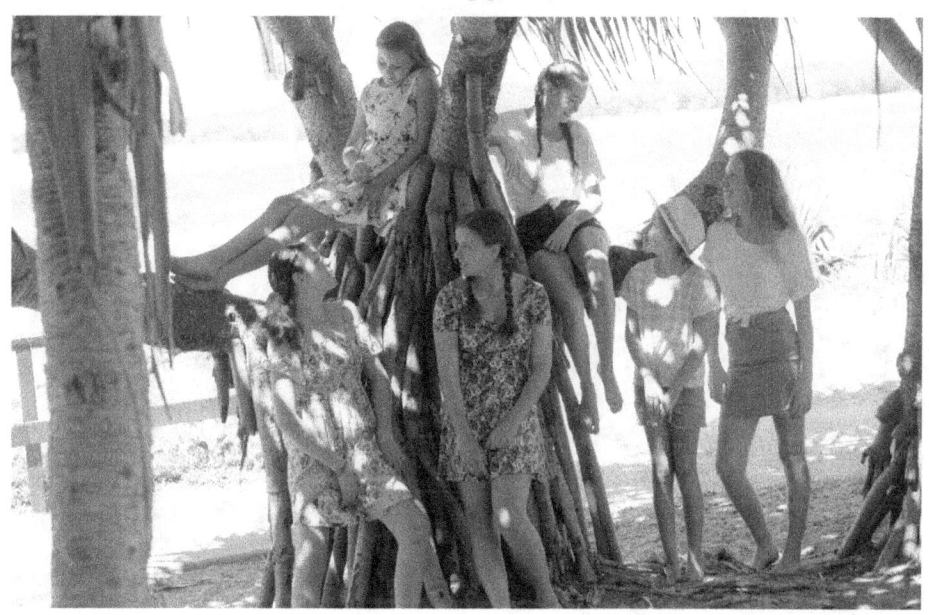

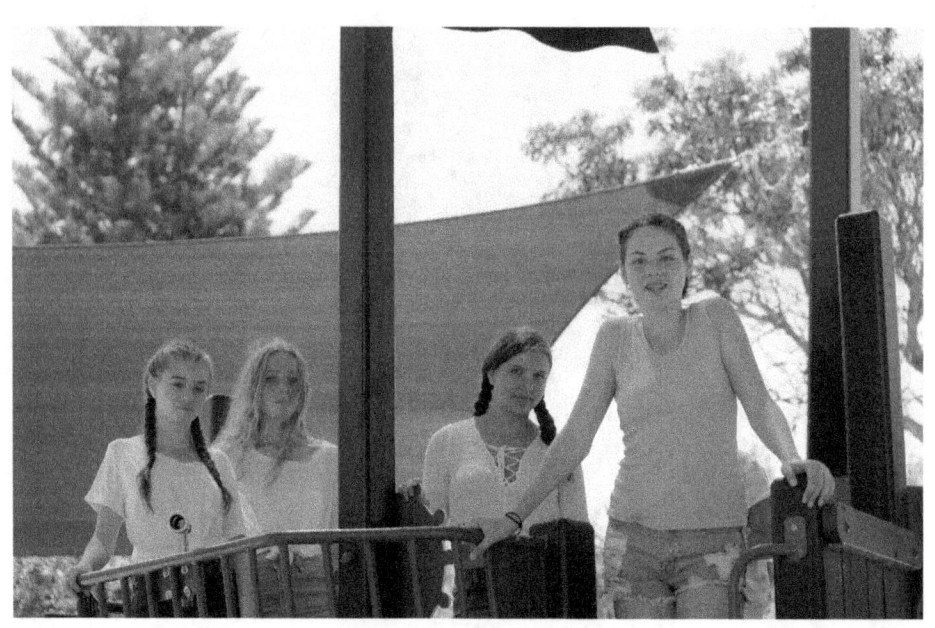

59

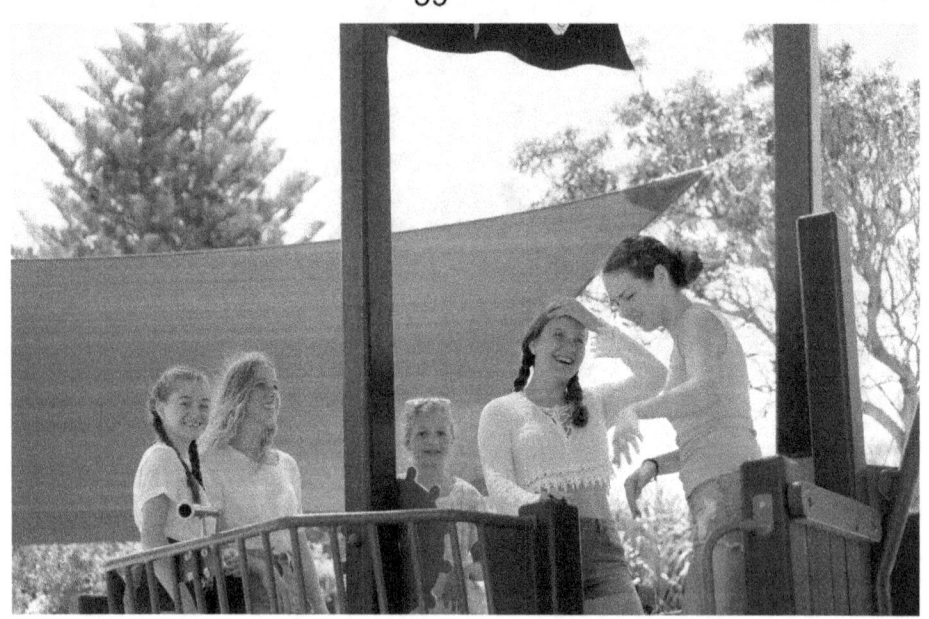

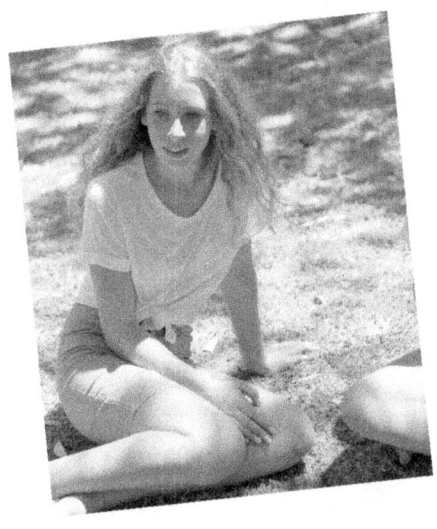 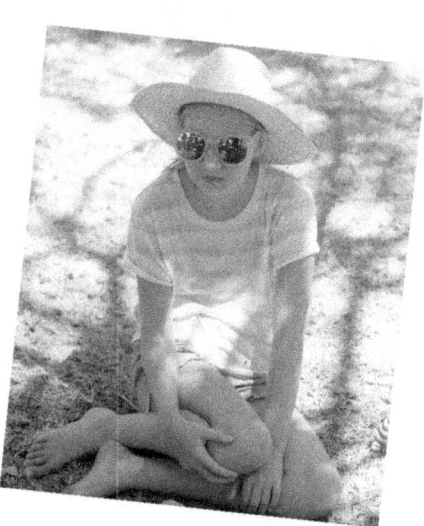

60

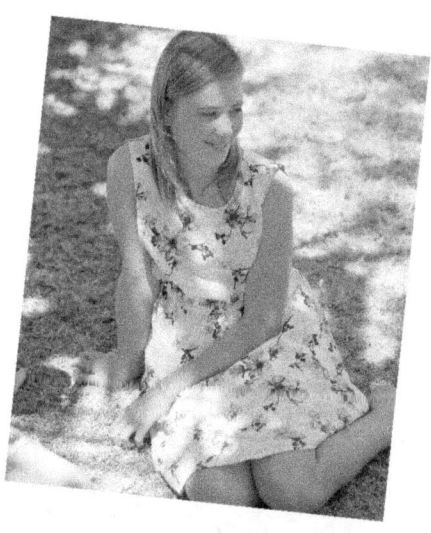 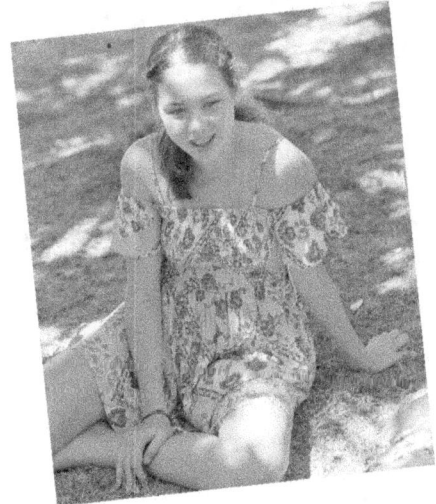

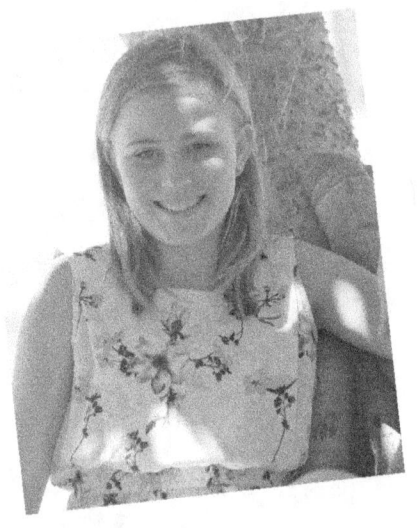 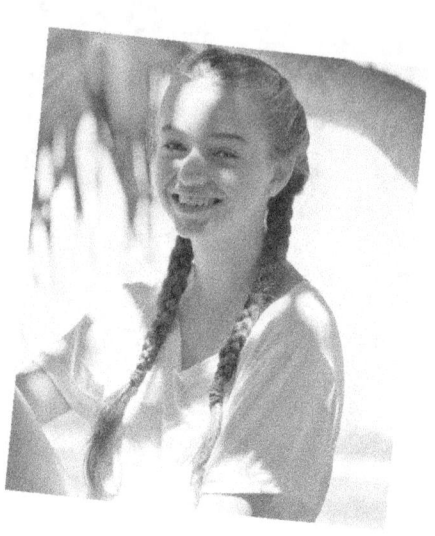

62

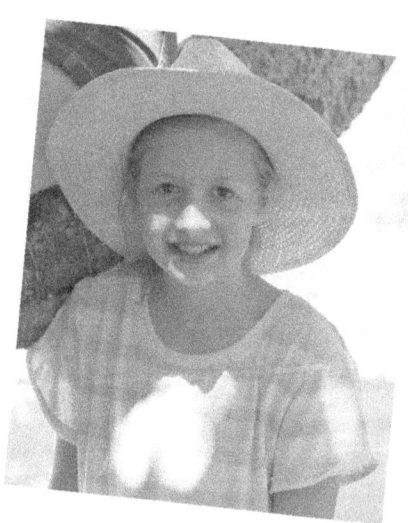 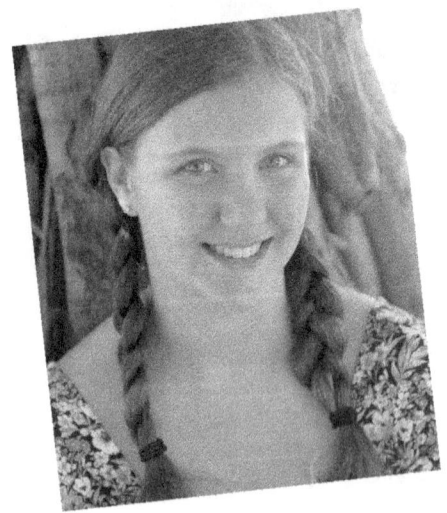

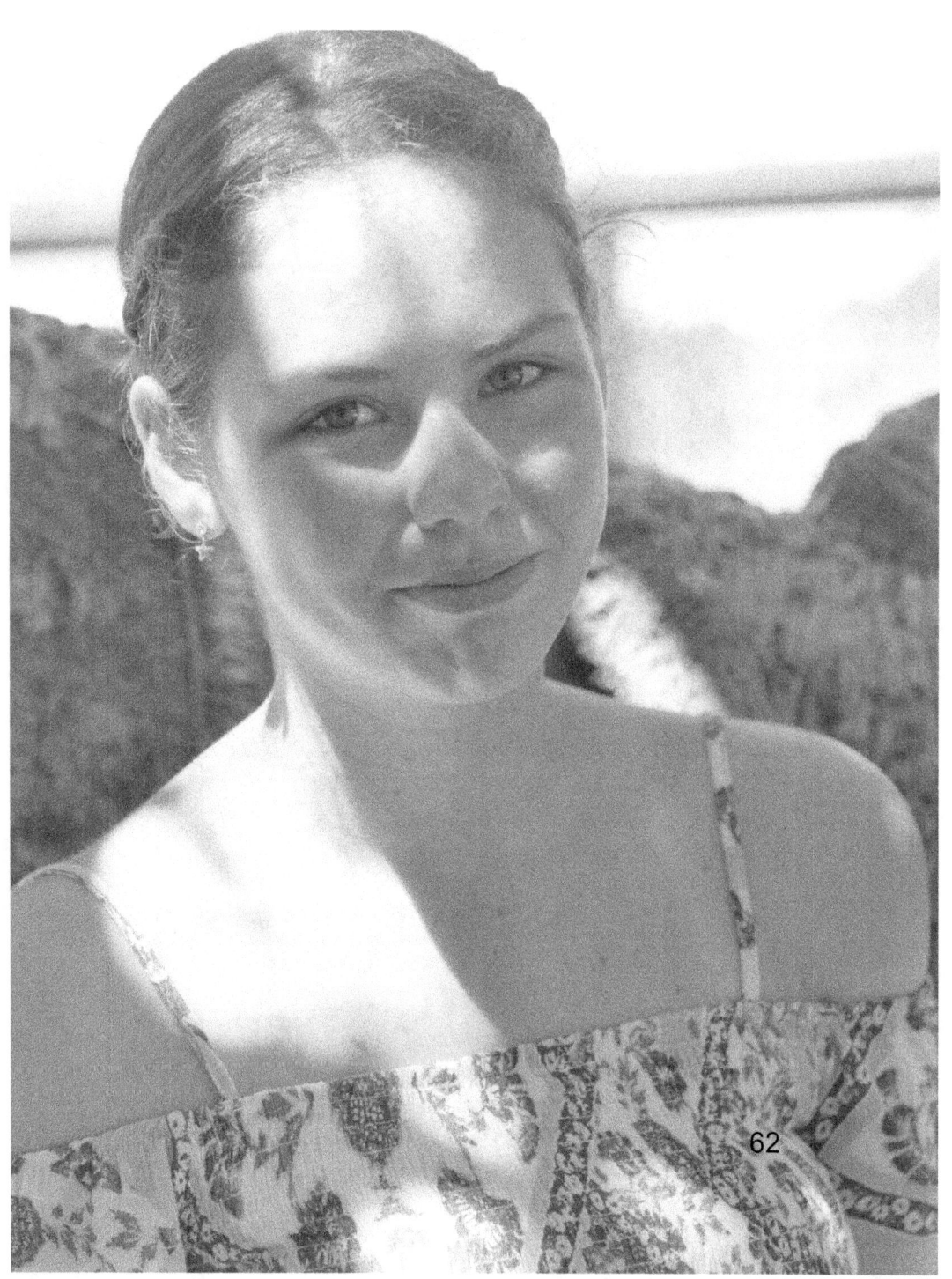

62

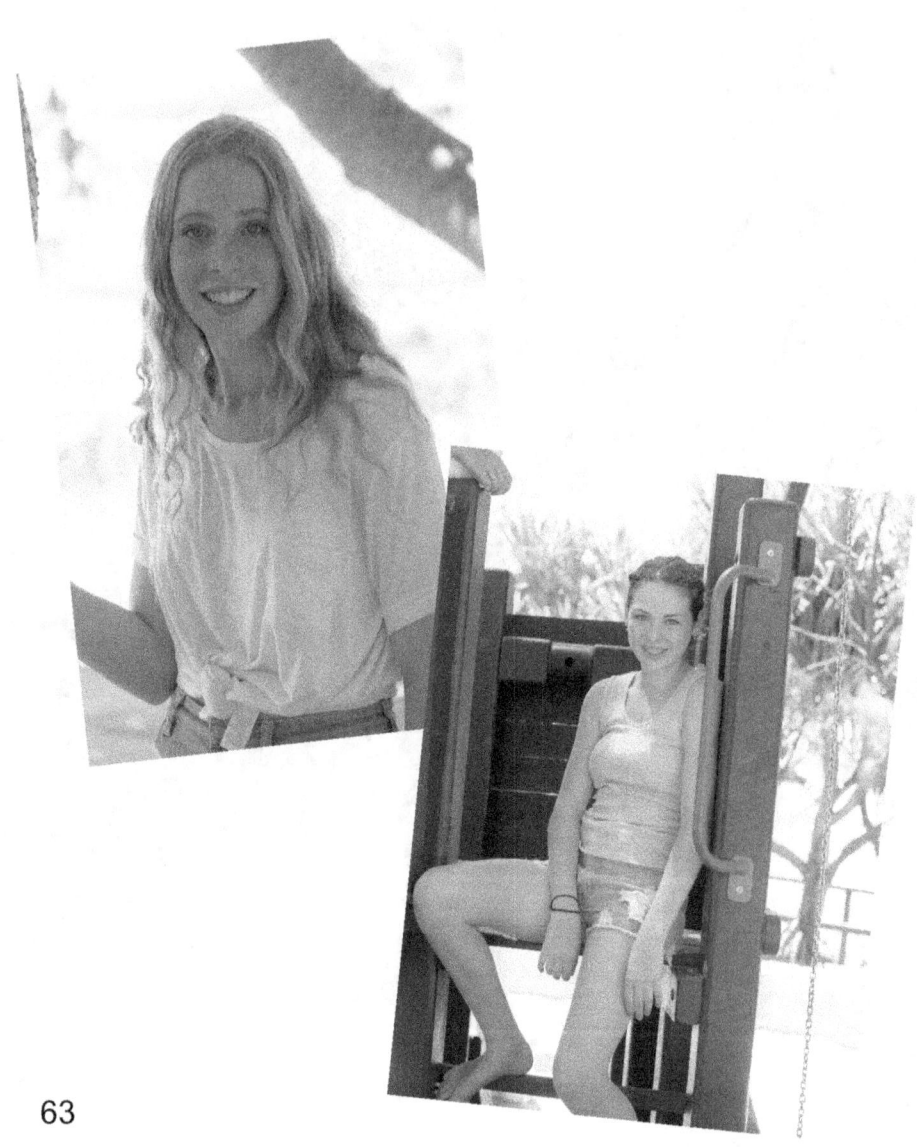

63

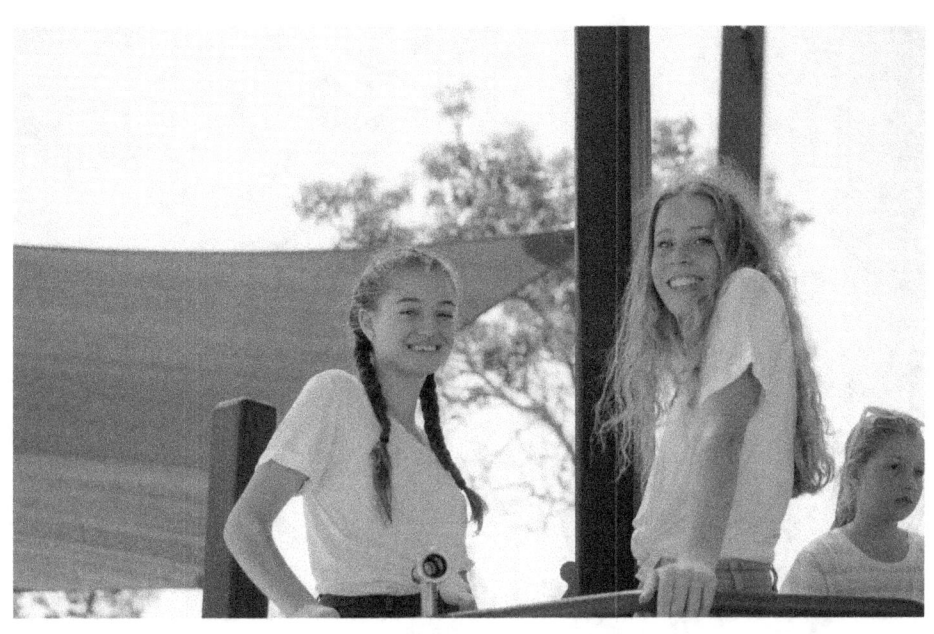

64

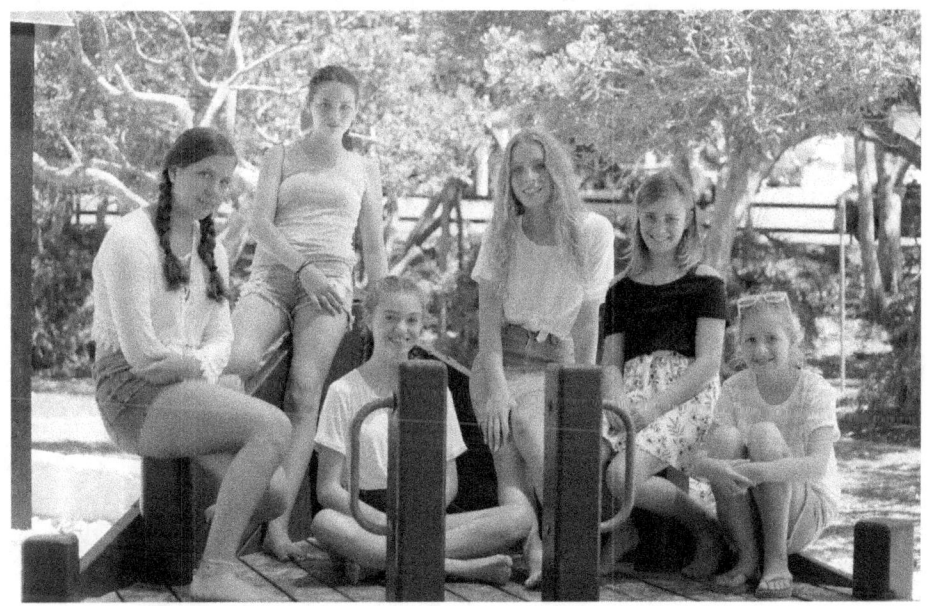

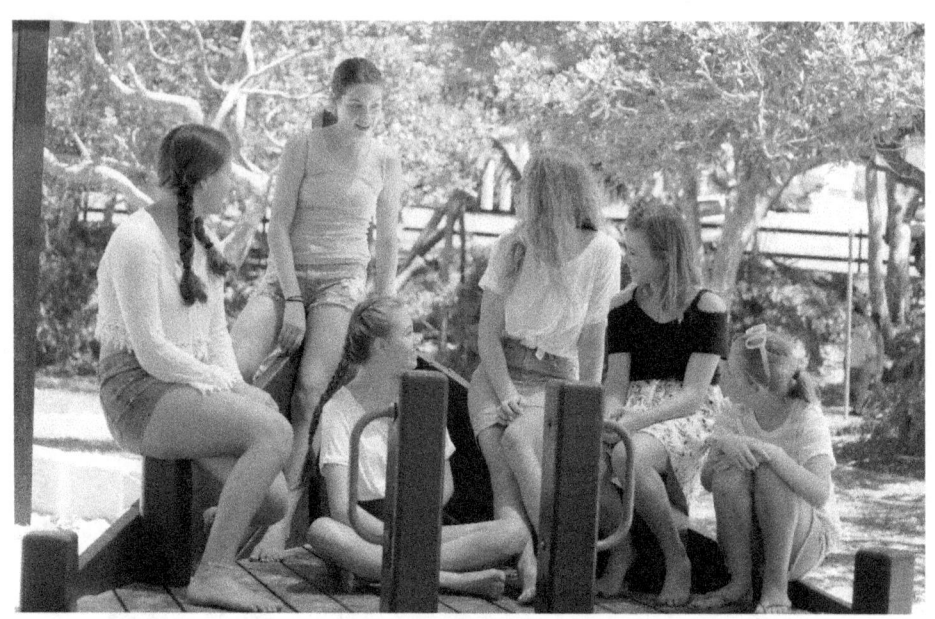

65

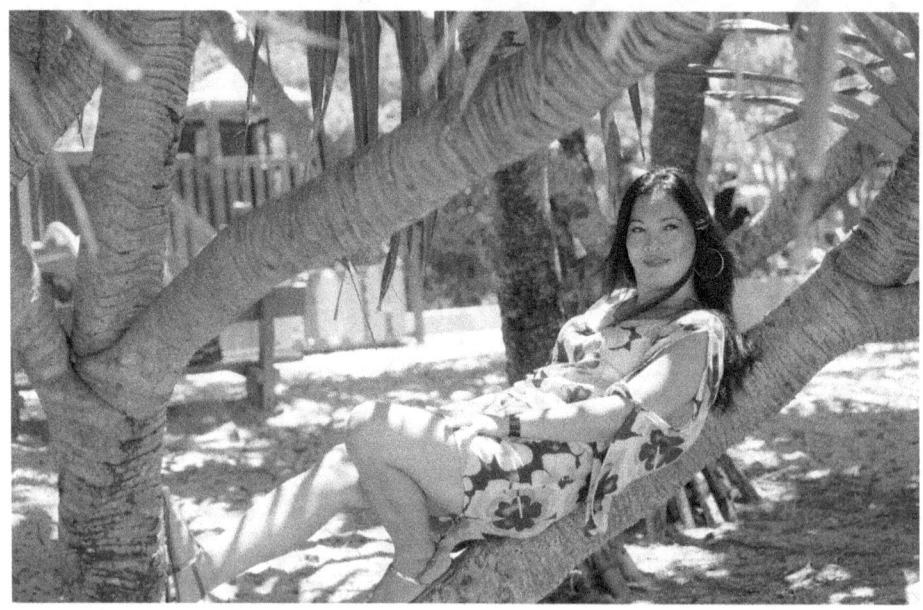

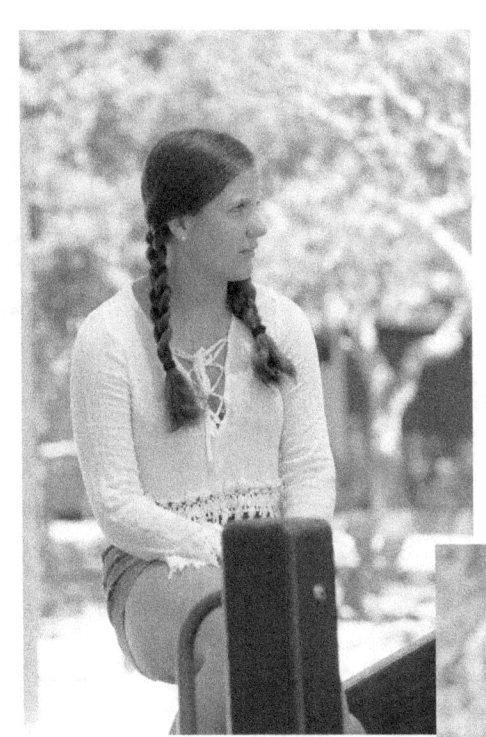

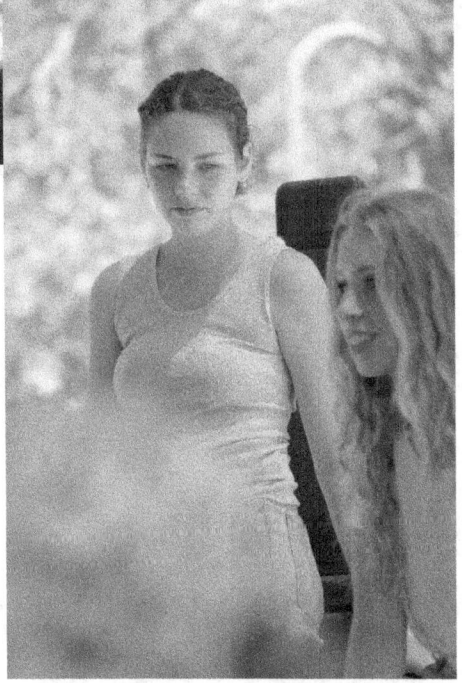

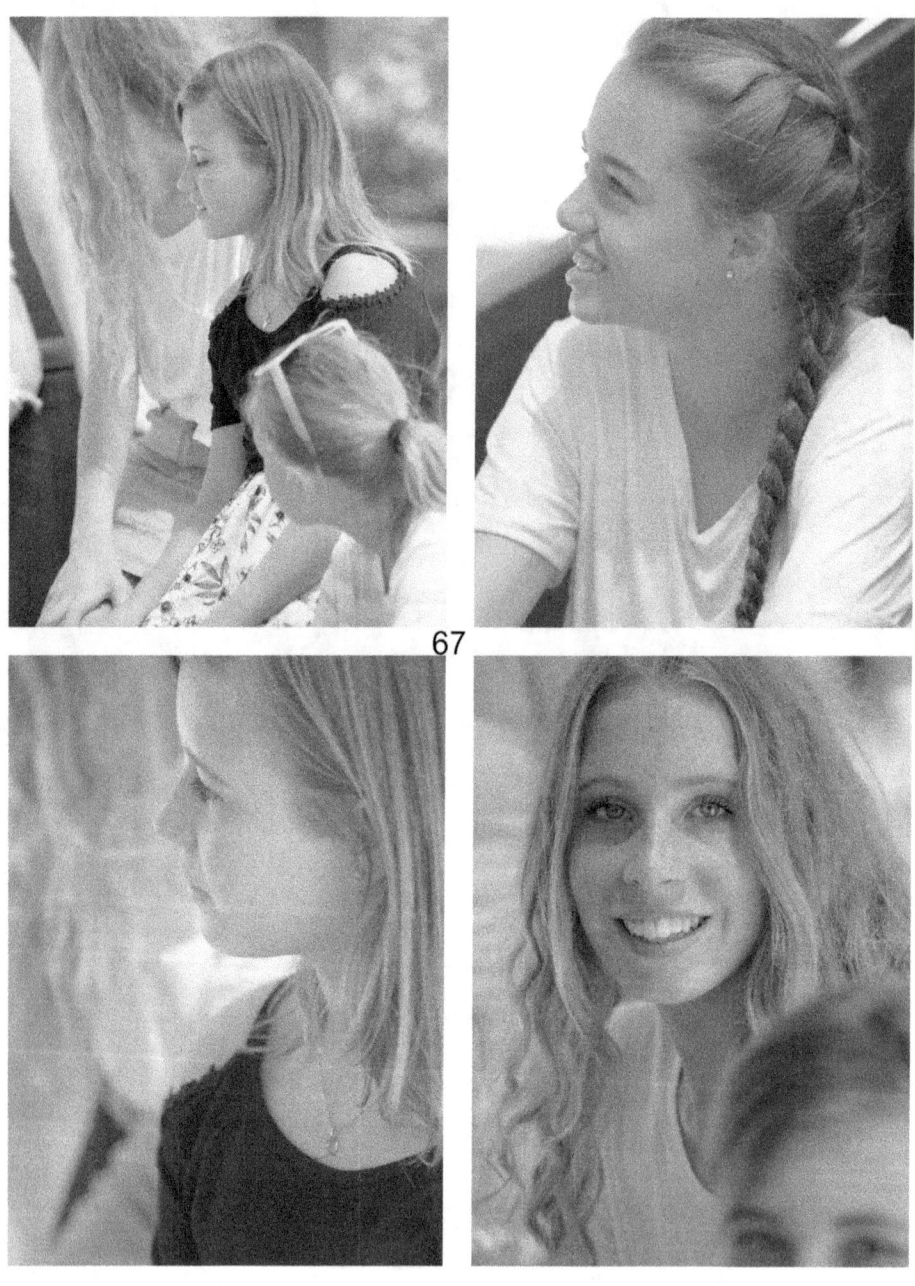

67

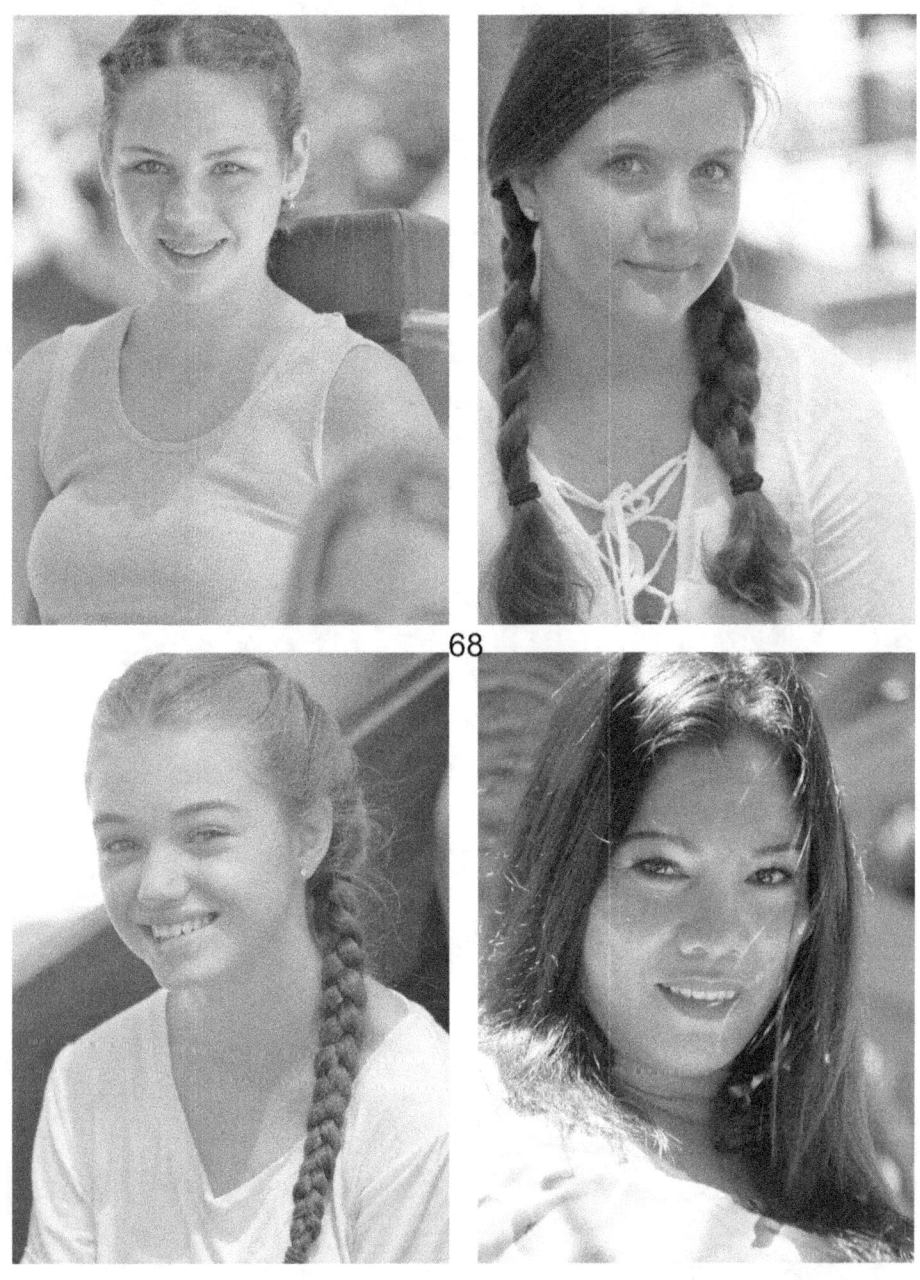

68

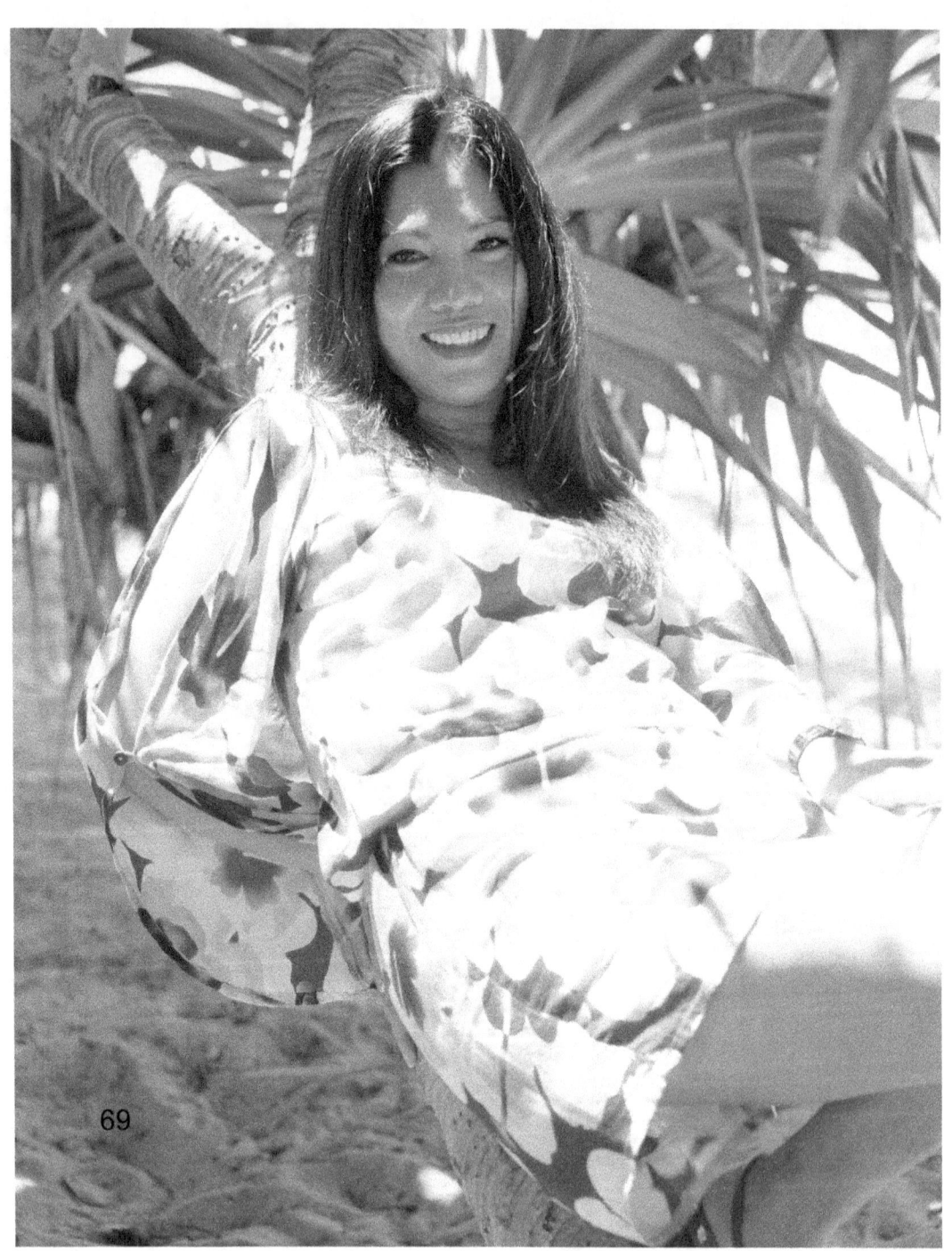

69

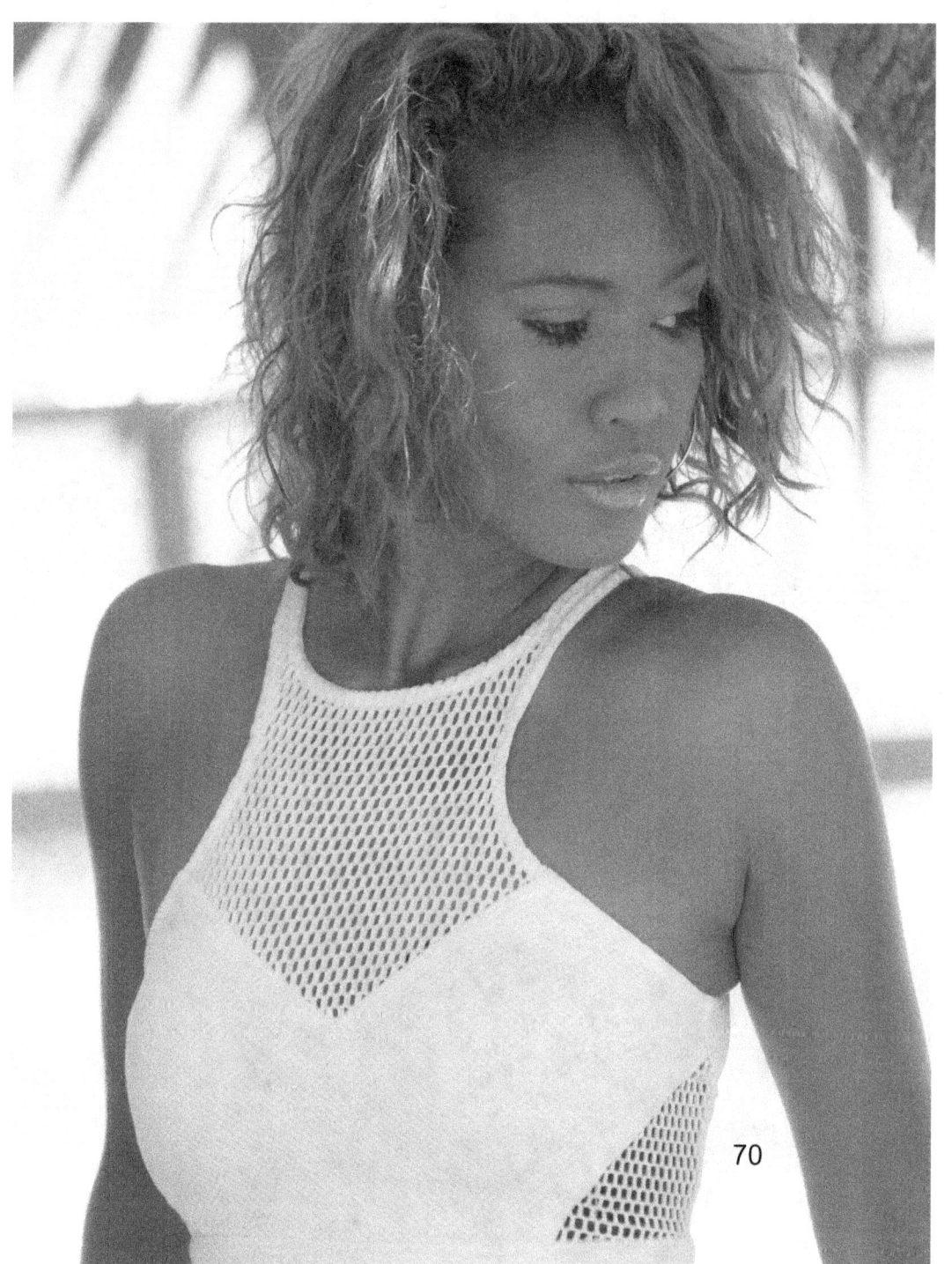

70

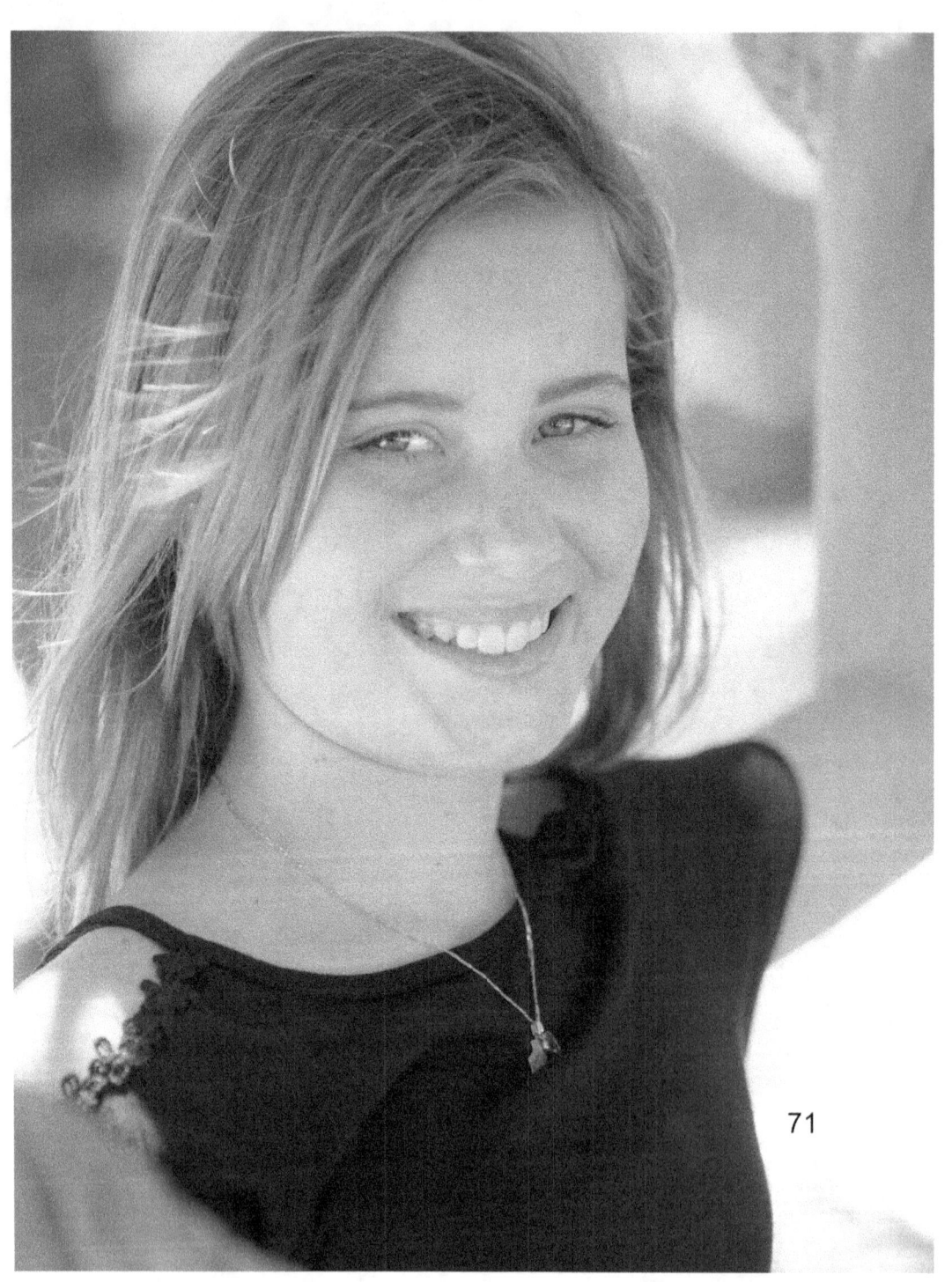

71

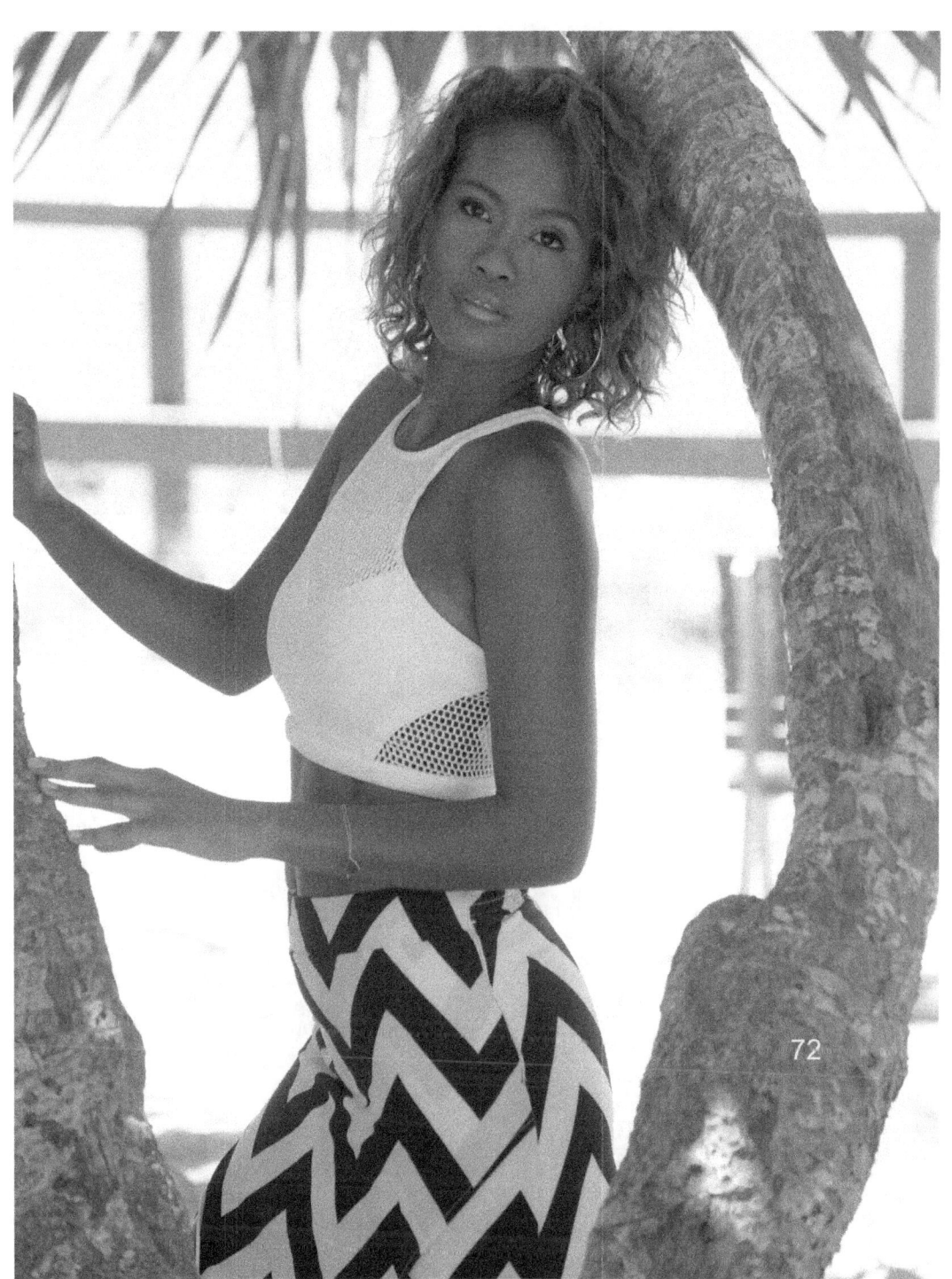

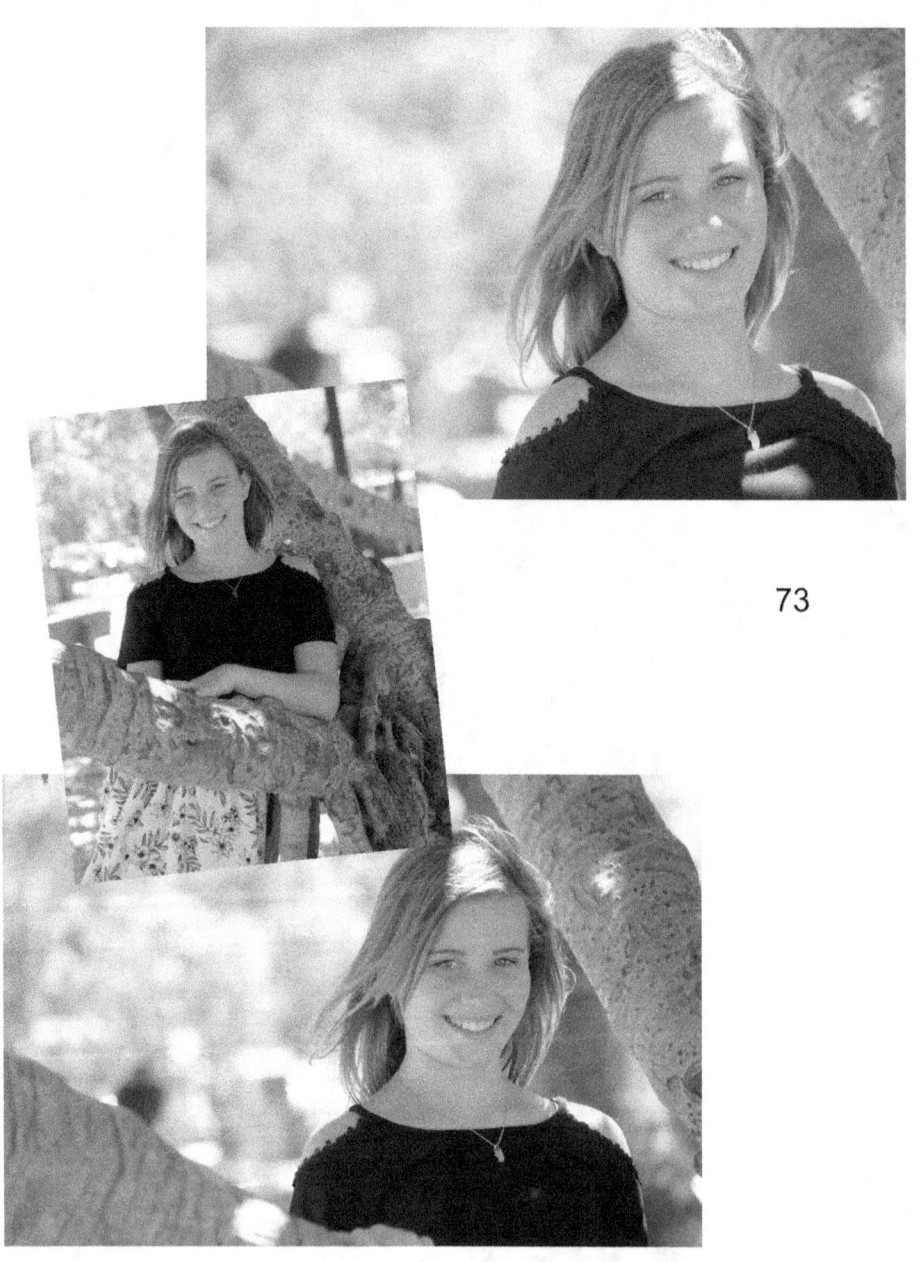

73

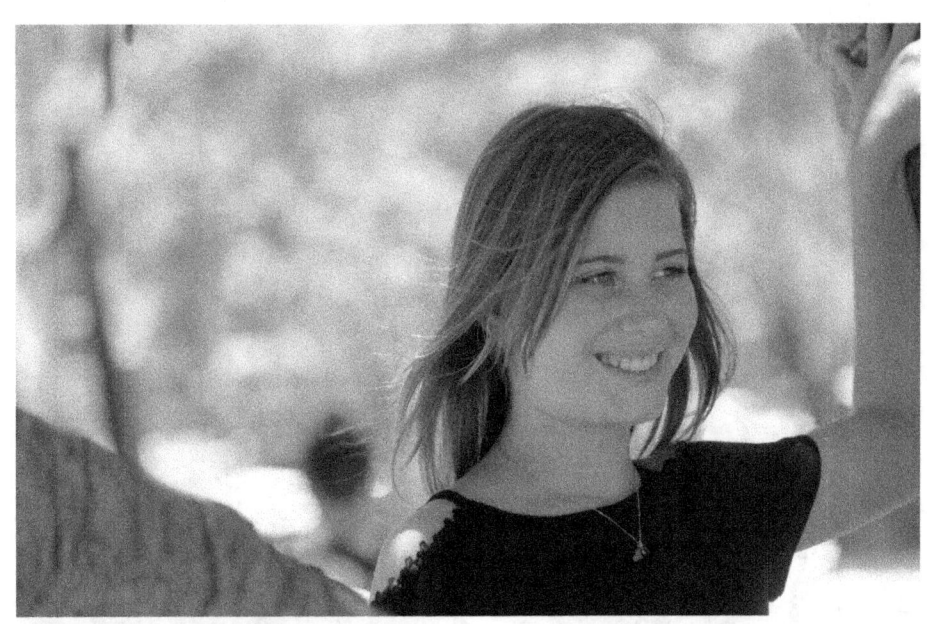

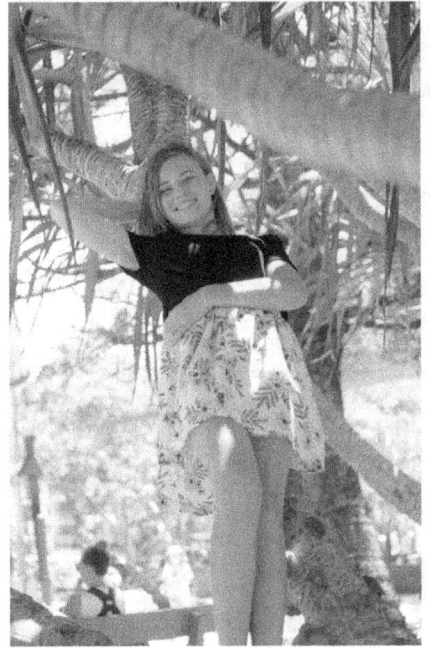

74

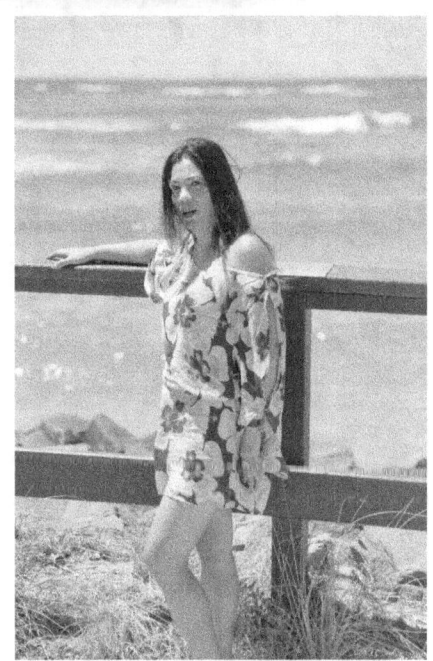

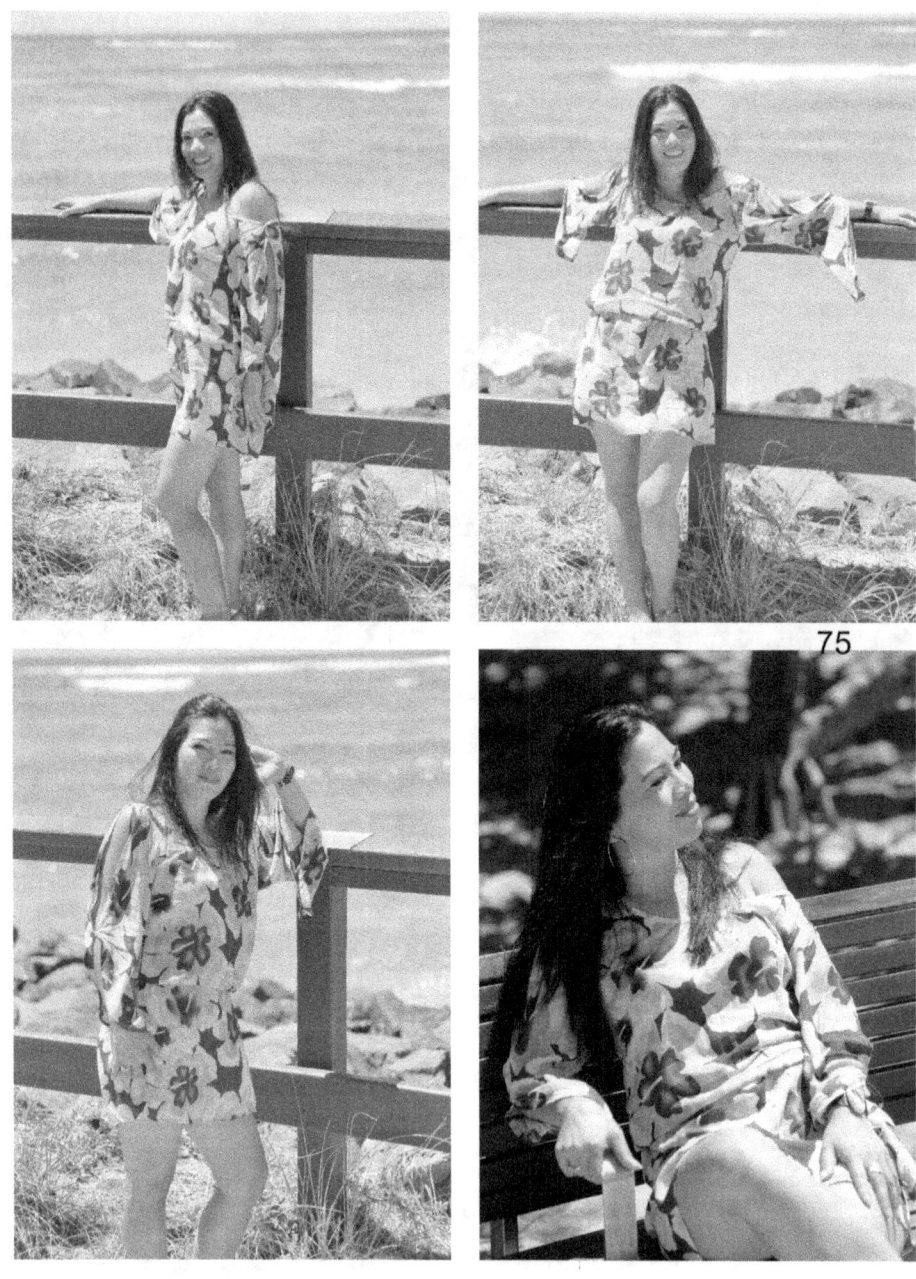

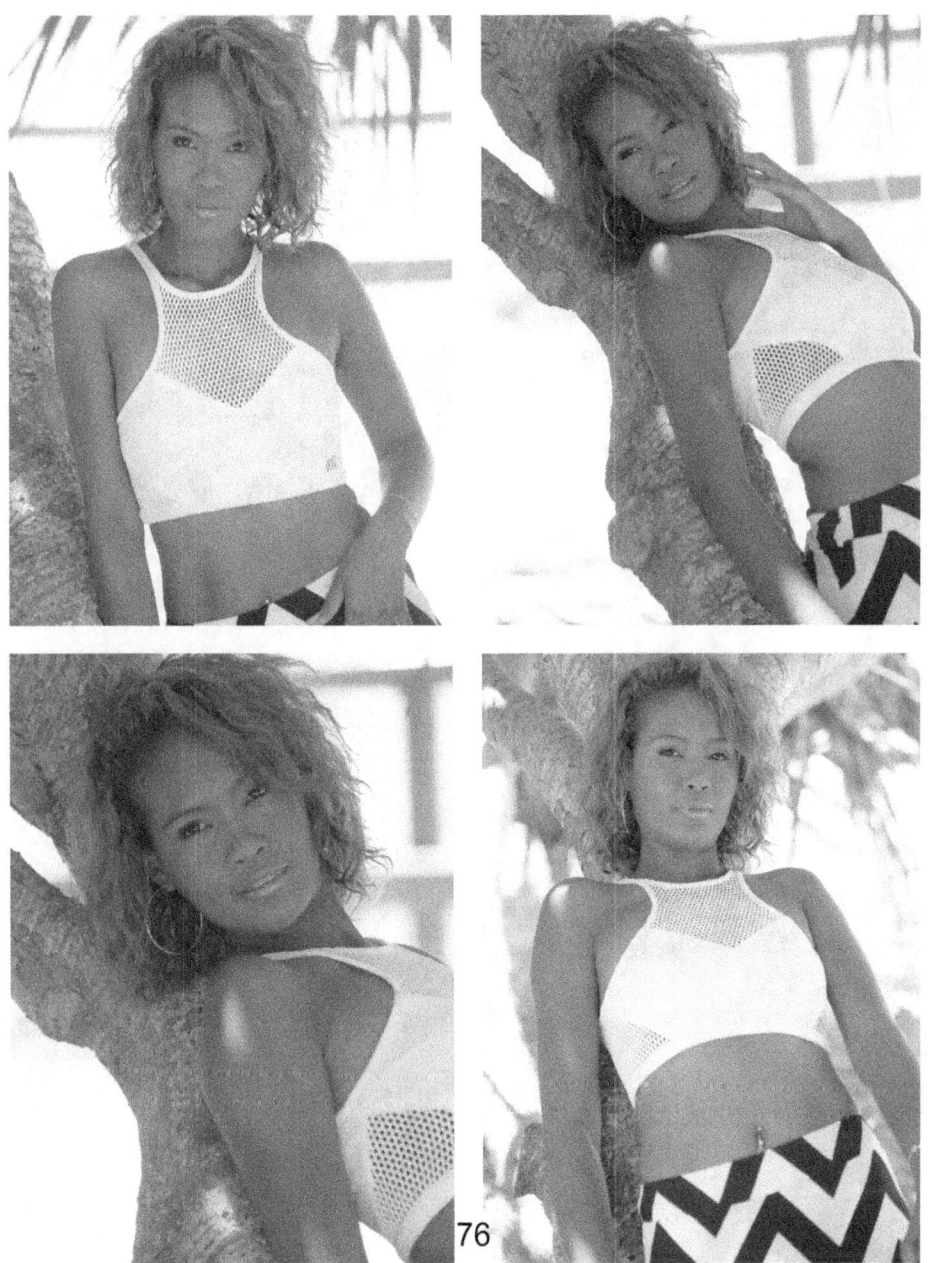

76

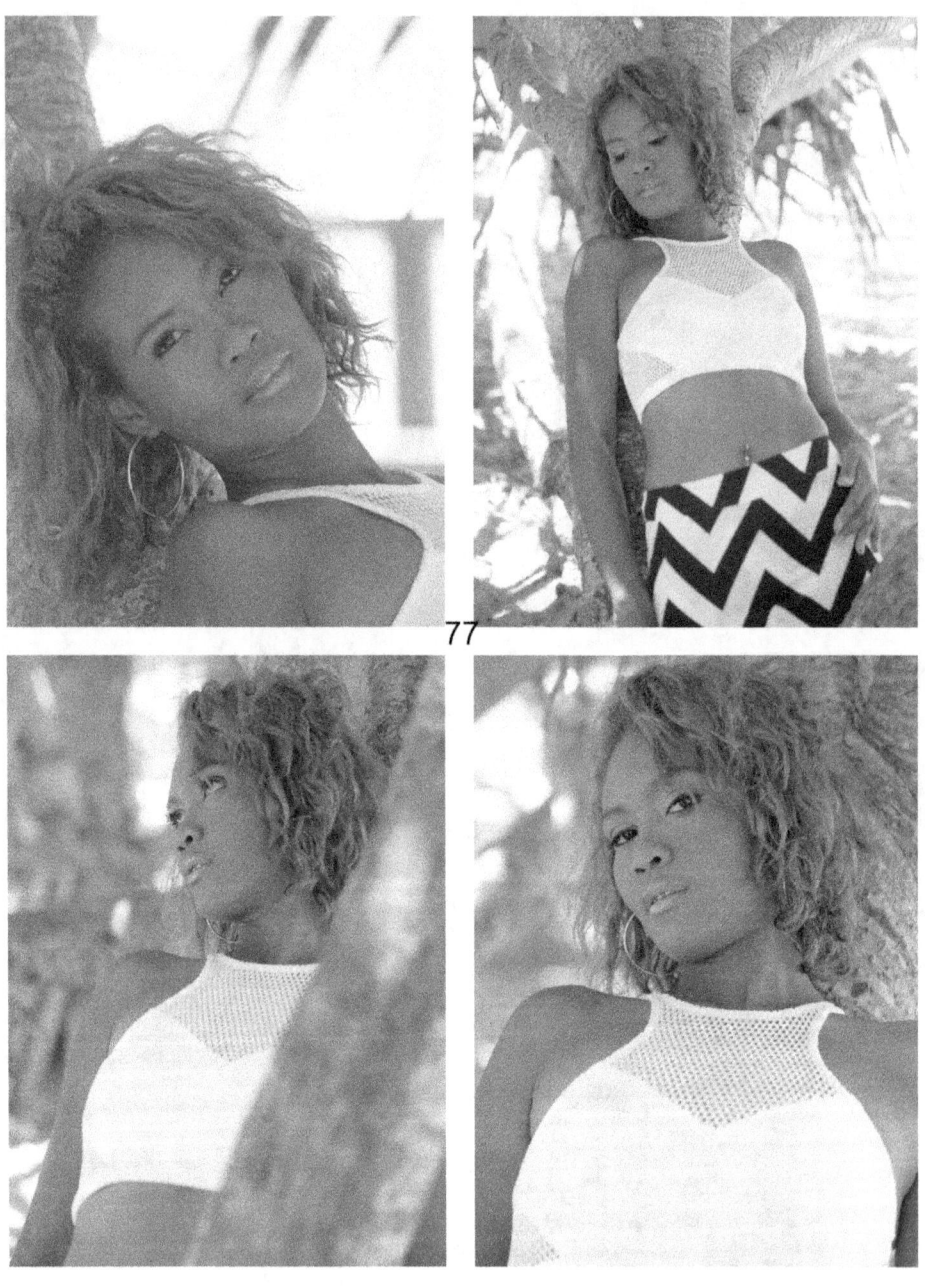

77

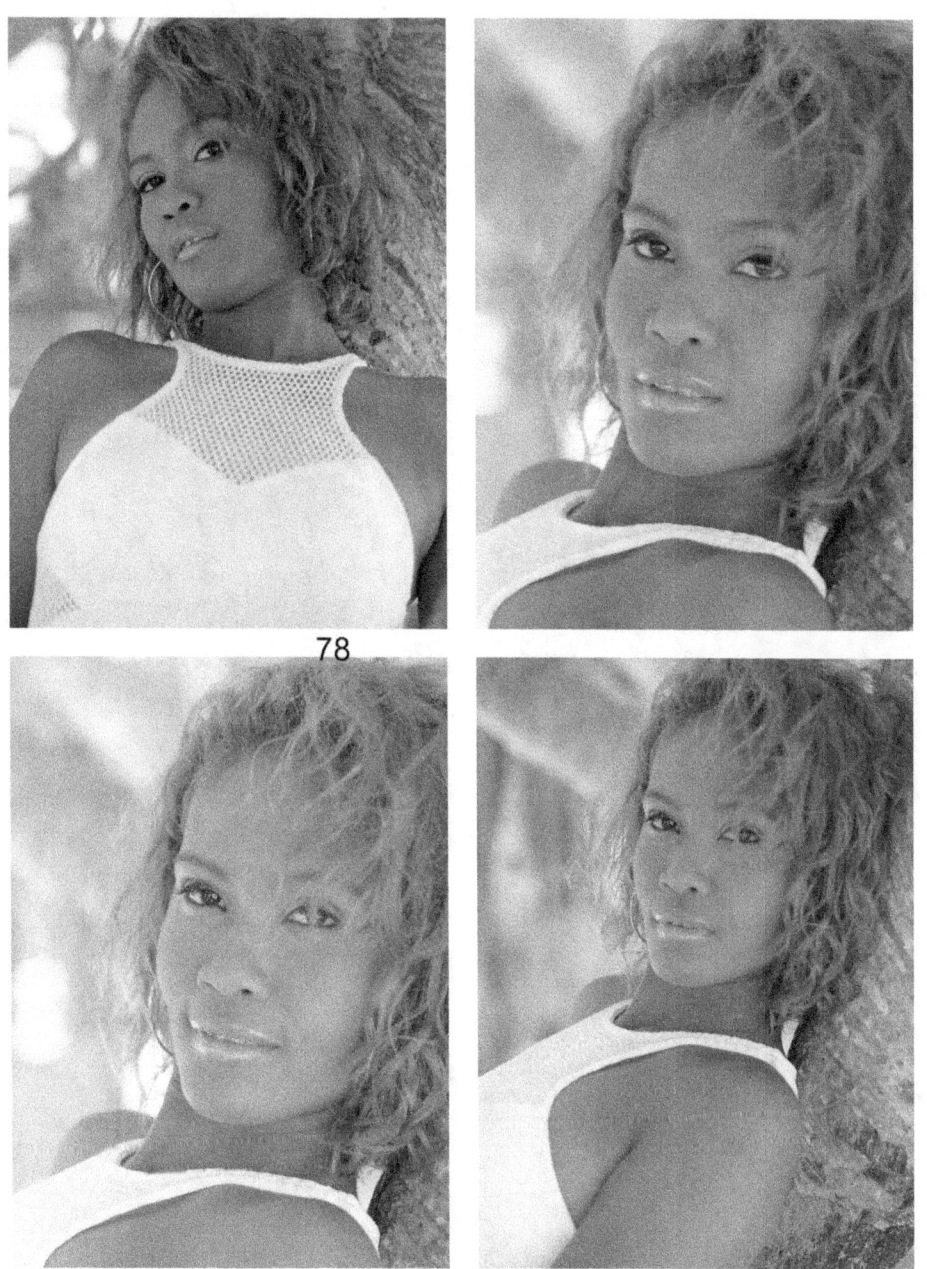

78

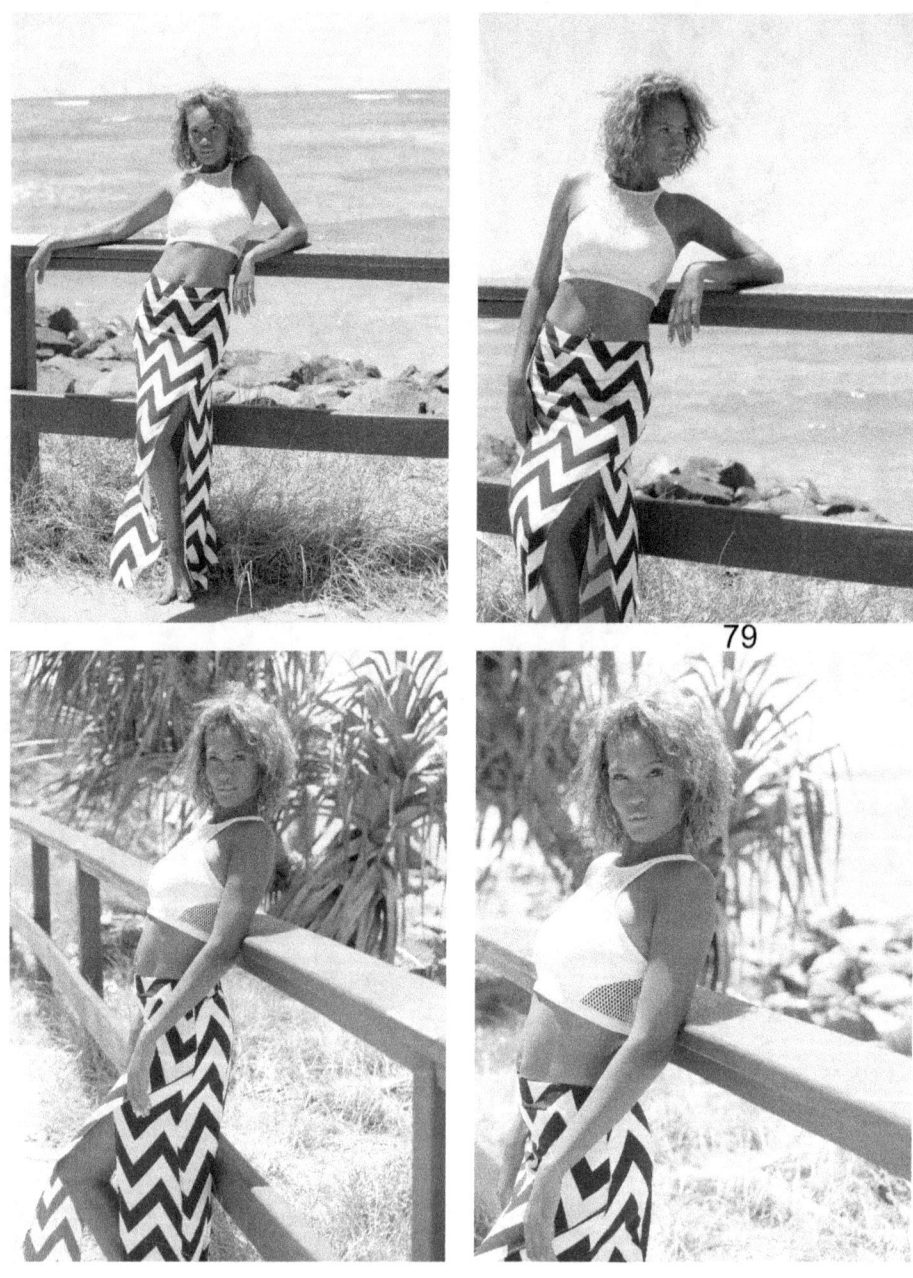

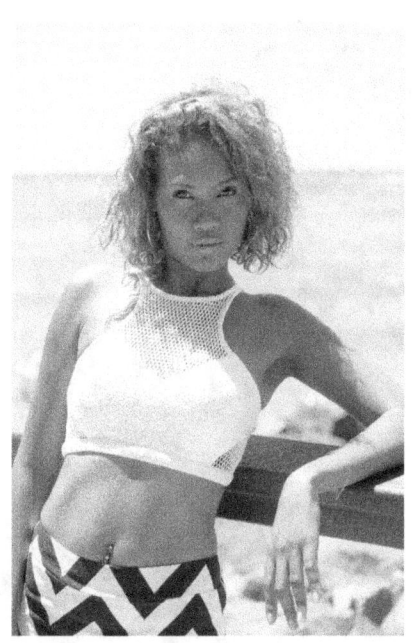

80

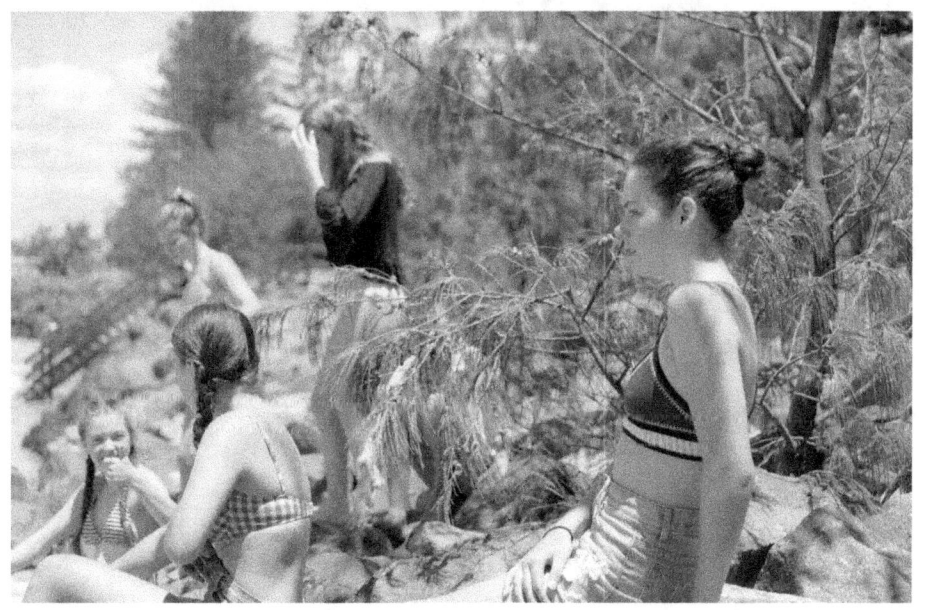

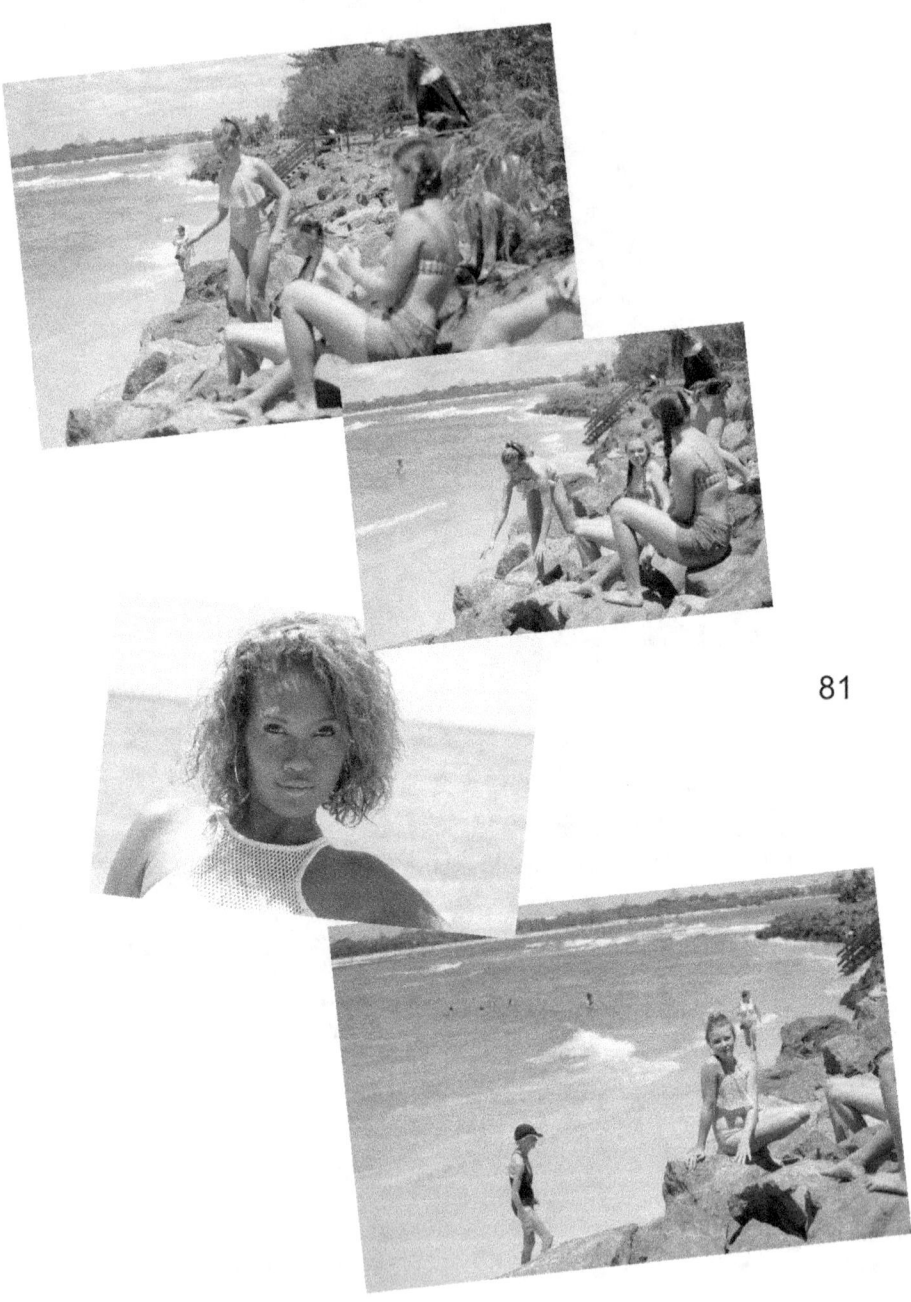

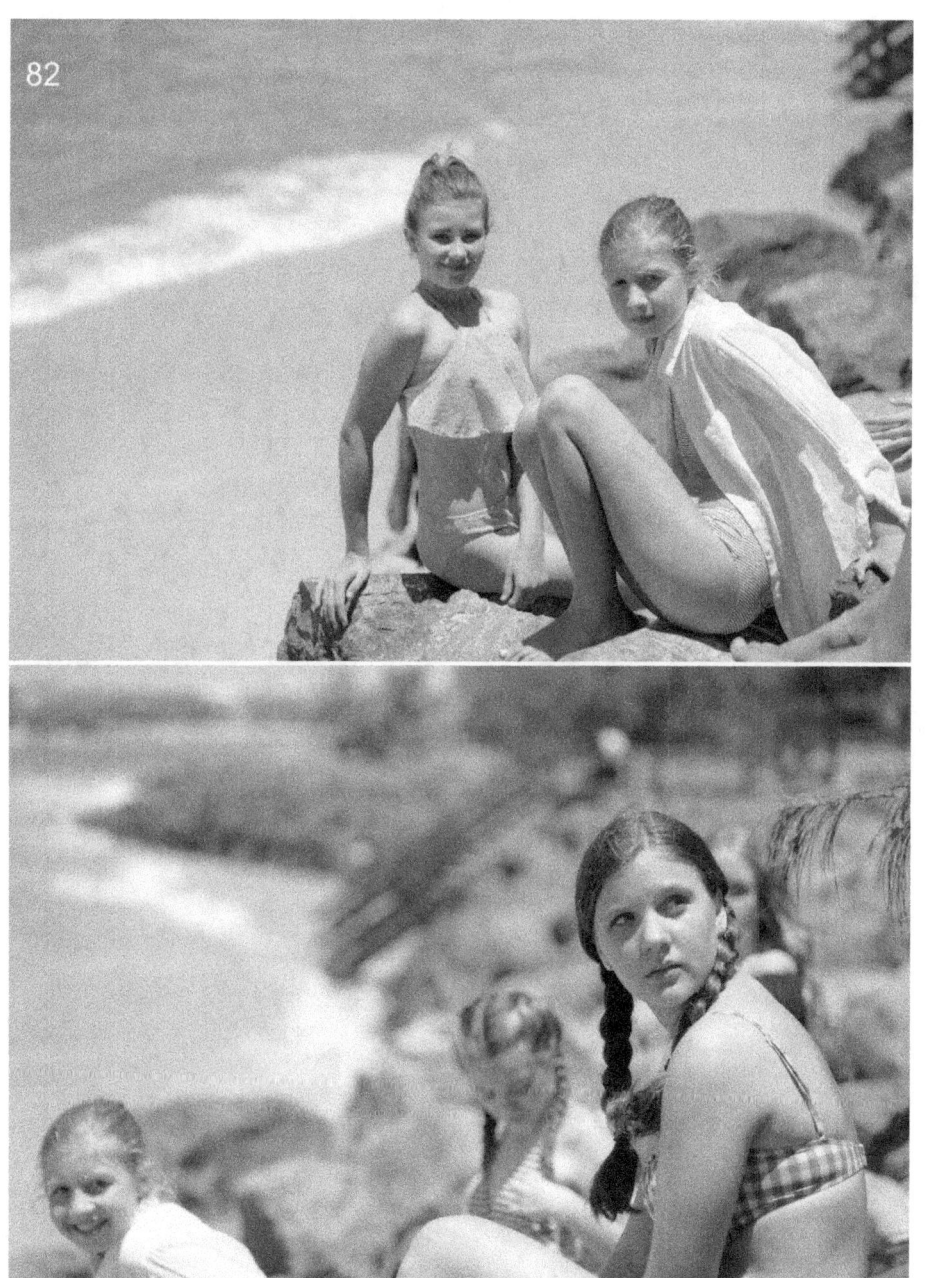

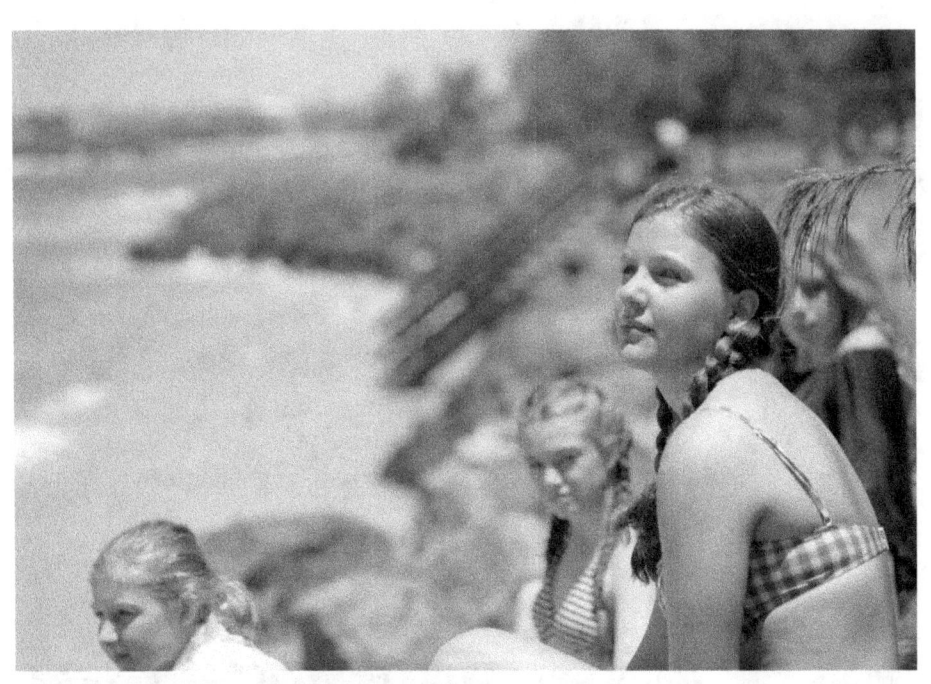

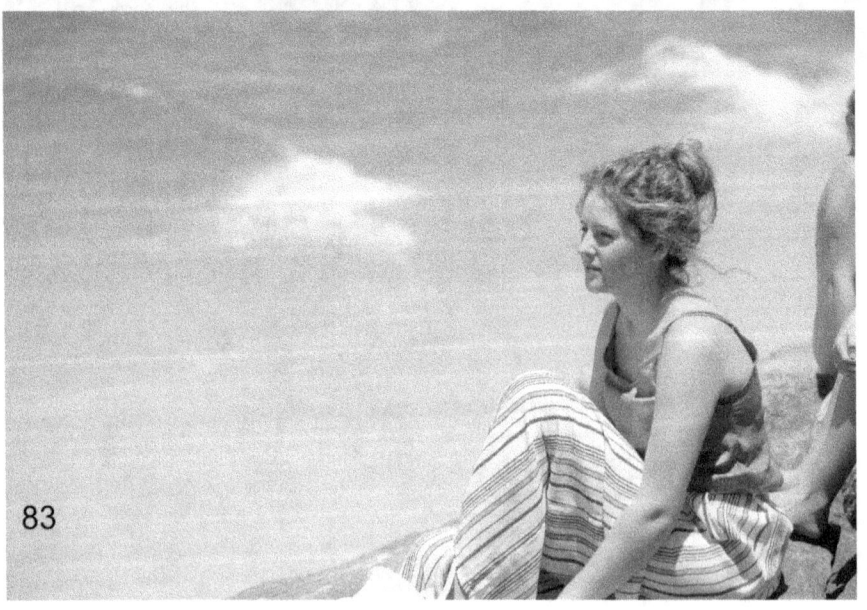

83

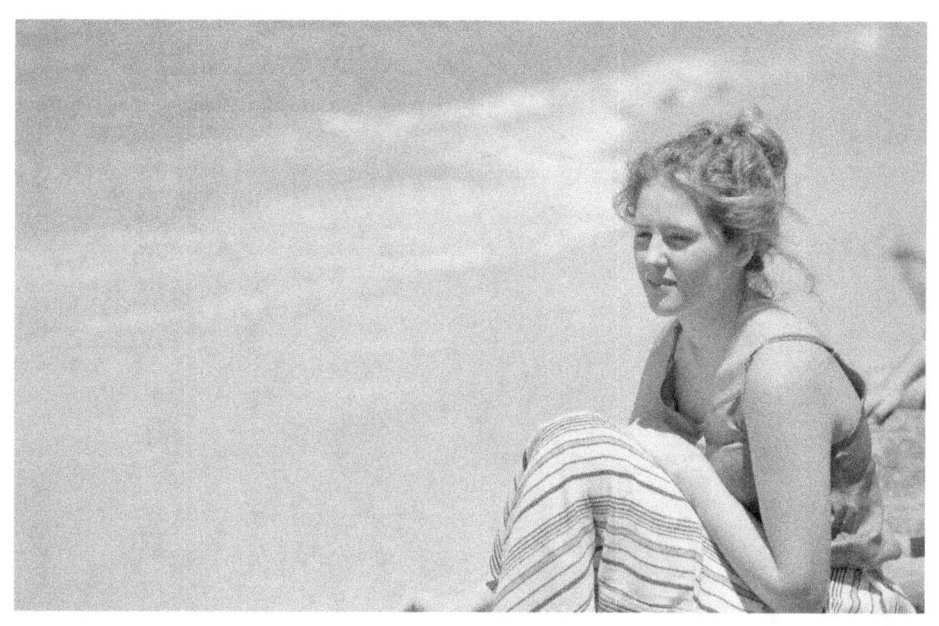

84

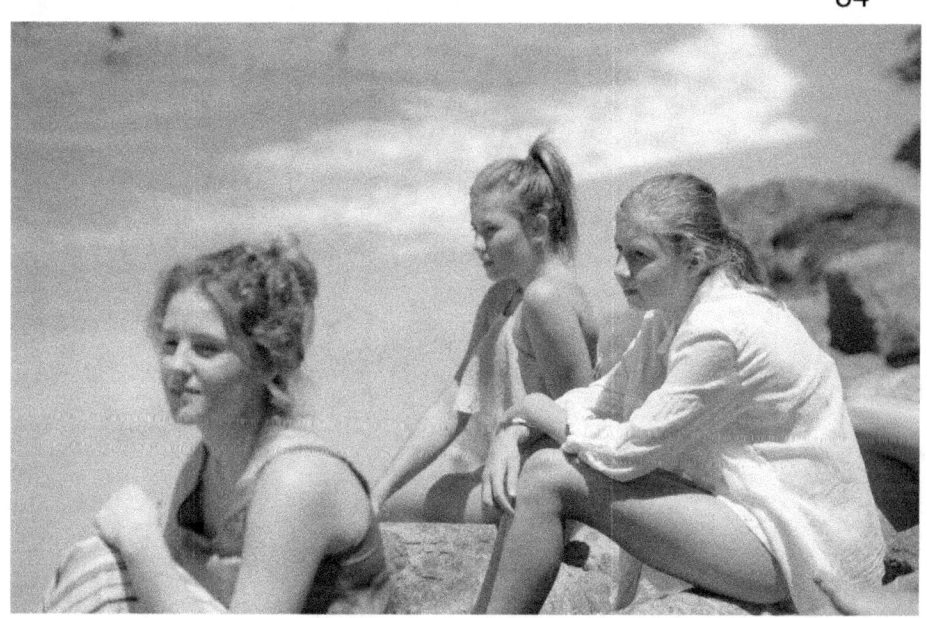

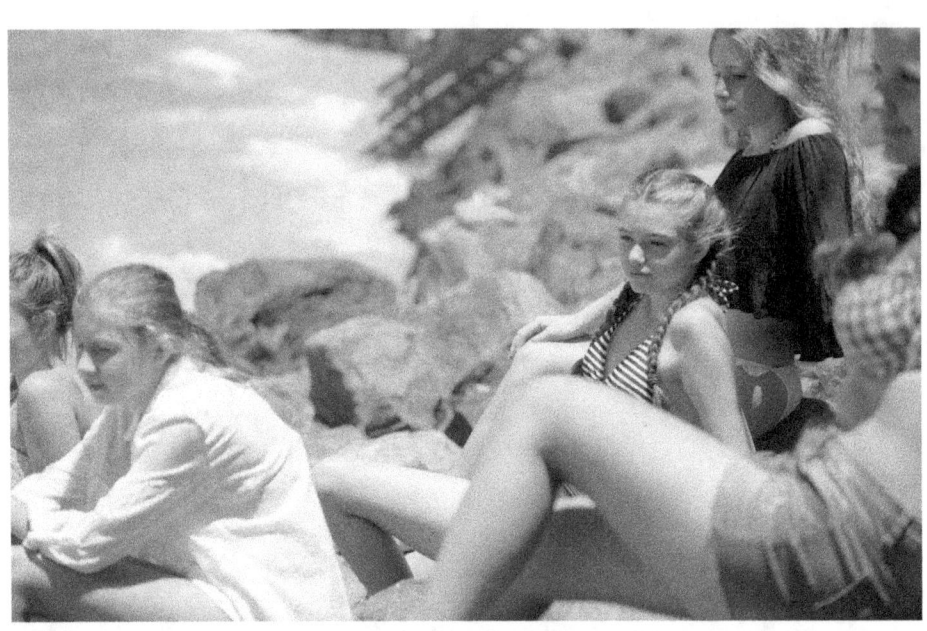

85

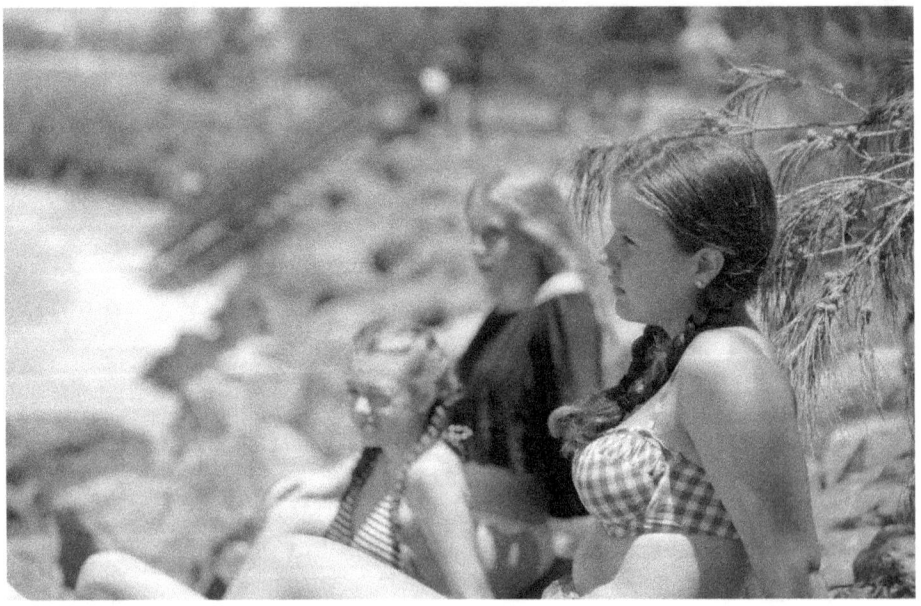

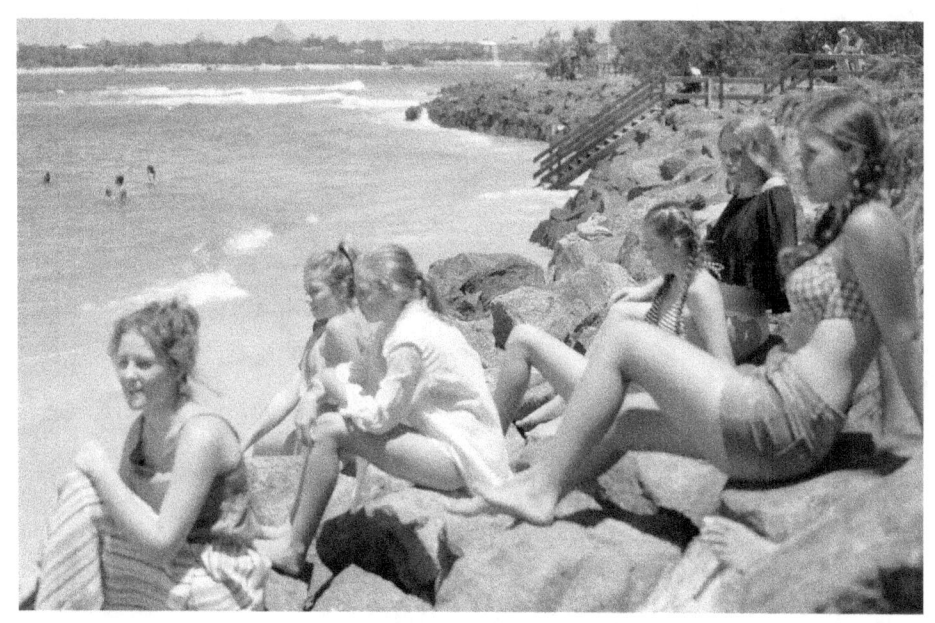

86

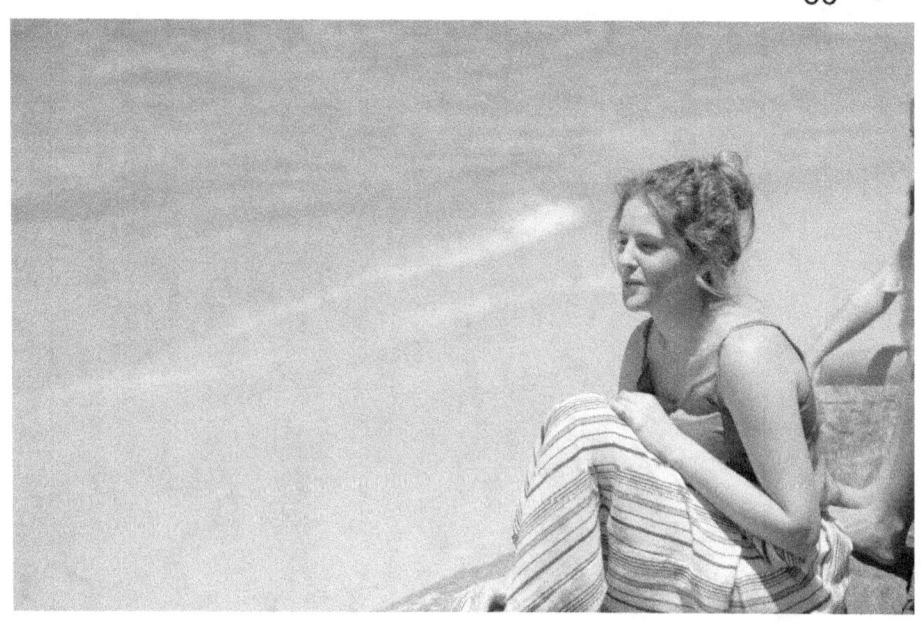

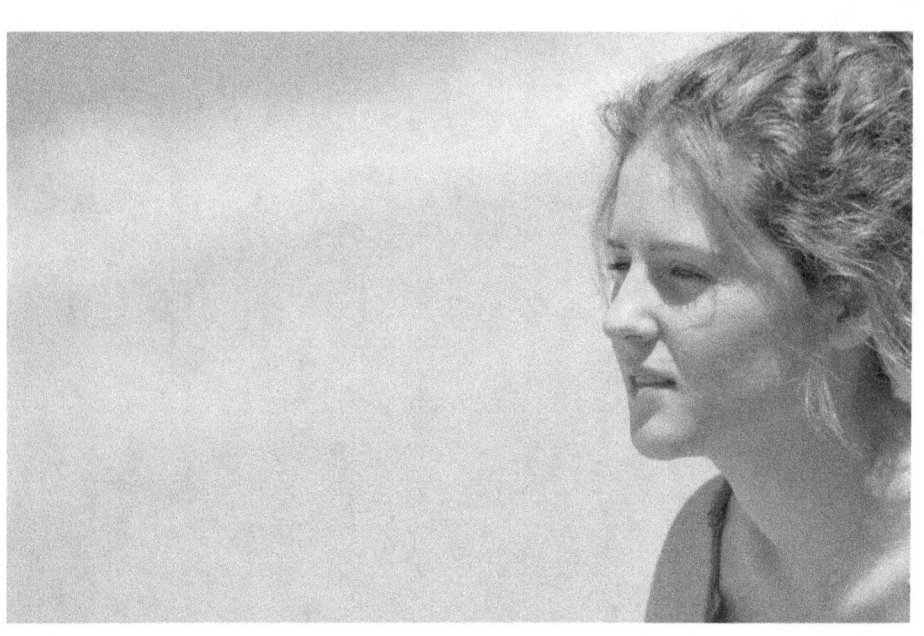

87

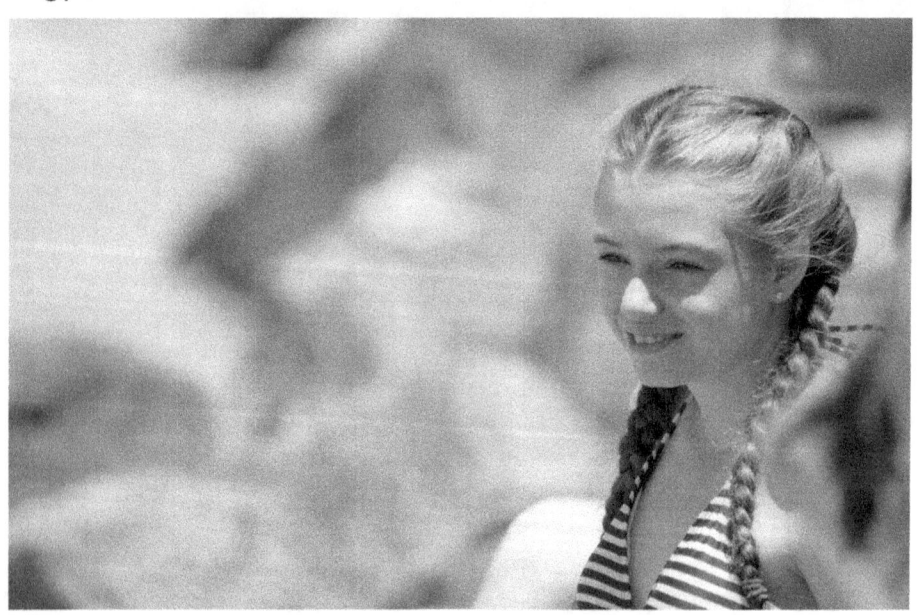

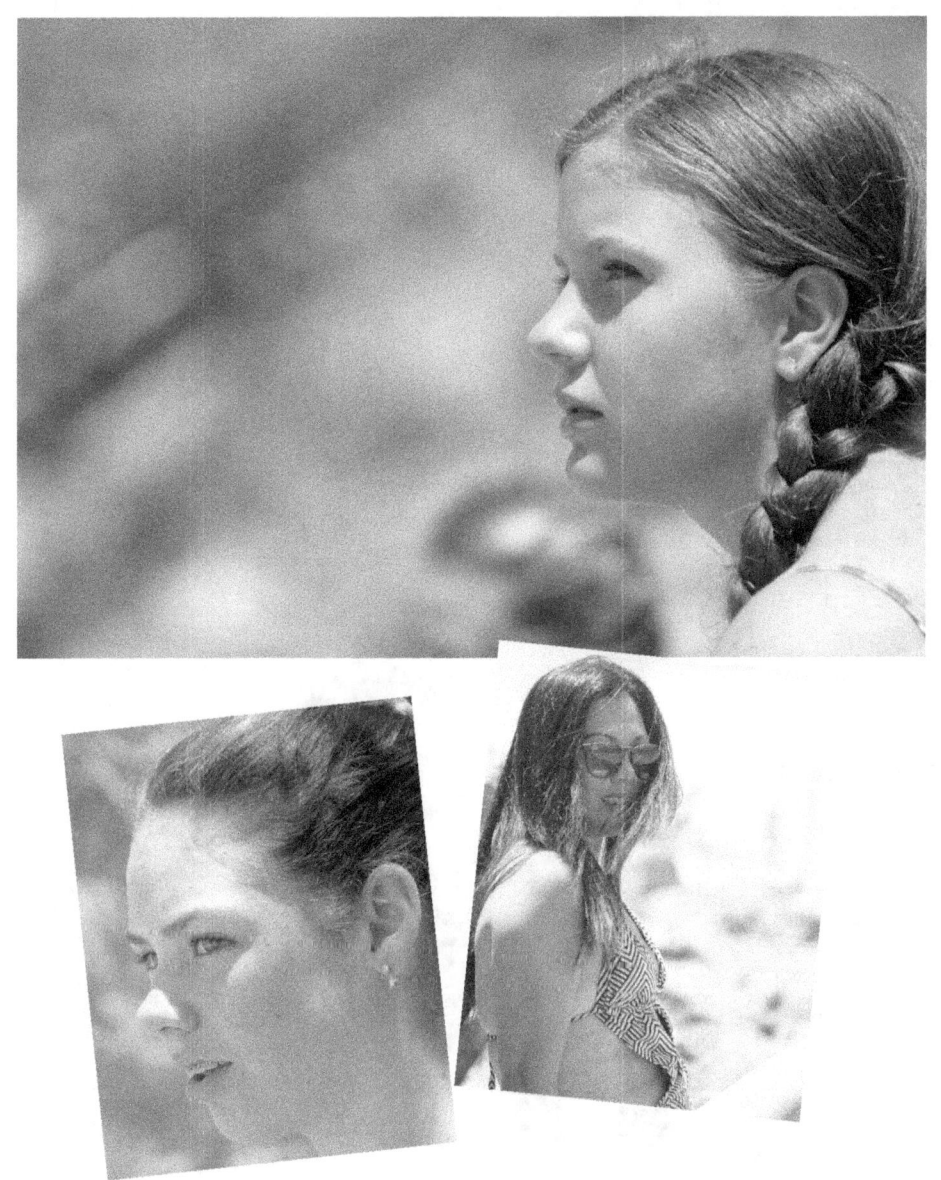

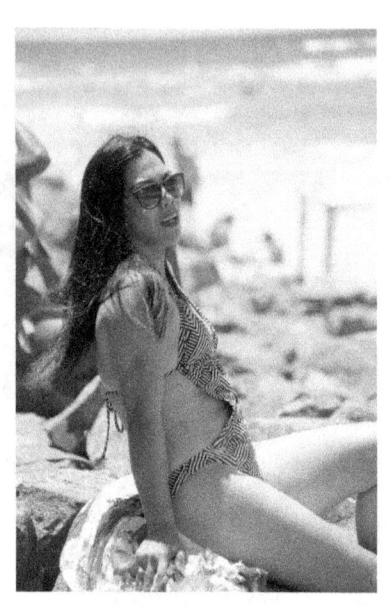
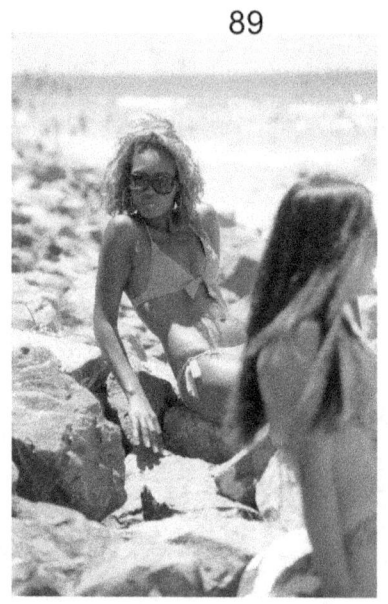
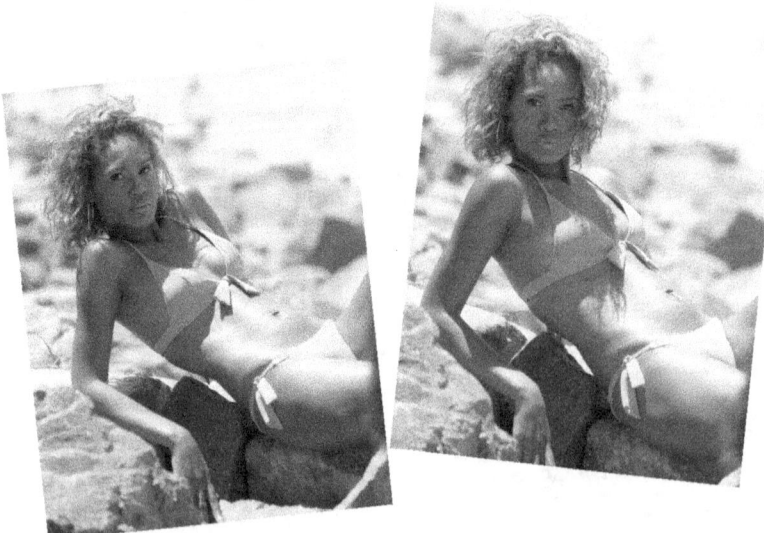

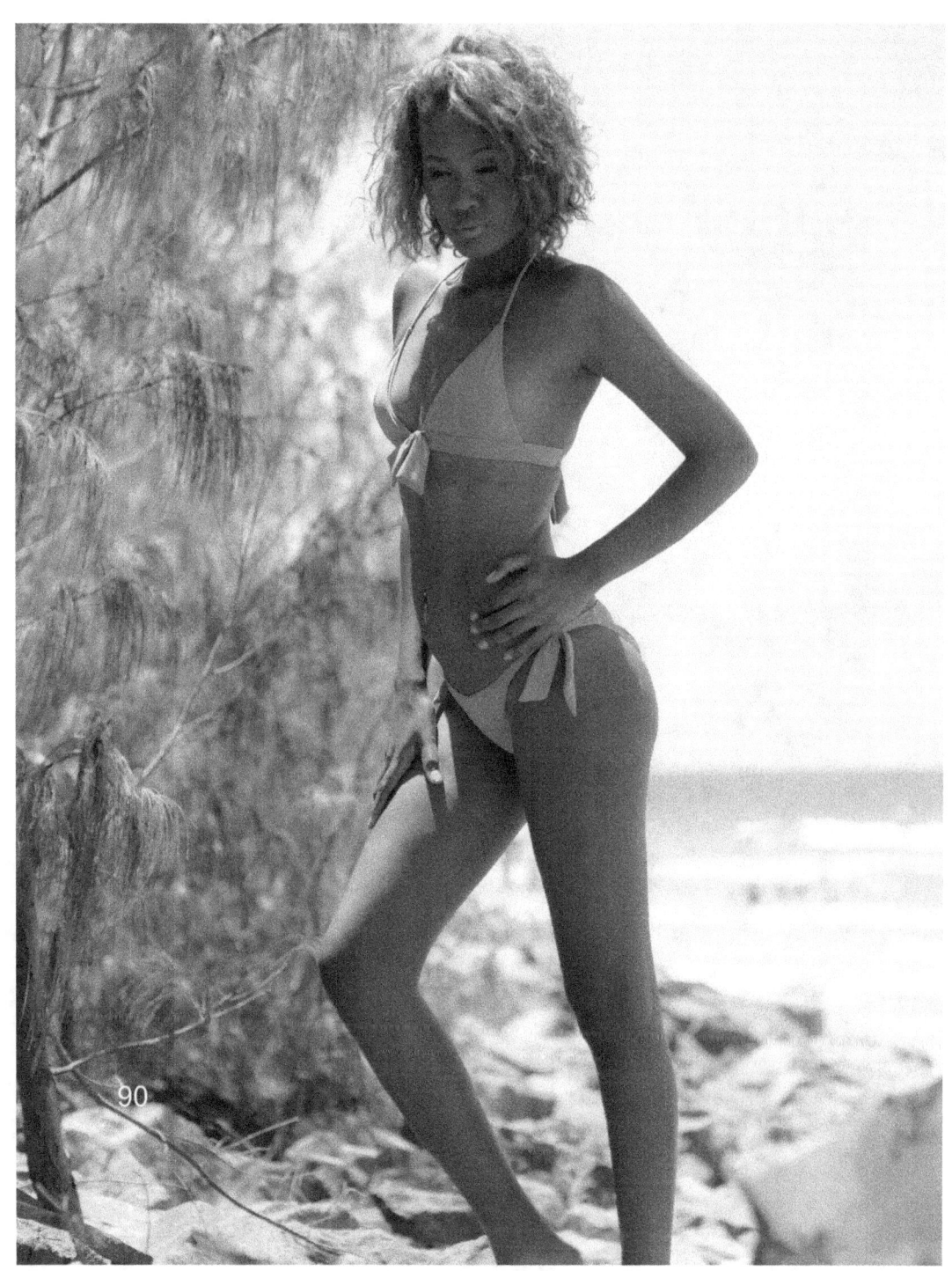

90

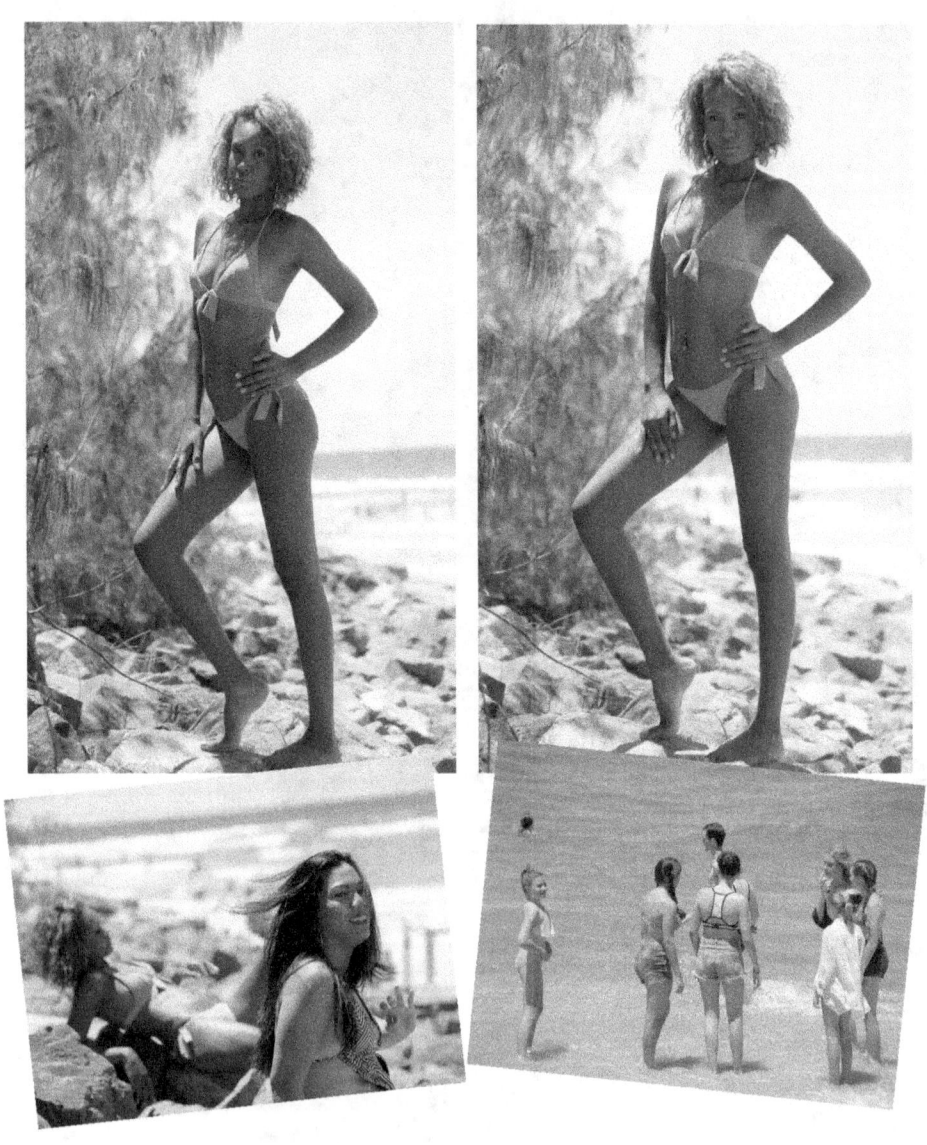

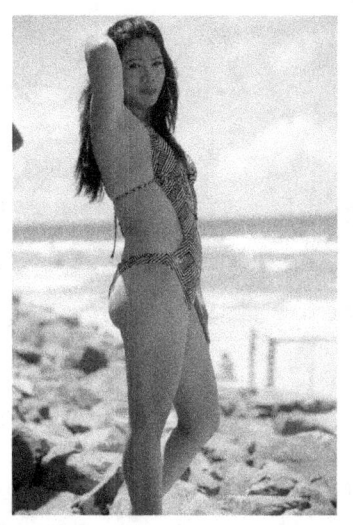

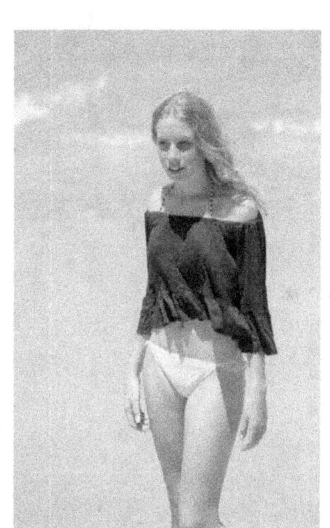

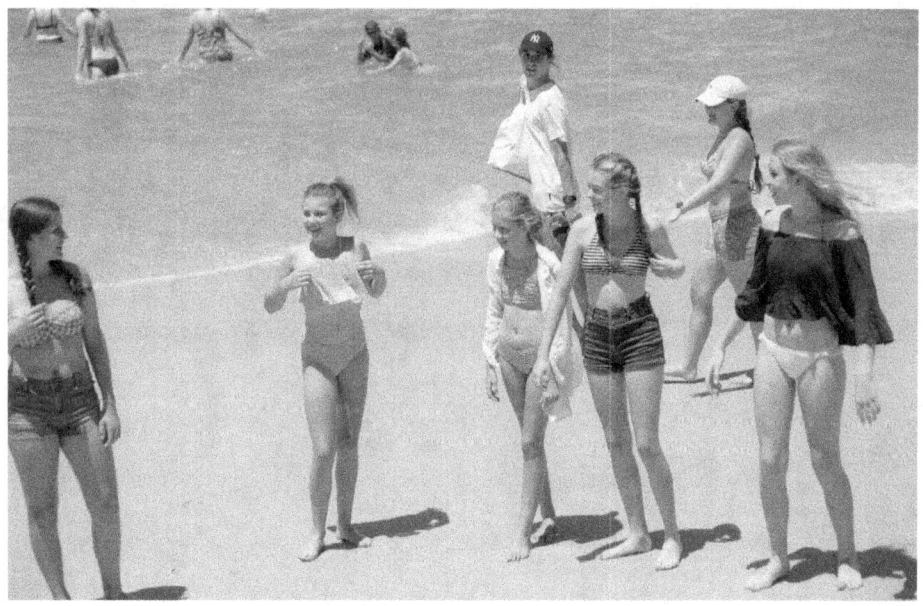

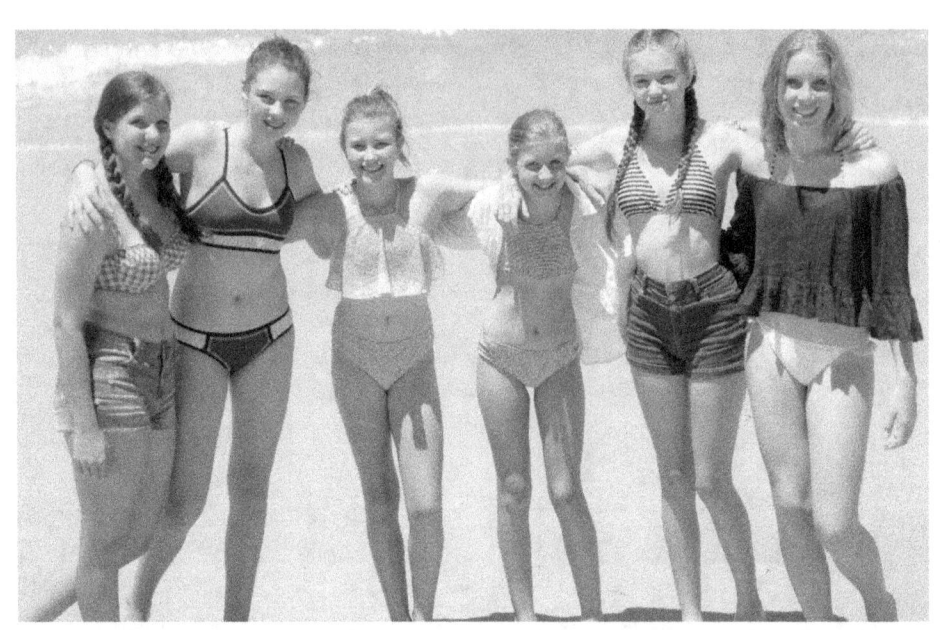

93

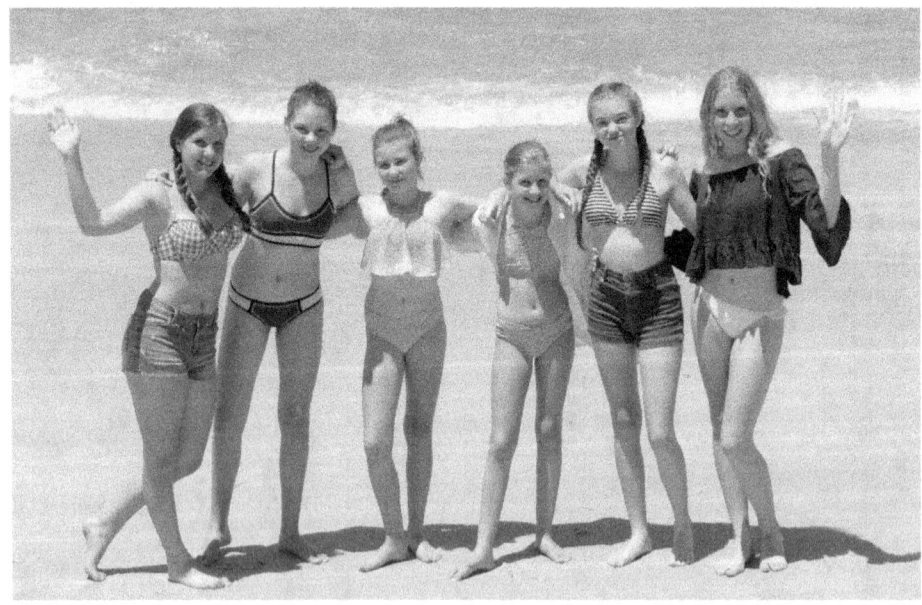

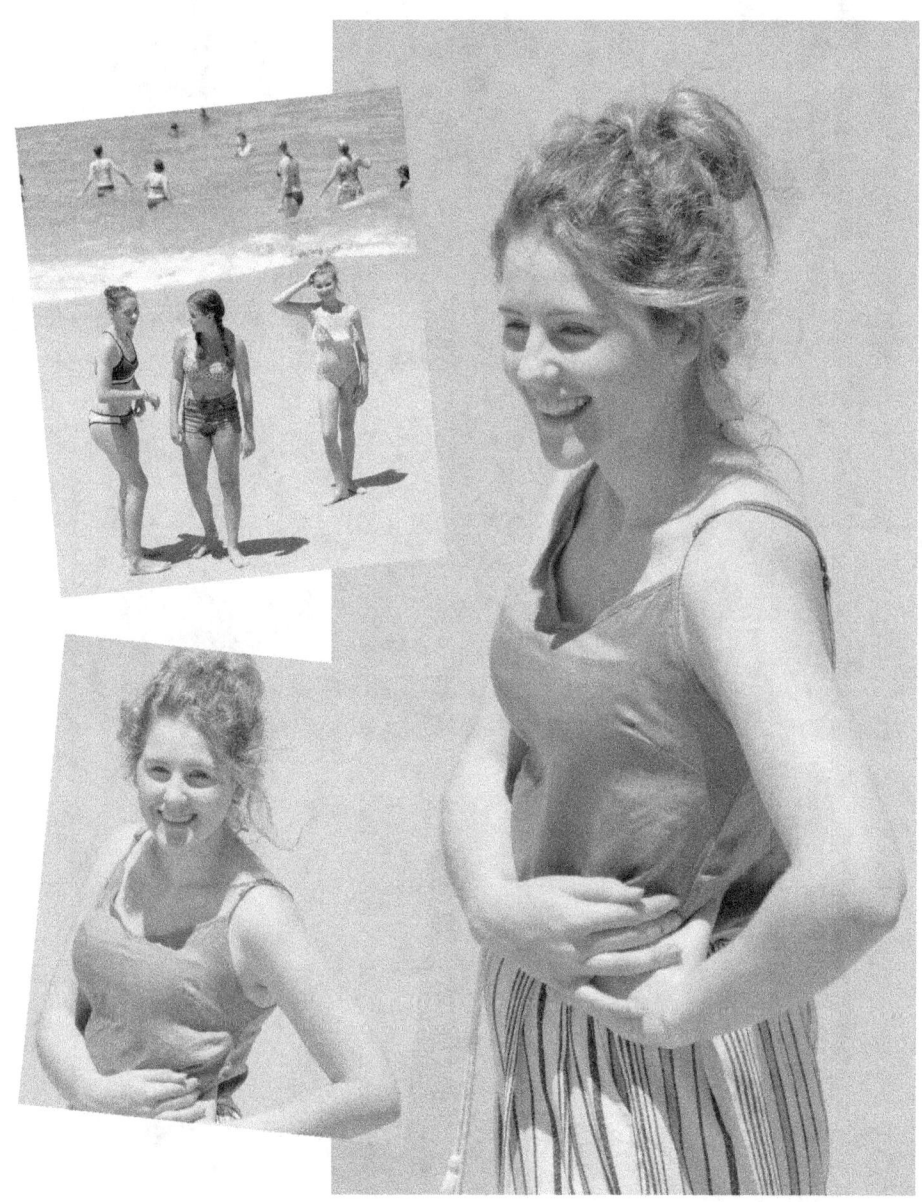

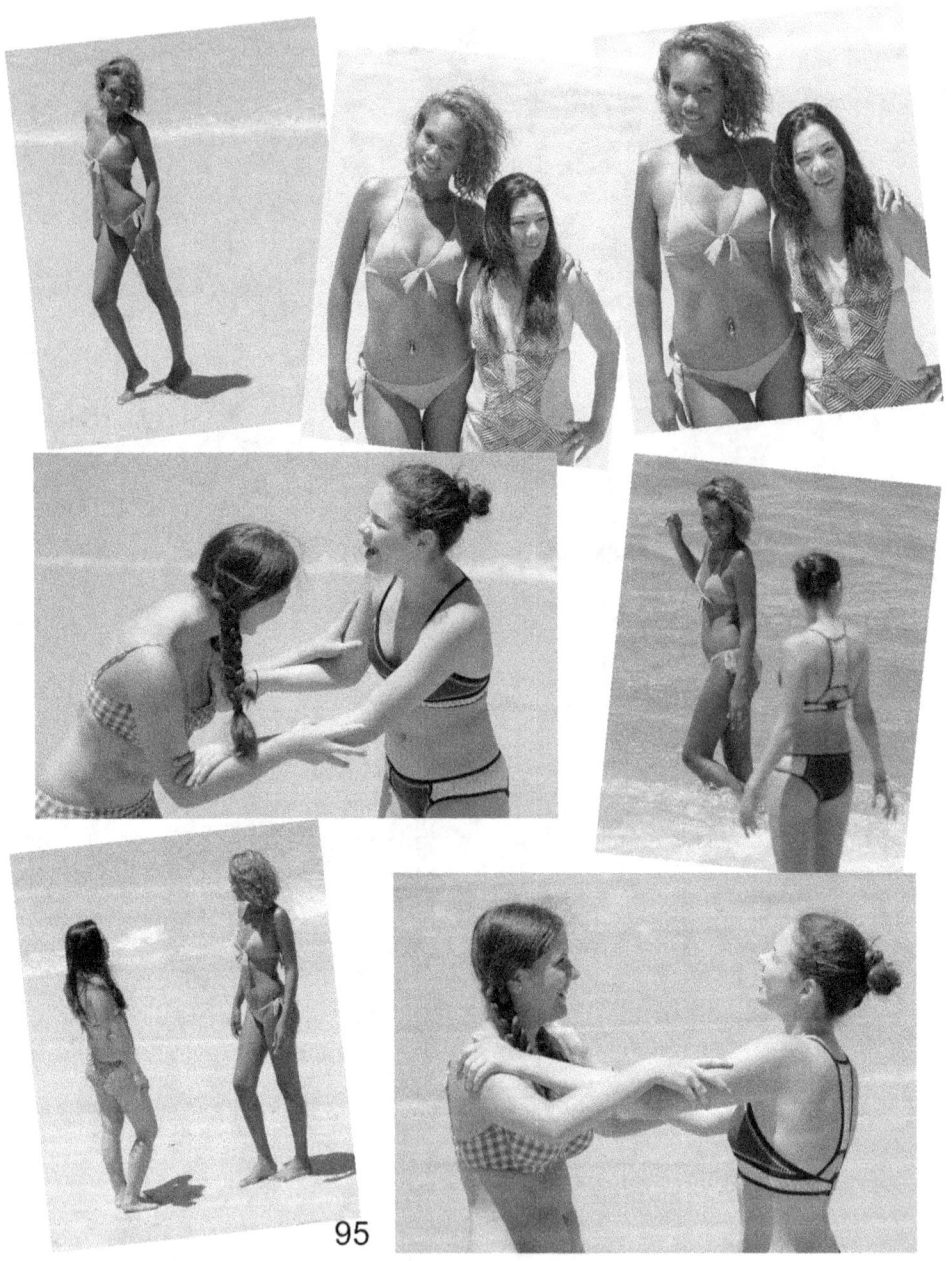

95

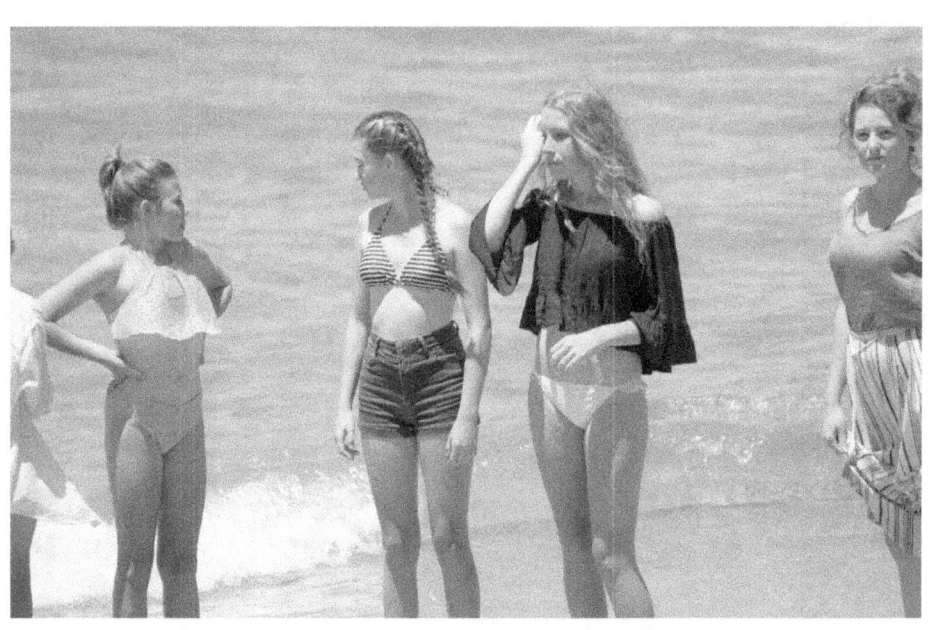

96

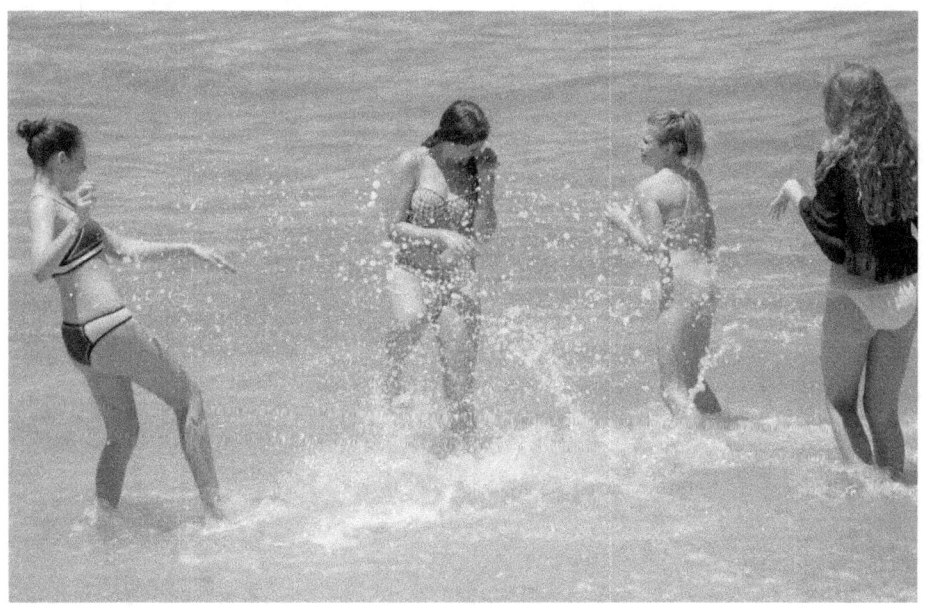

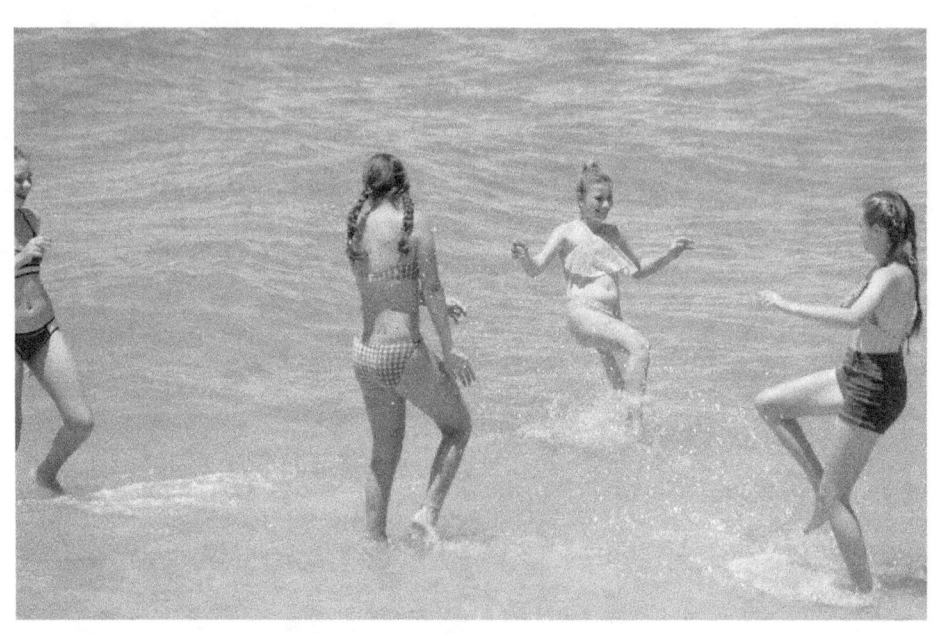

97

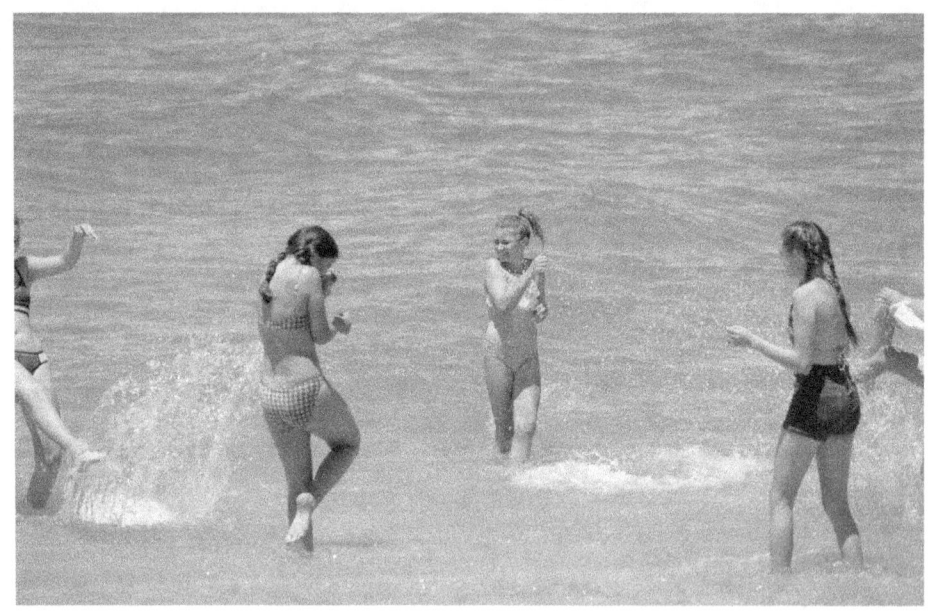

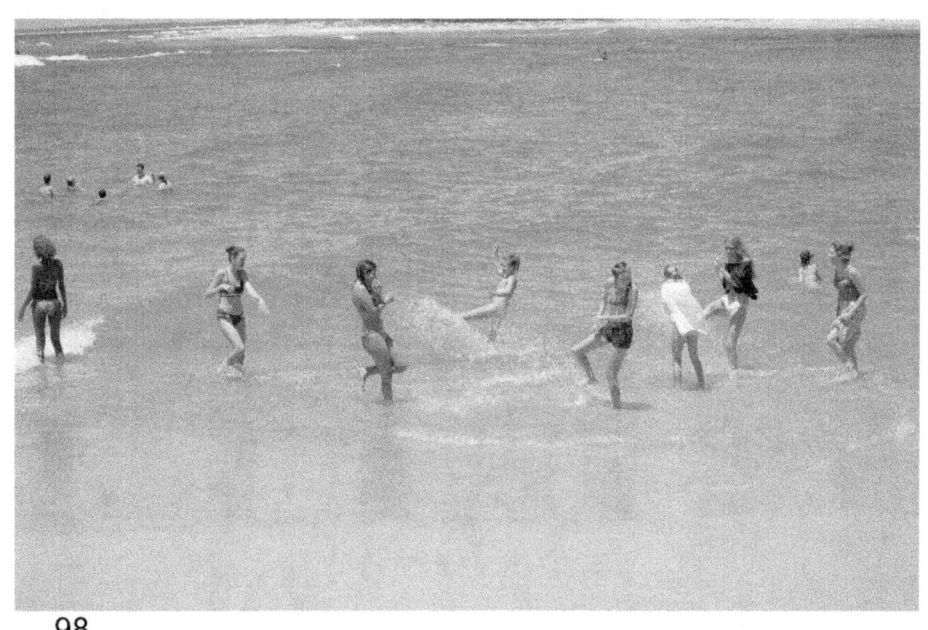

98

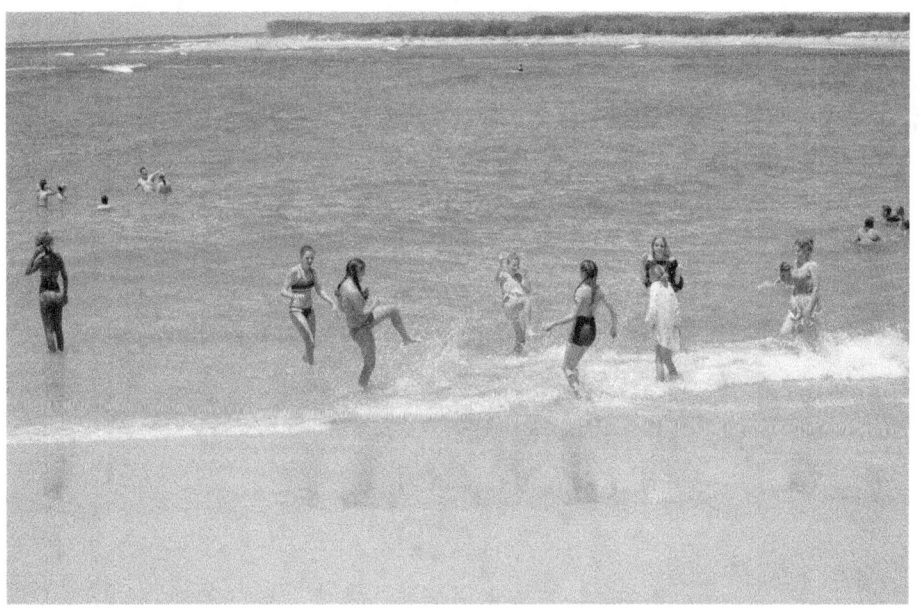

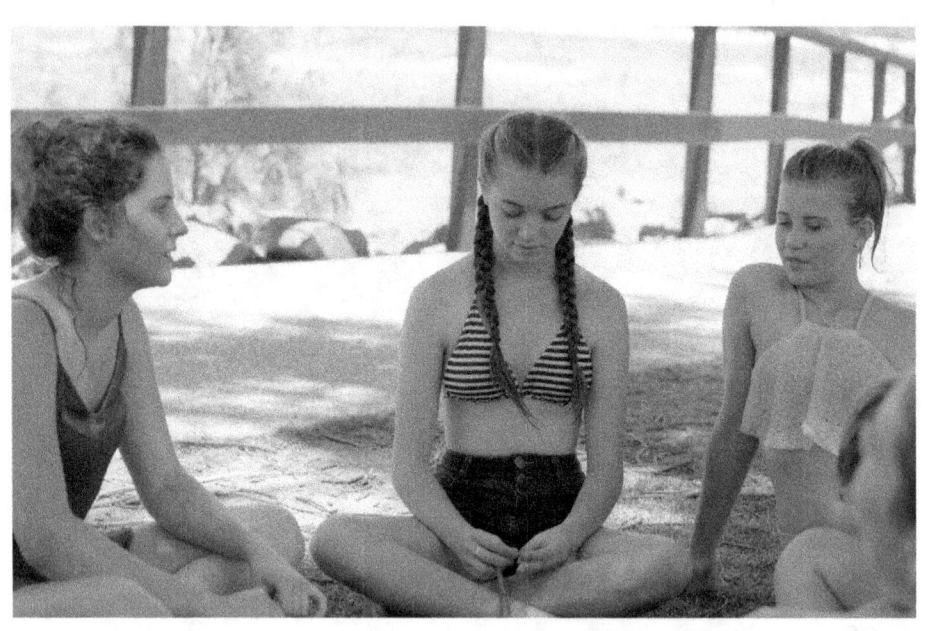

99

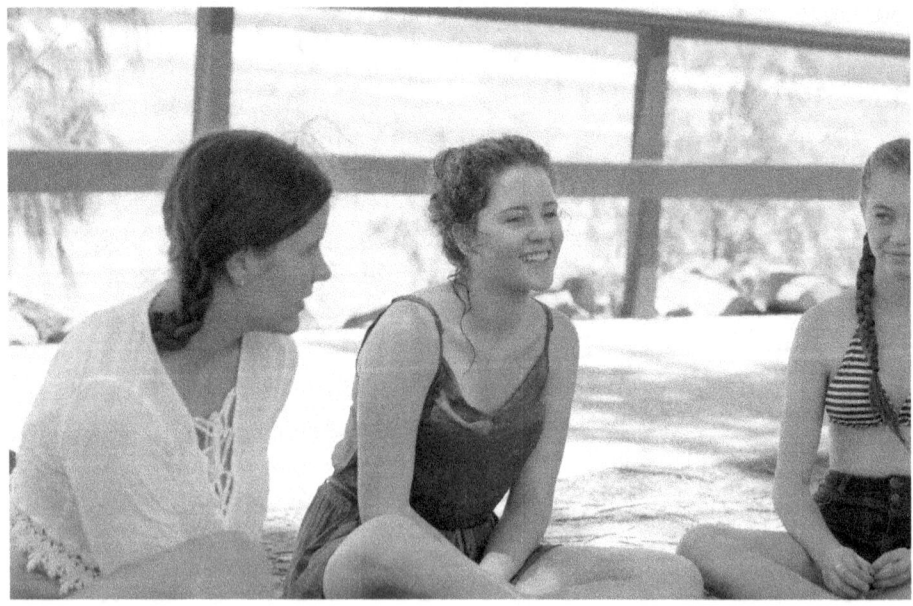

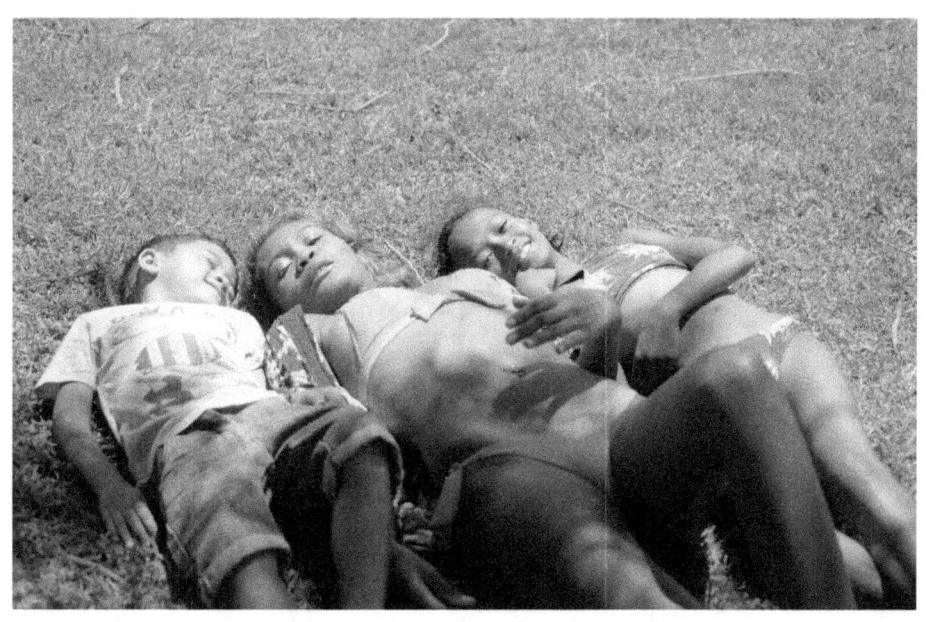

100

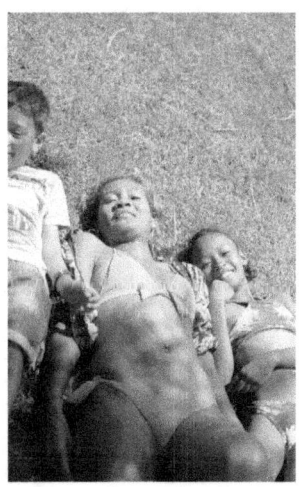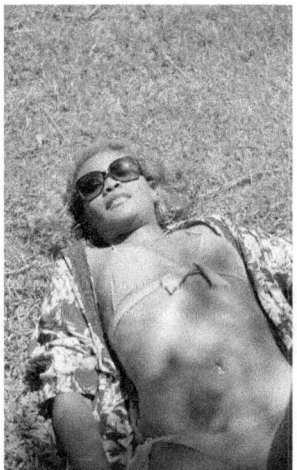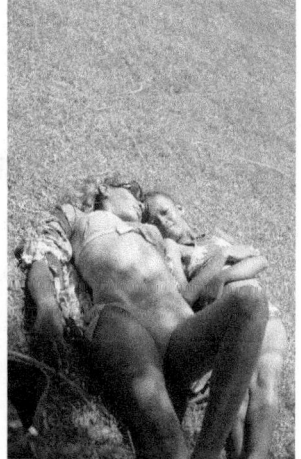

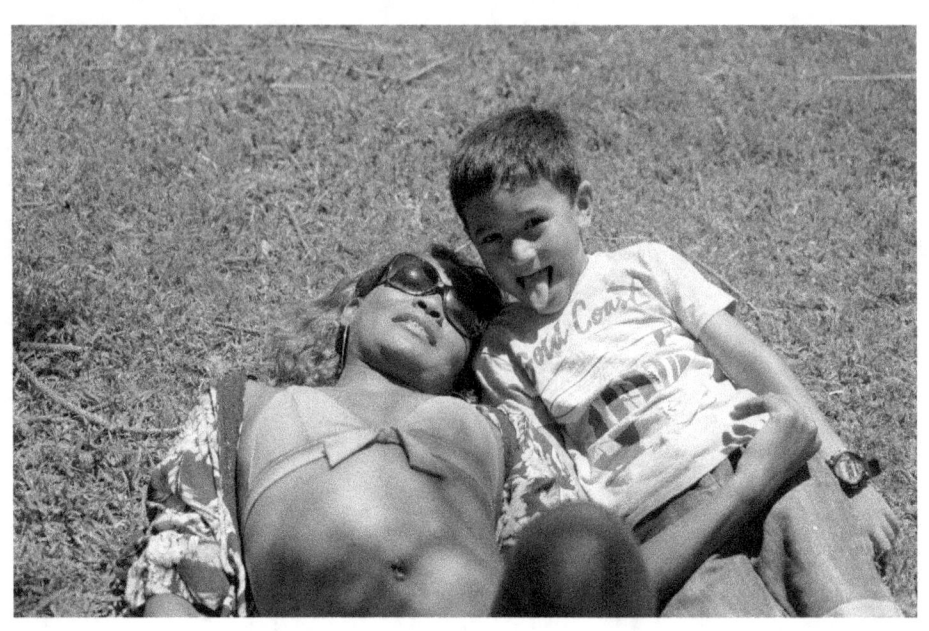

101

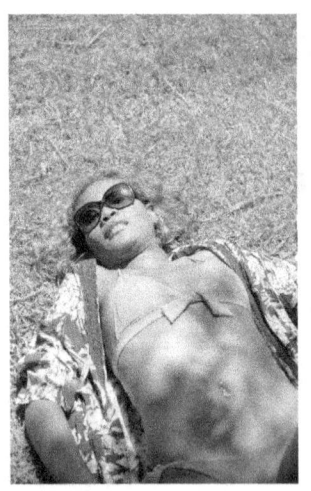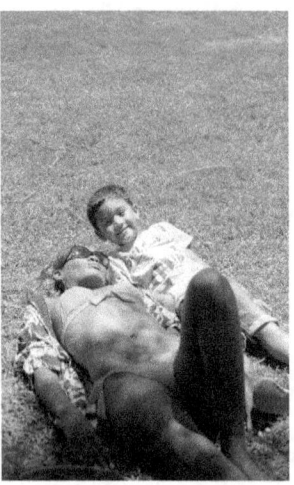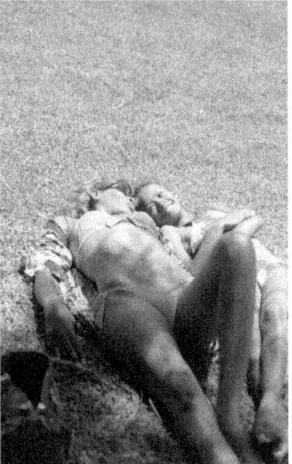

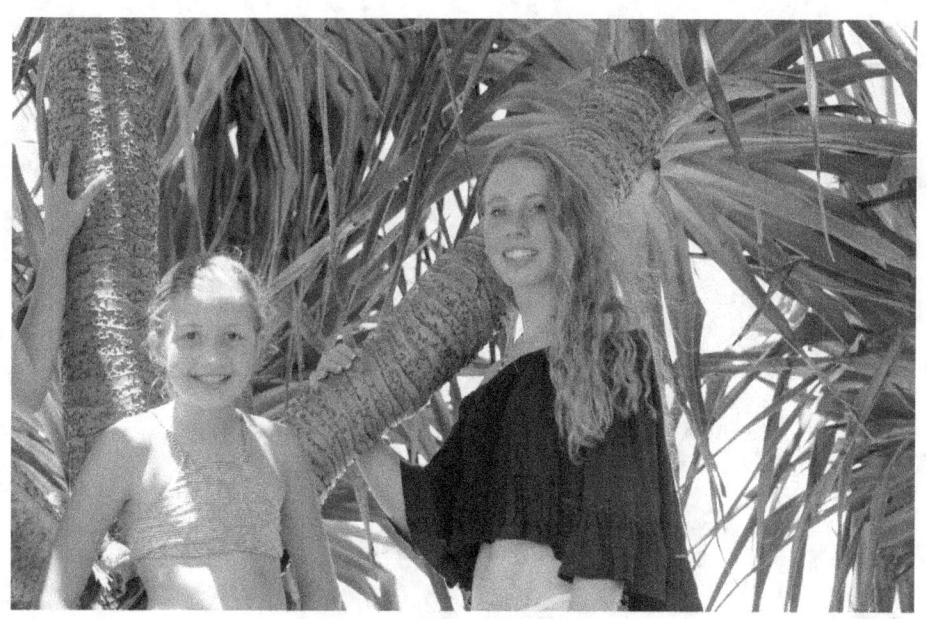

102

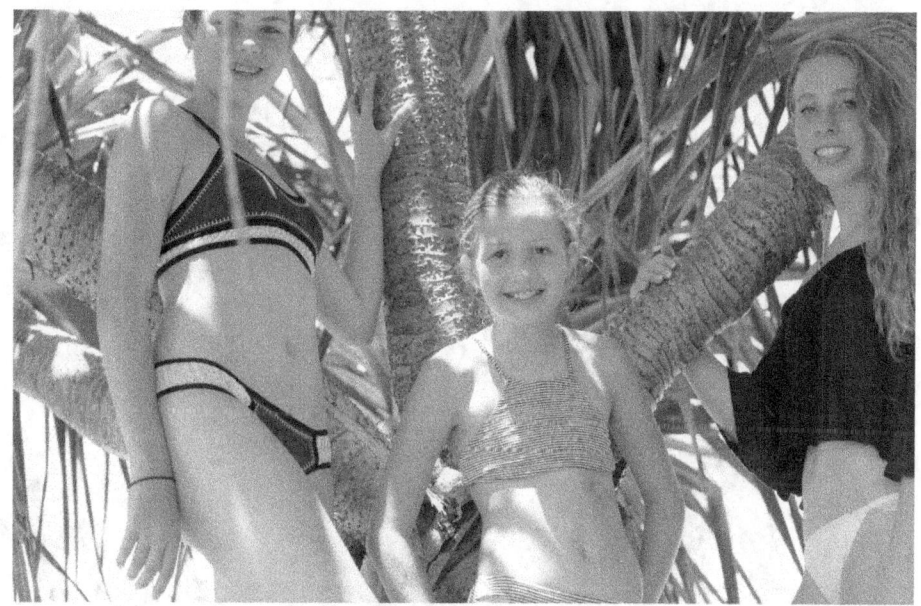

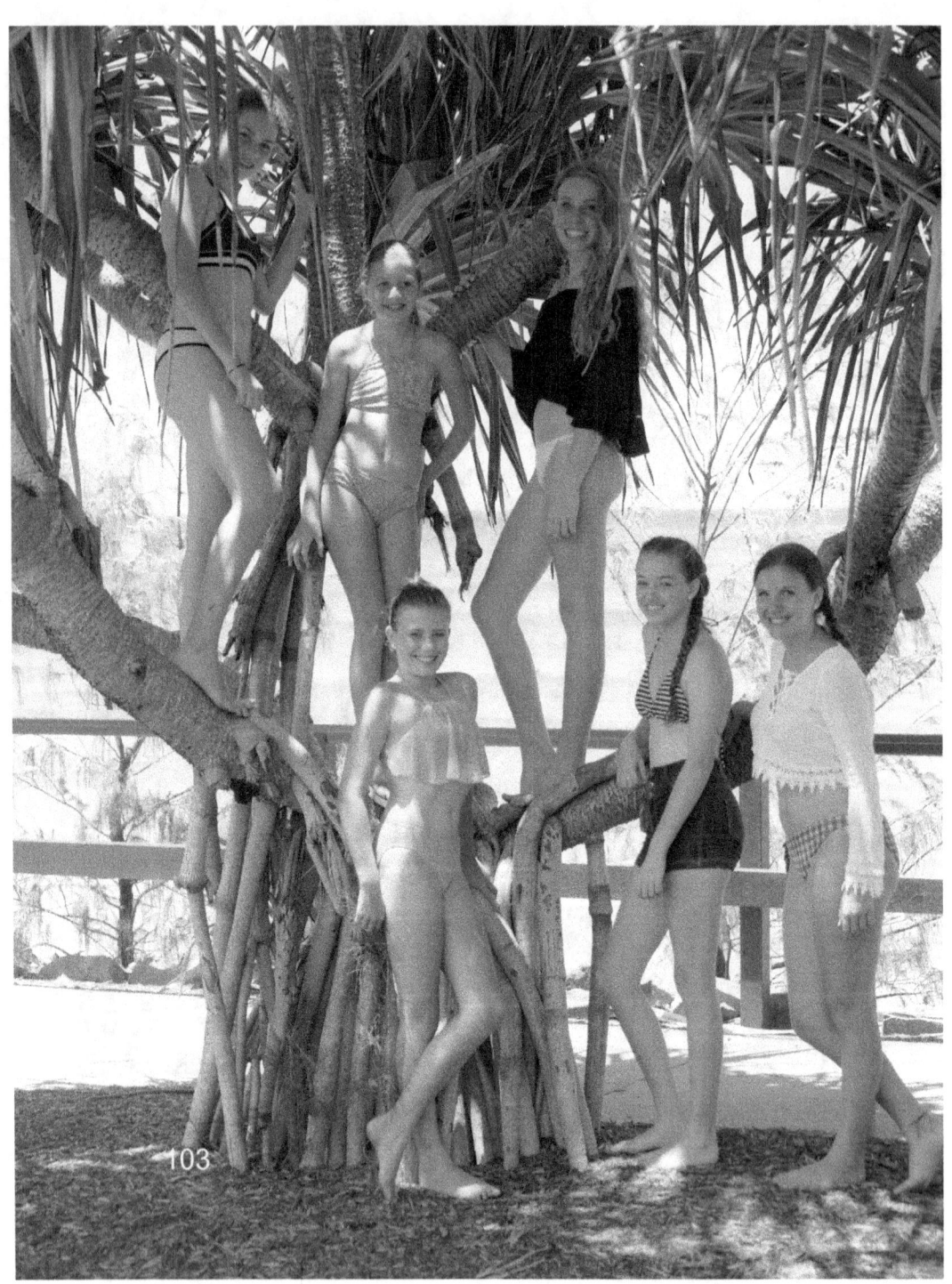

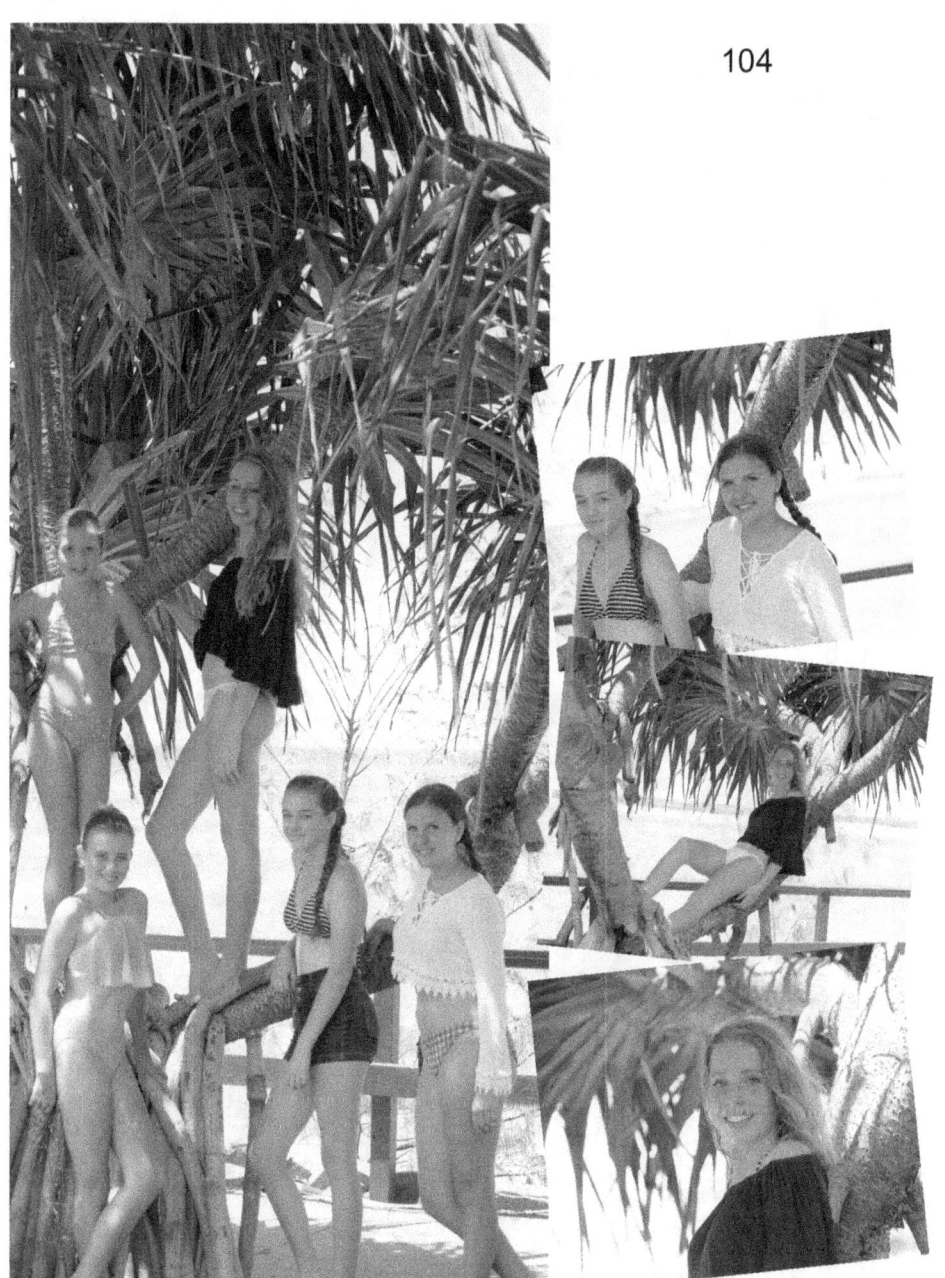

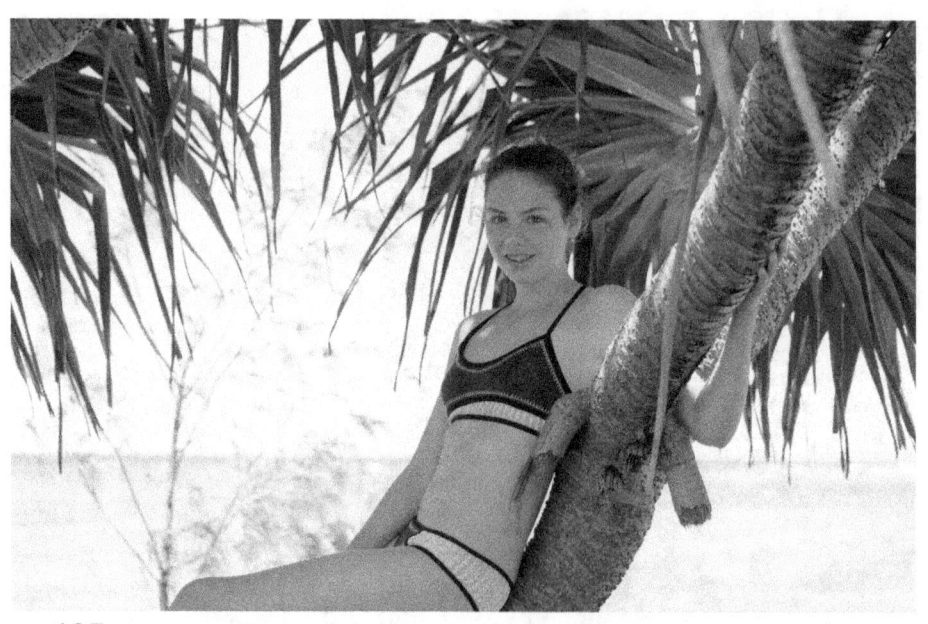

105

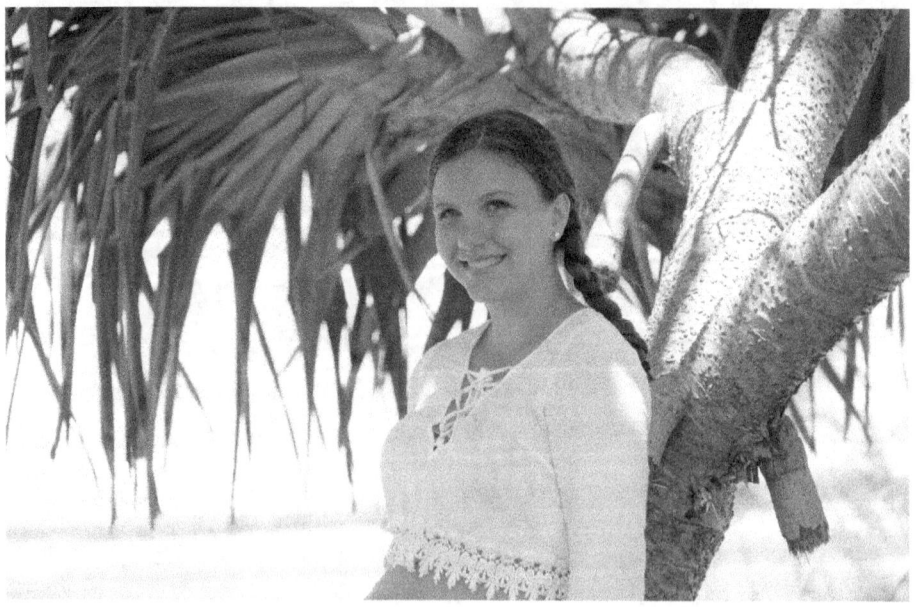

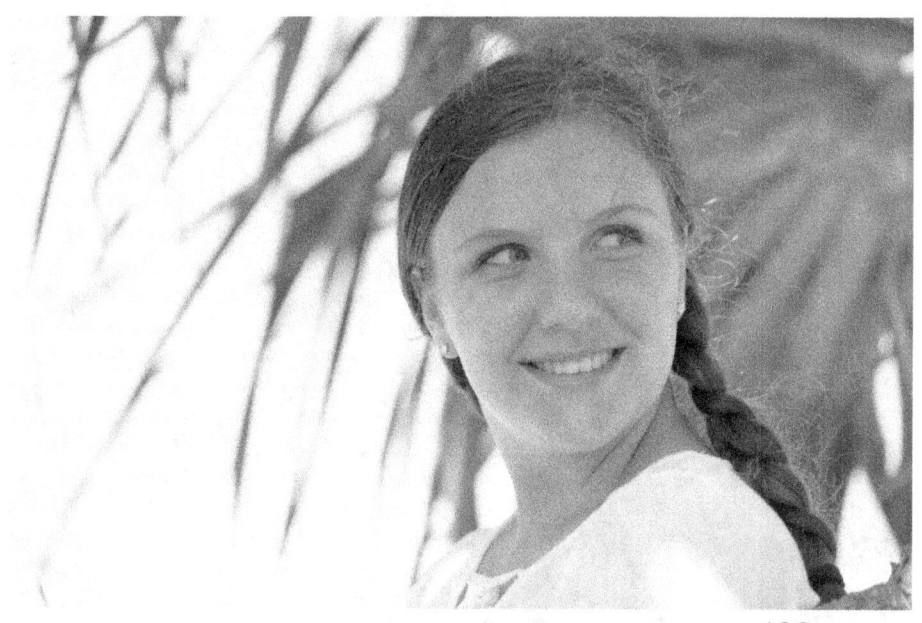

106

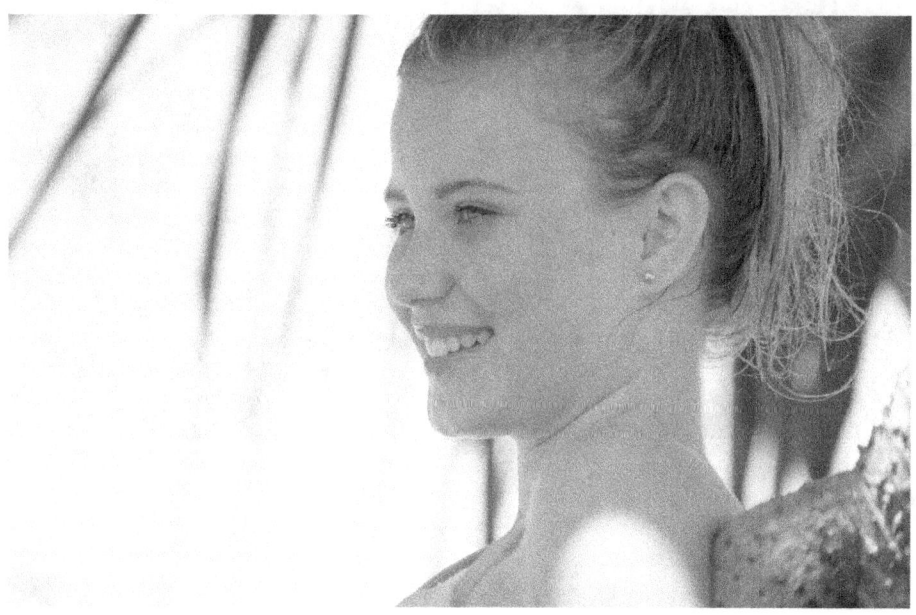

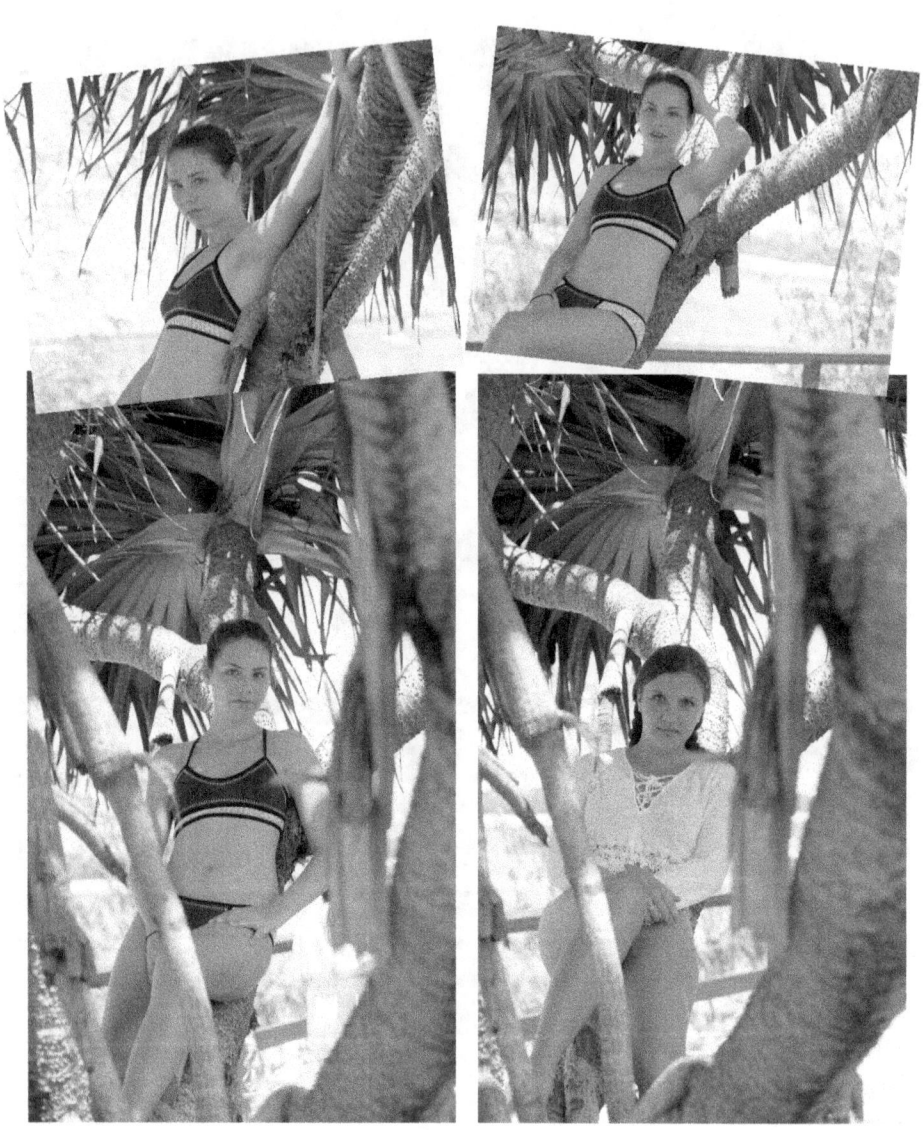

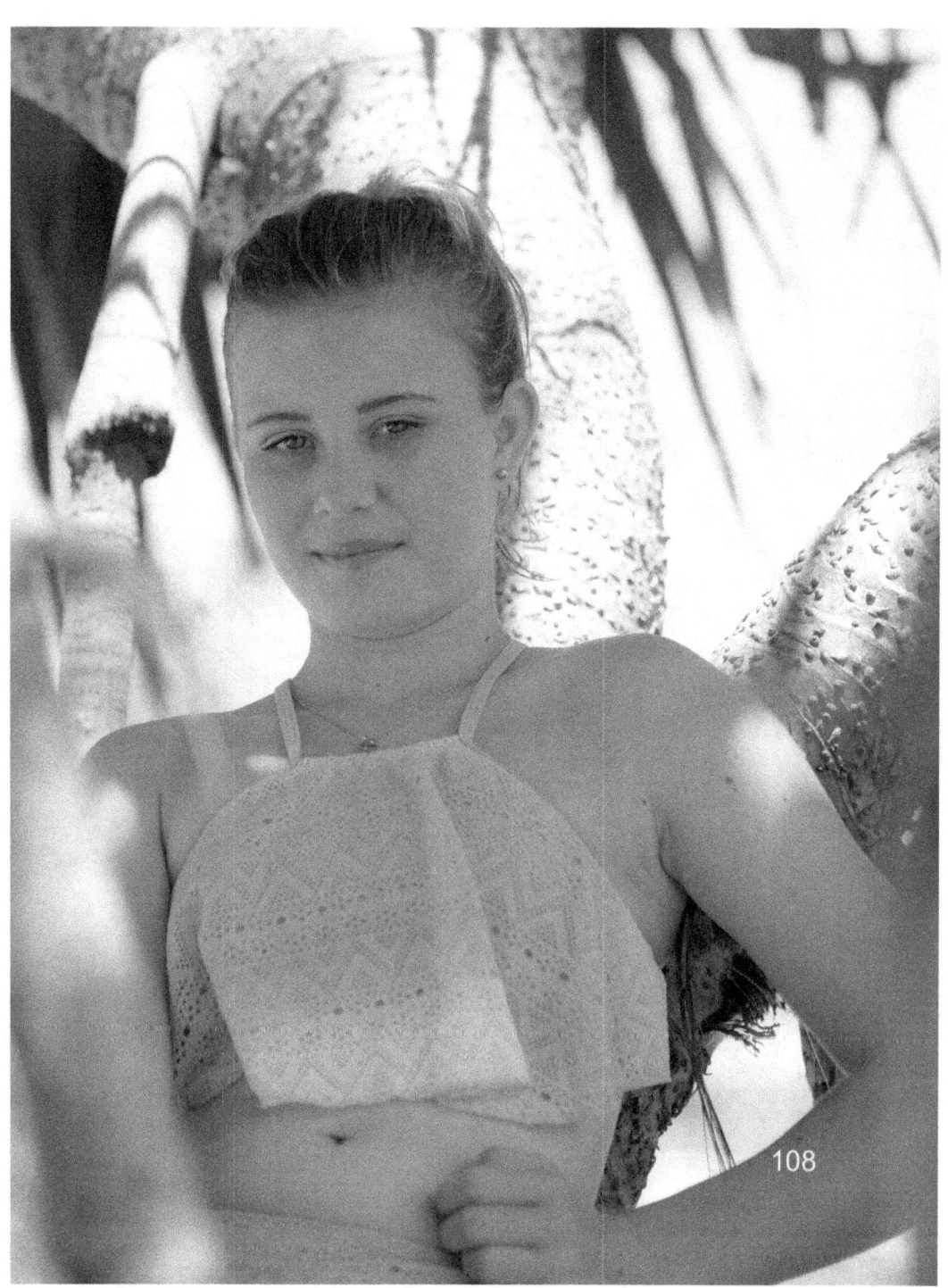
108

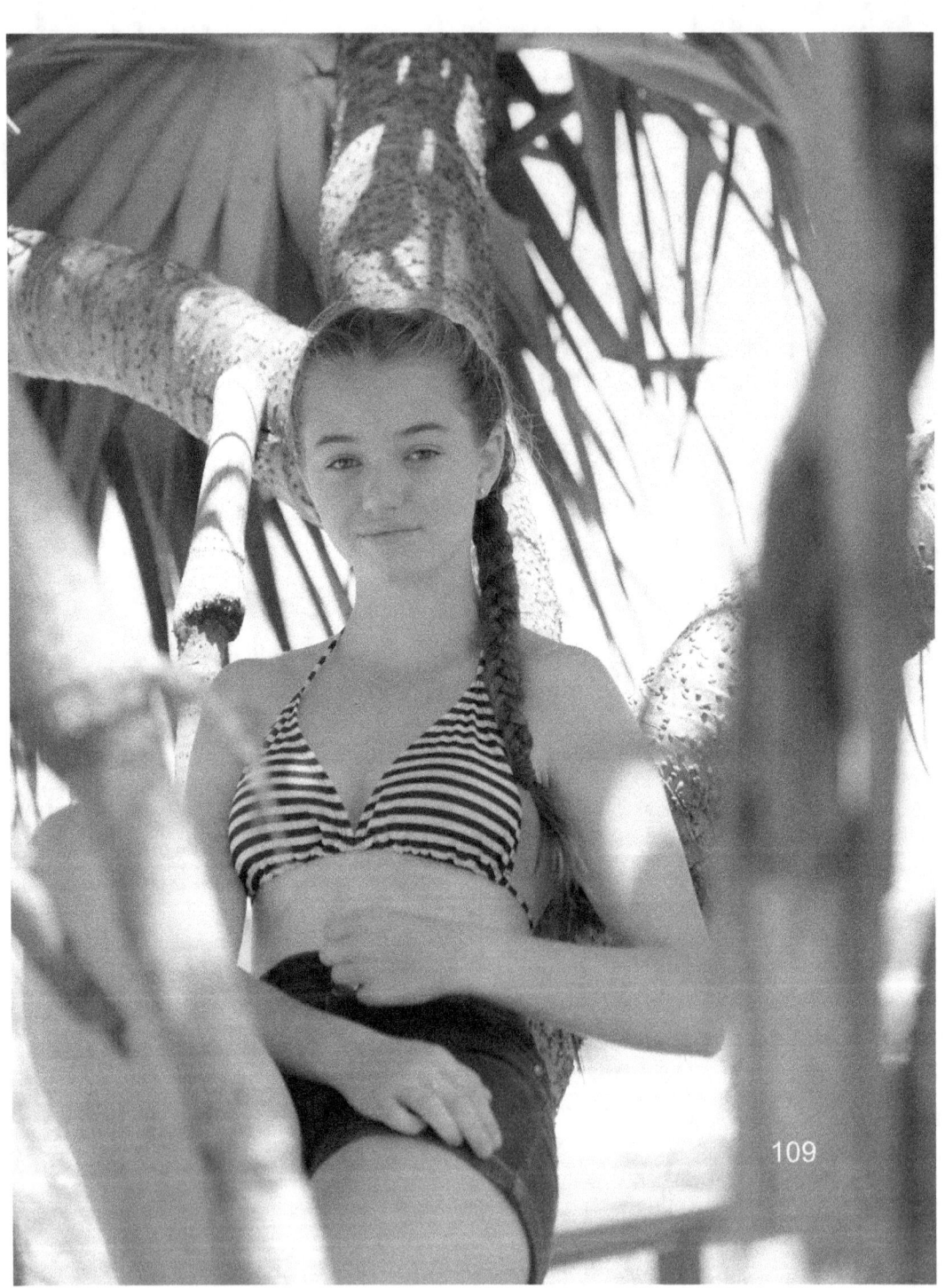

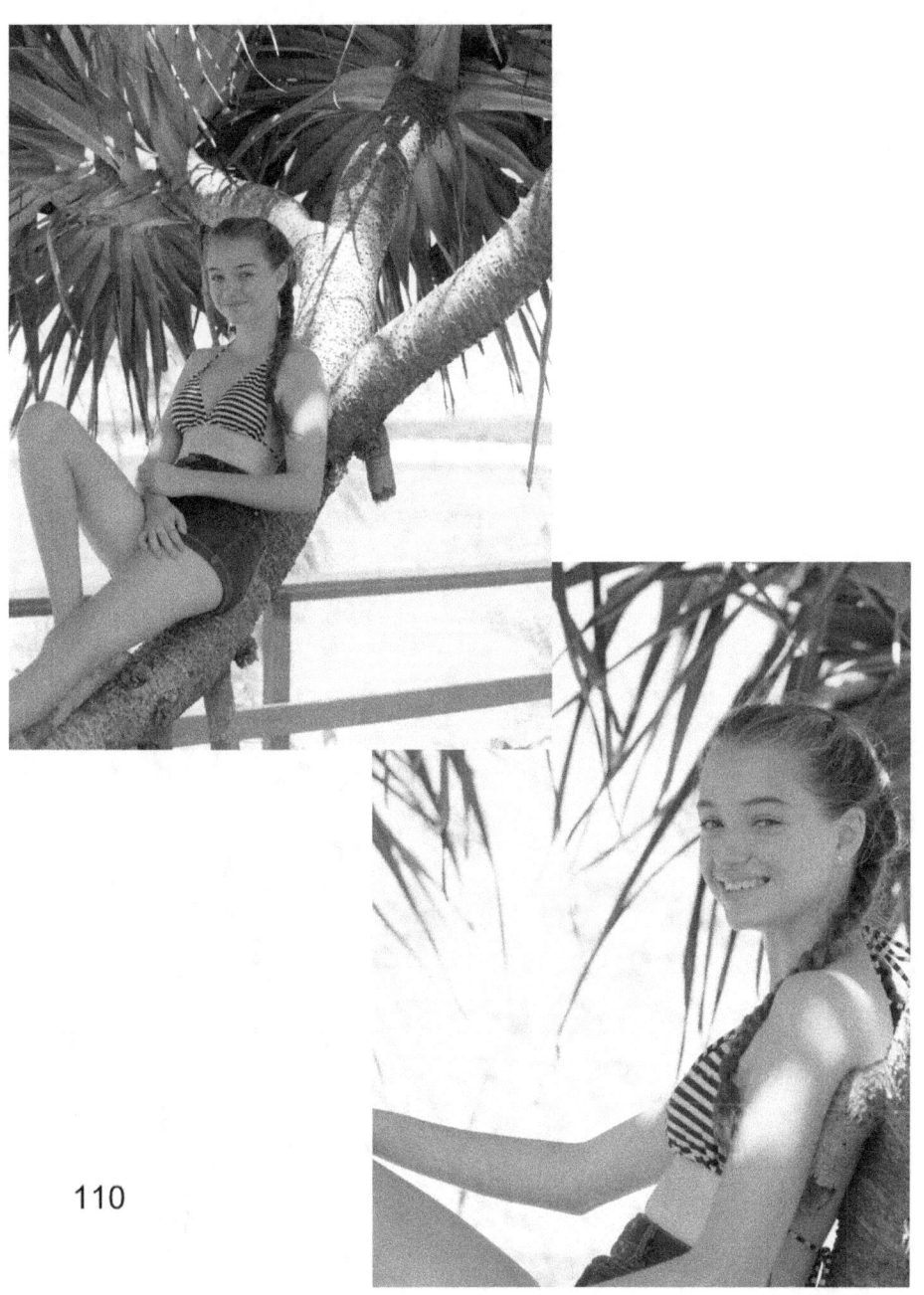

110

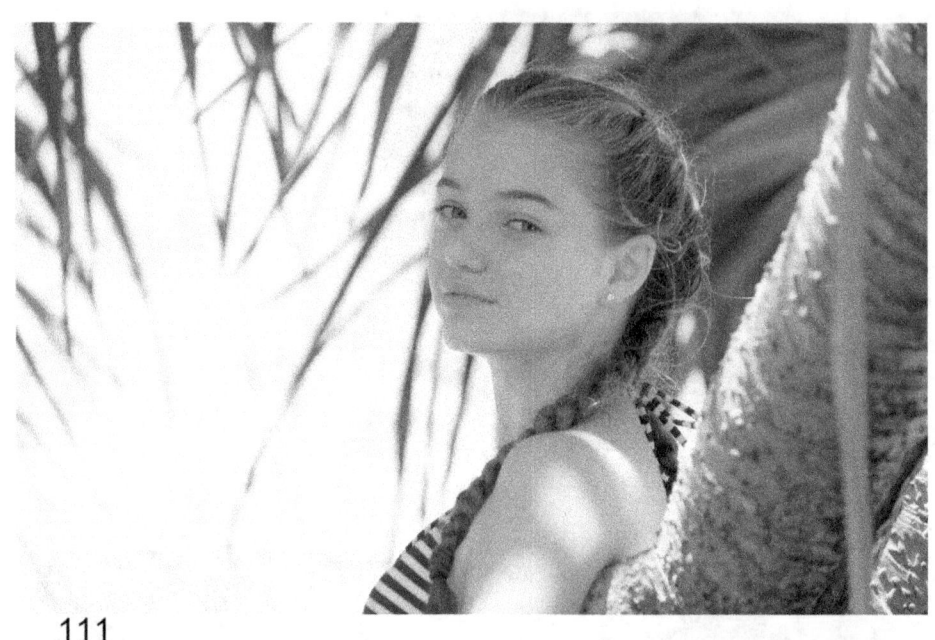

111

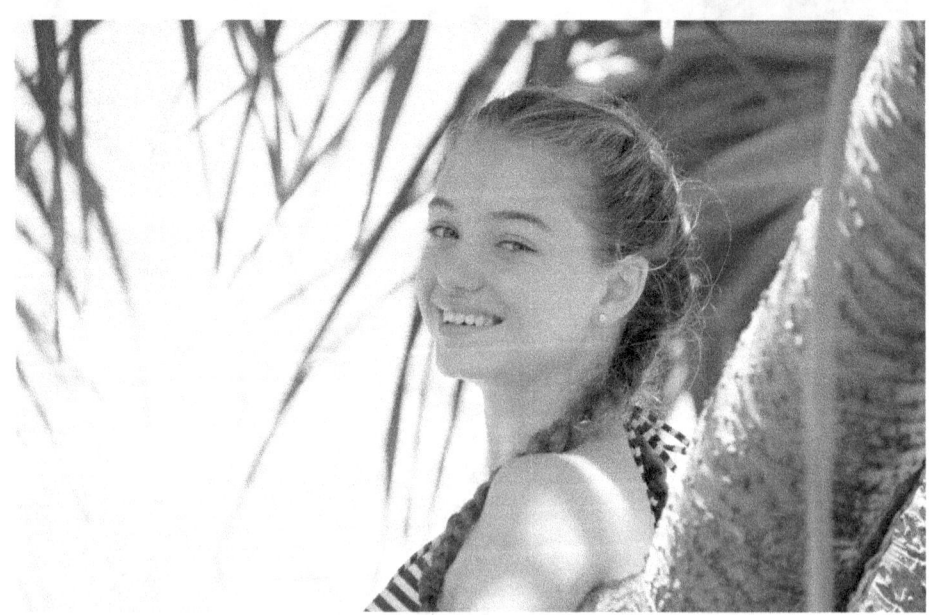

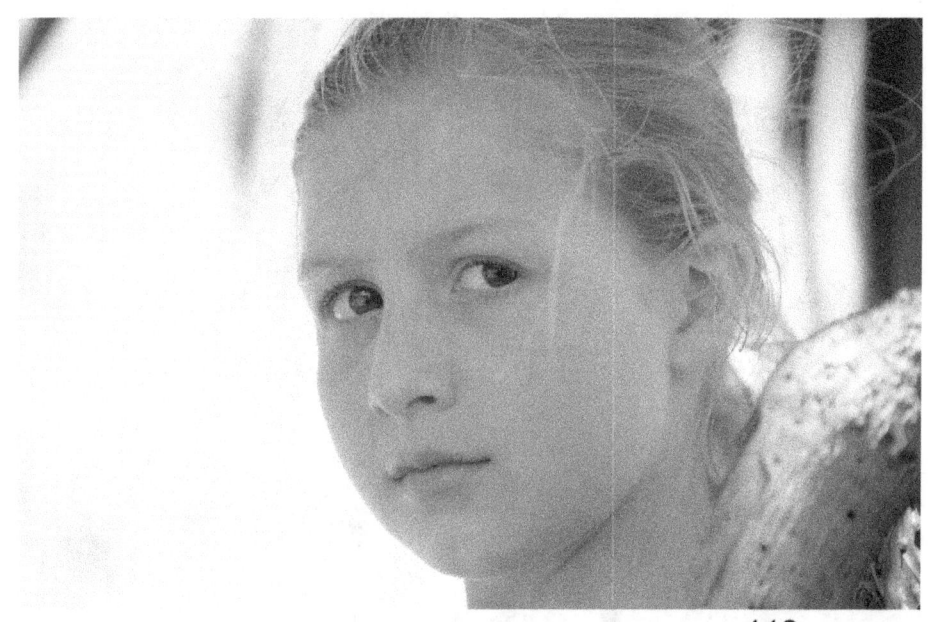

112

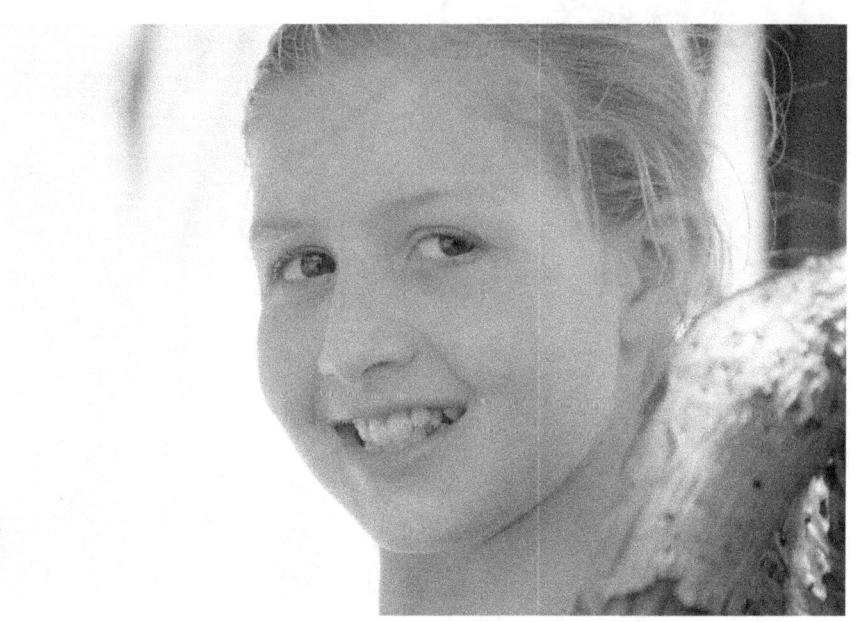

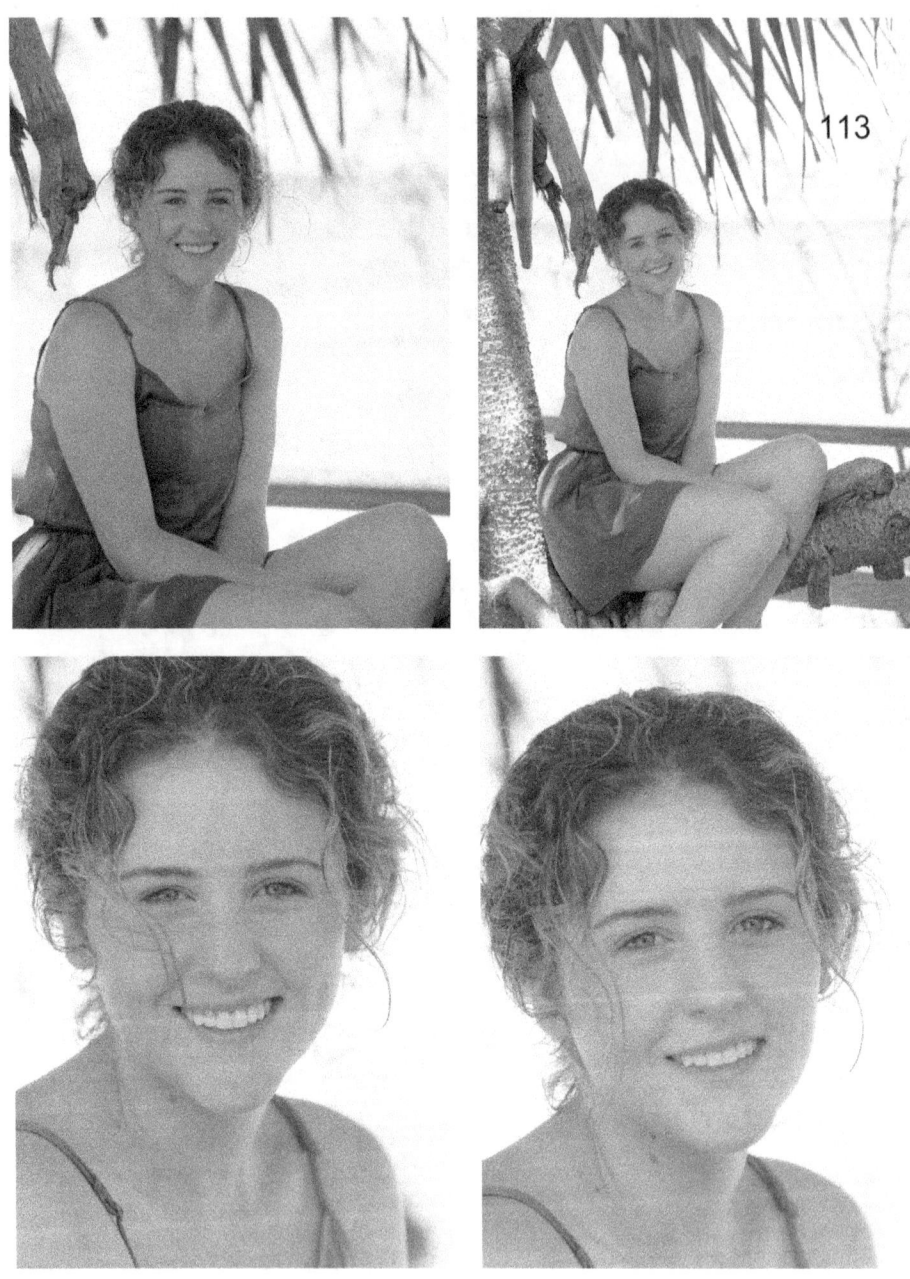

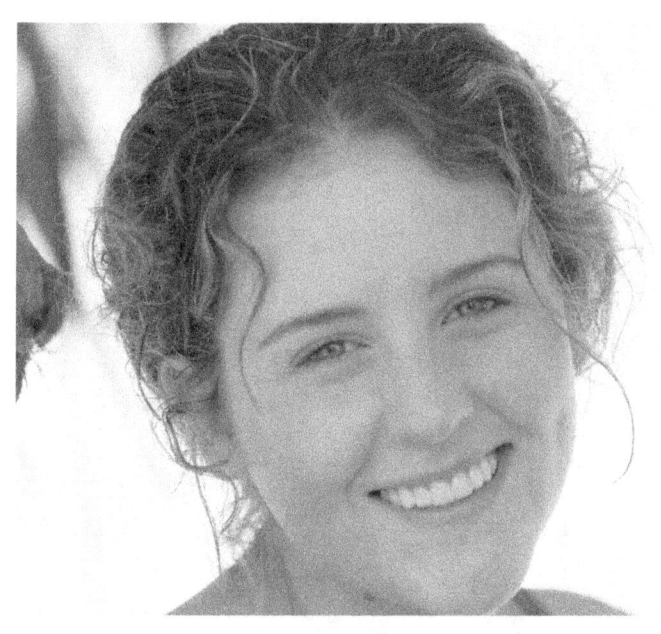

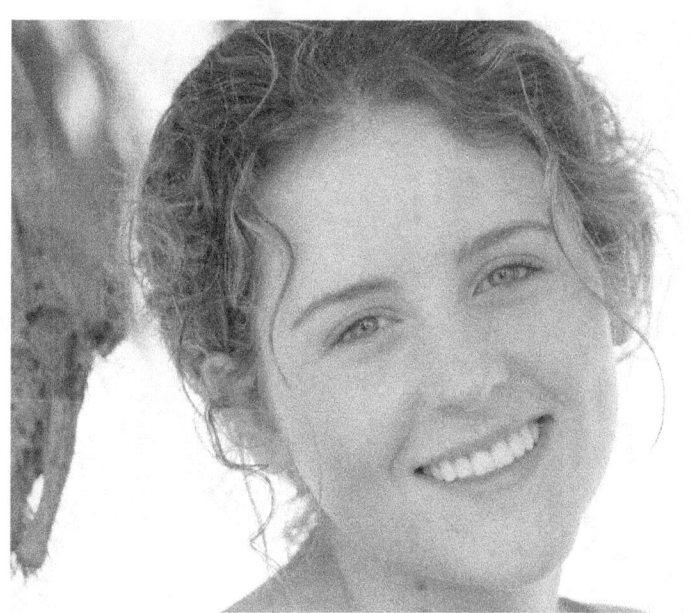

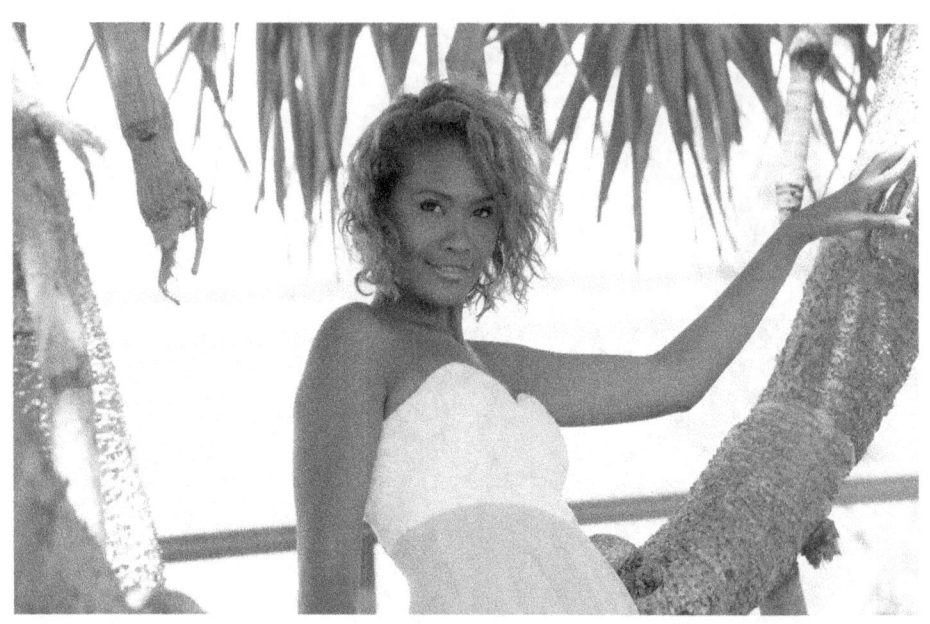

115

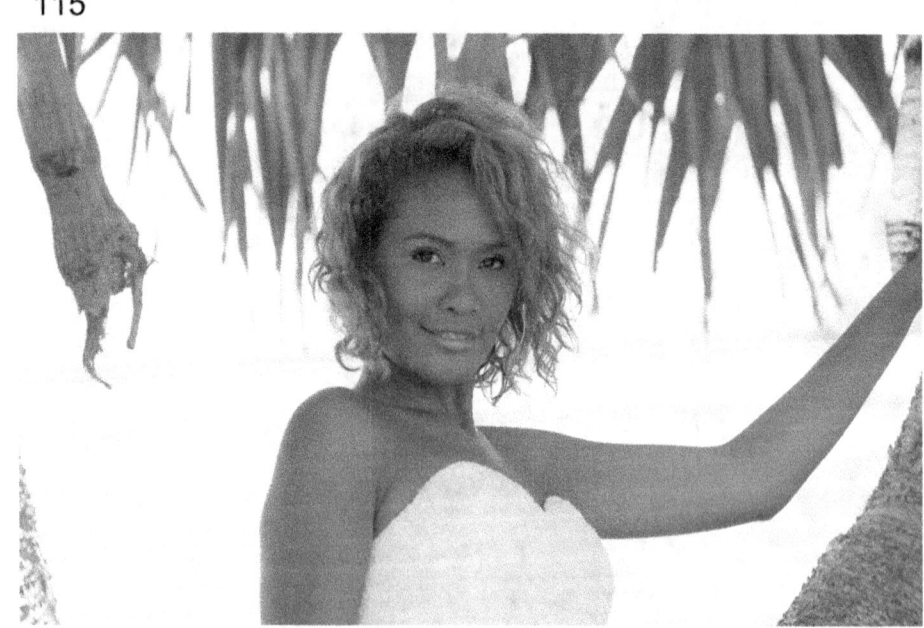

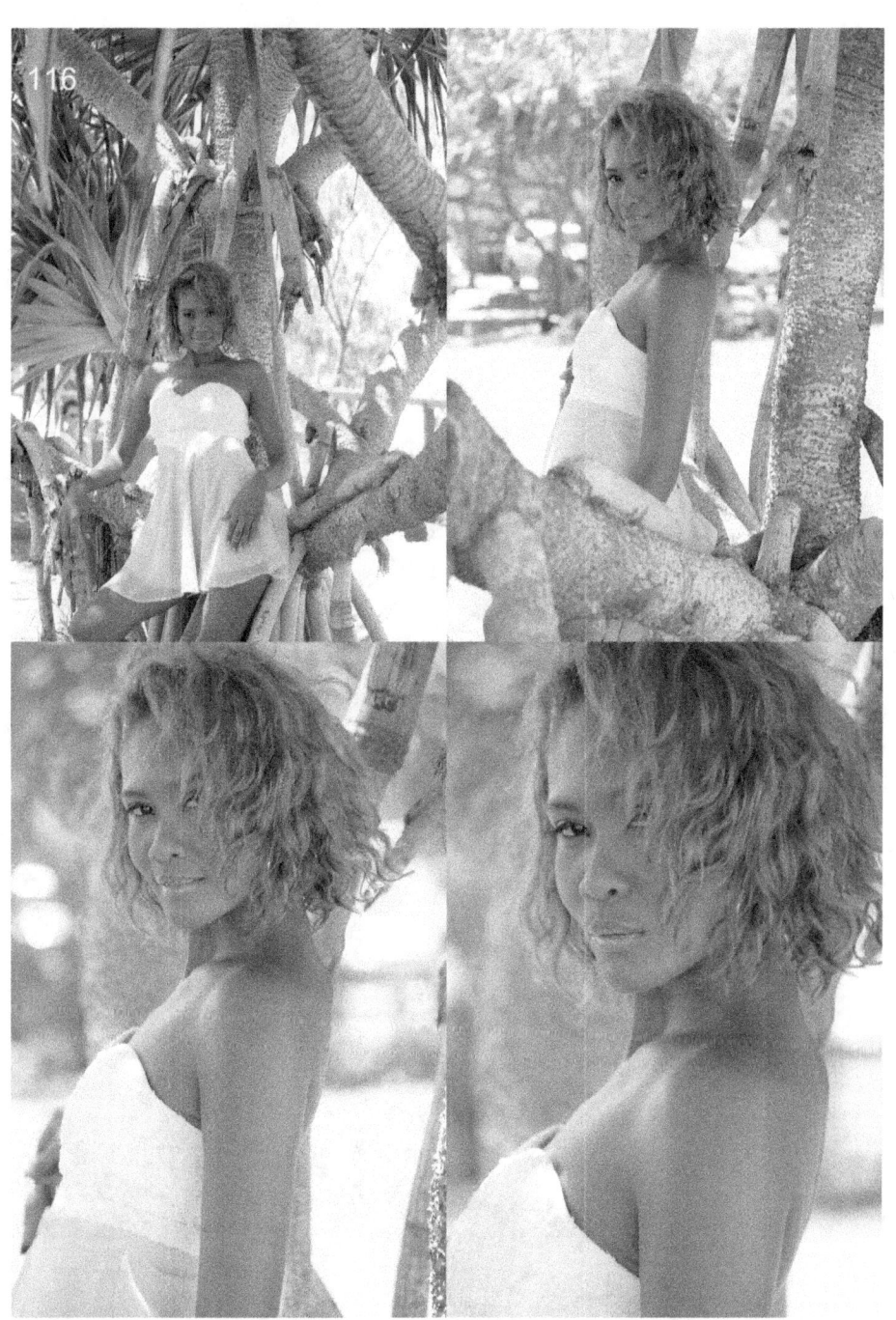

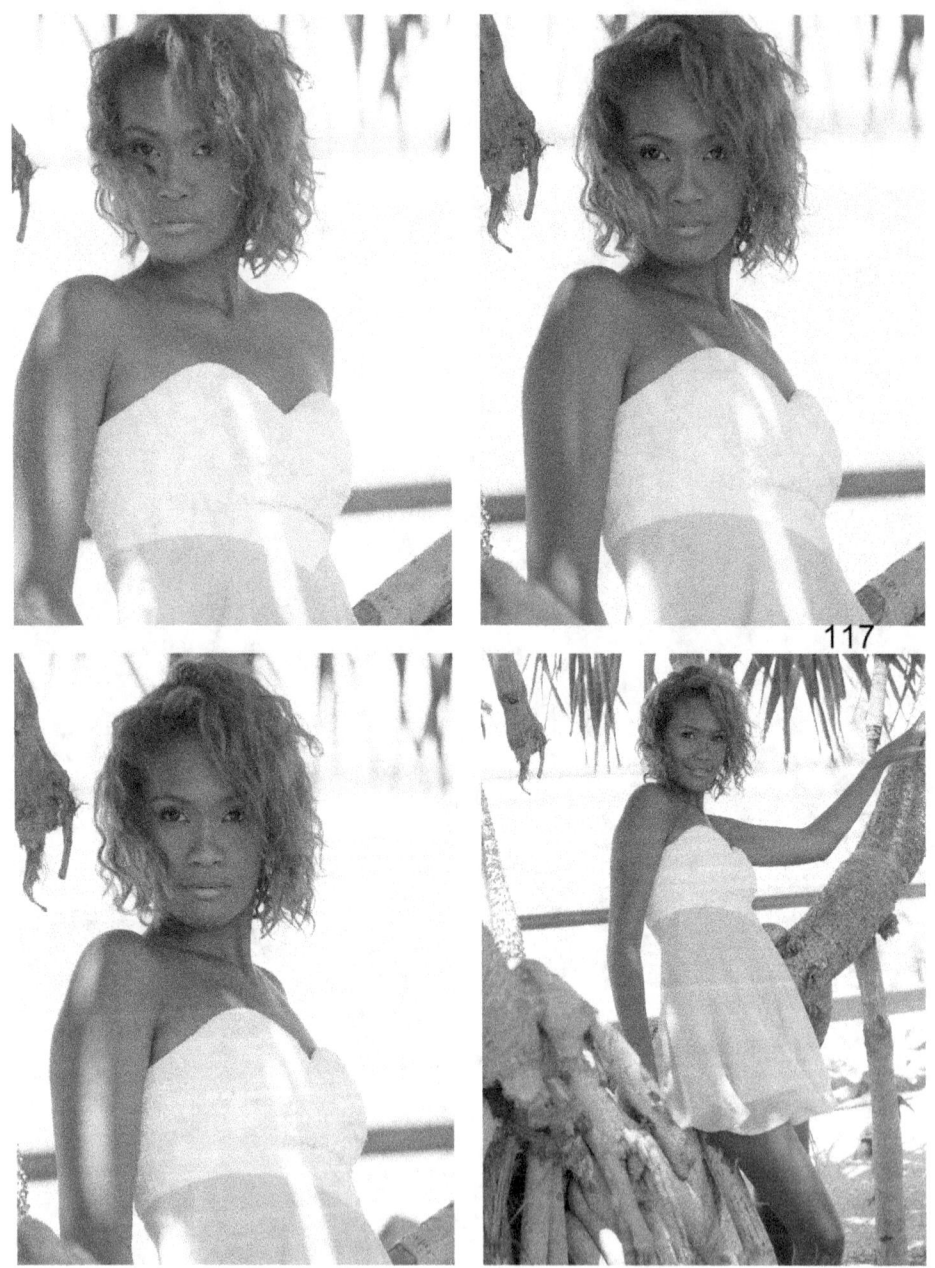

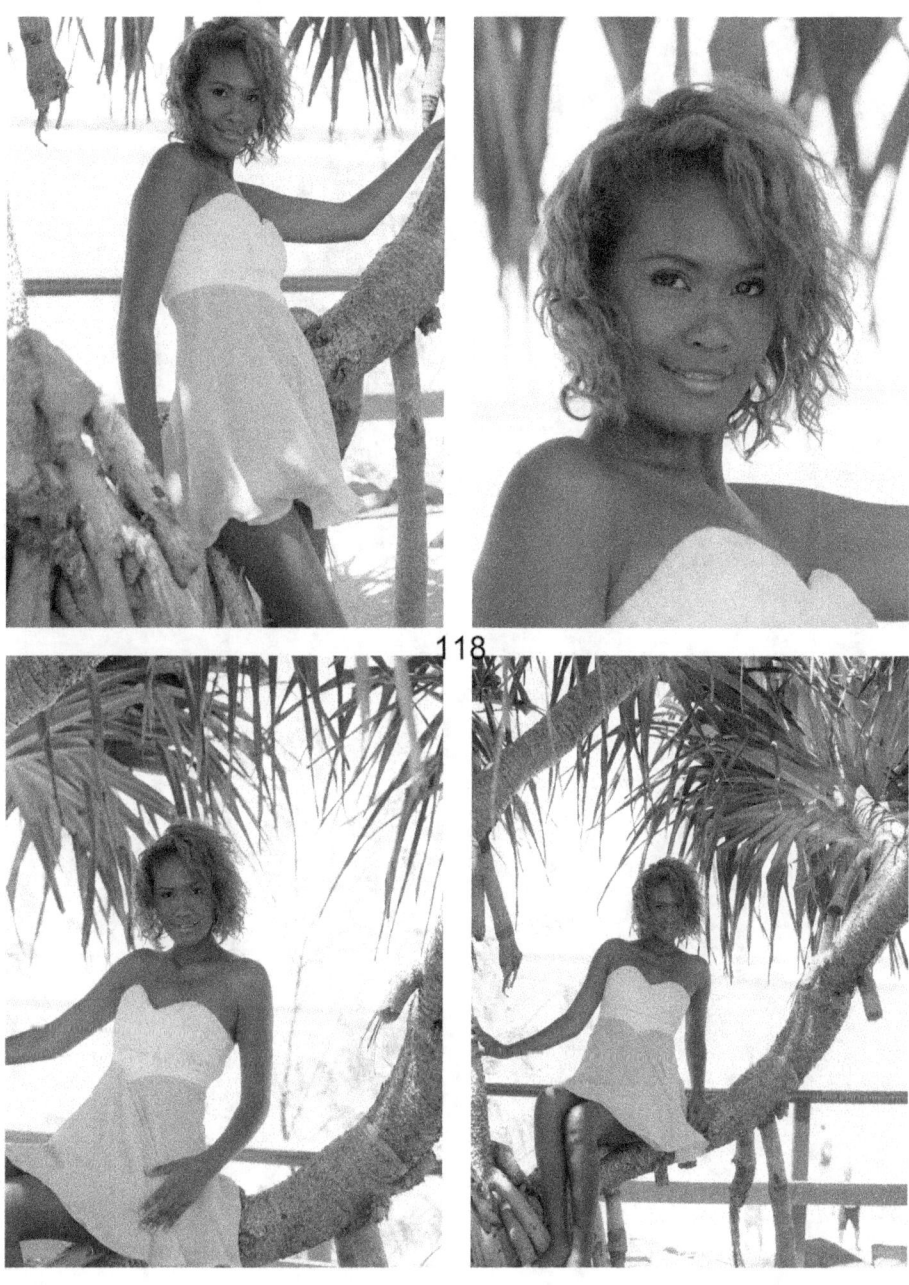

118

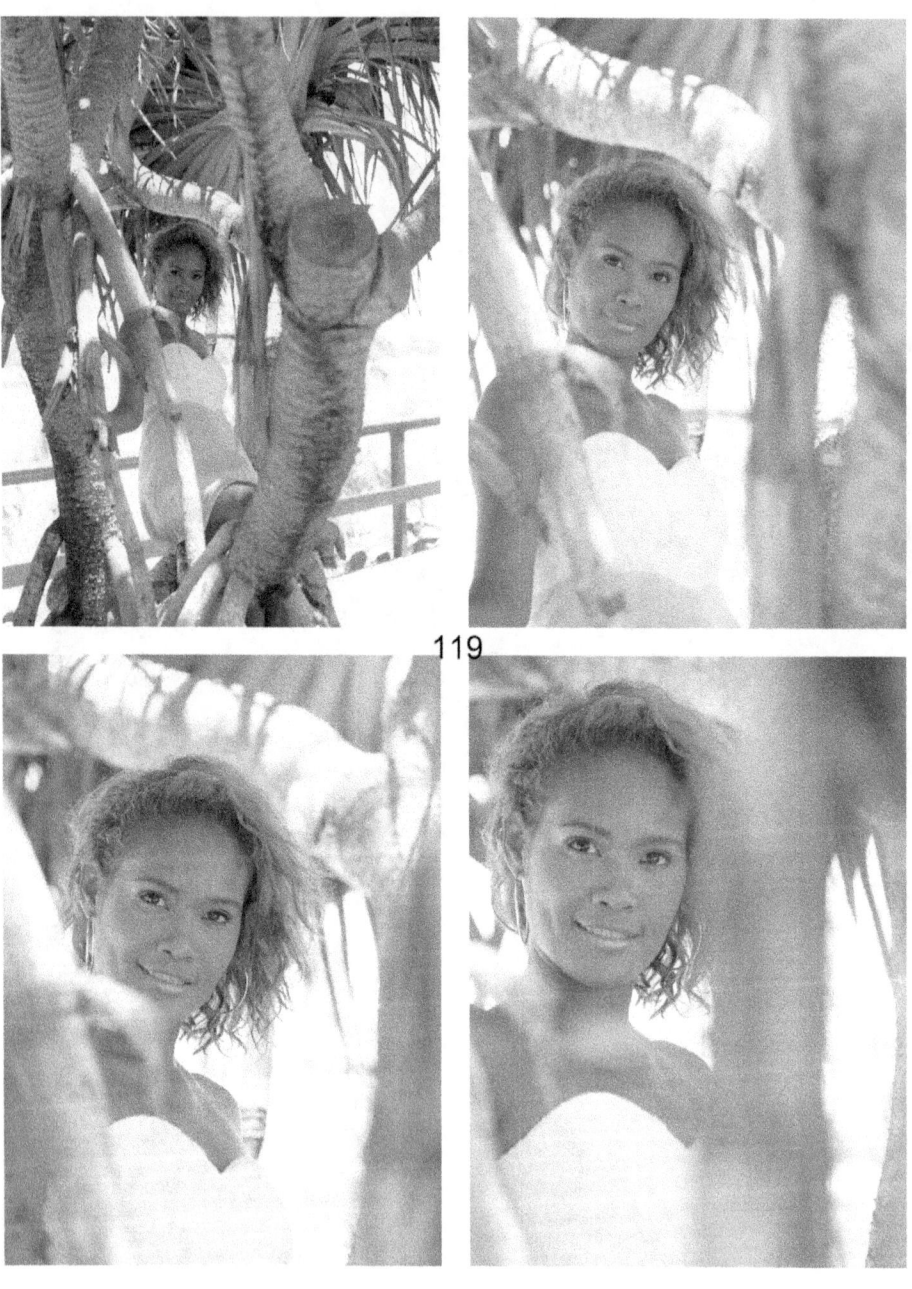

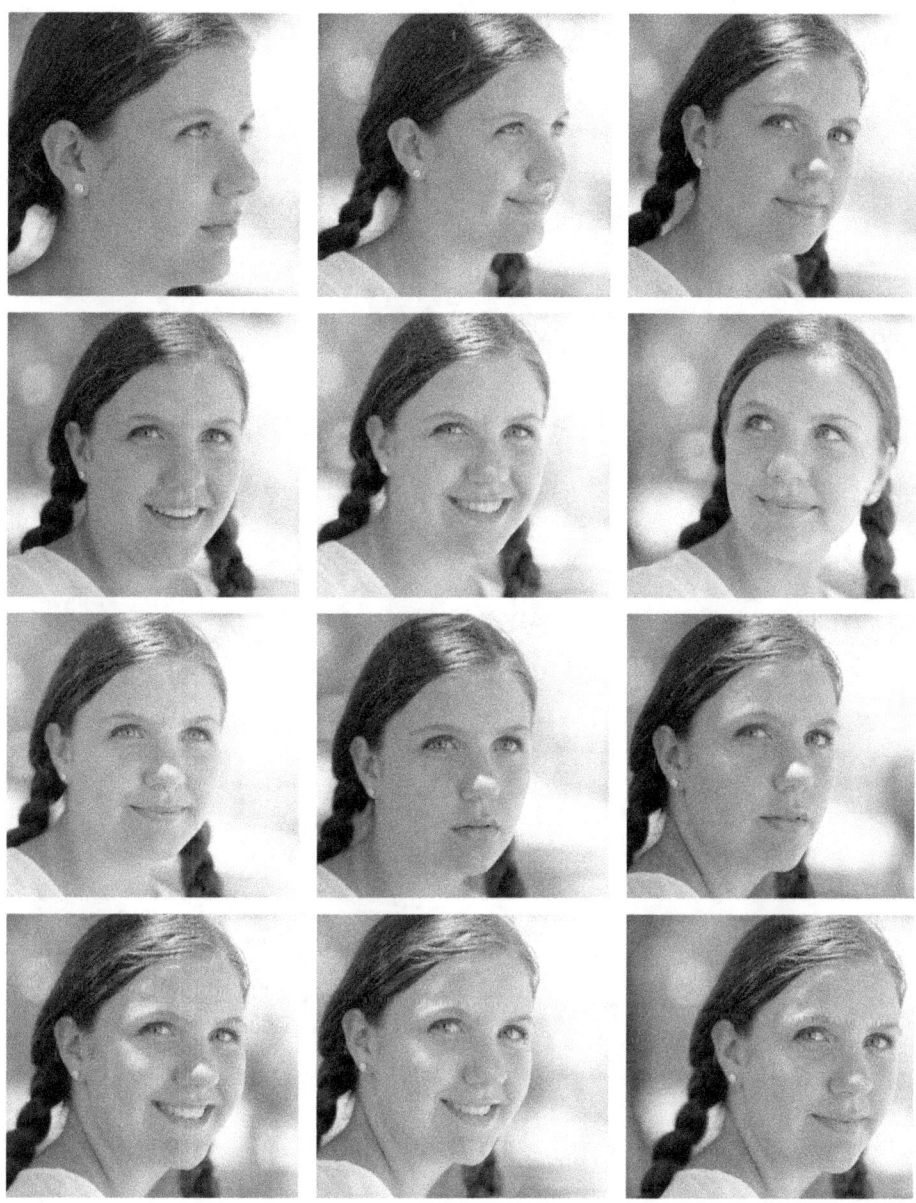

120

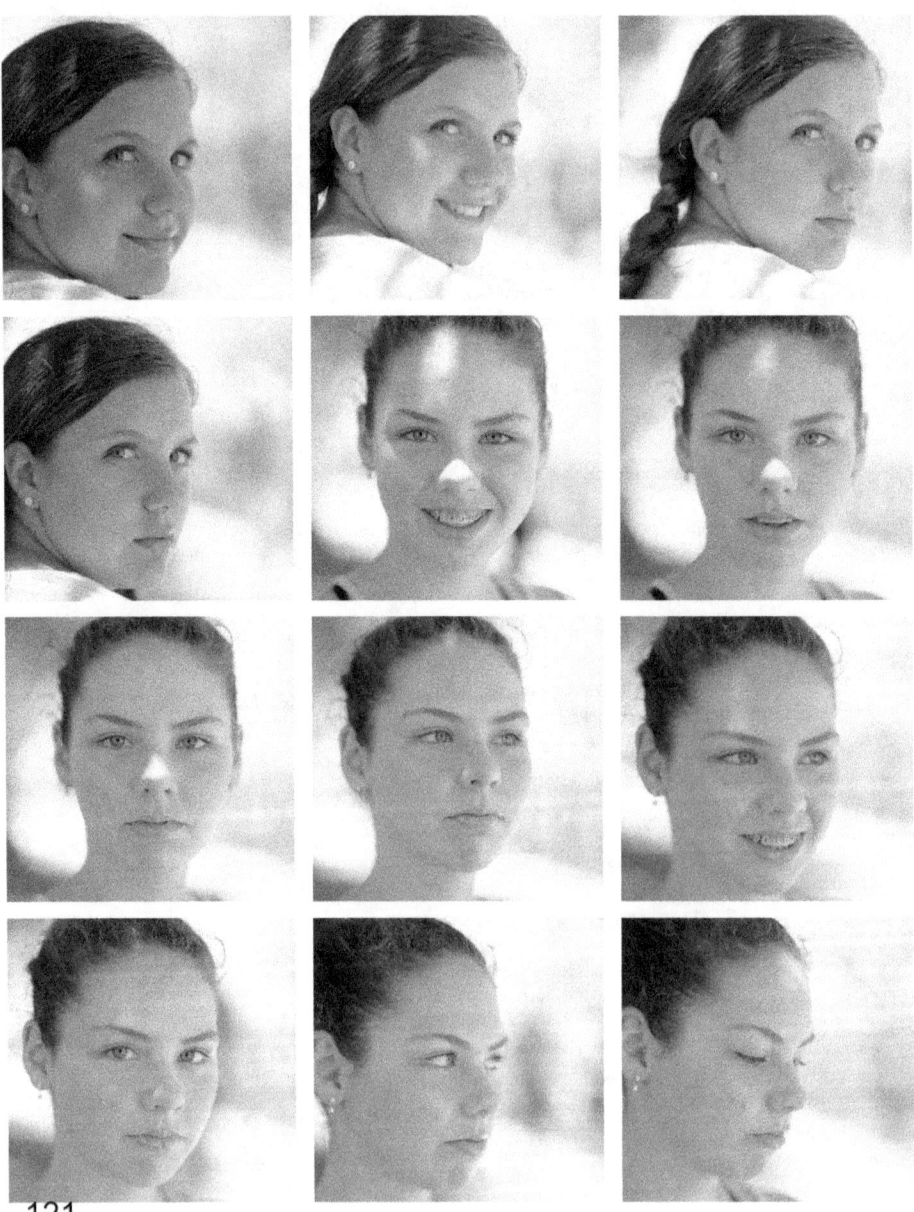

121

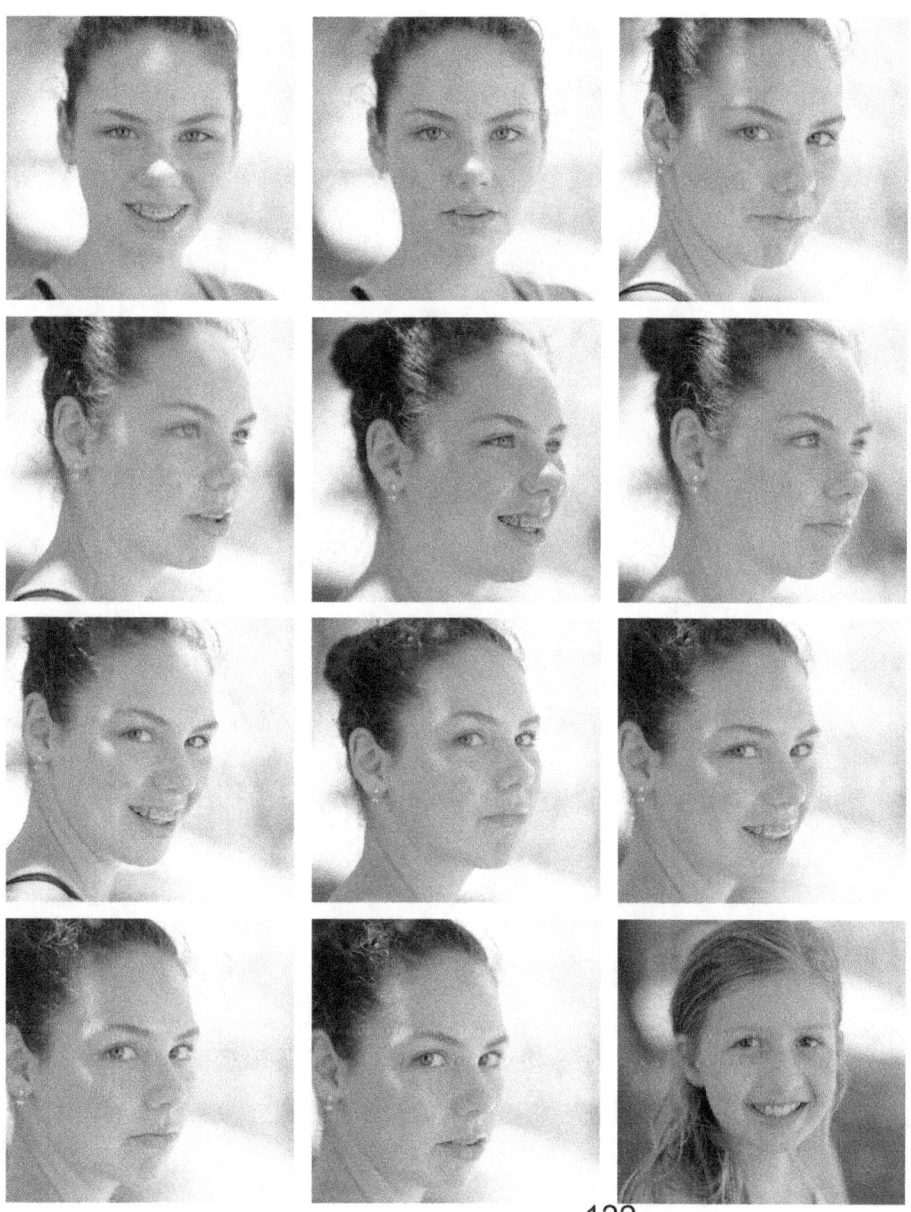

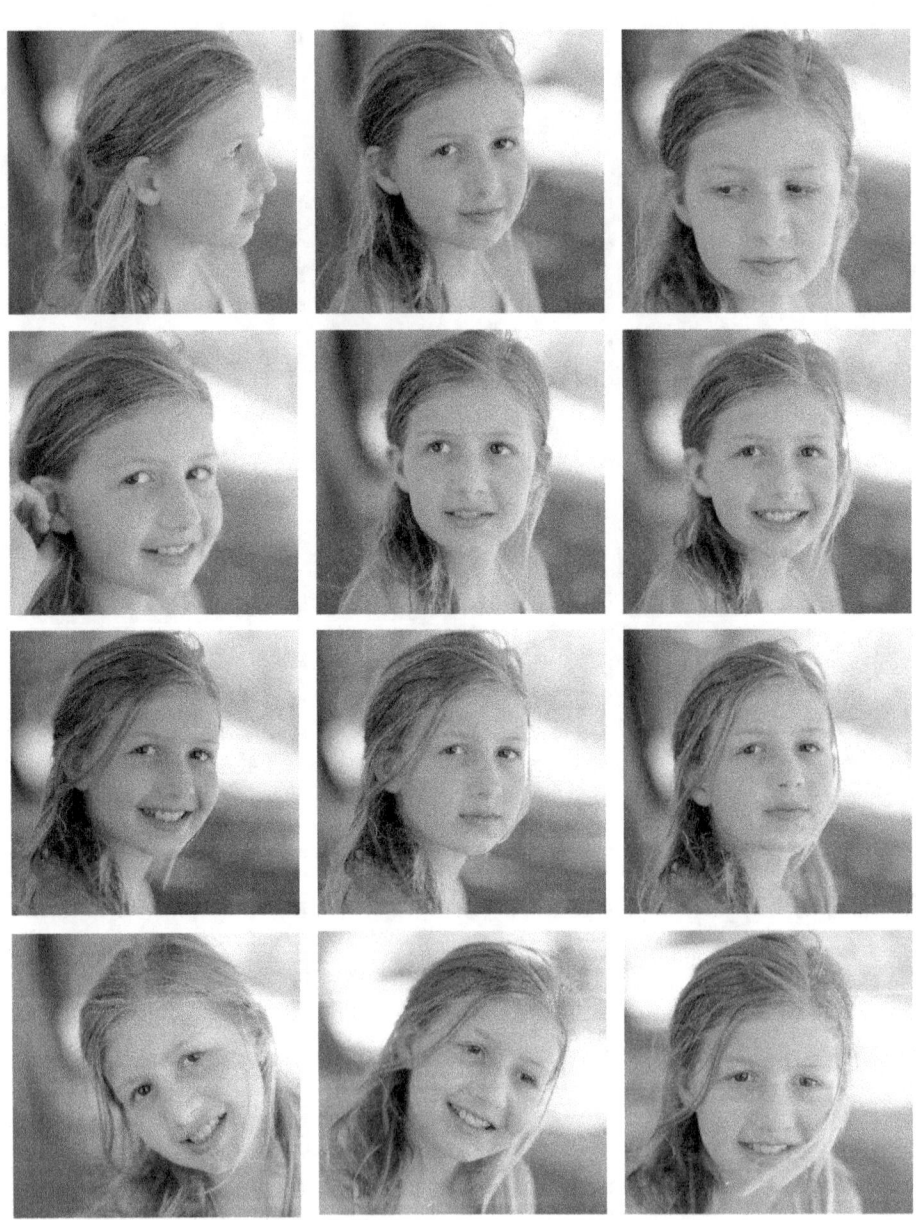

123

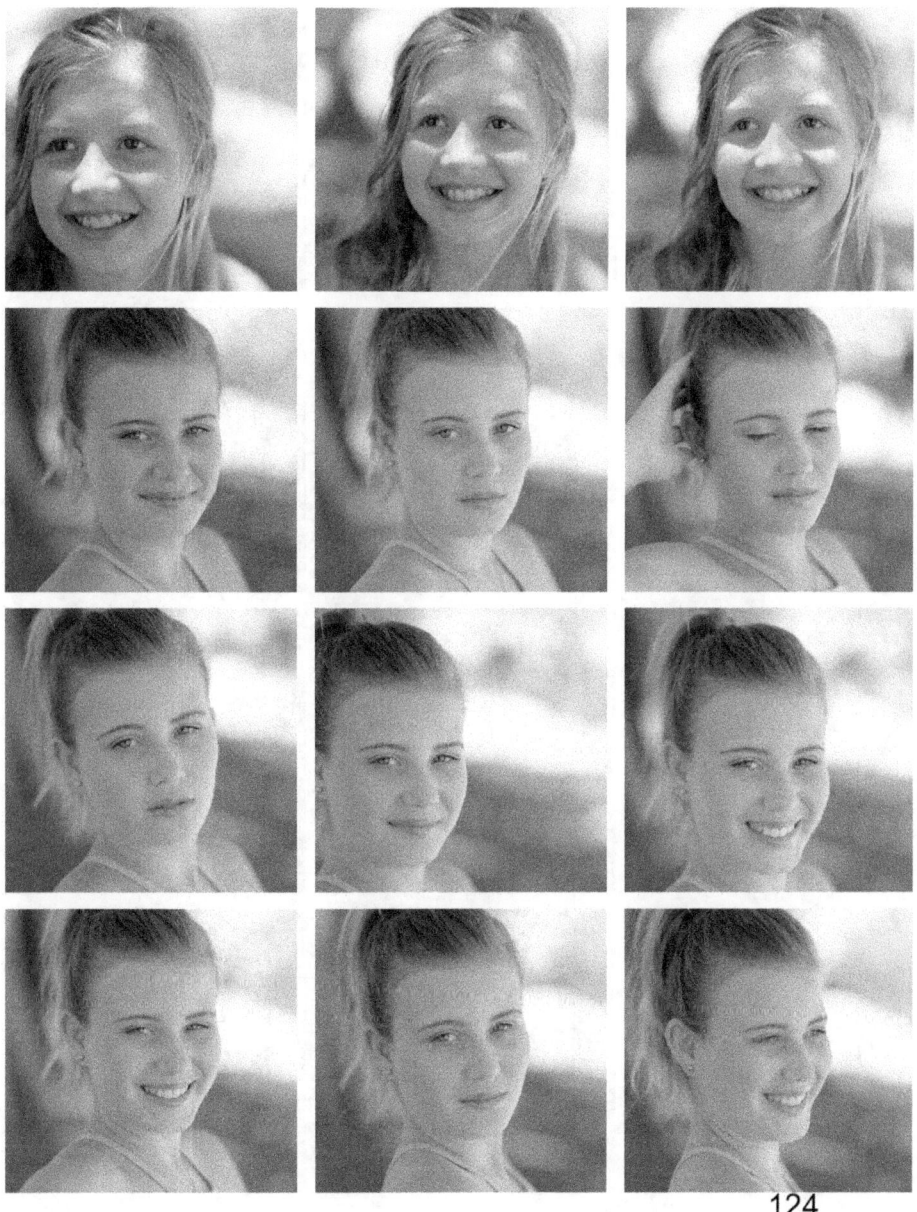

124

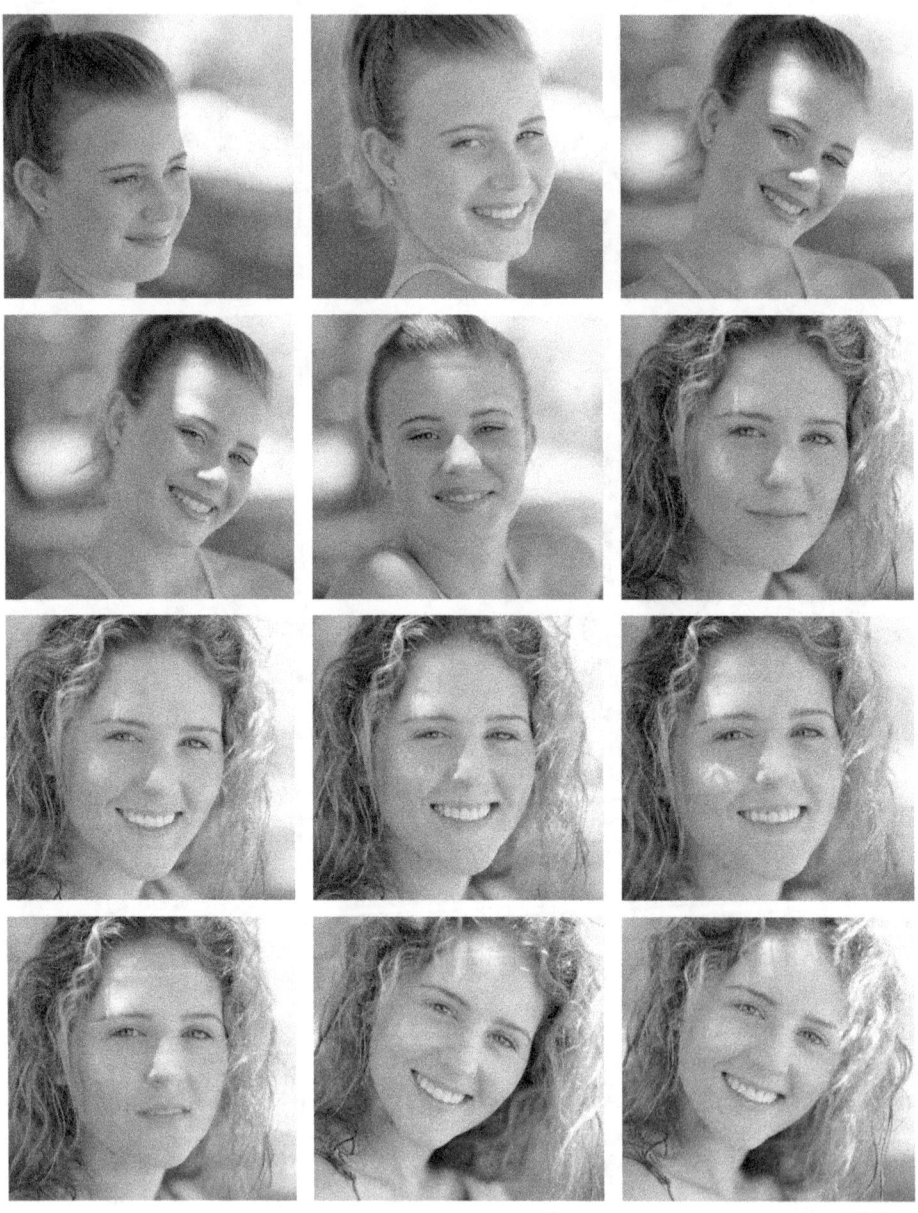

125

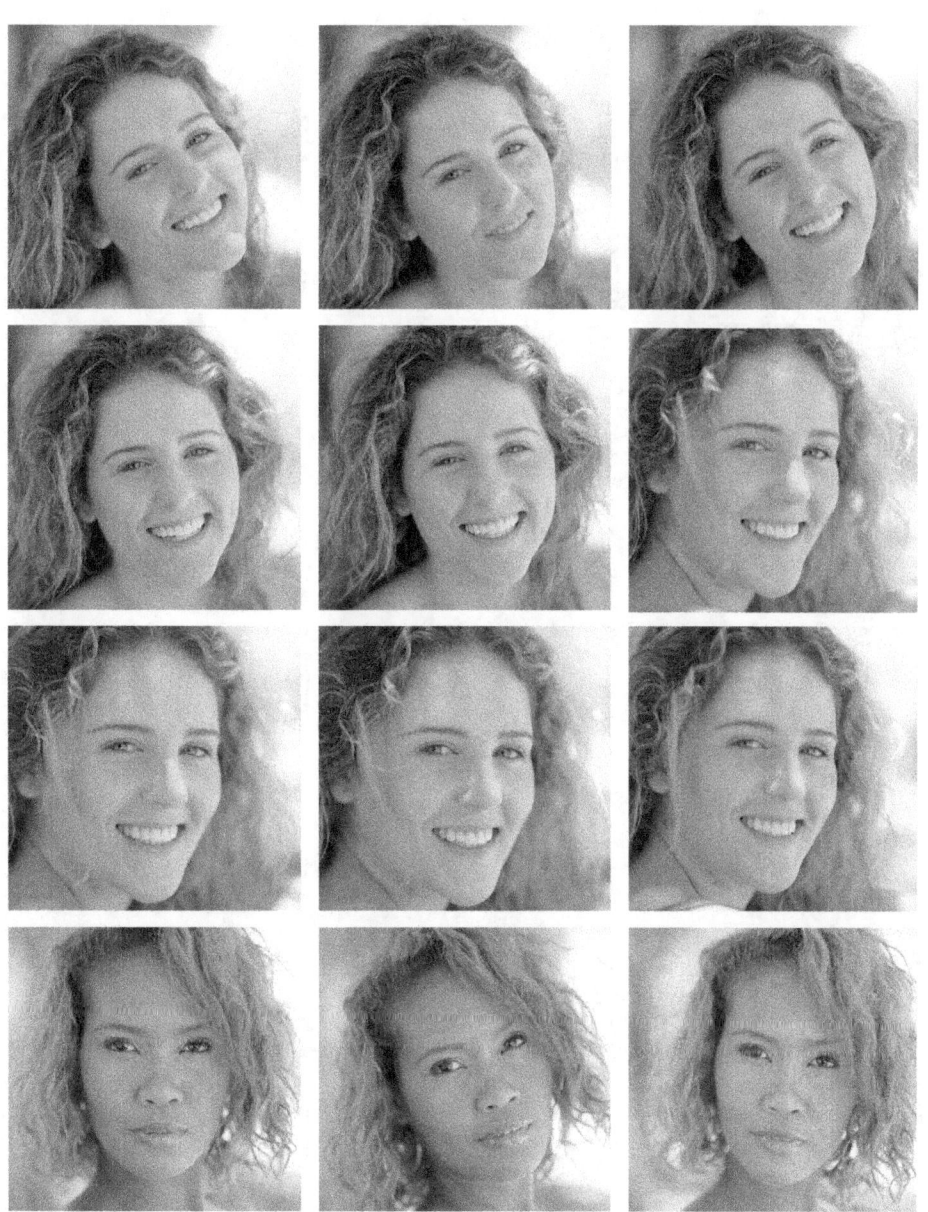

126

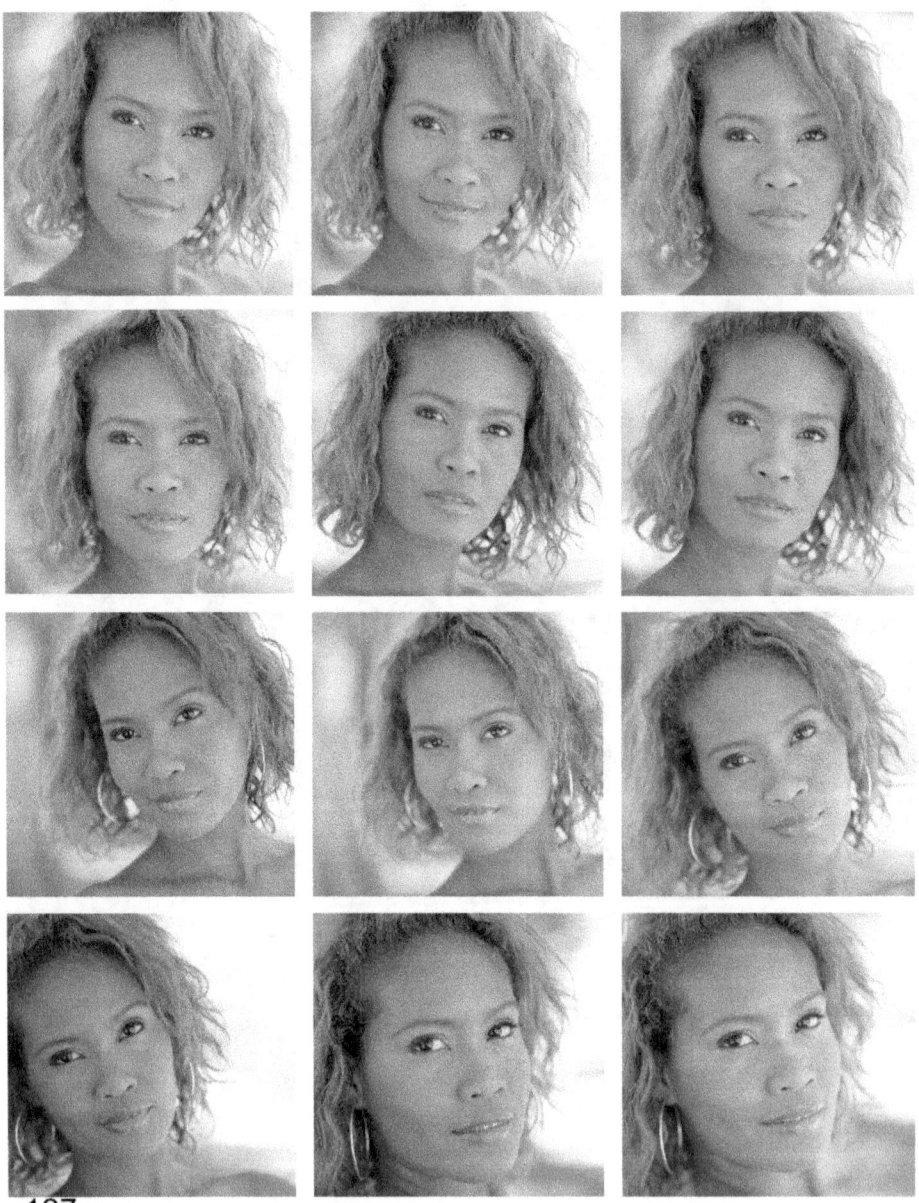

127

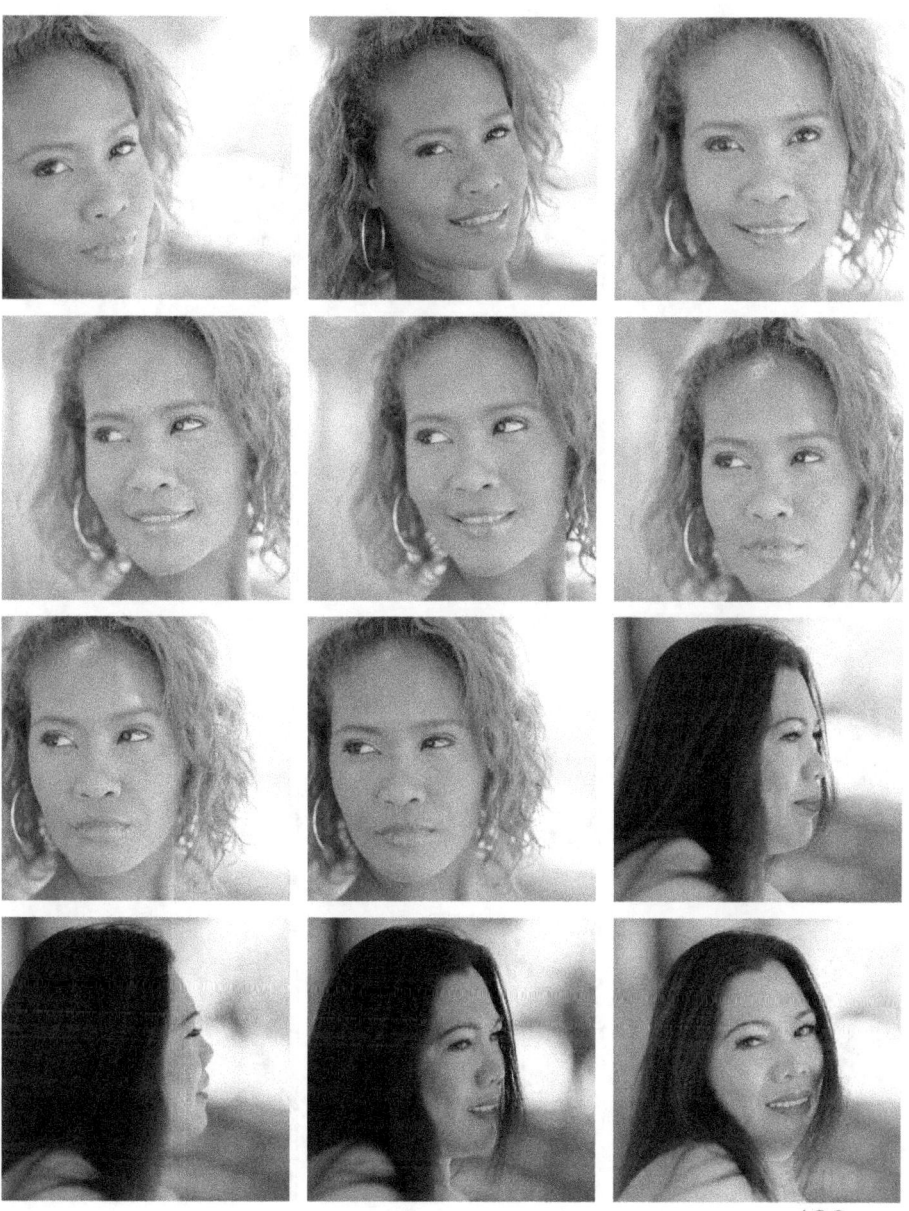

128

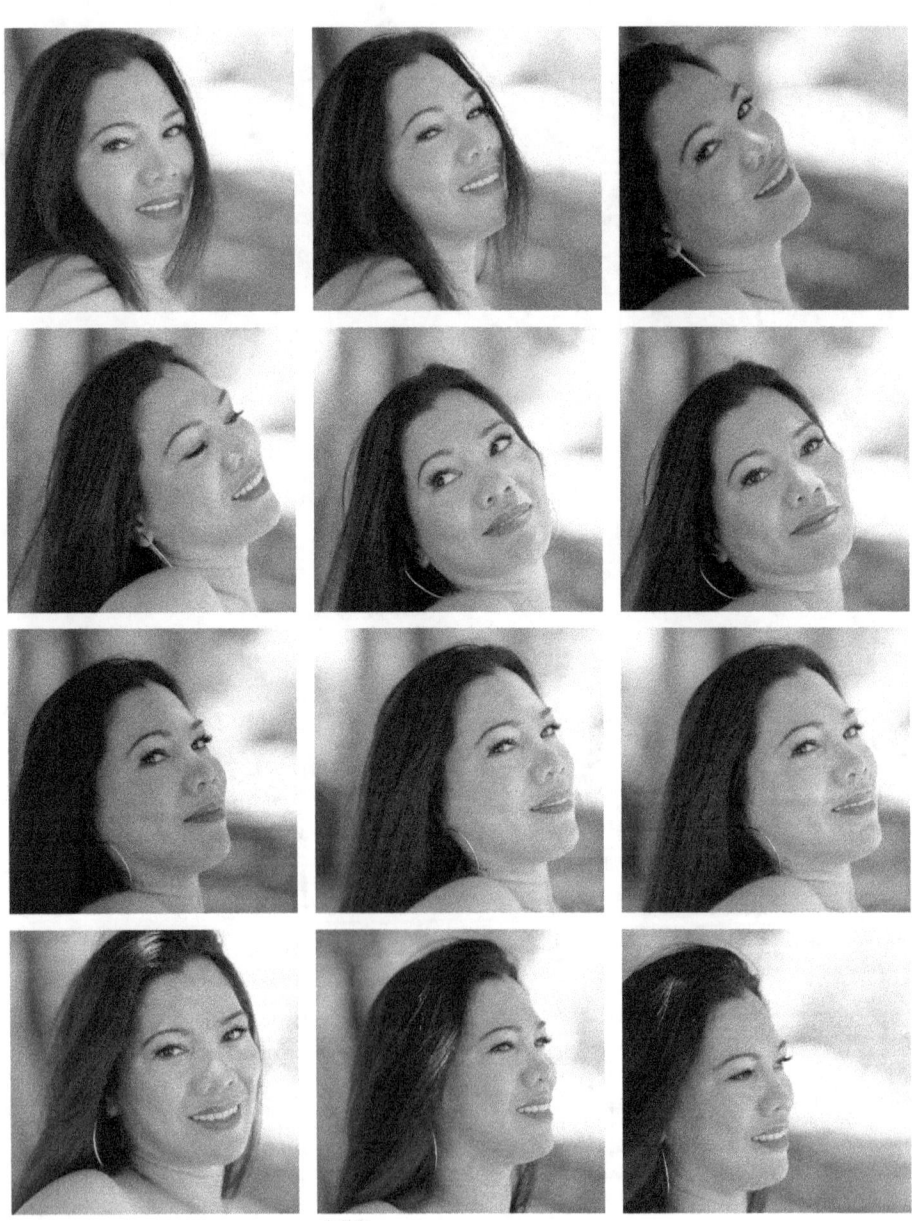

129

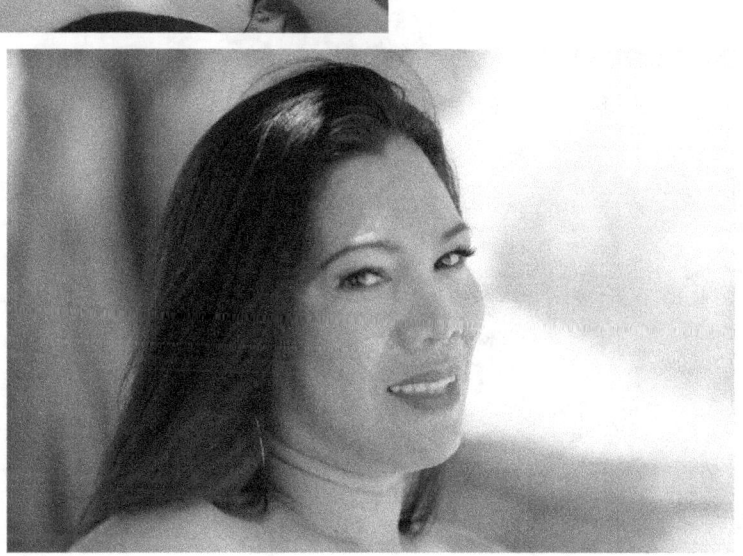

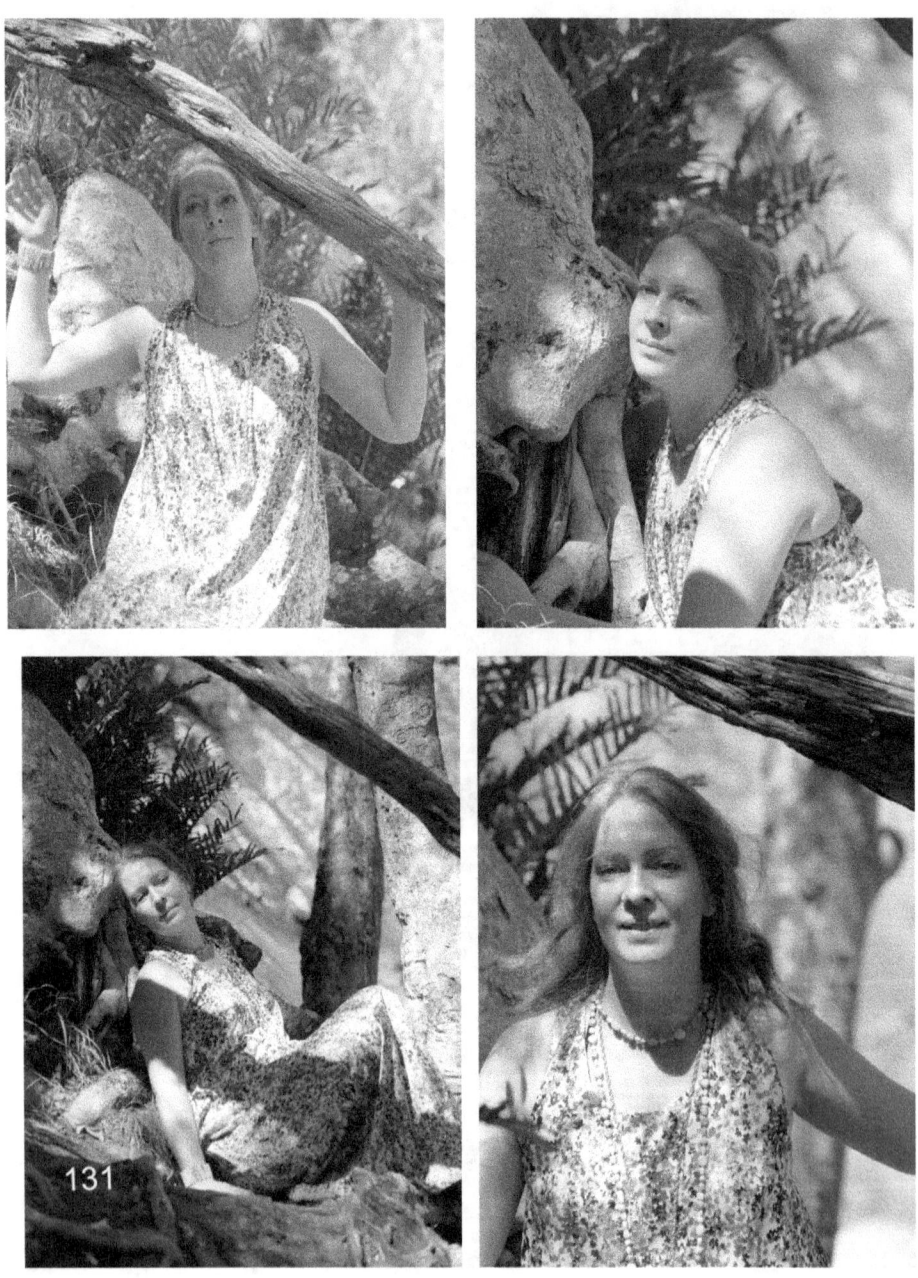

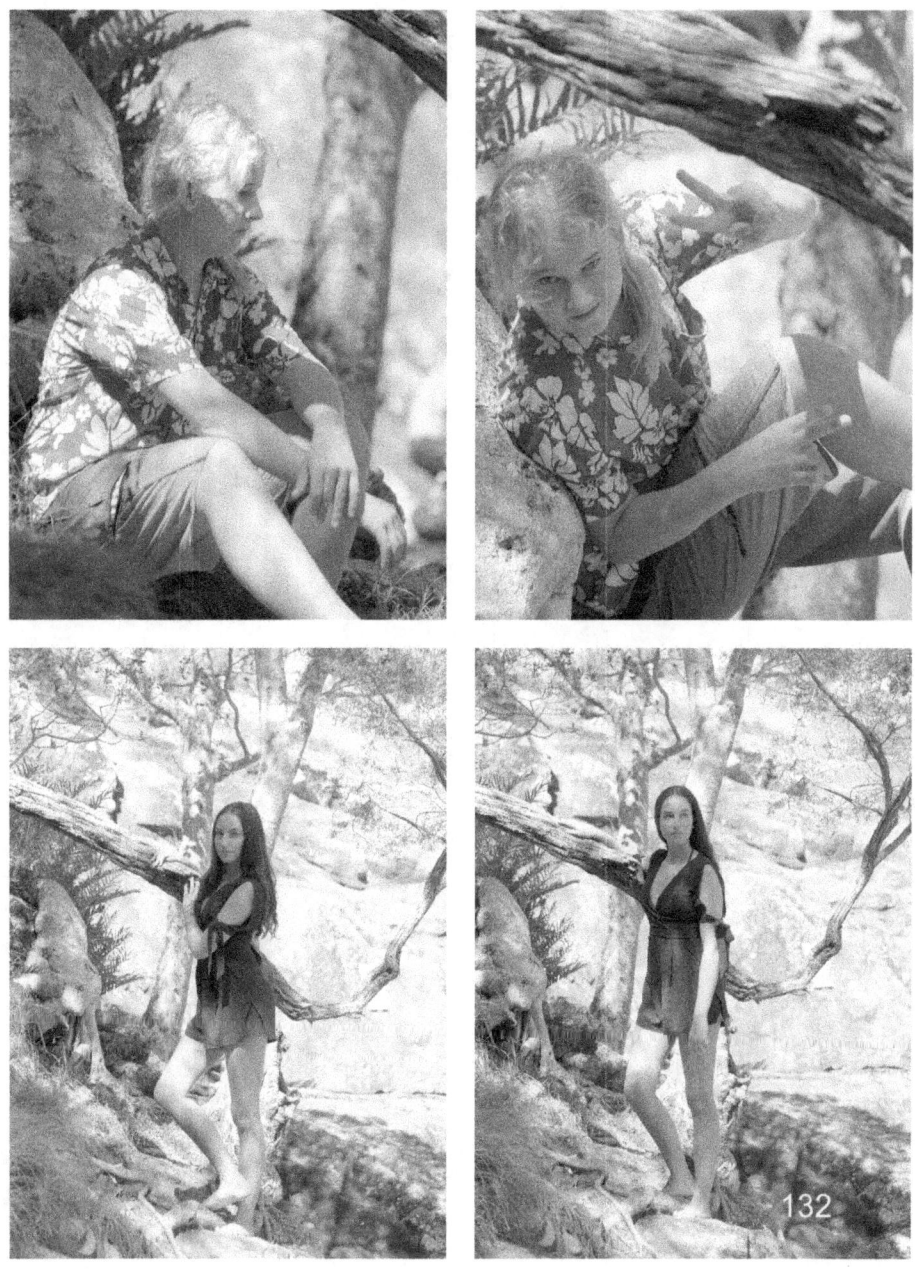

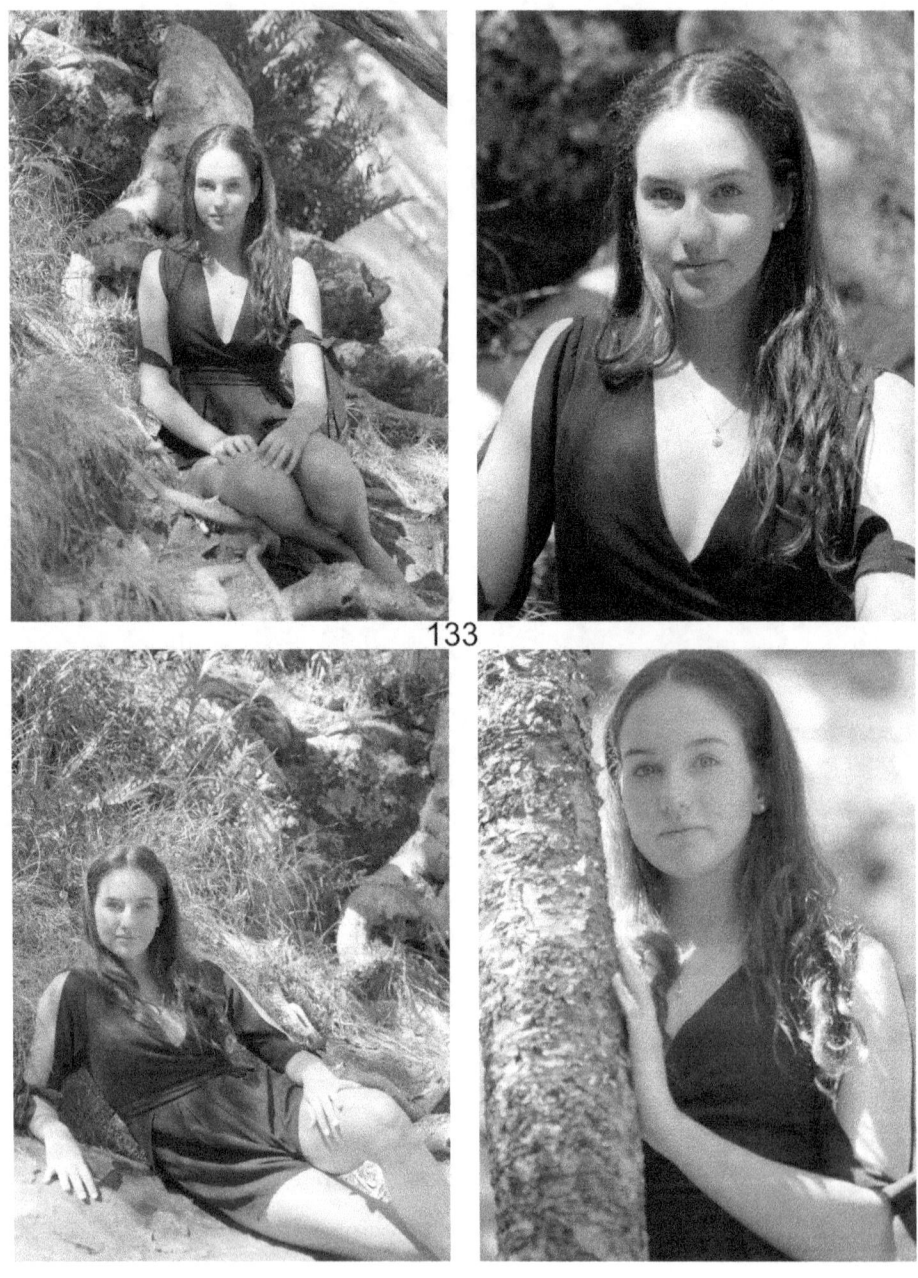

133

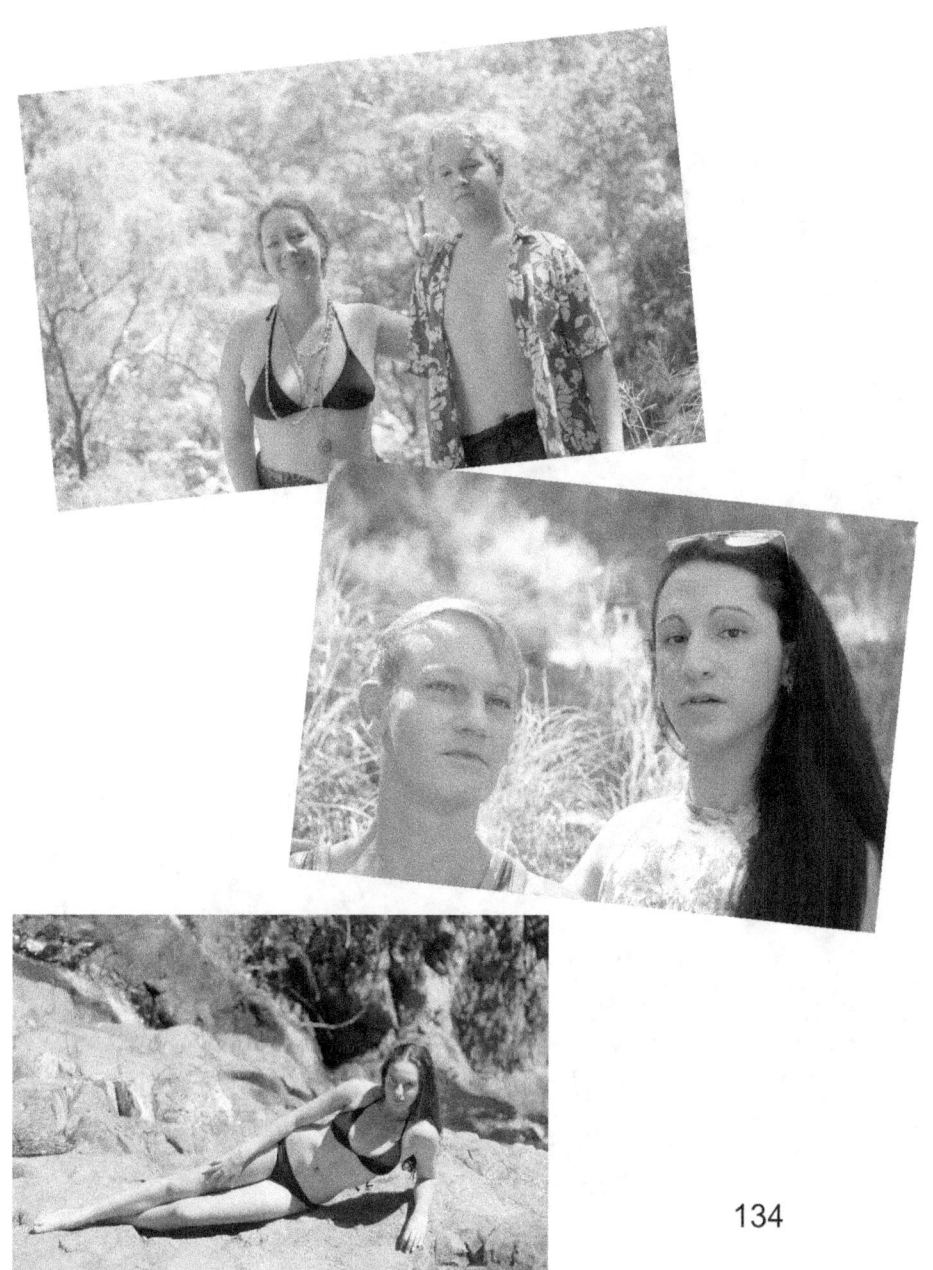

134

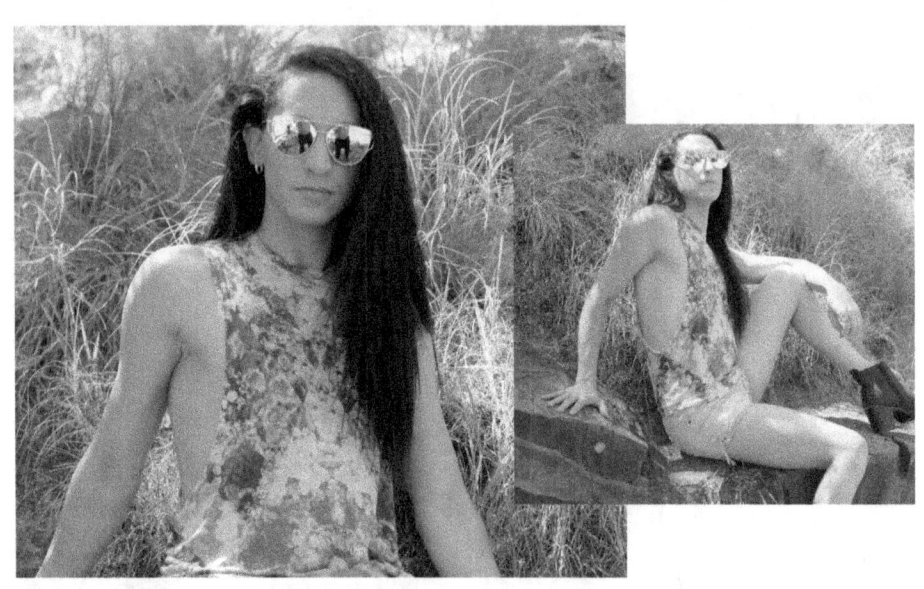

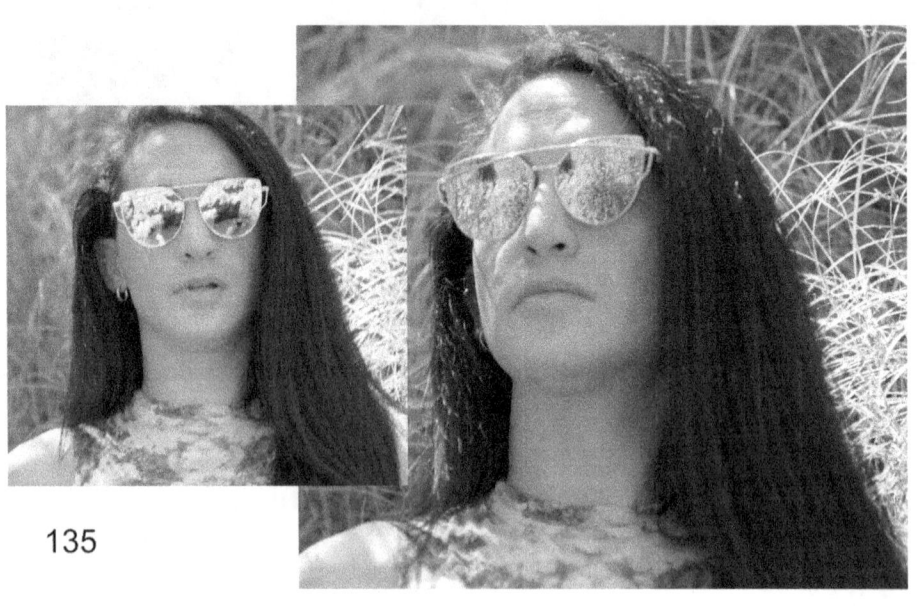

135

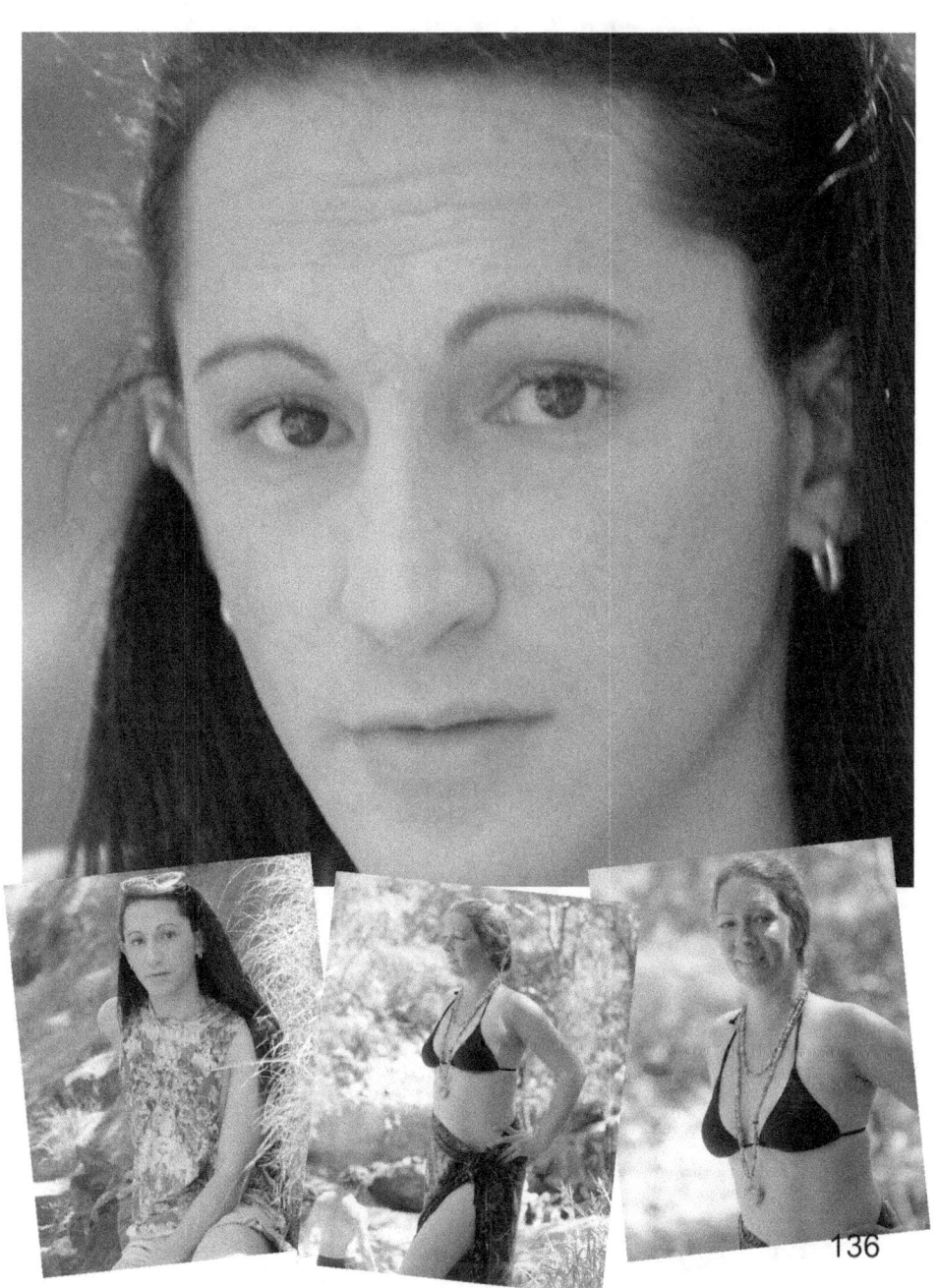

136

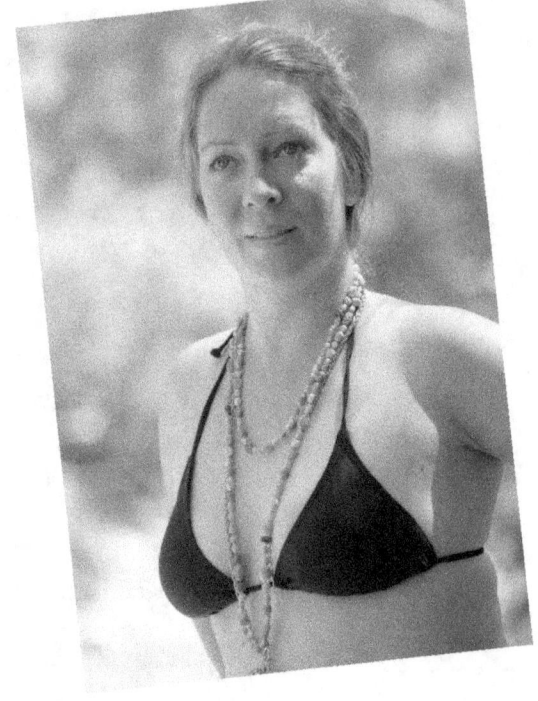

137

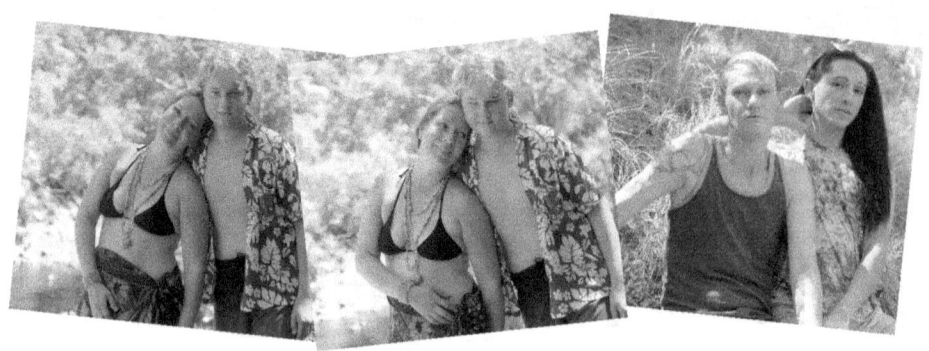

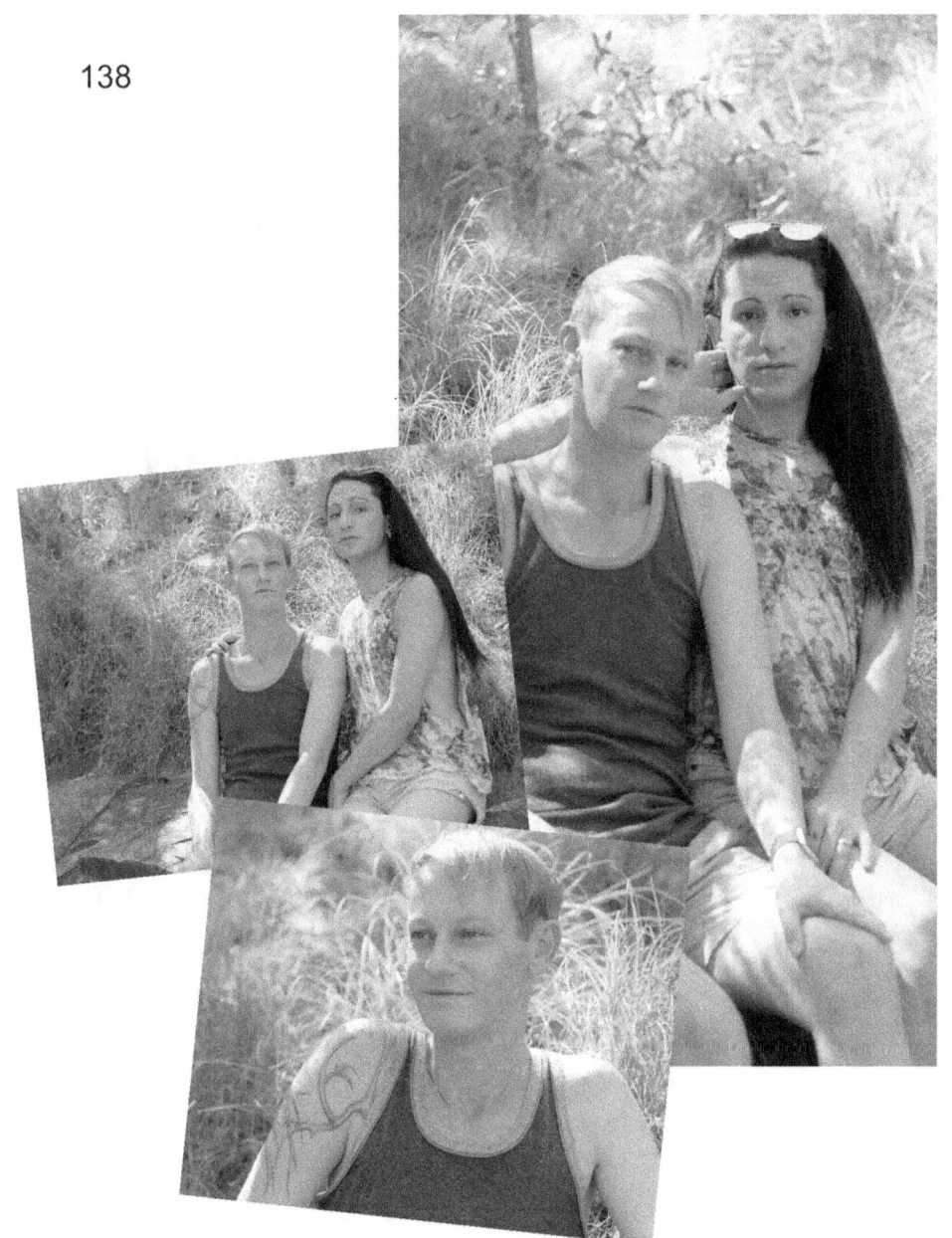

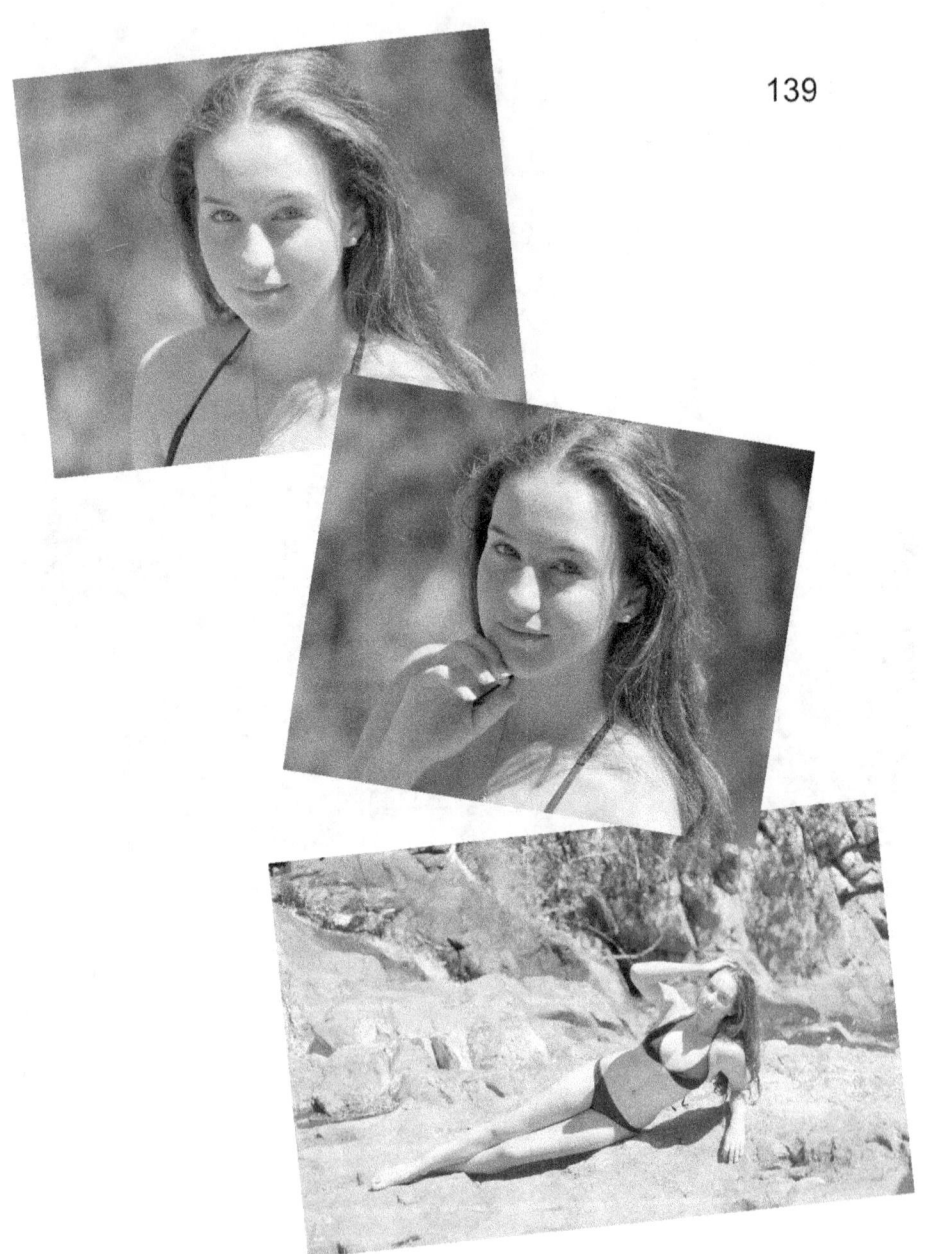

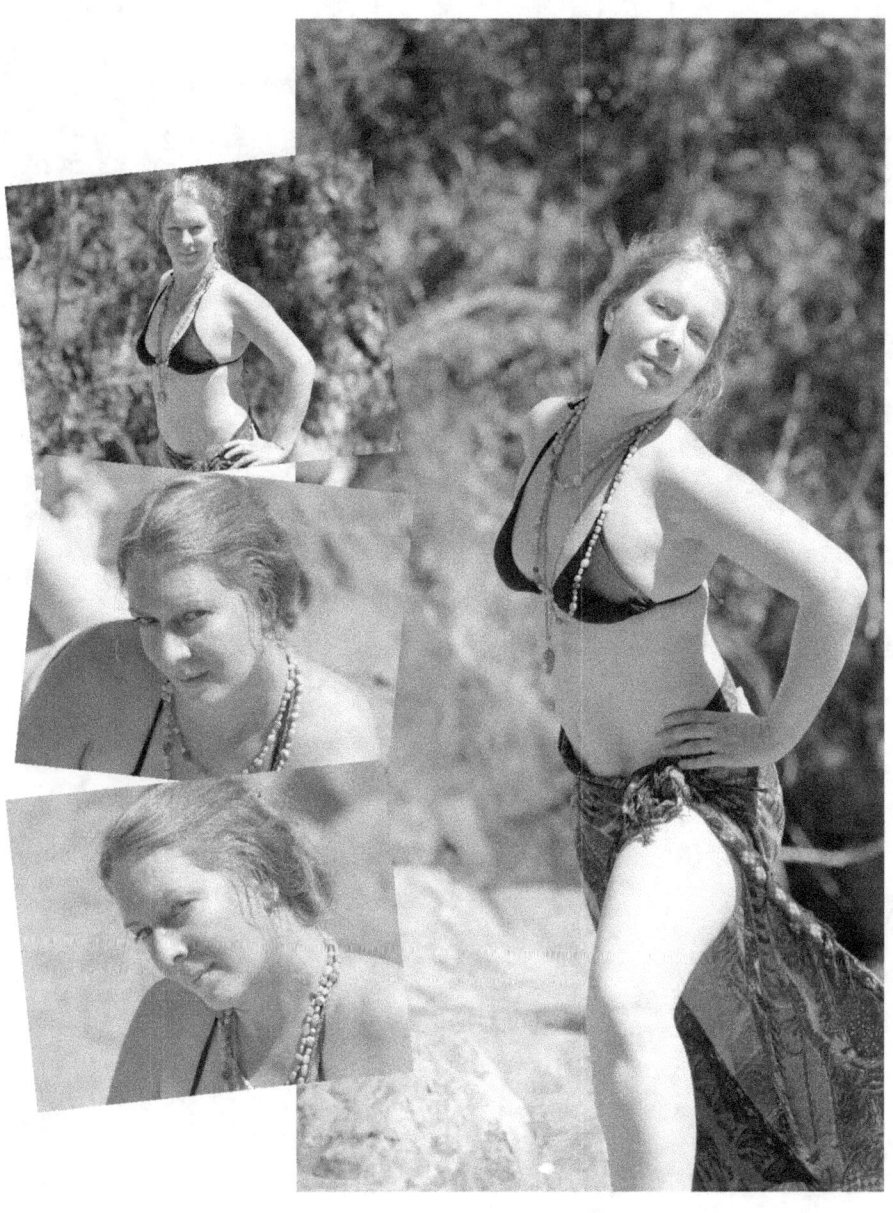

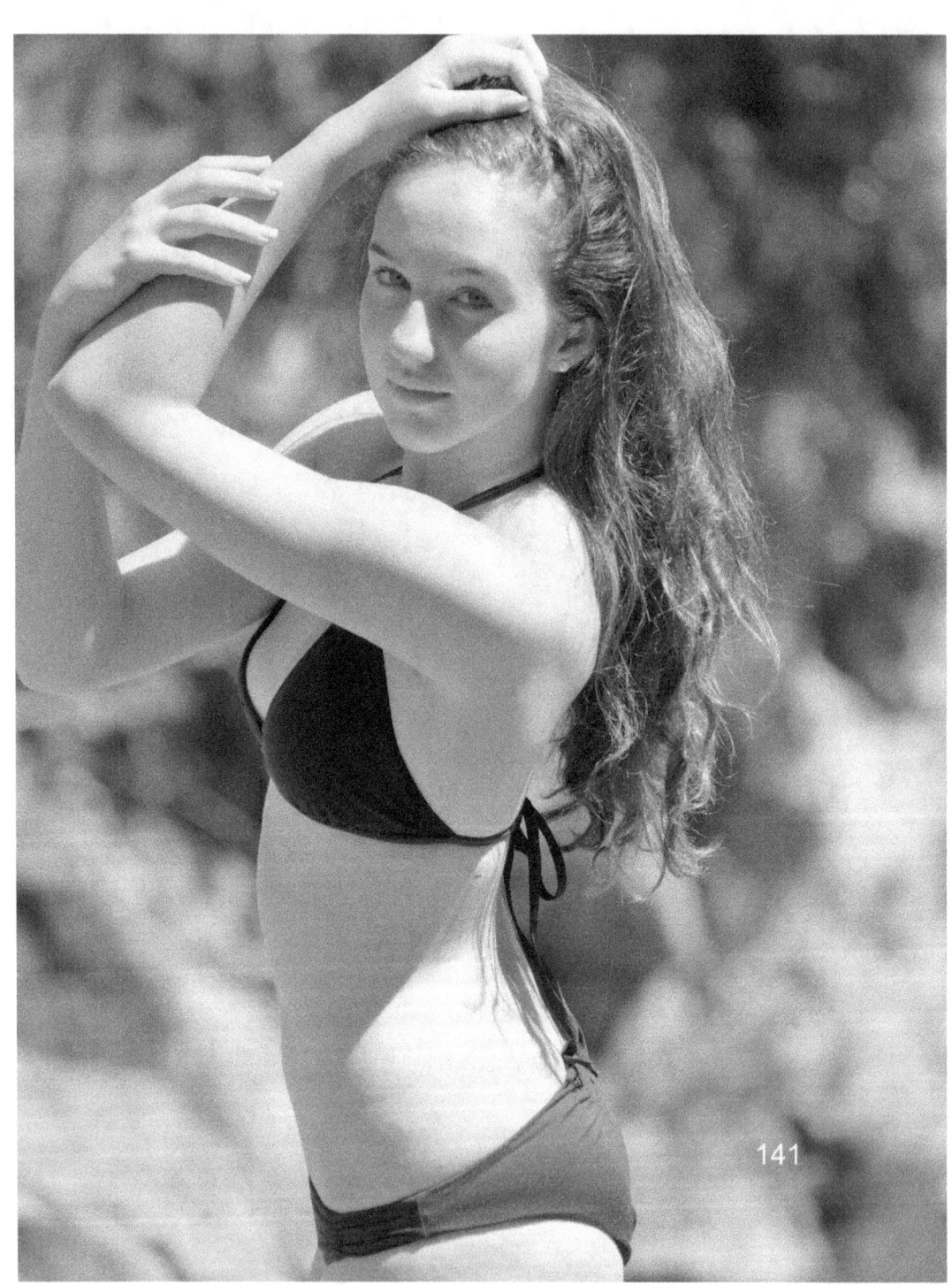

141

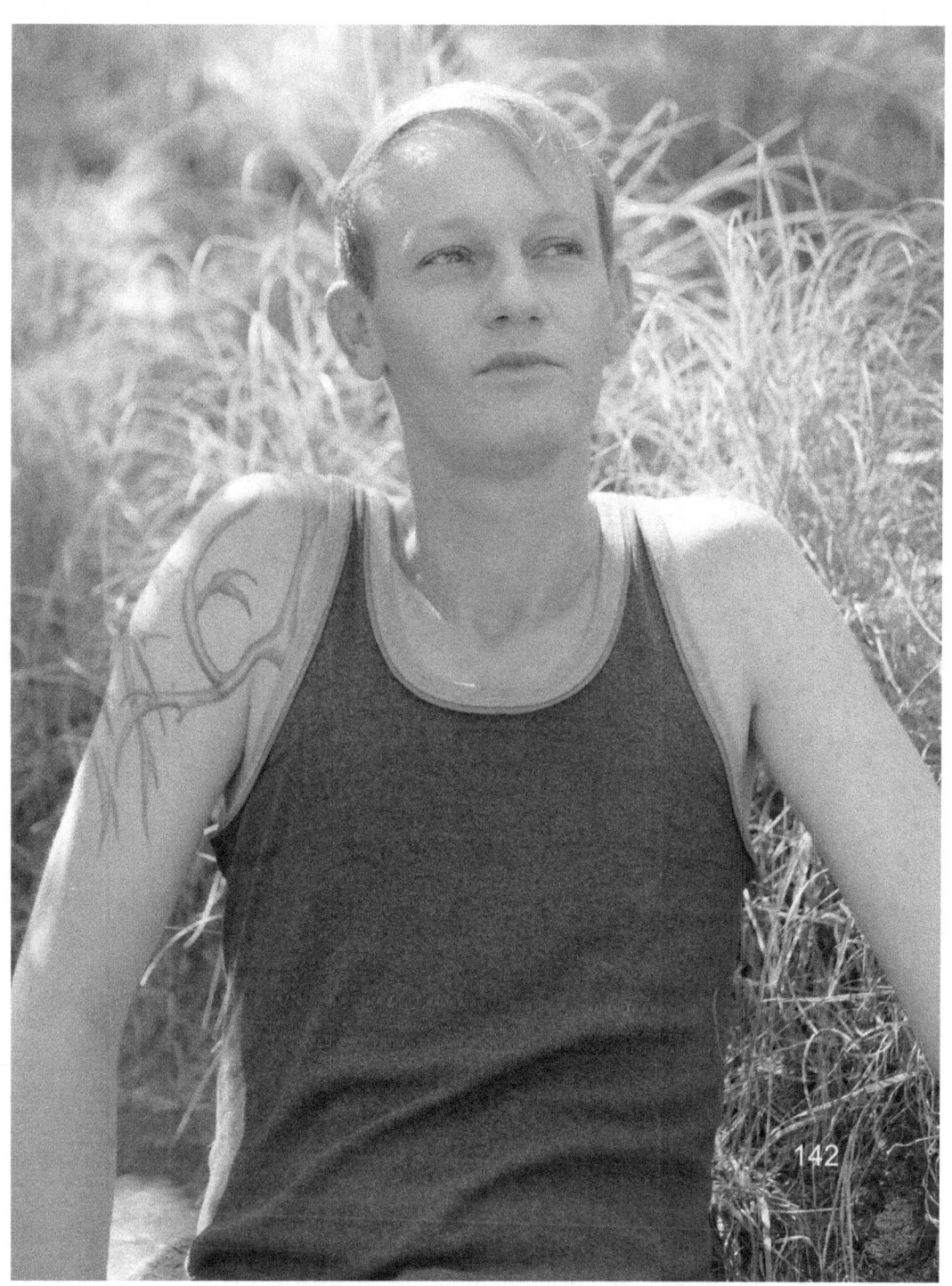

142

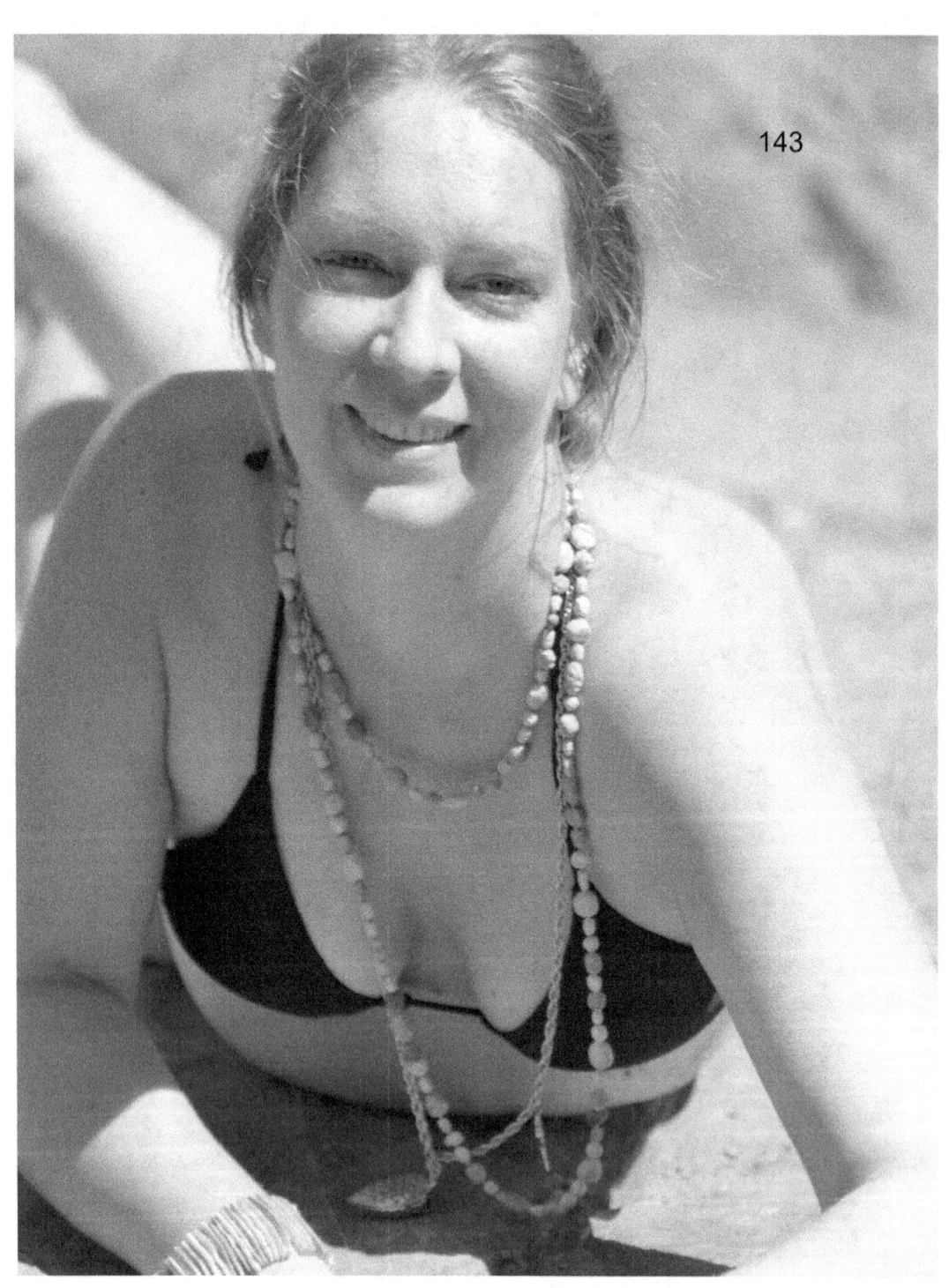

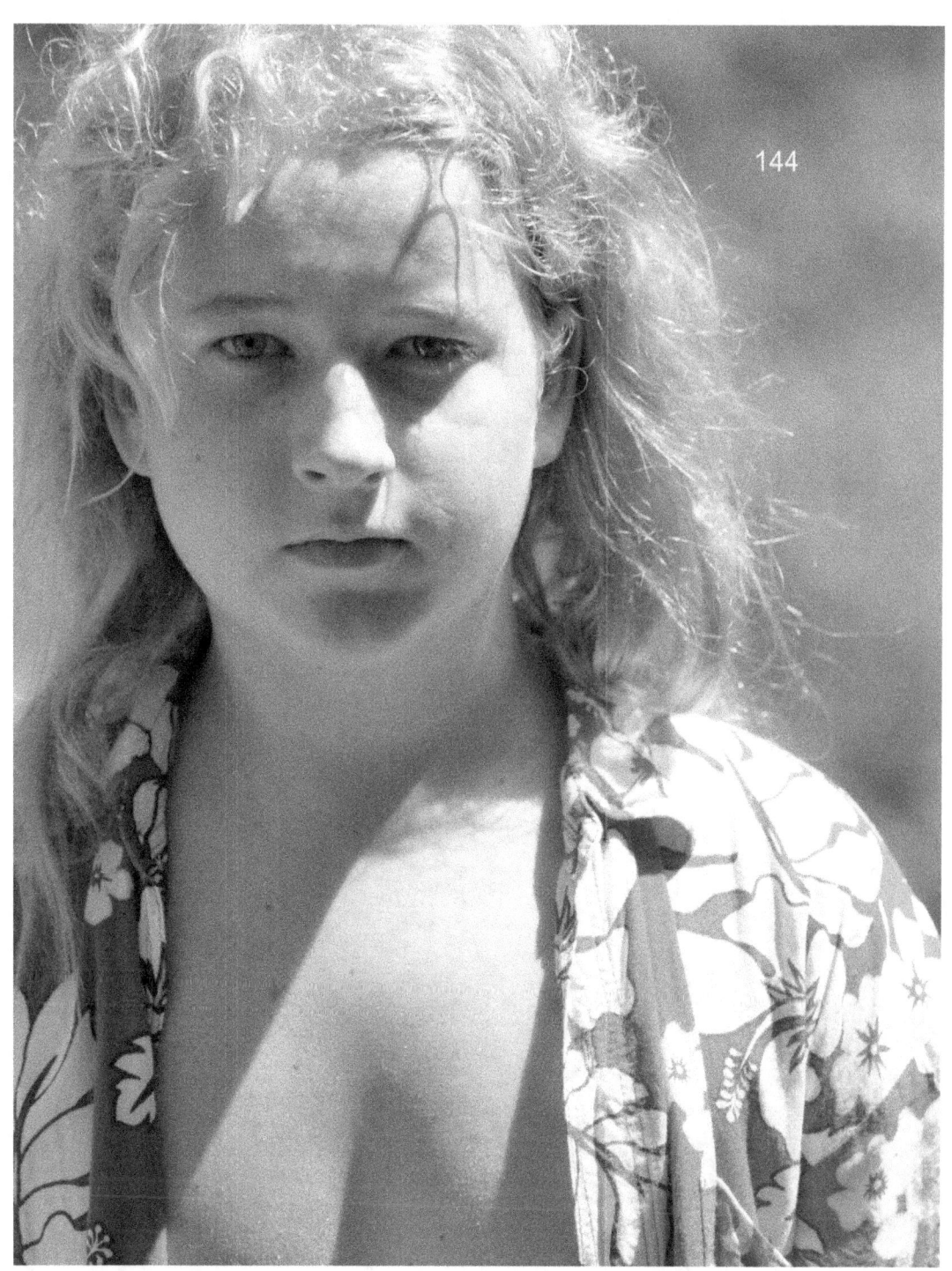

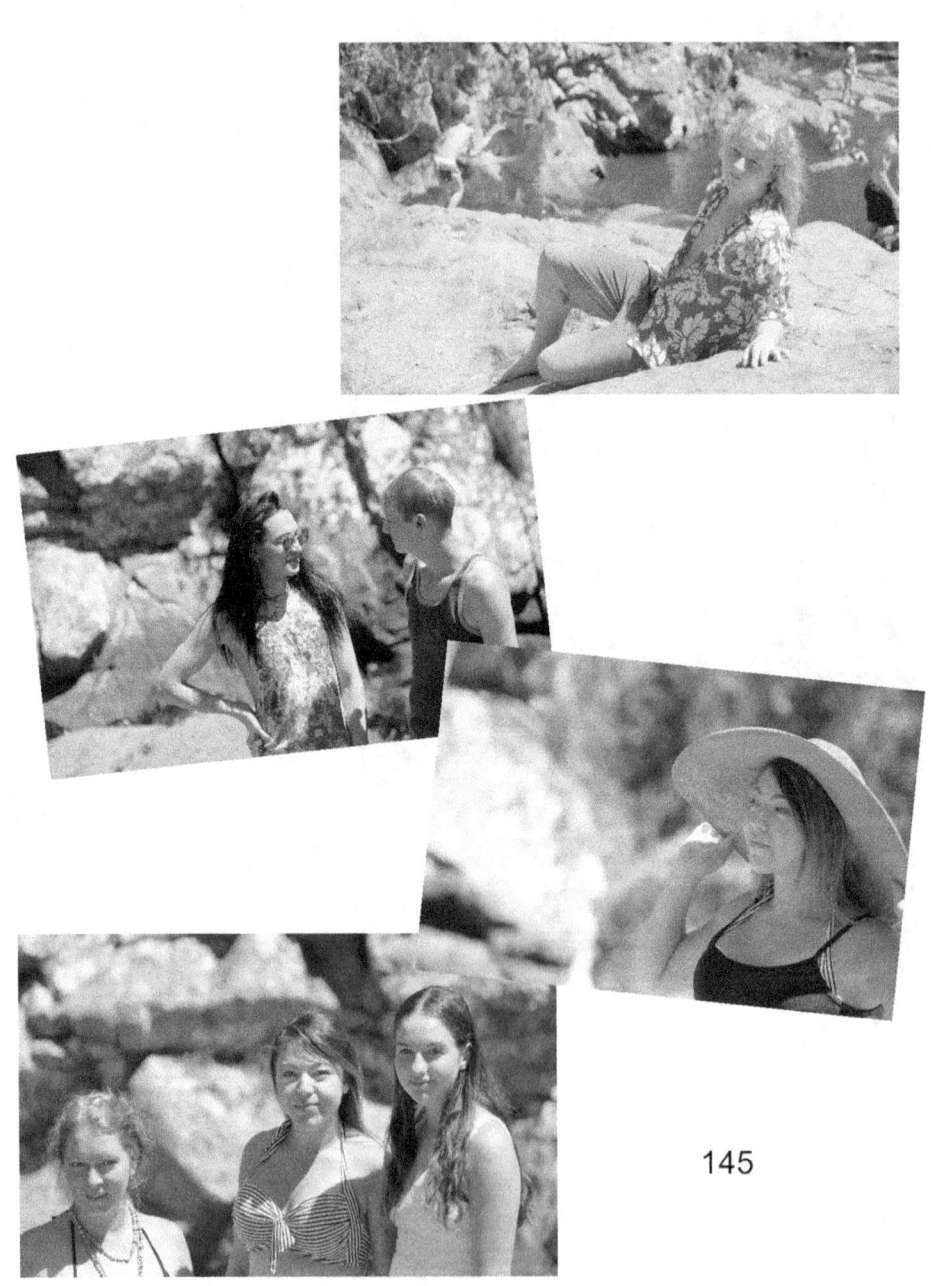

145

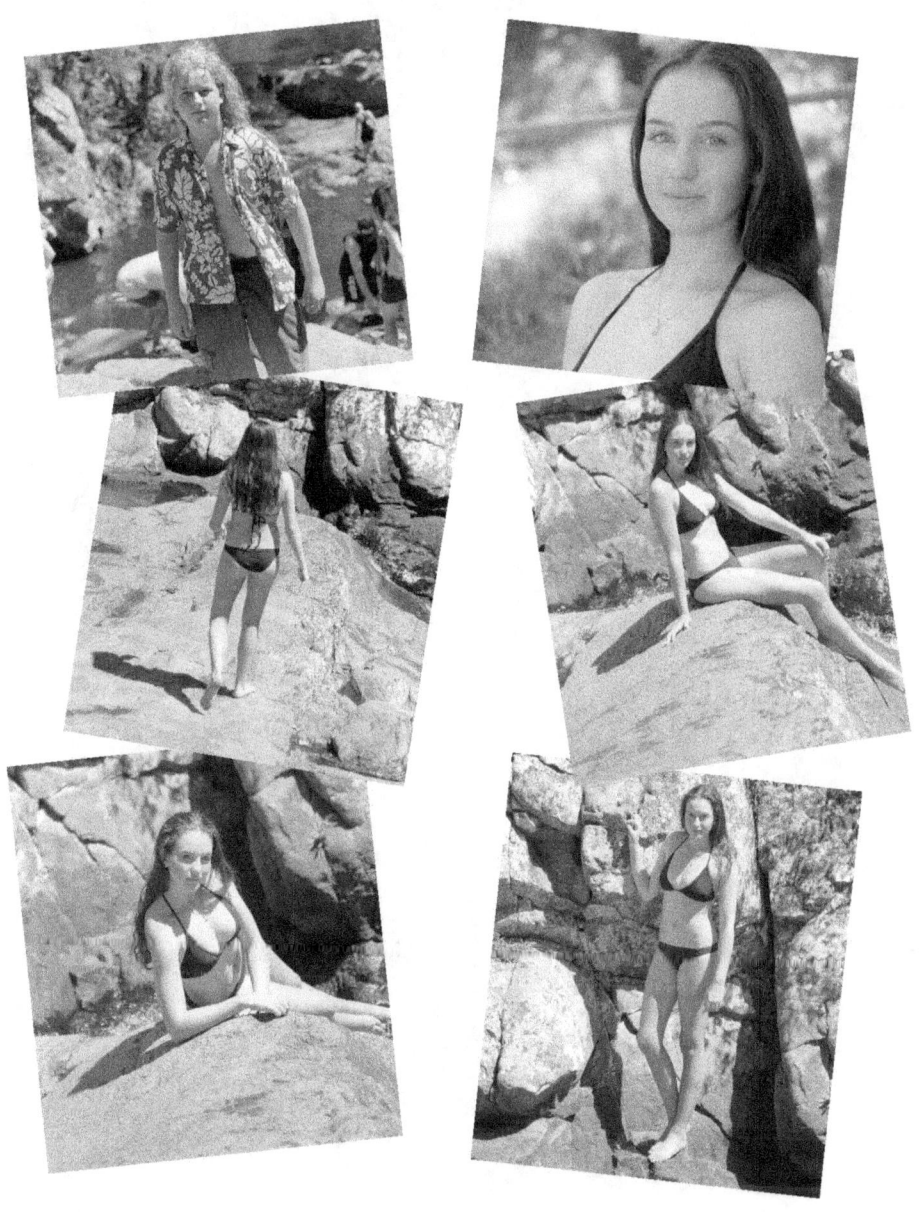

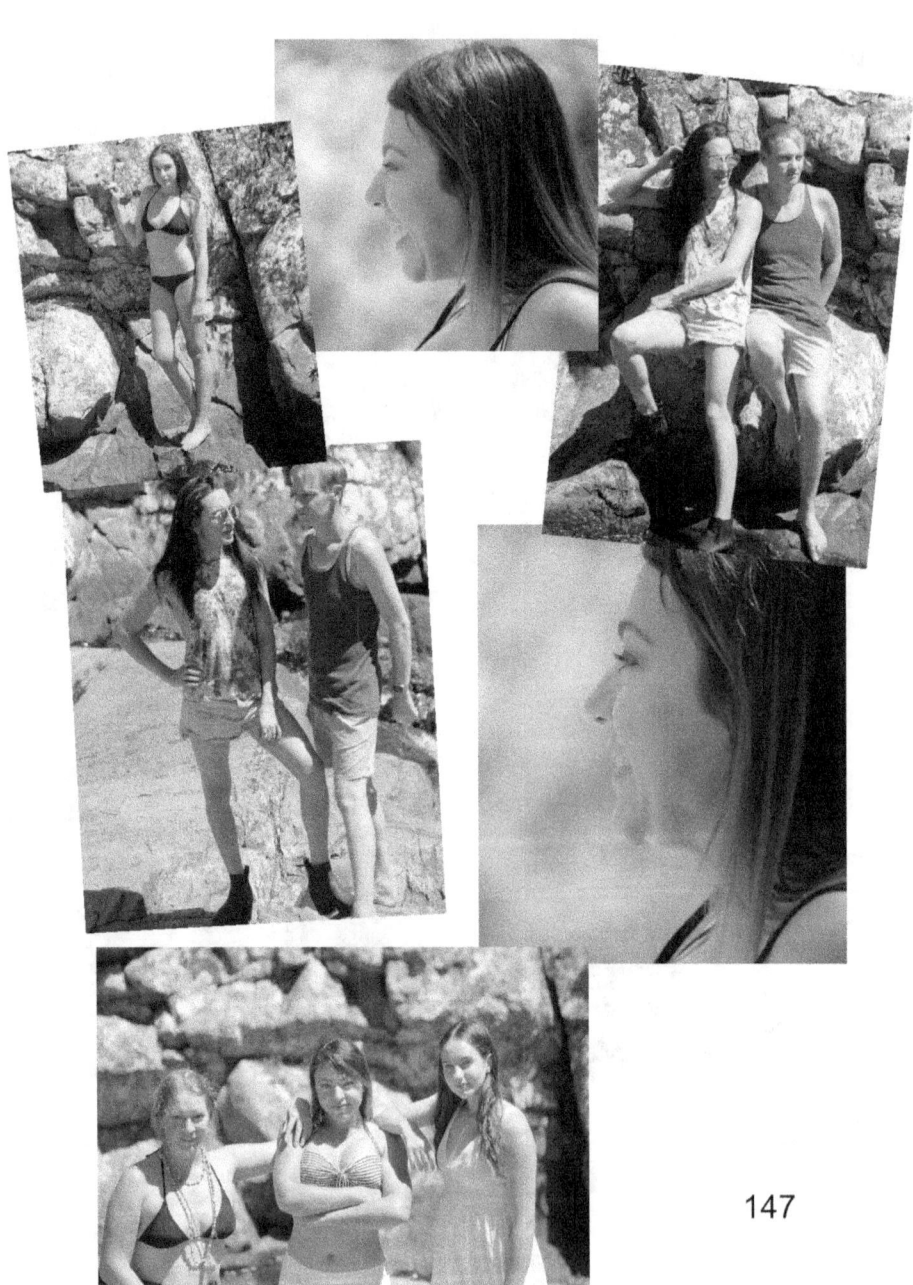

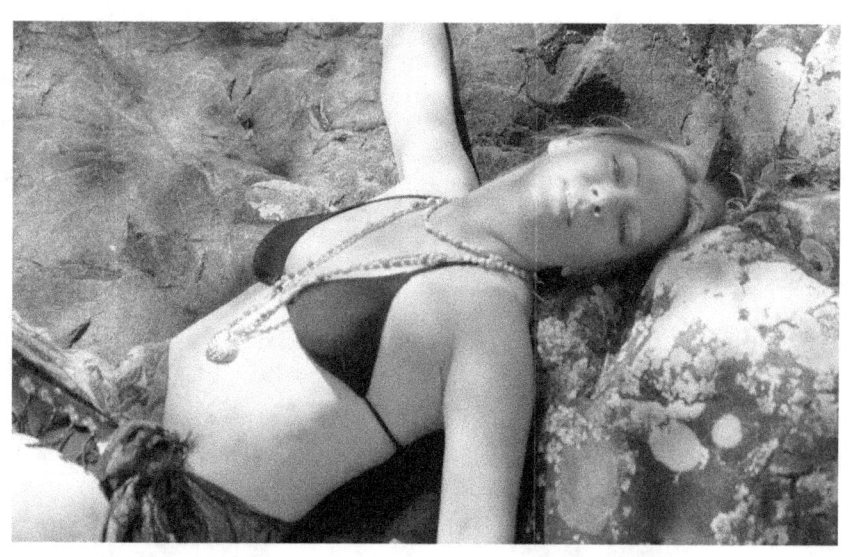

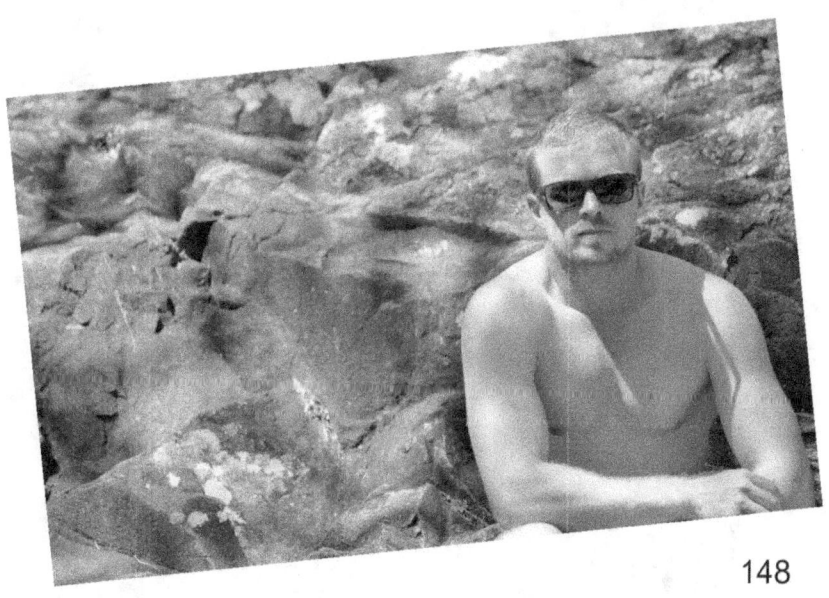

148

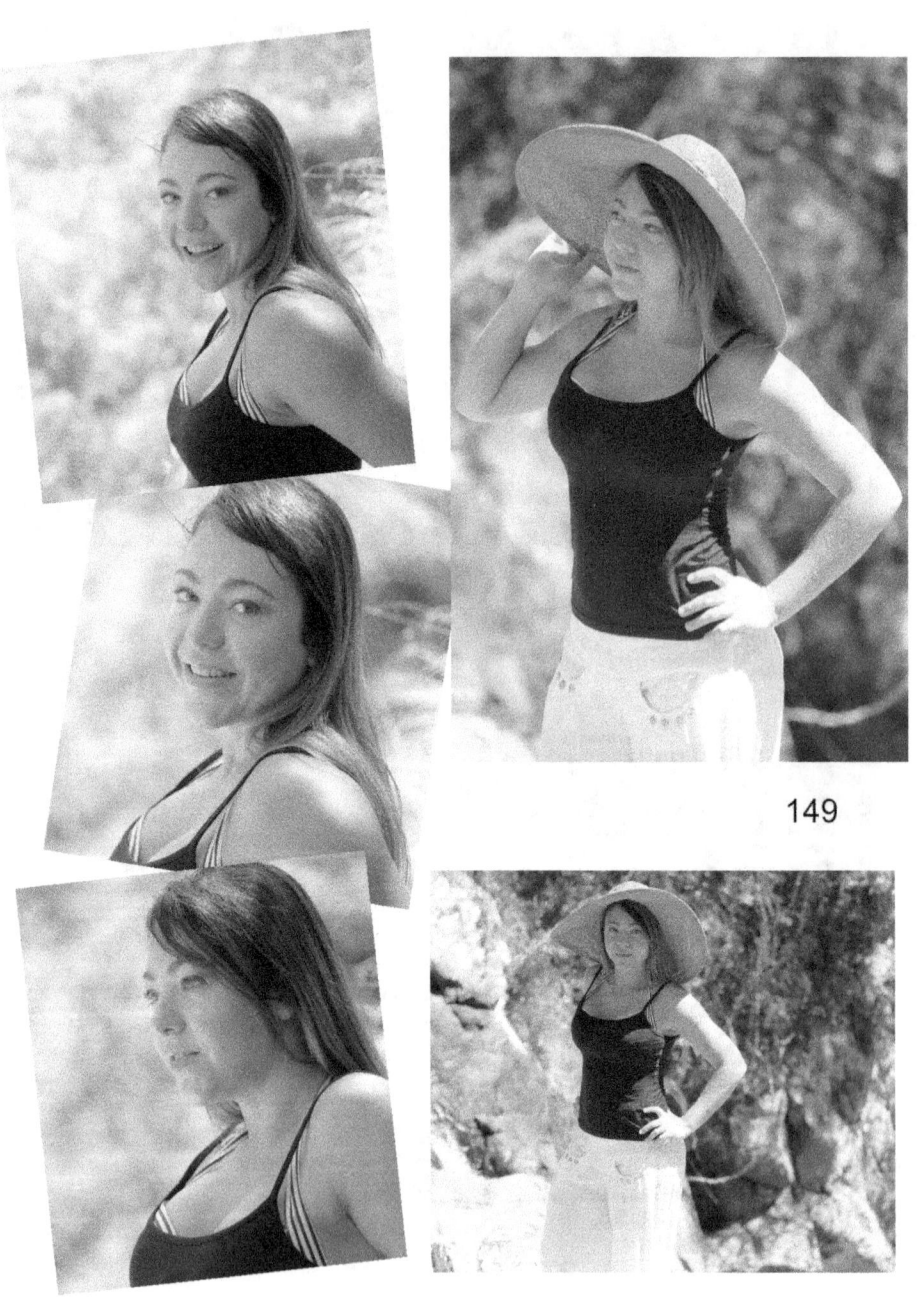

149

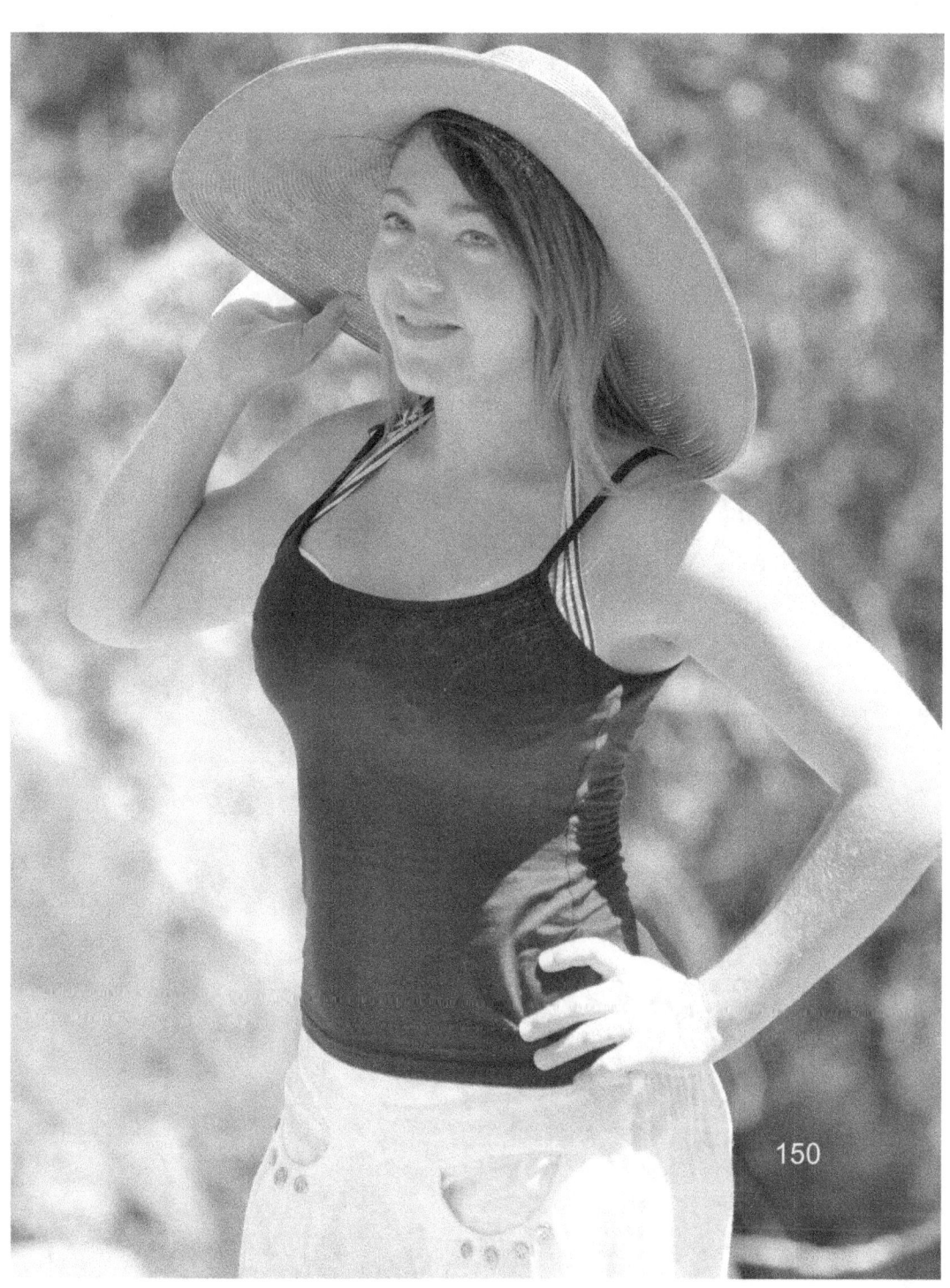

150

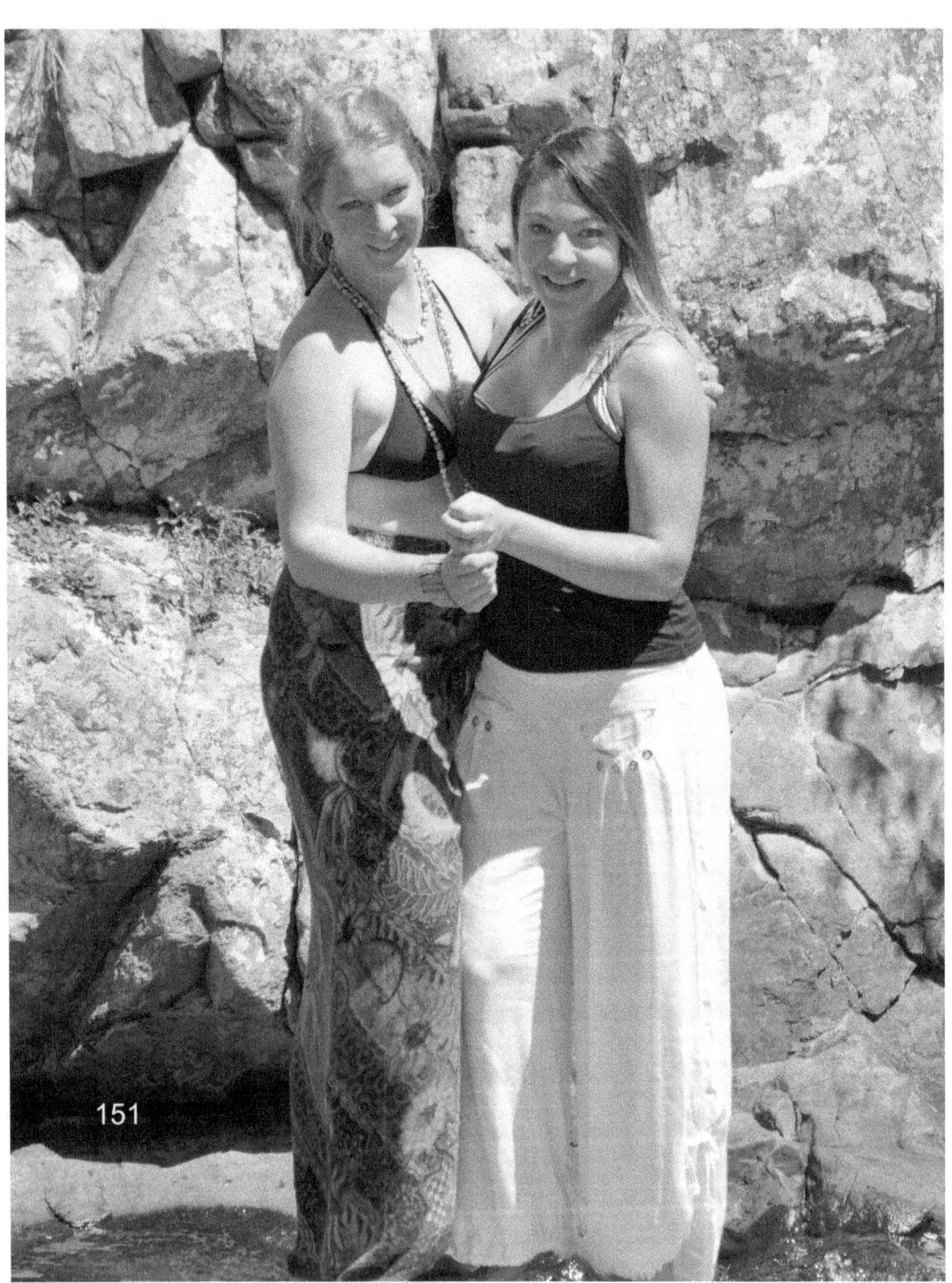

151

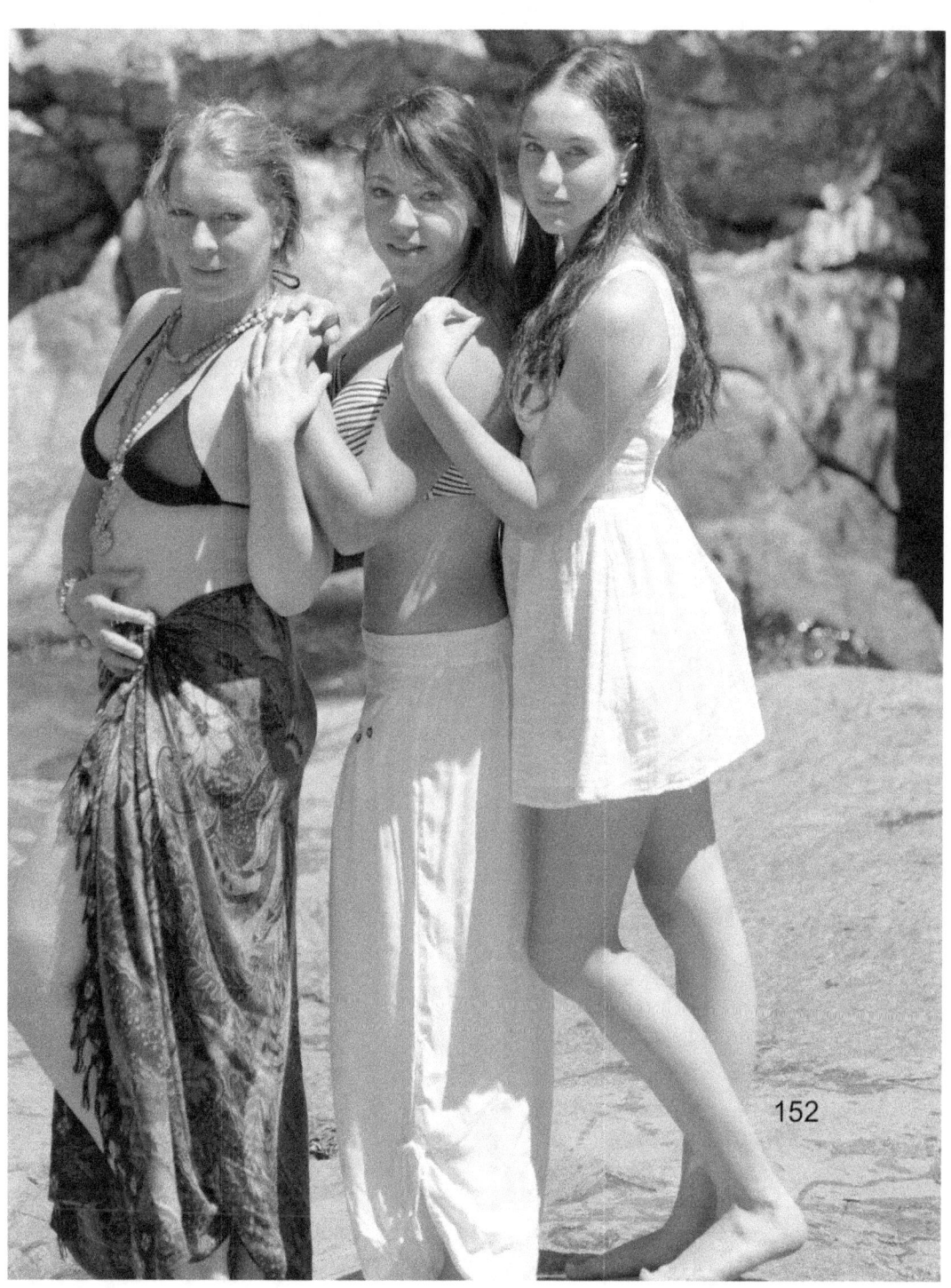

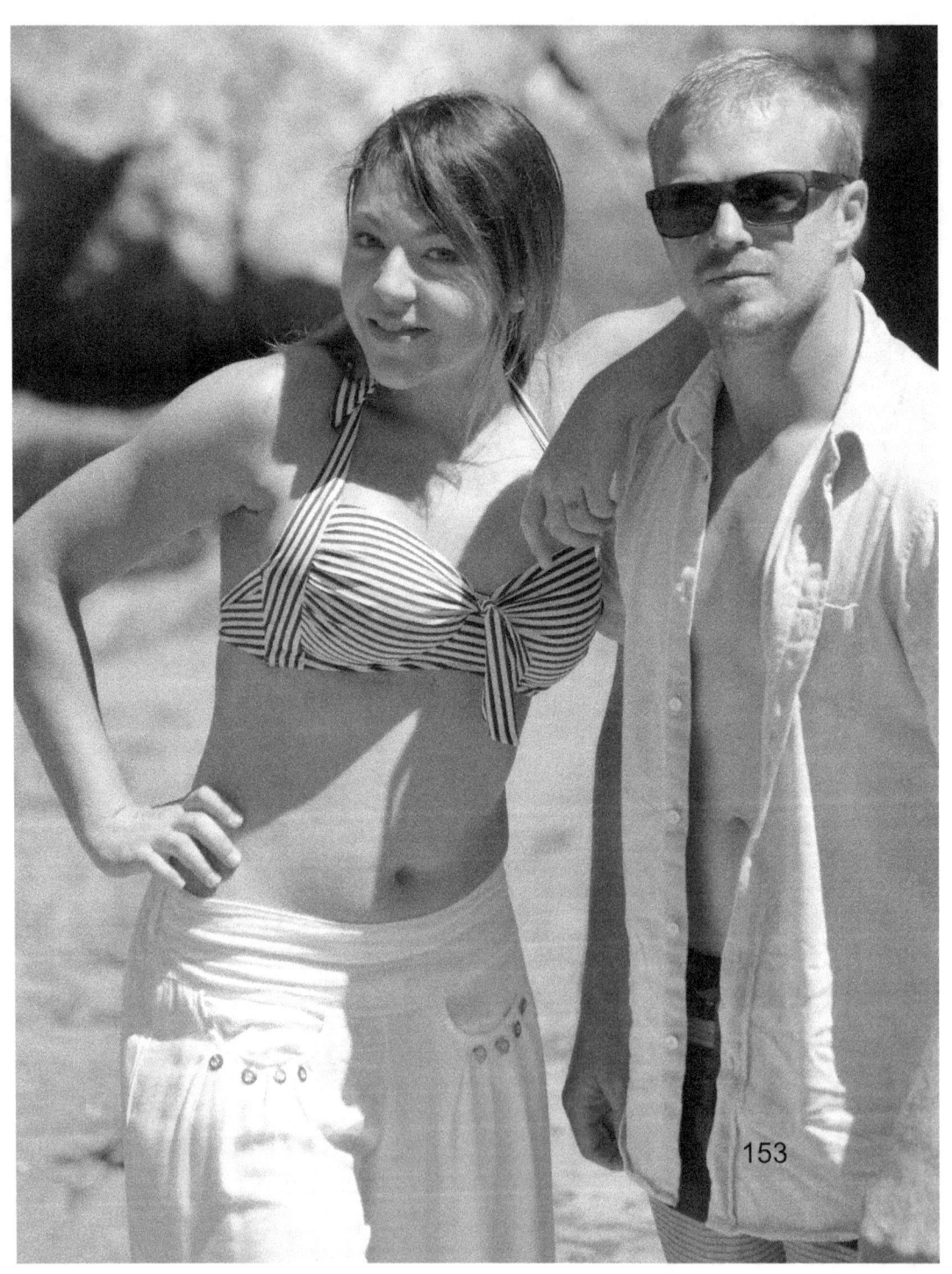

153

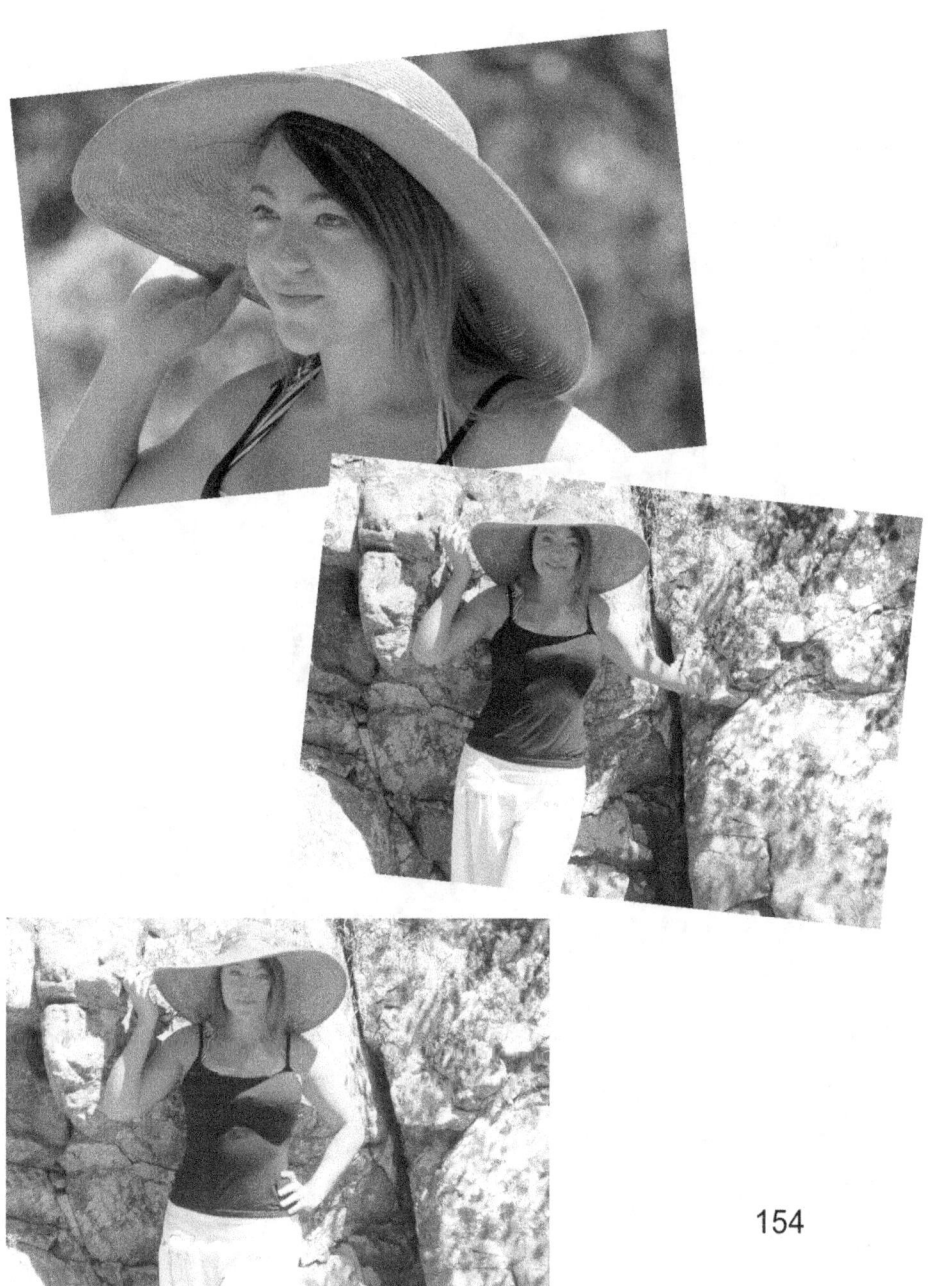

154

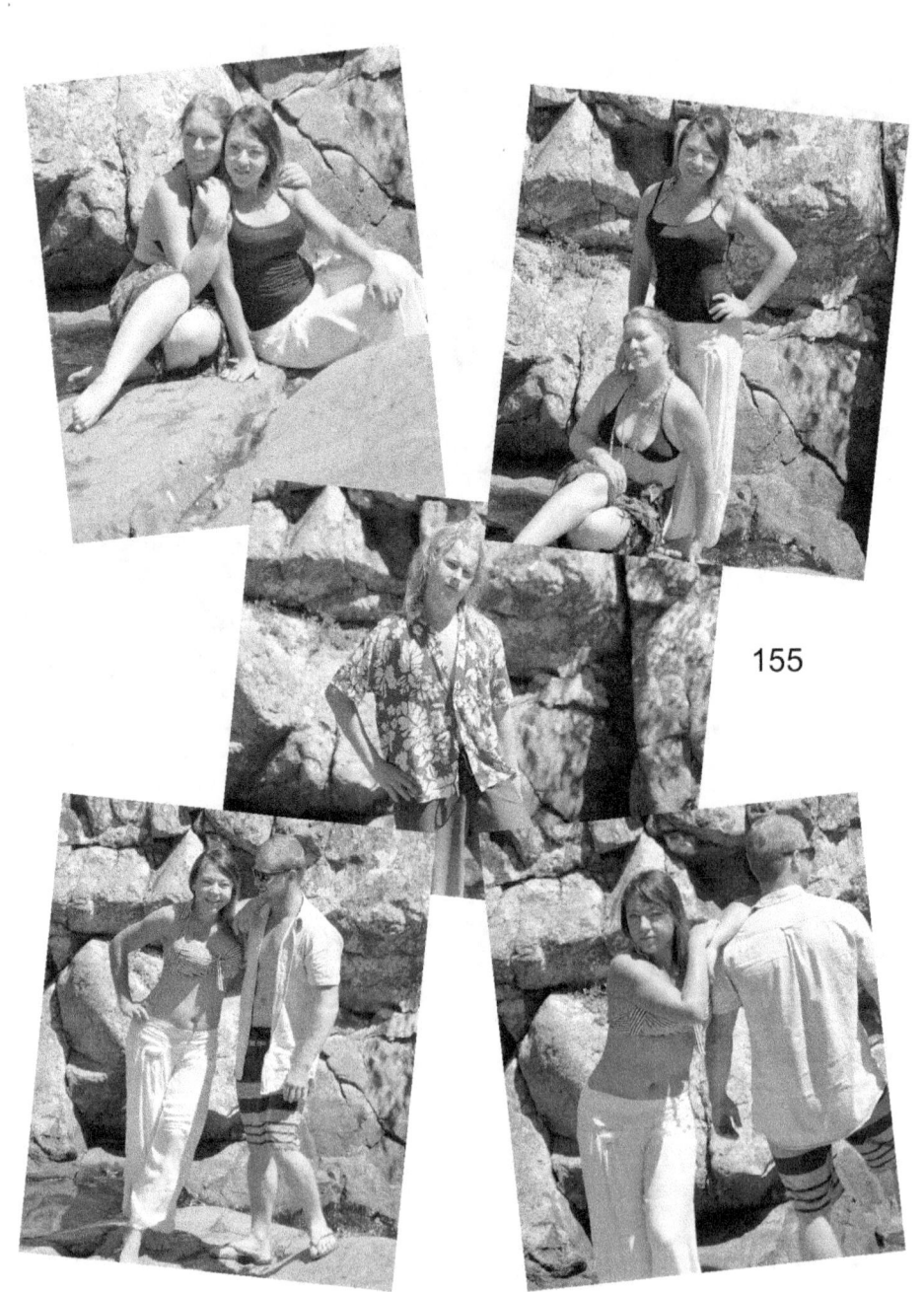

155

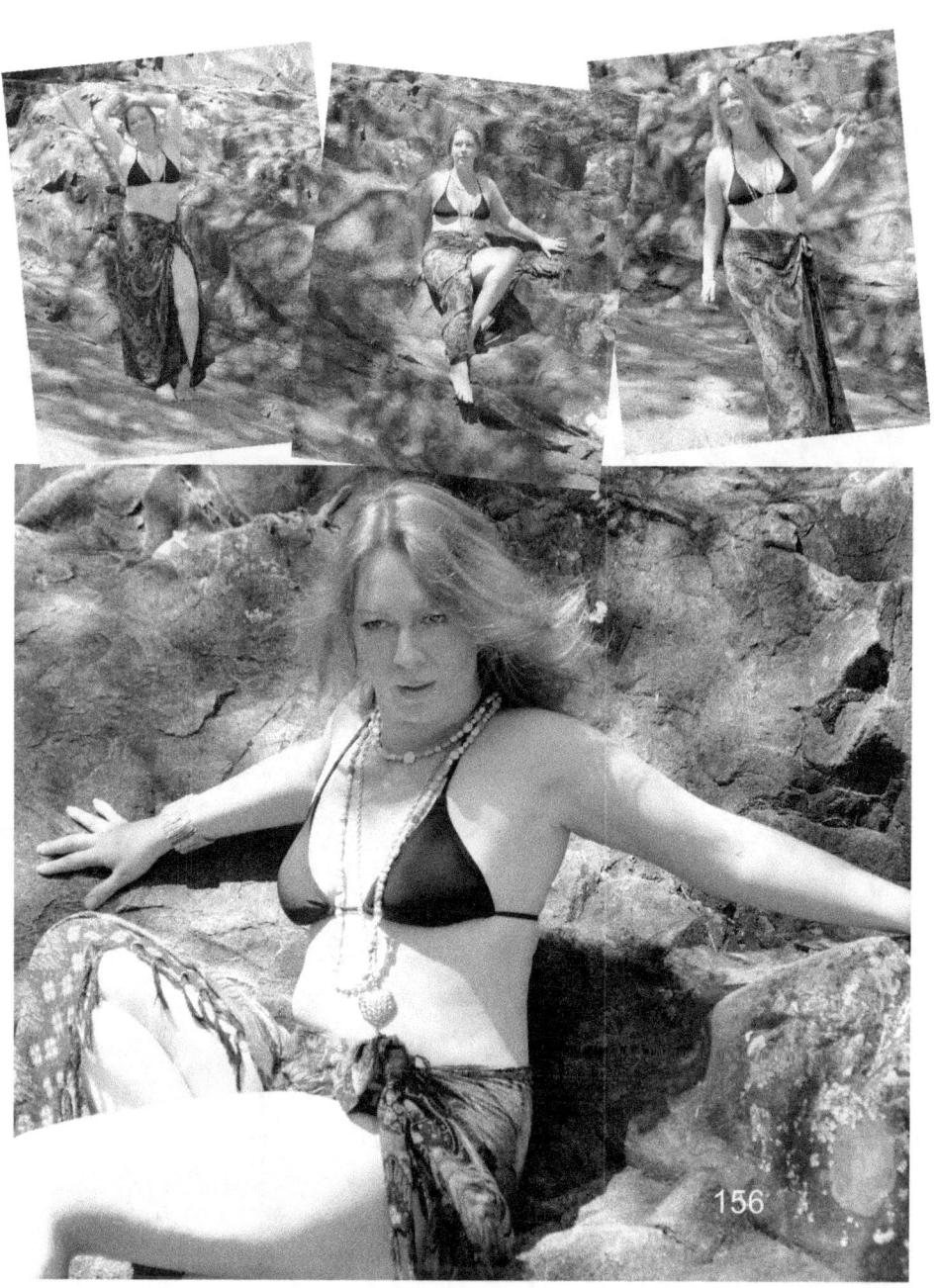

156

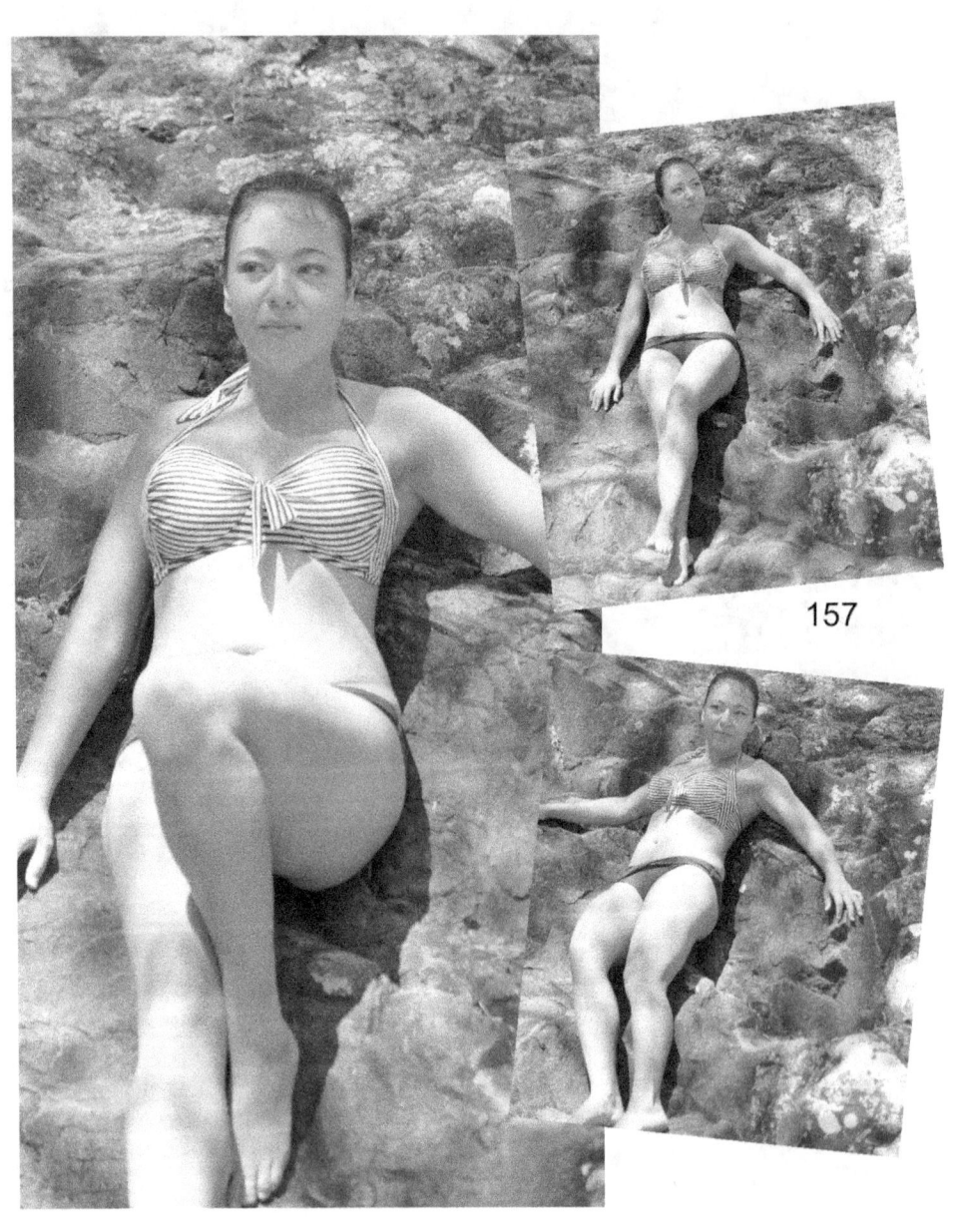

157

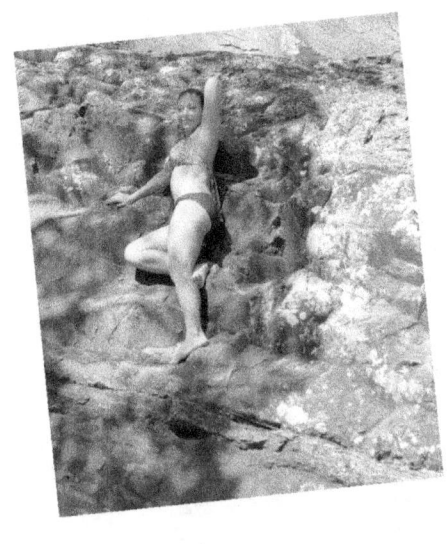
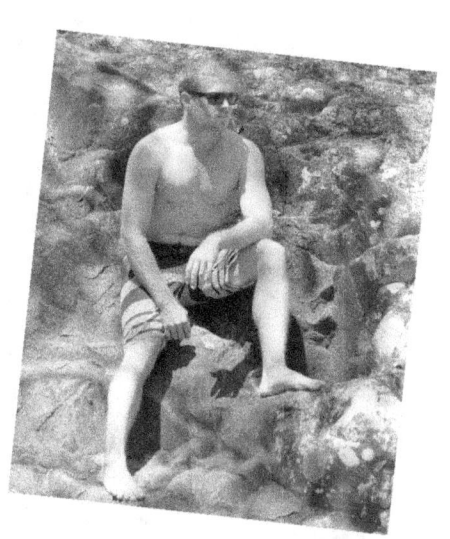

158

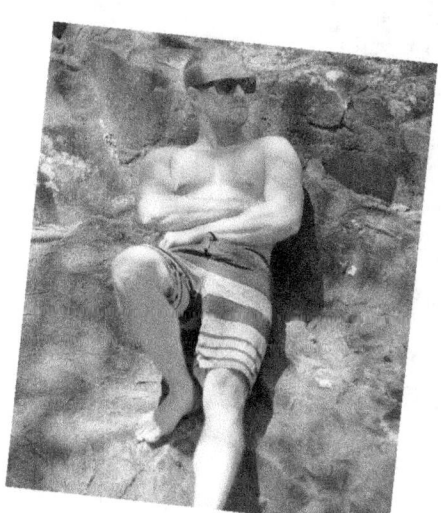
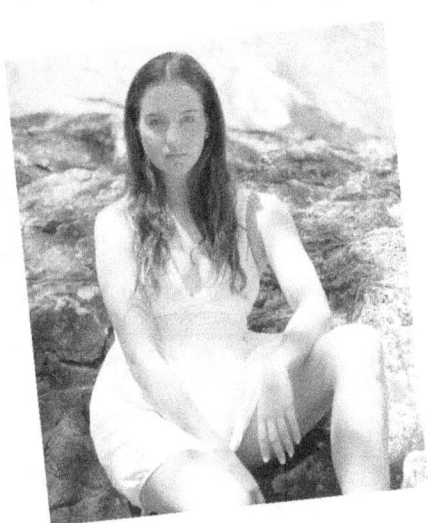

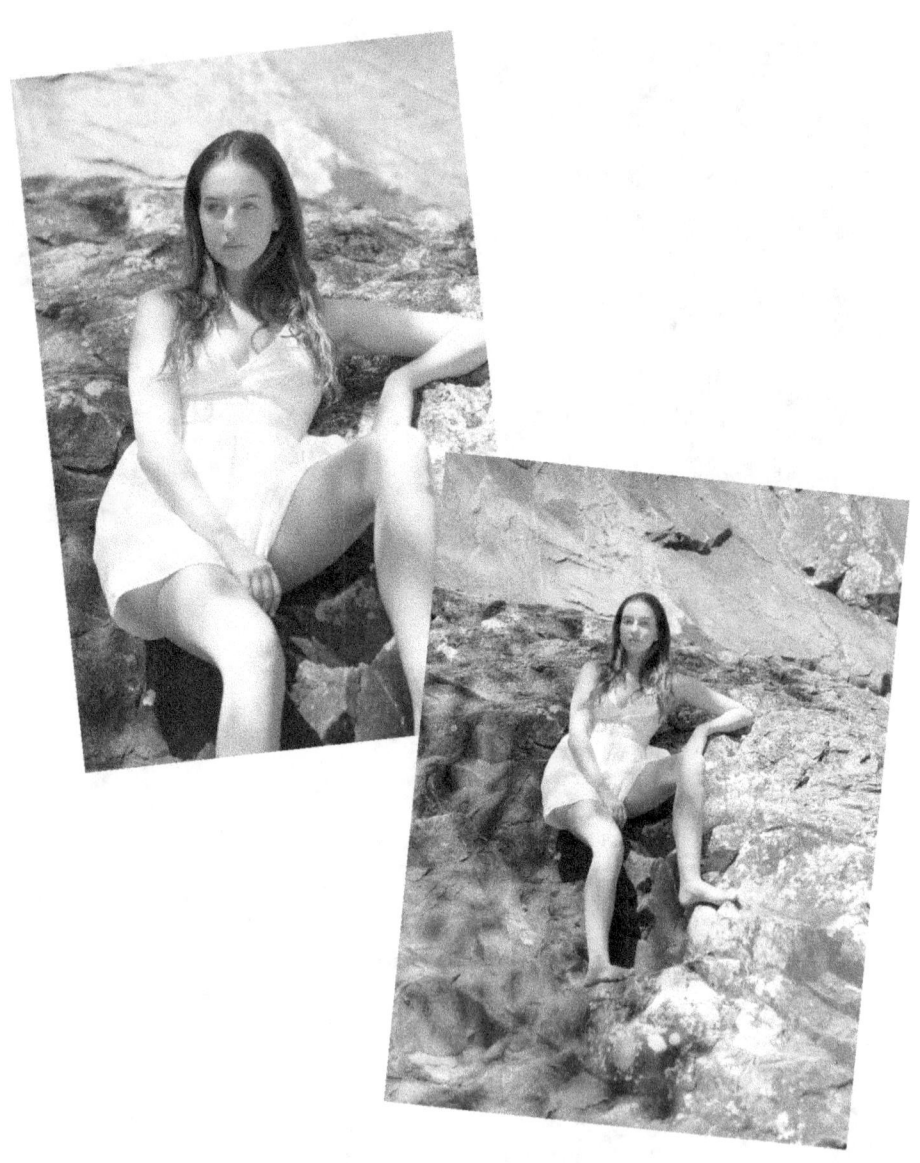

159

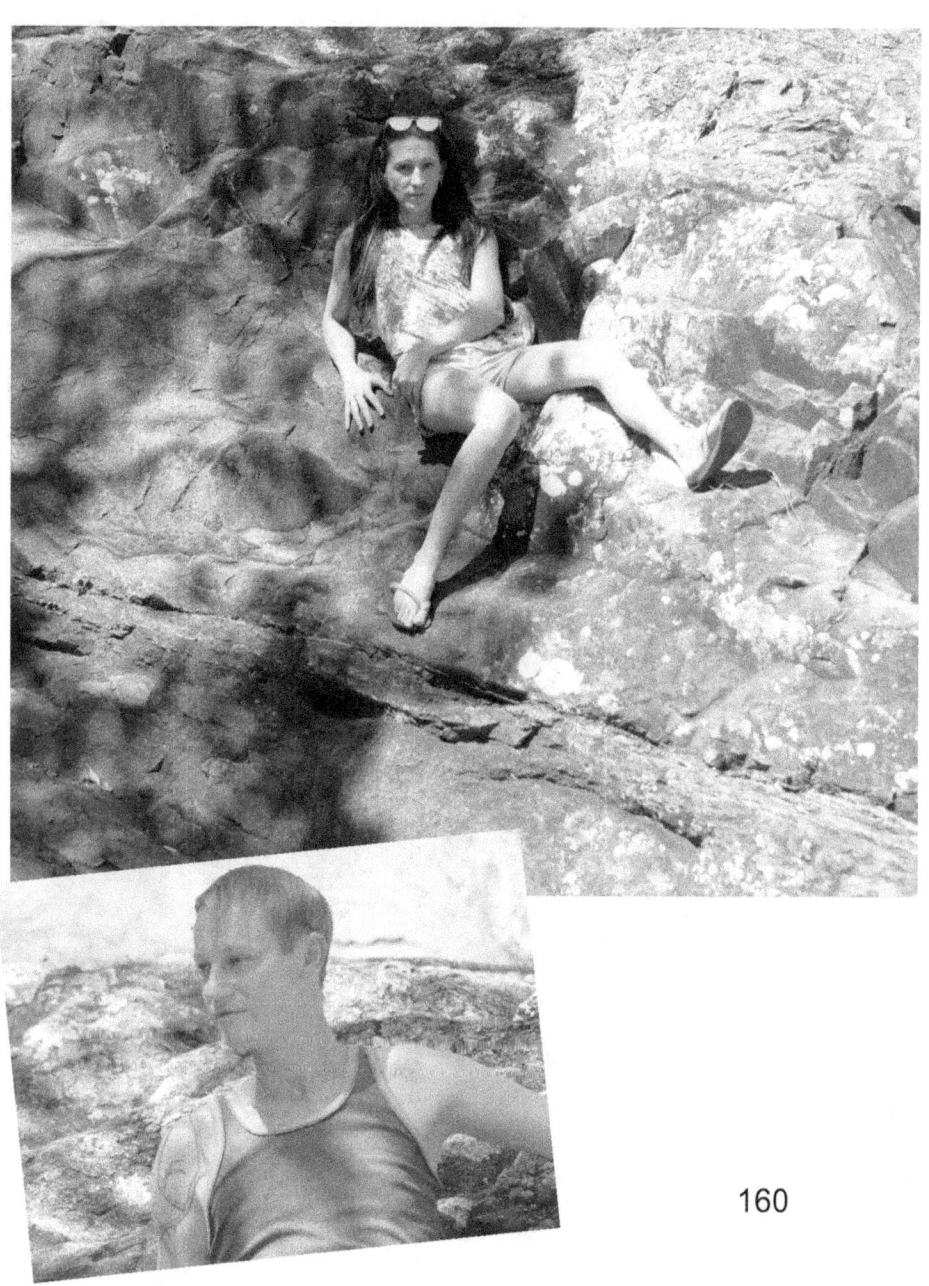

160

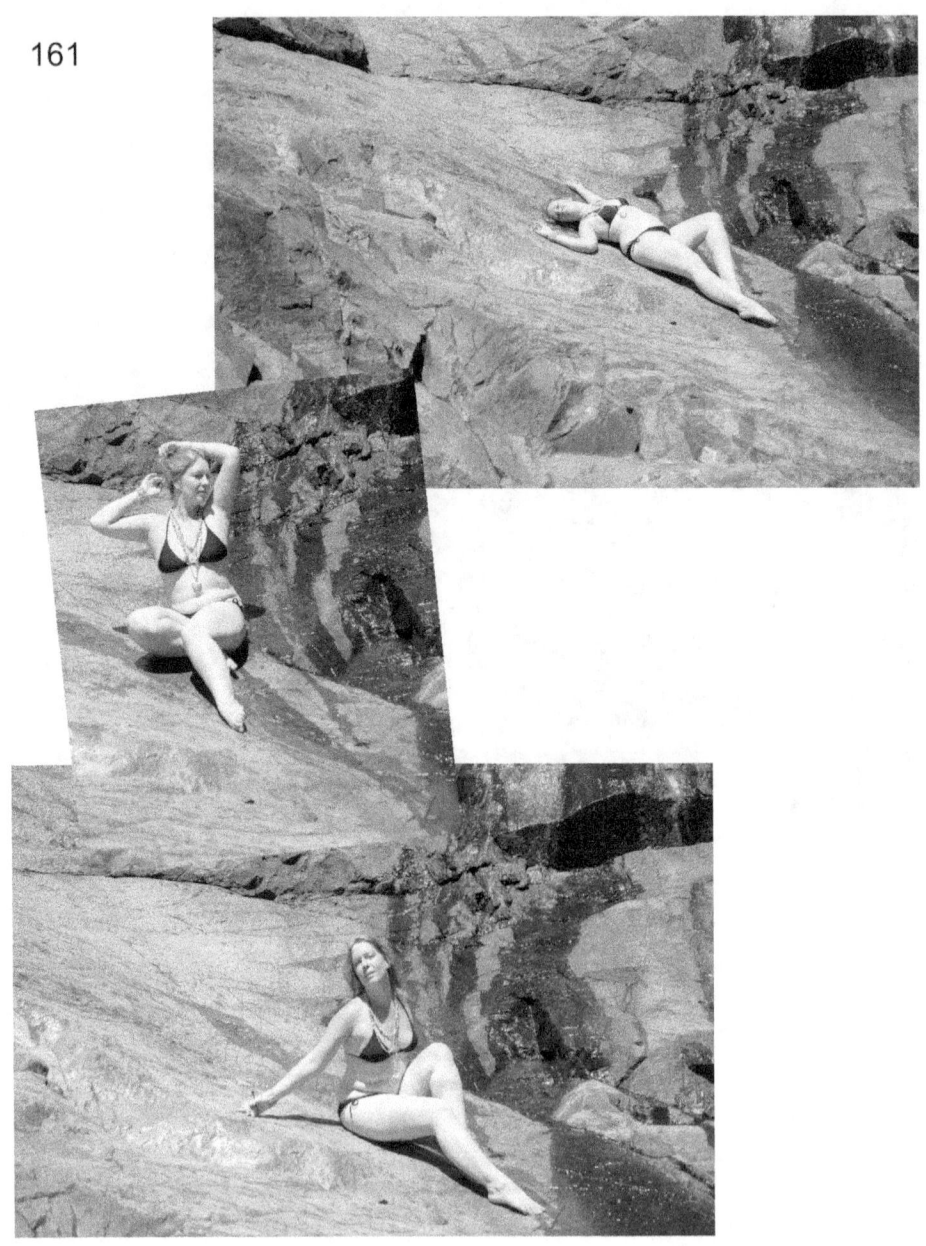

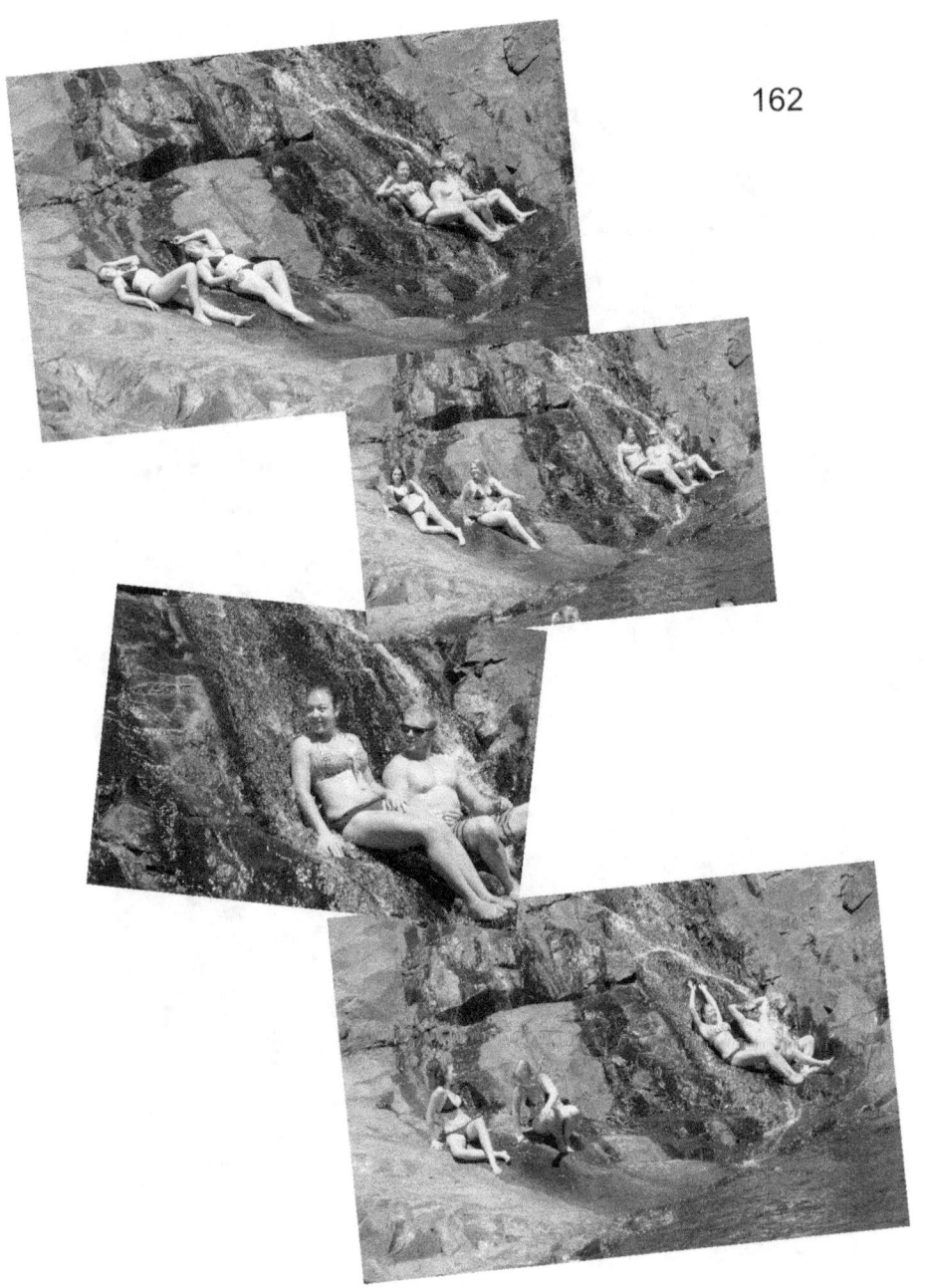

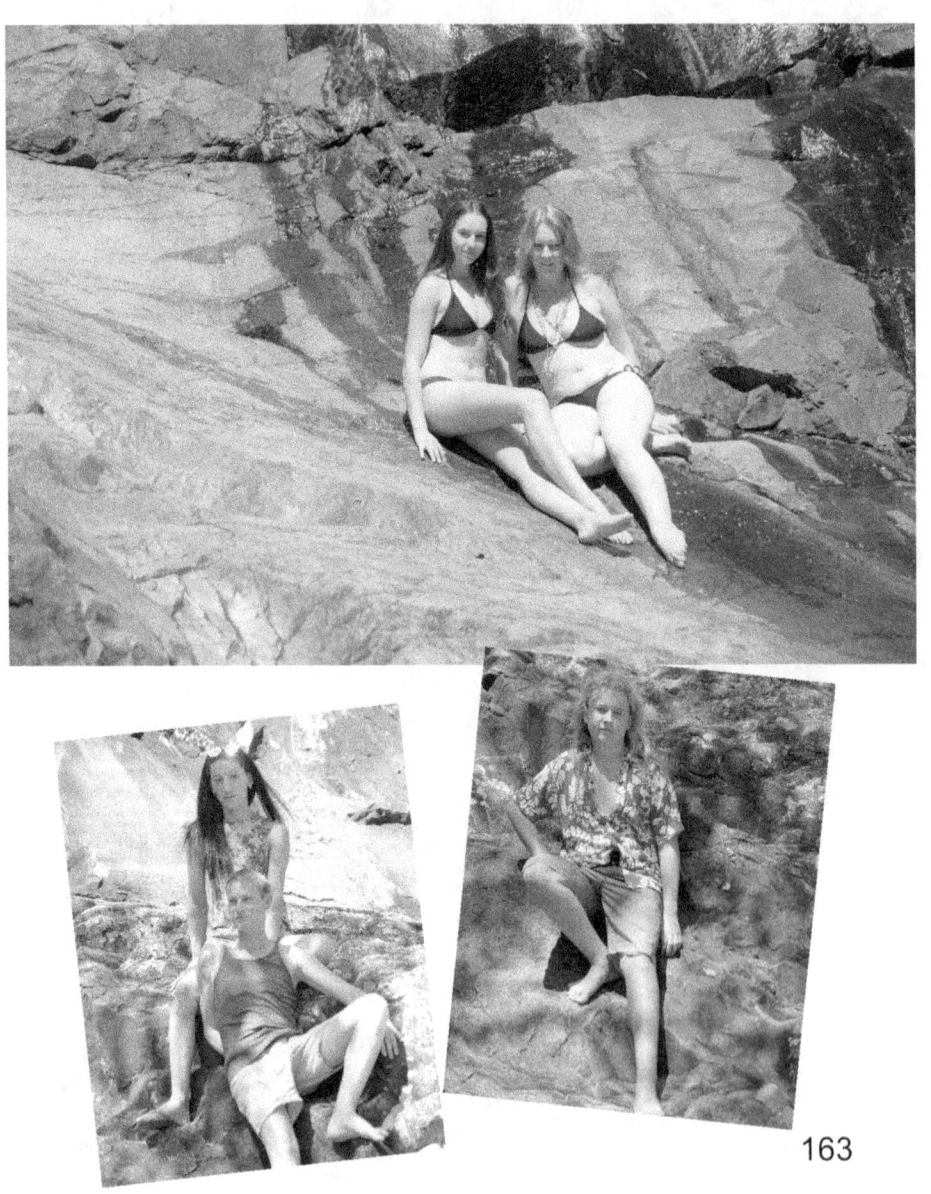

163

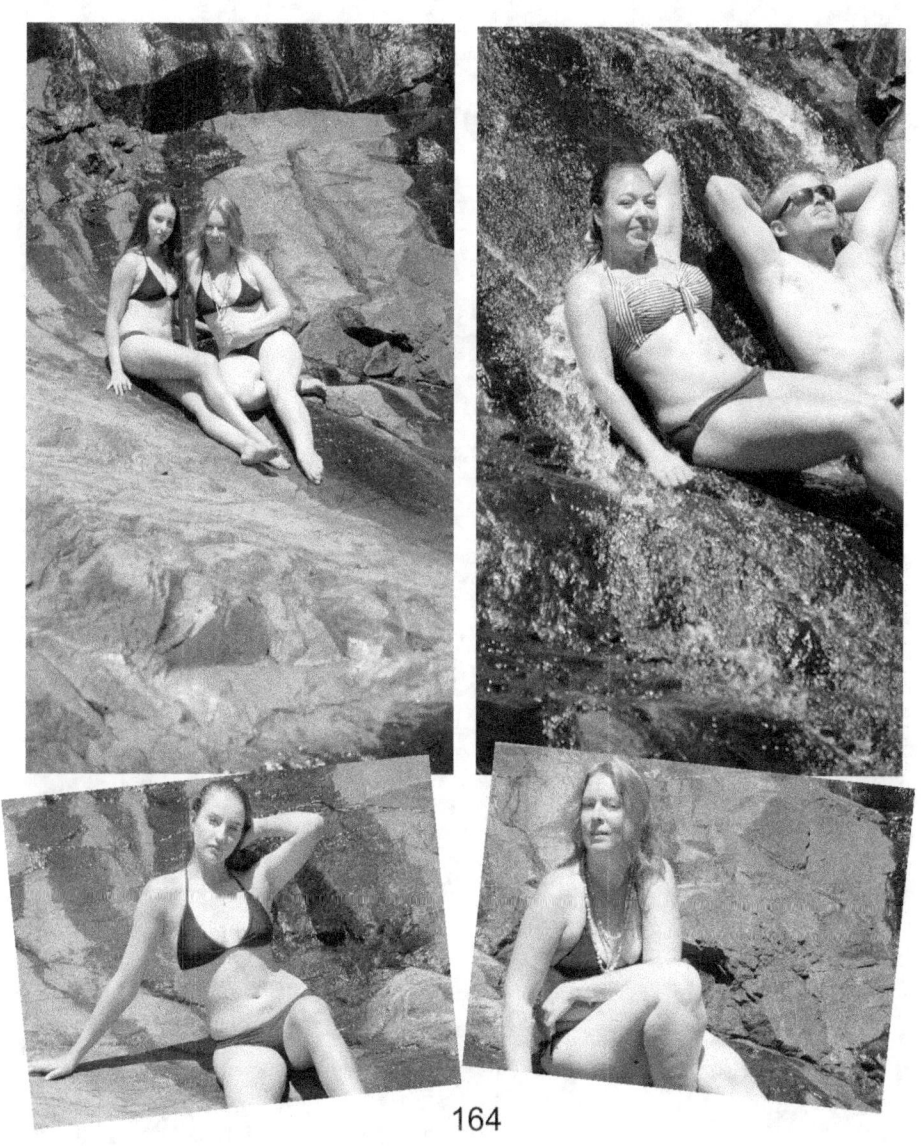

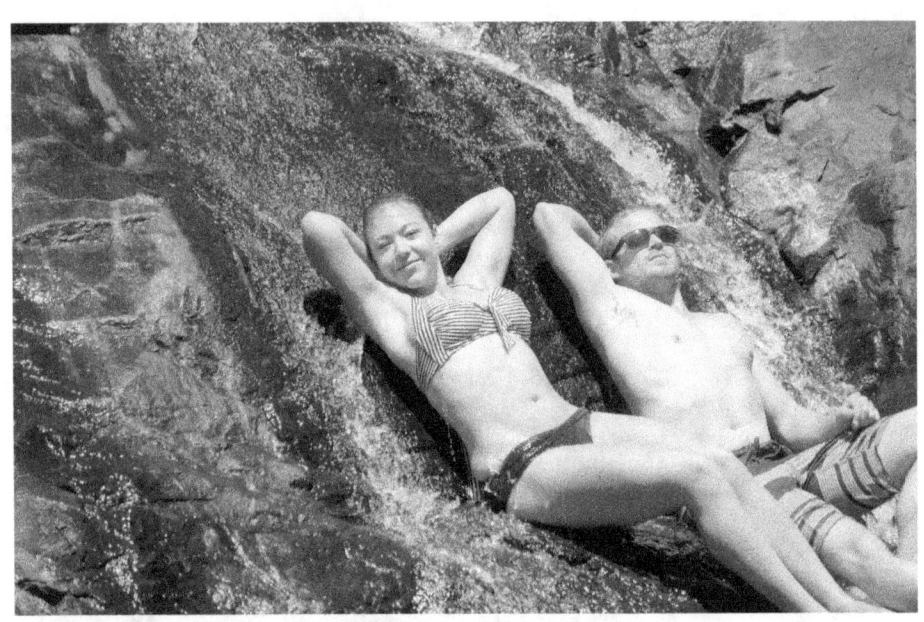

165

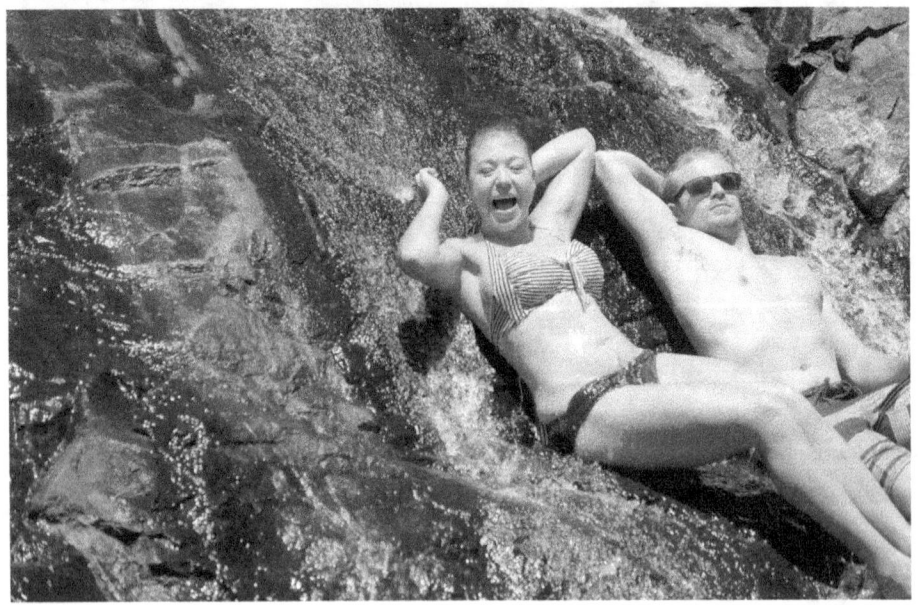

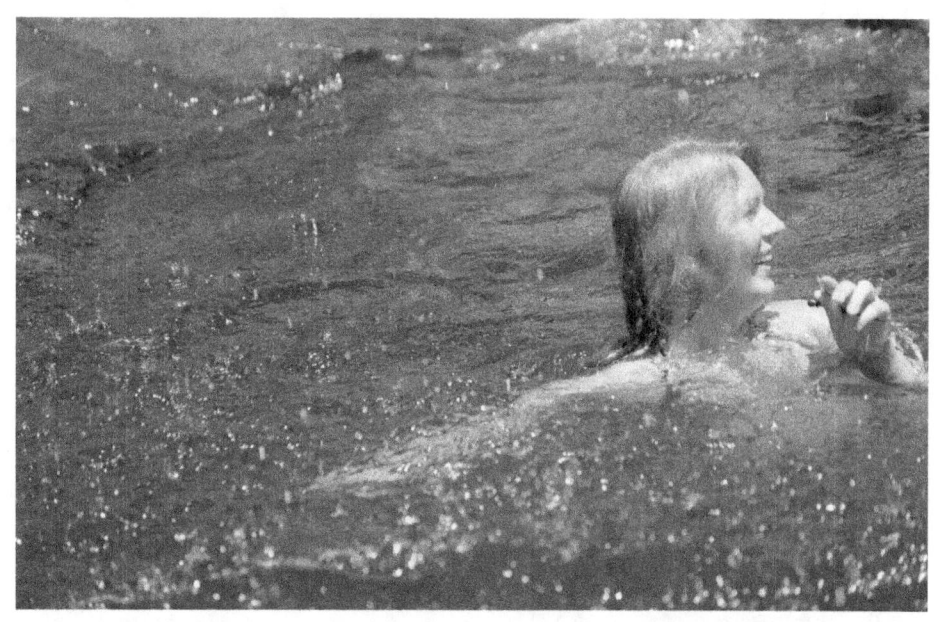

166

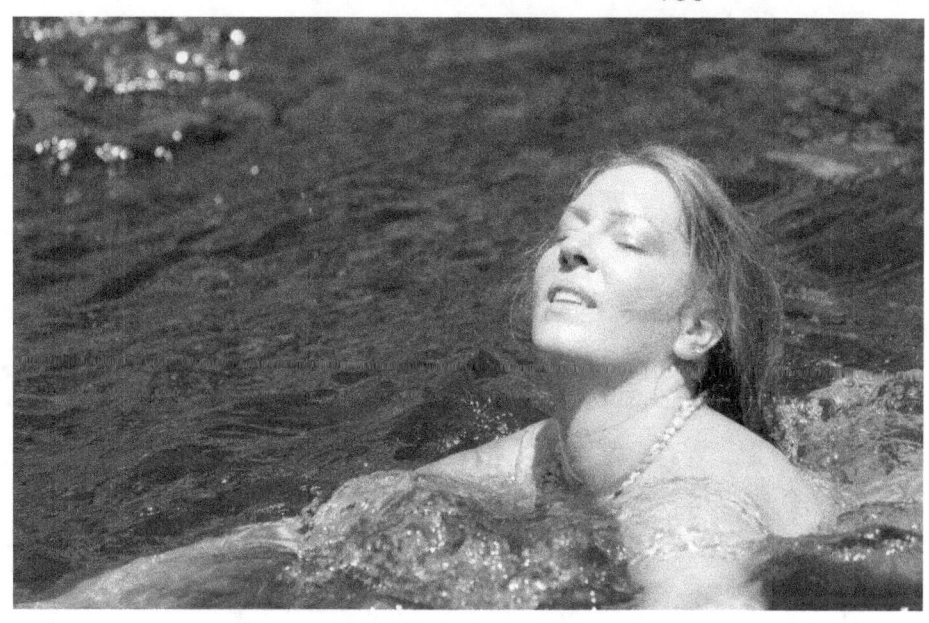

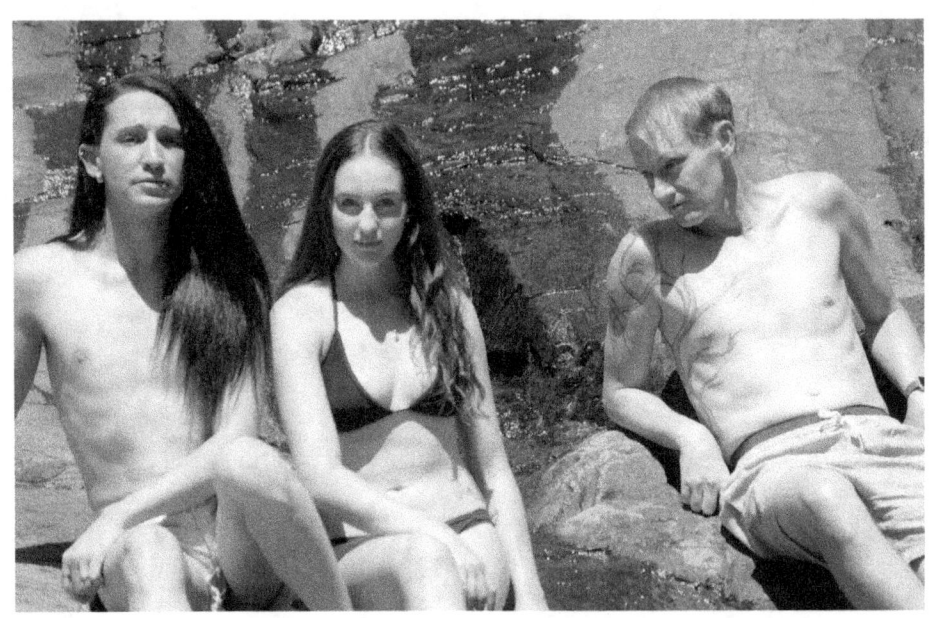

167

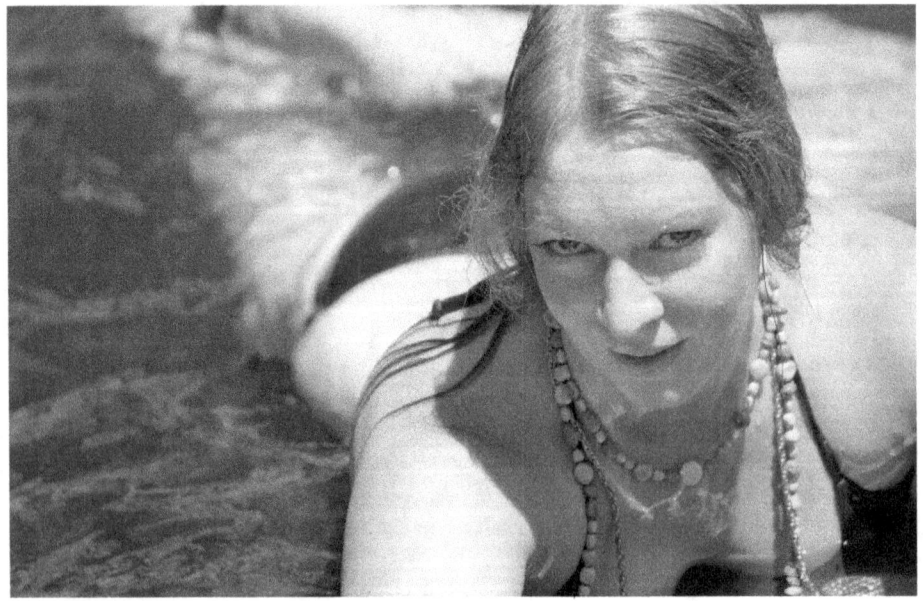

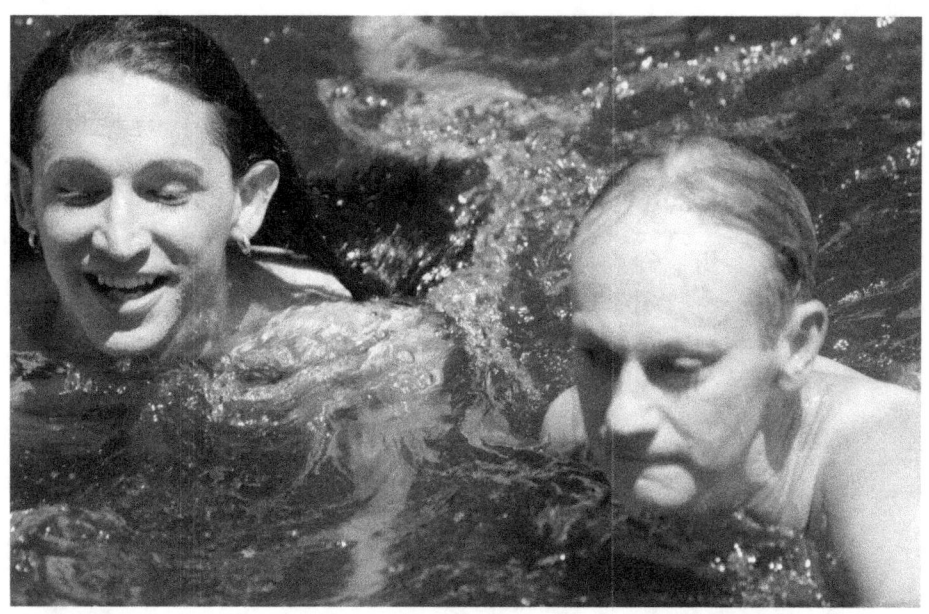

168

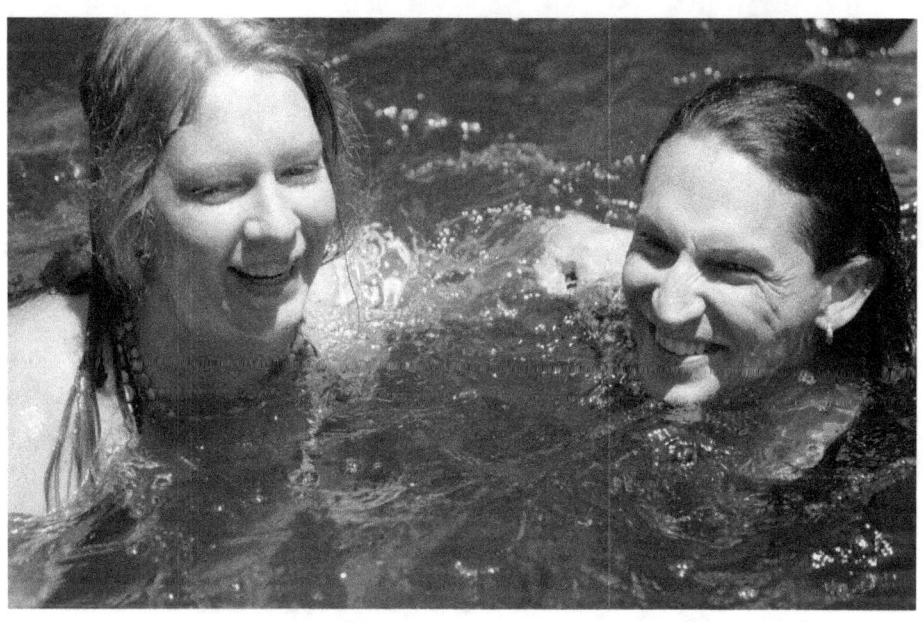

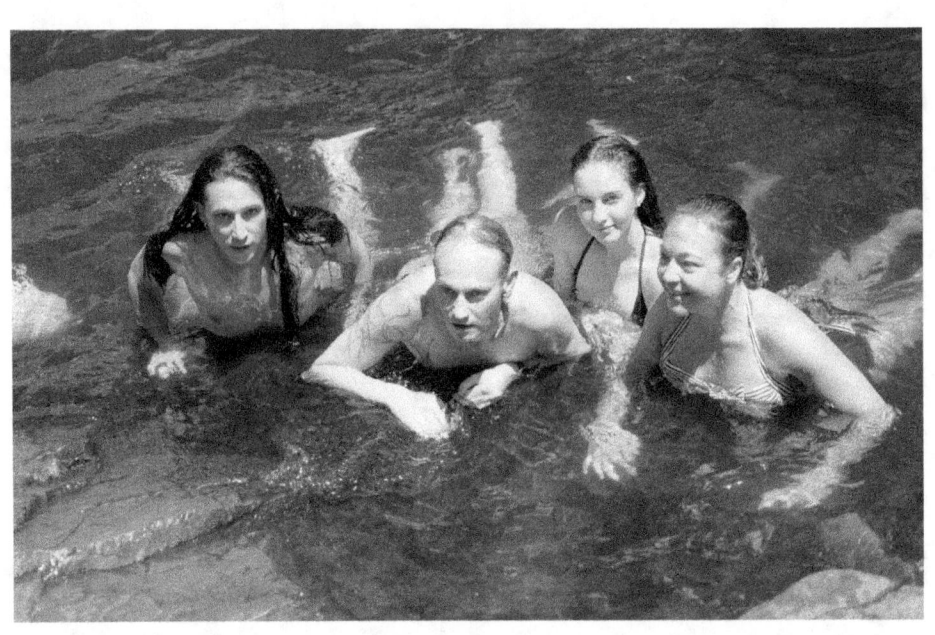

169

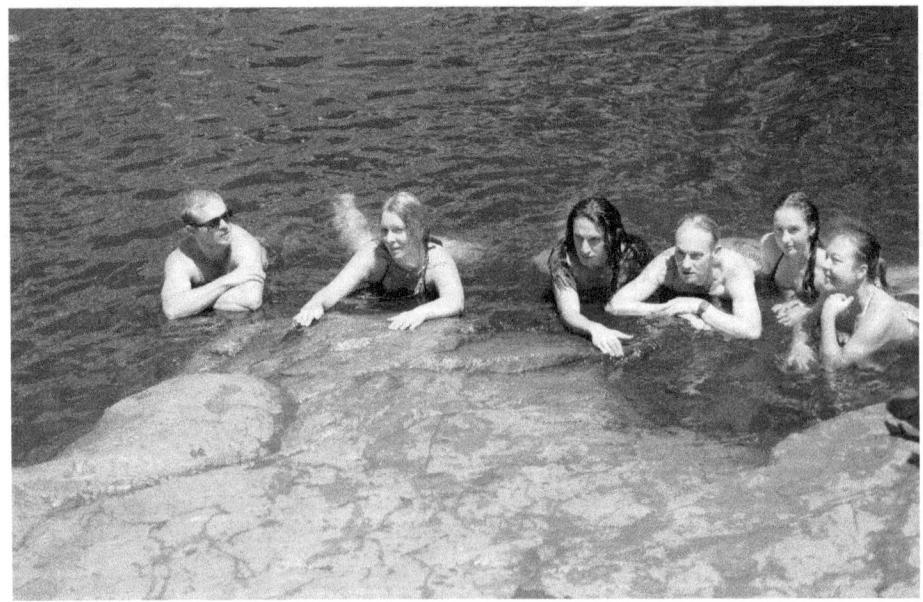

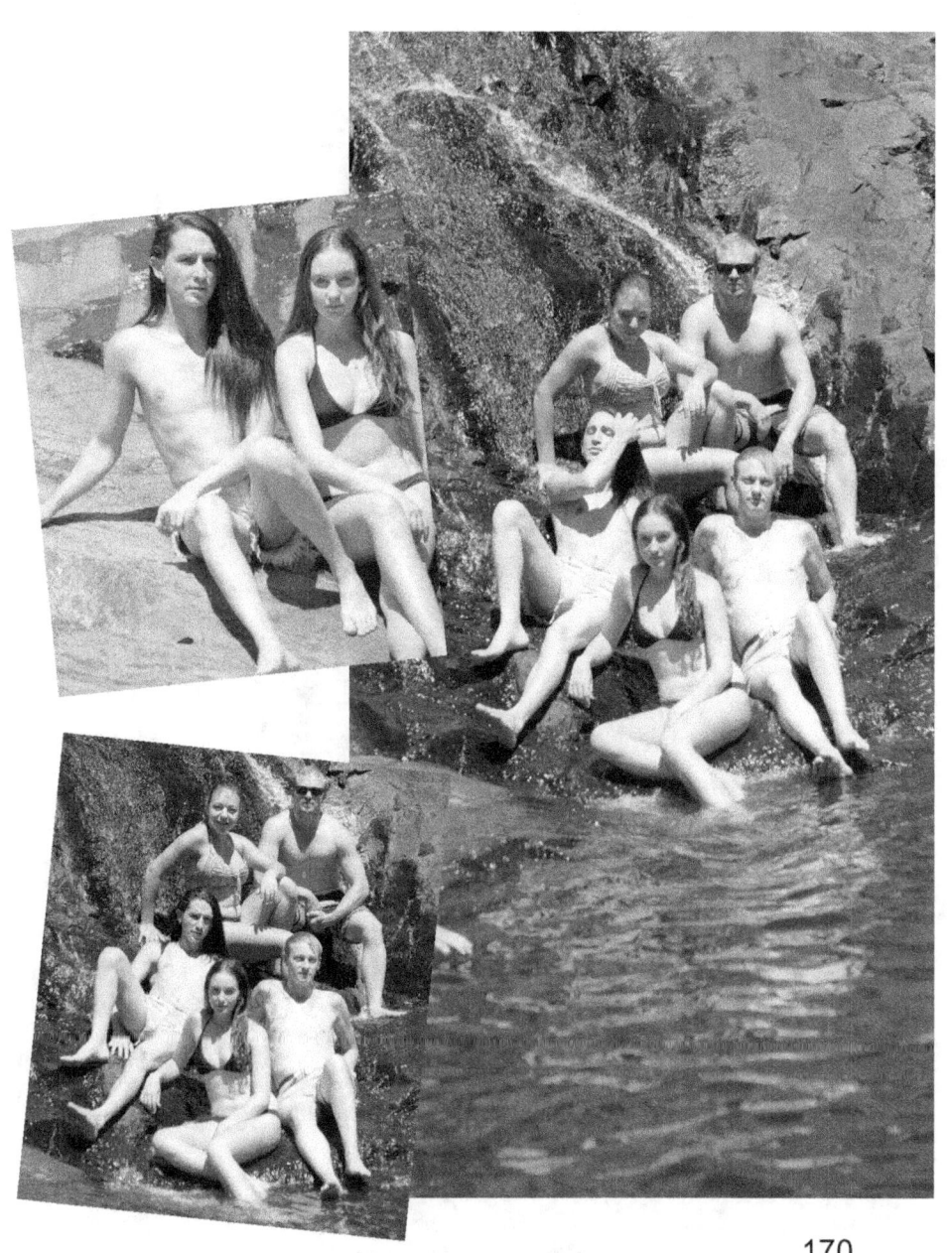

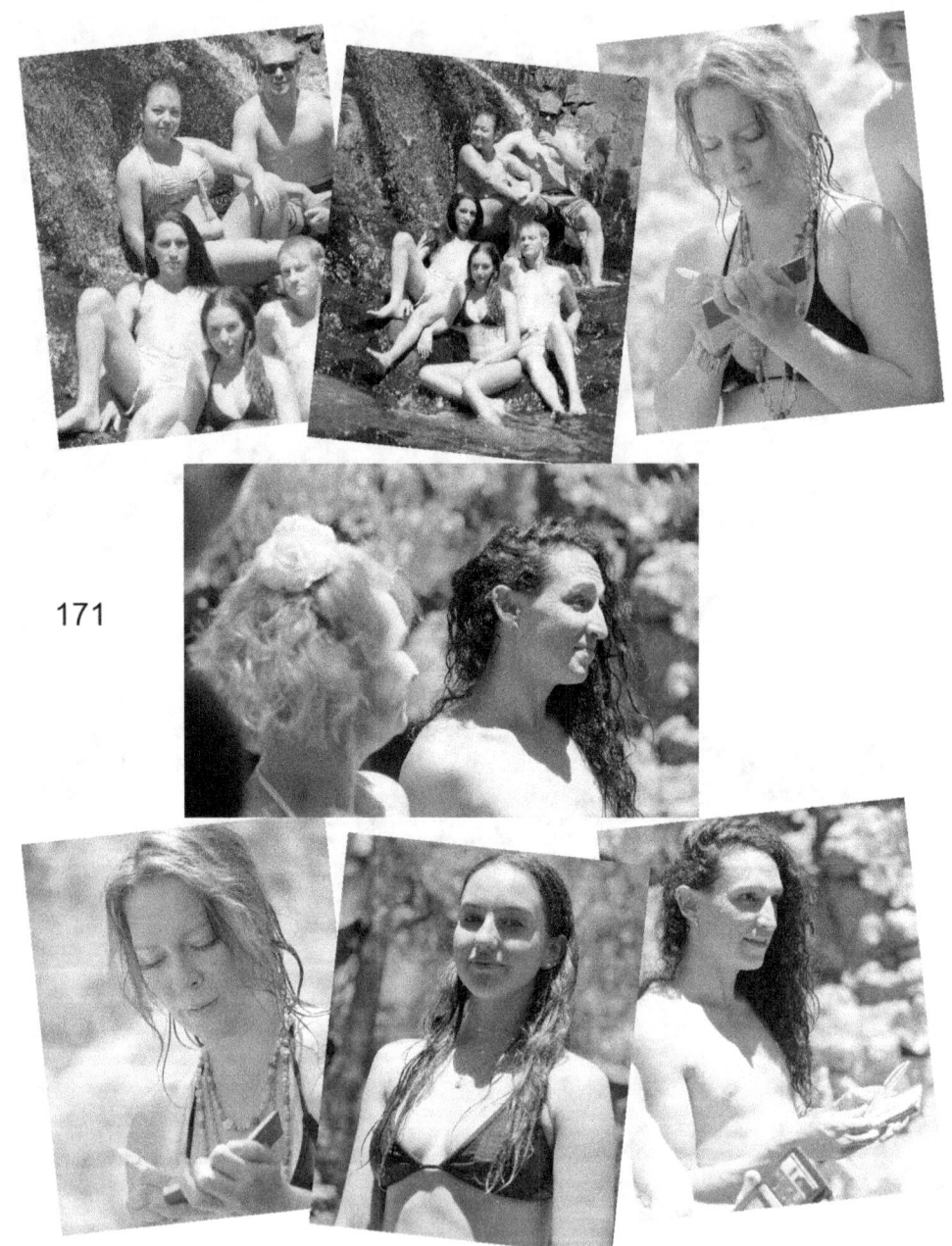

171

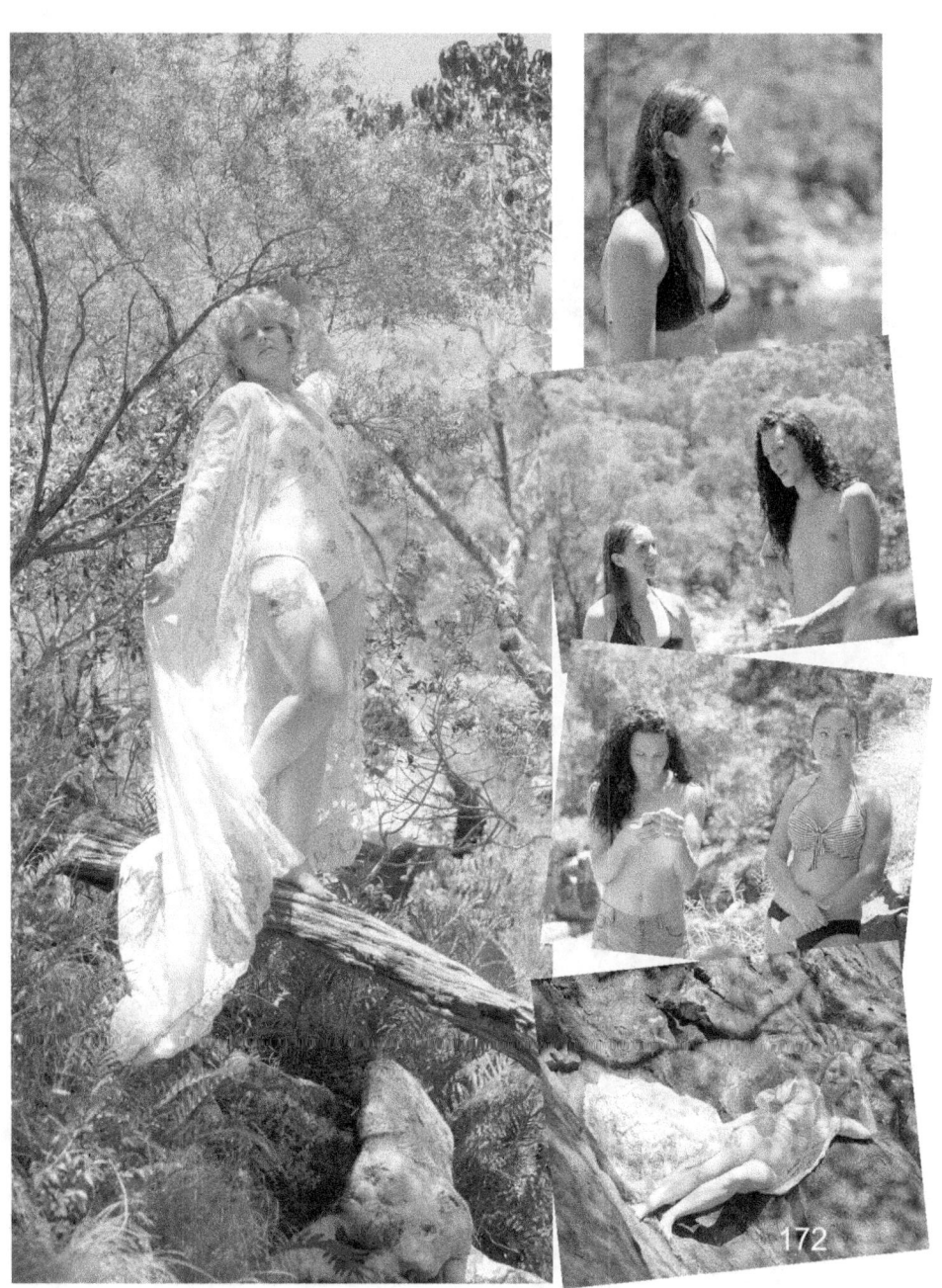

172

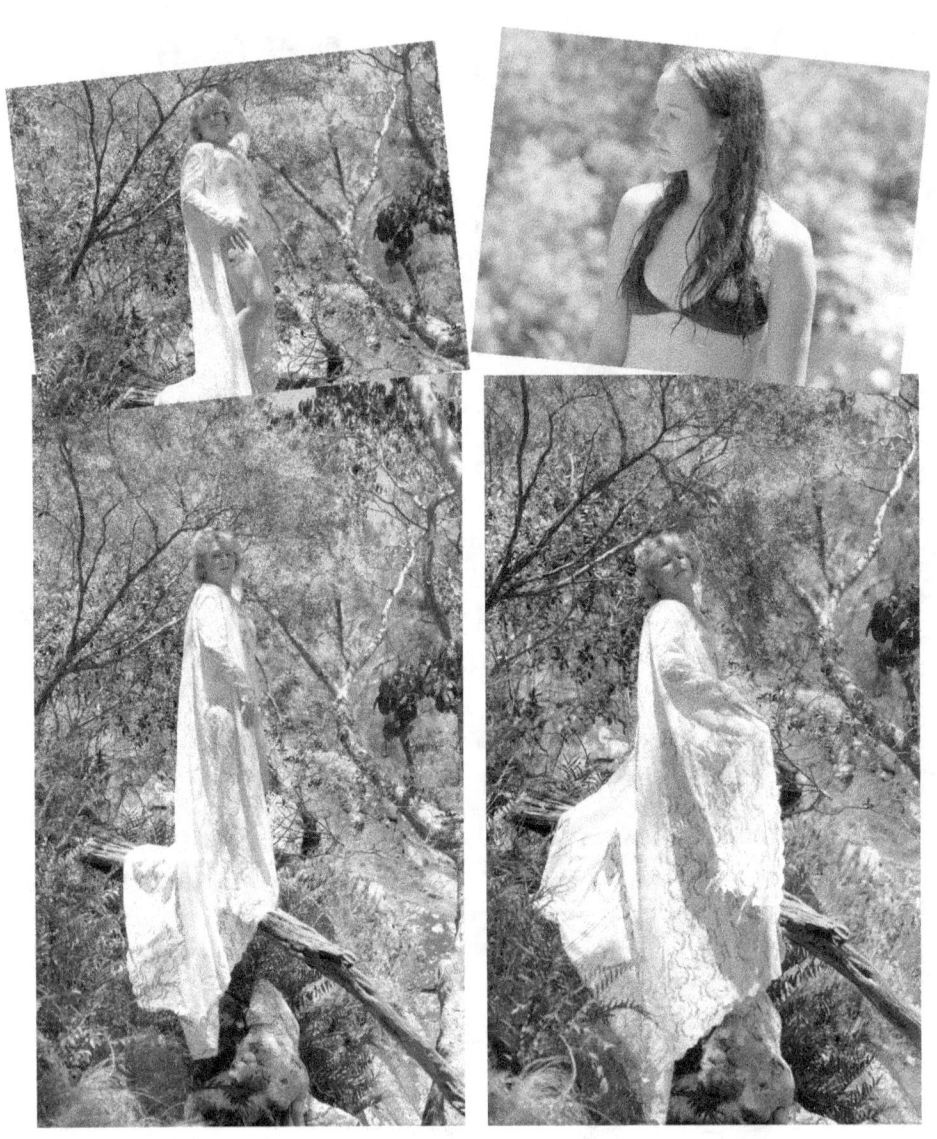

173

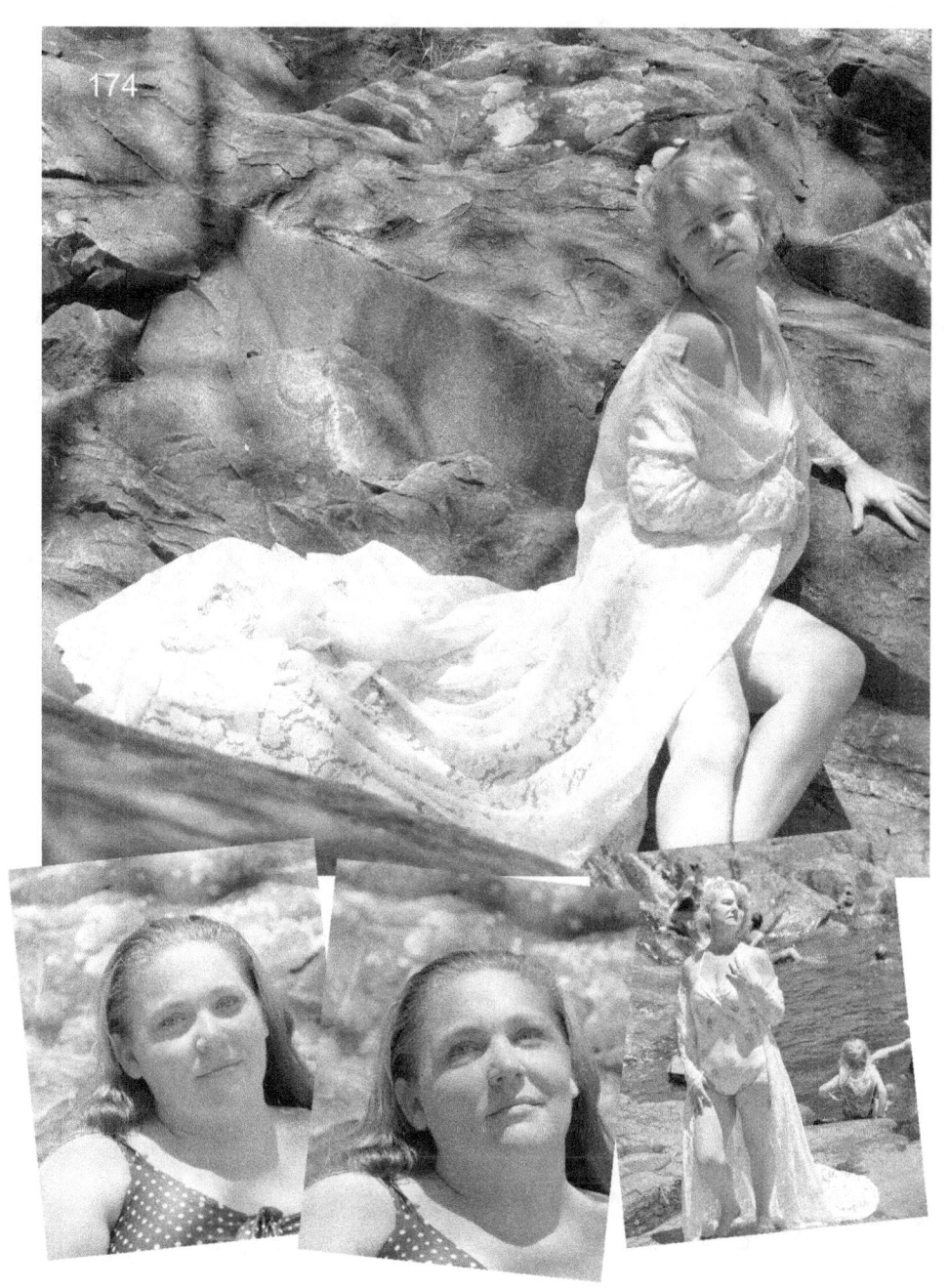

174

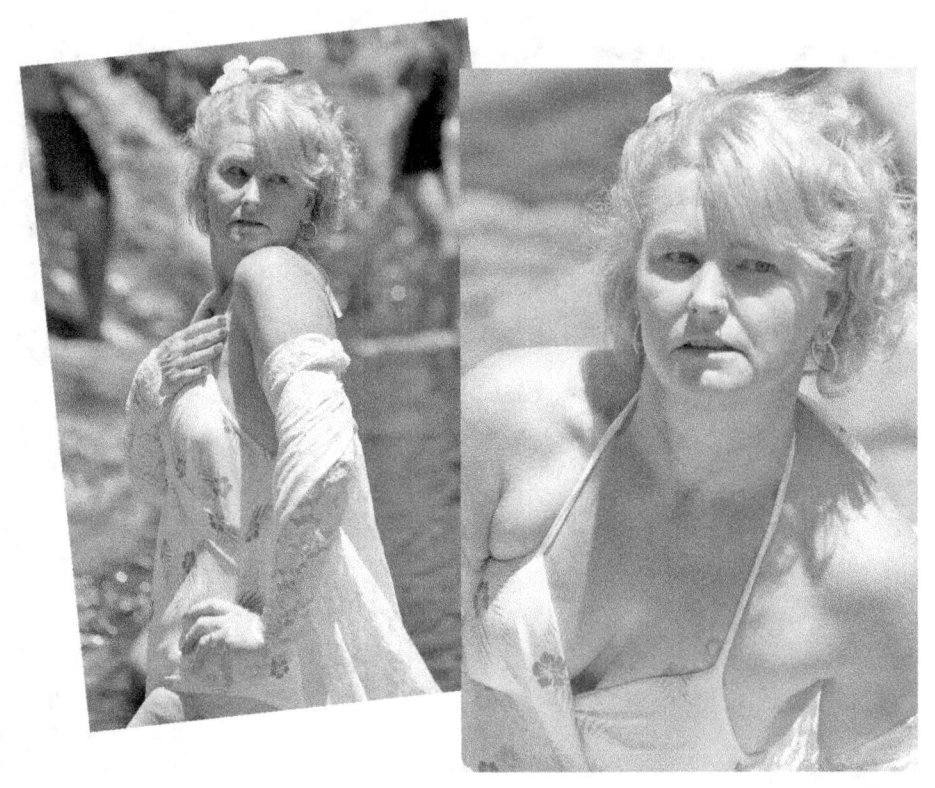

175

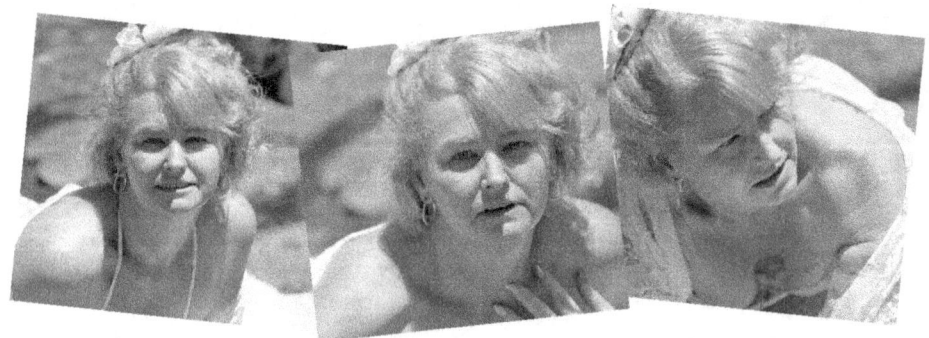

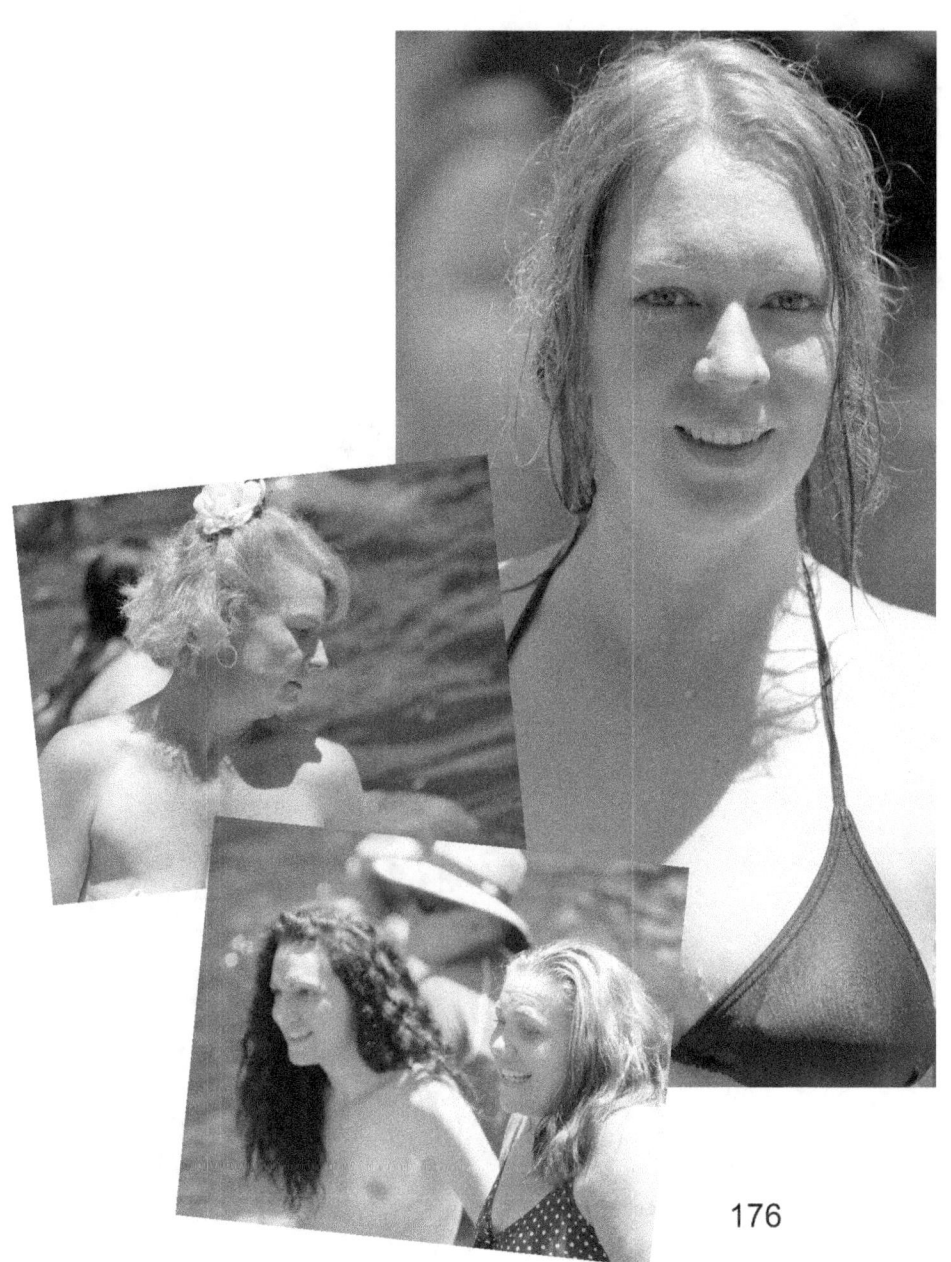

176

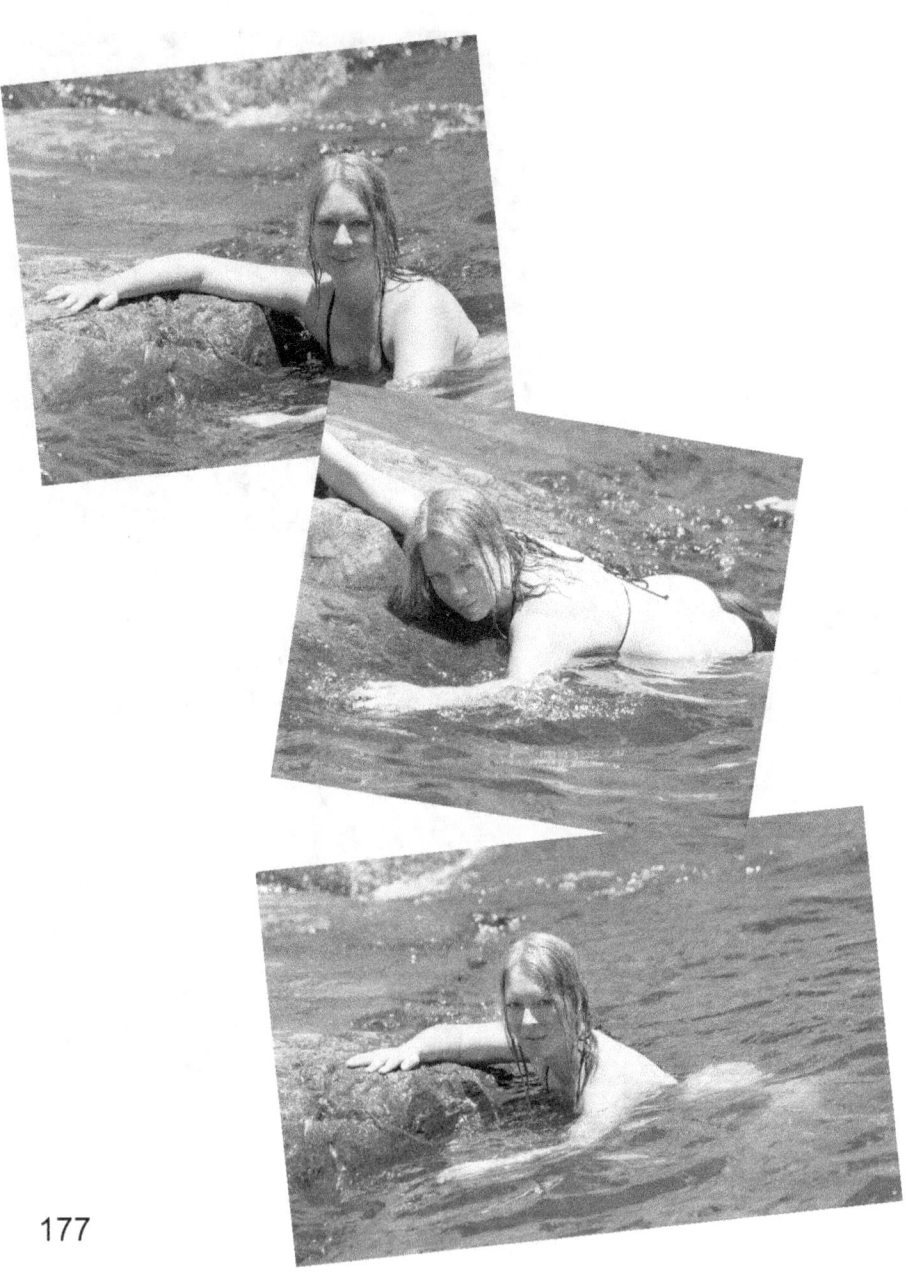

177

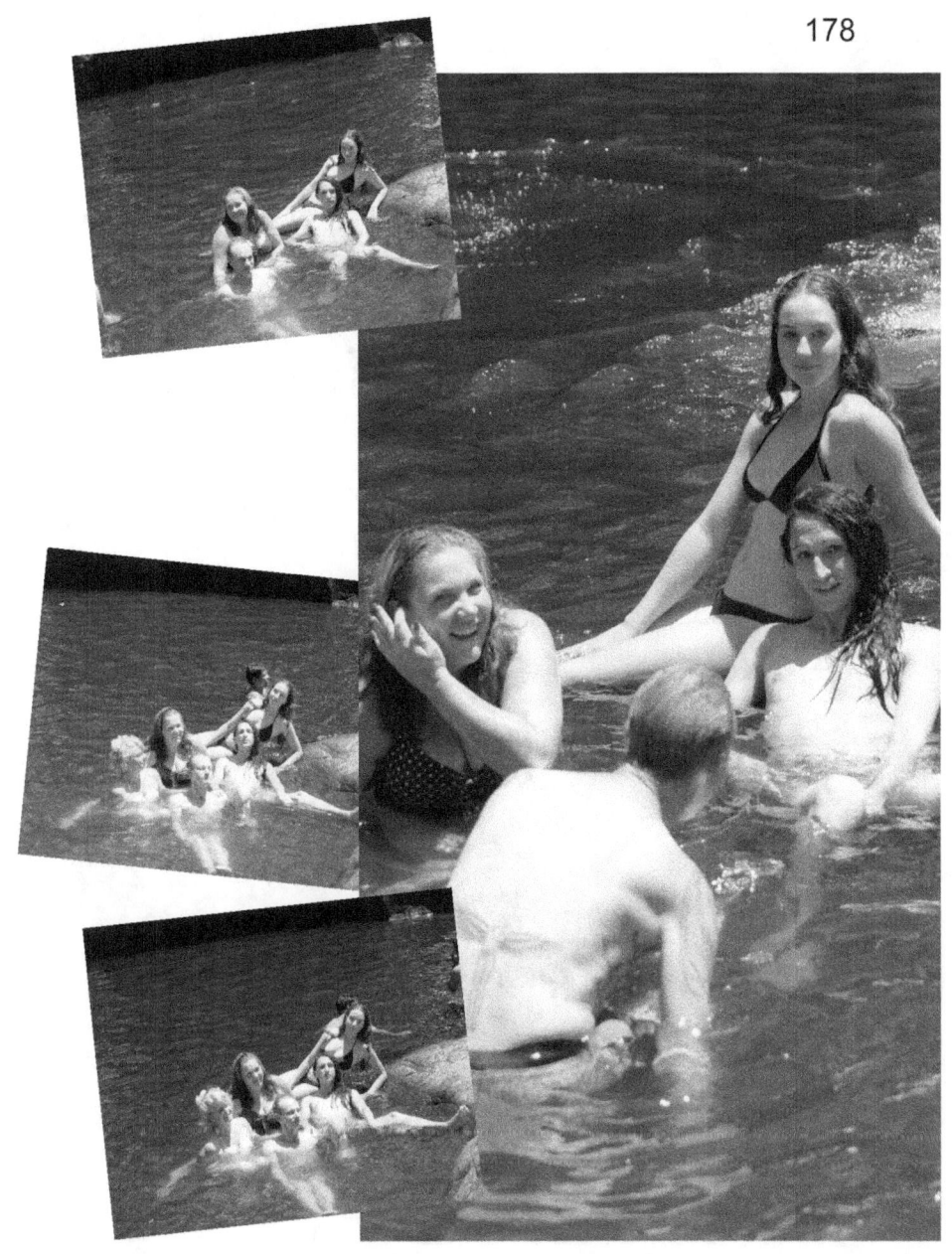

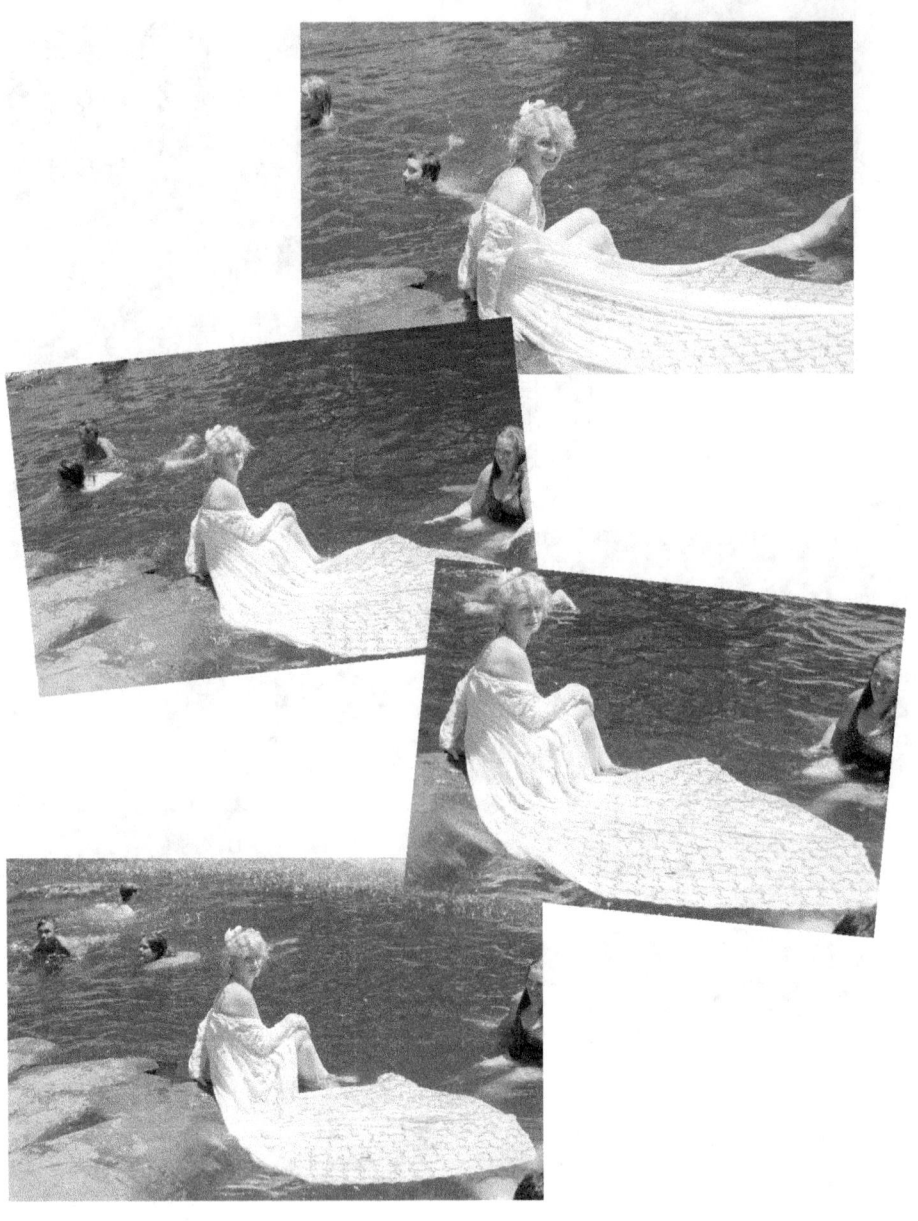

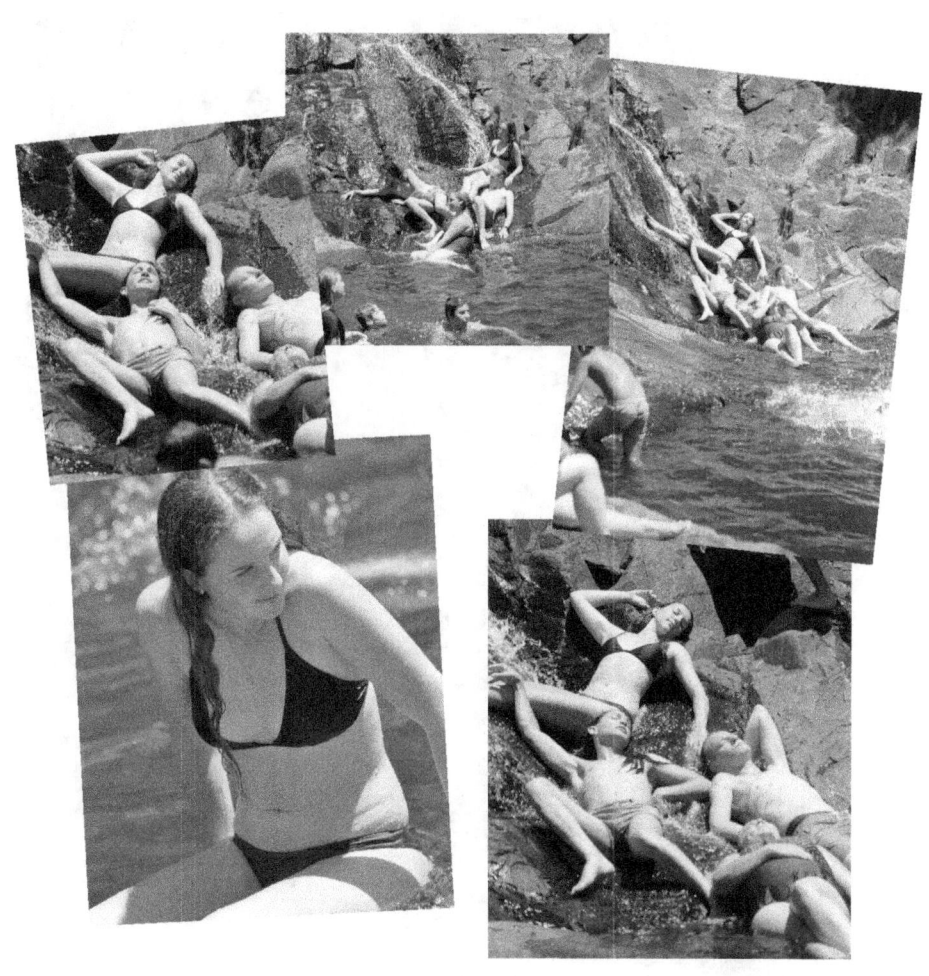

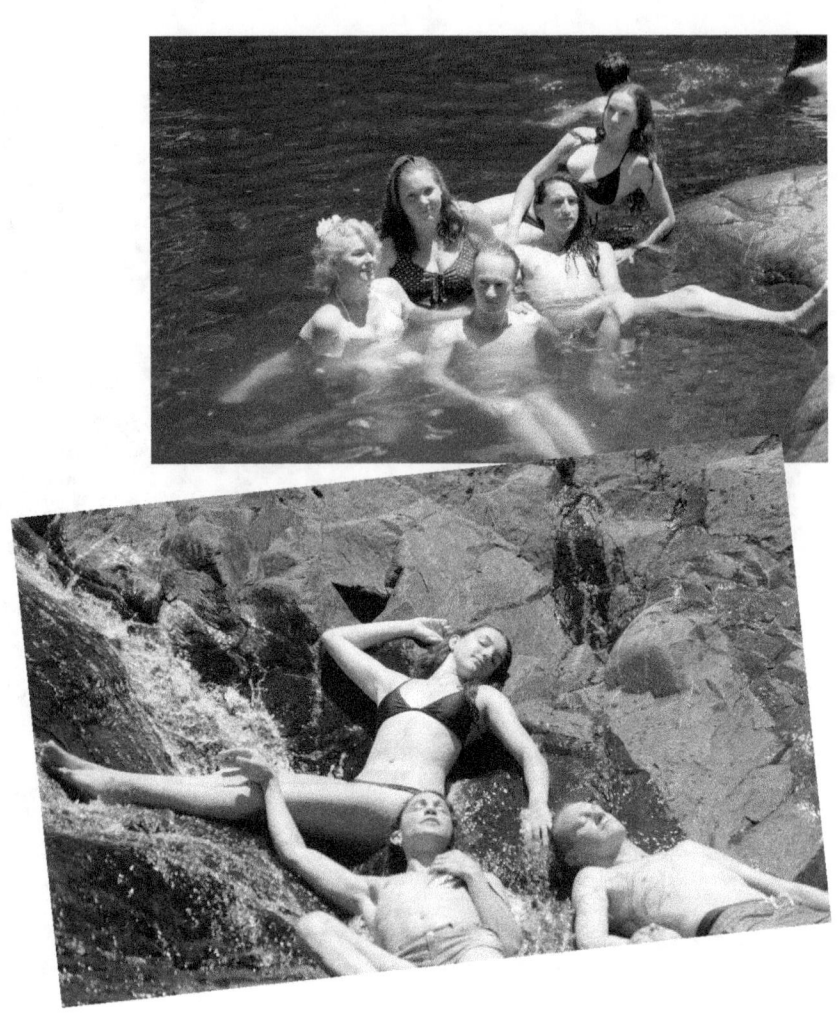

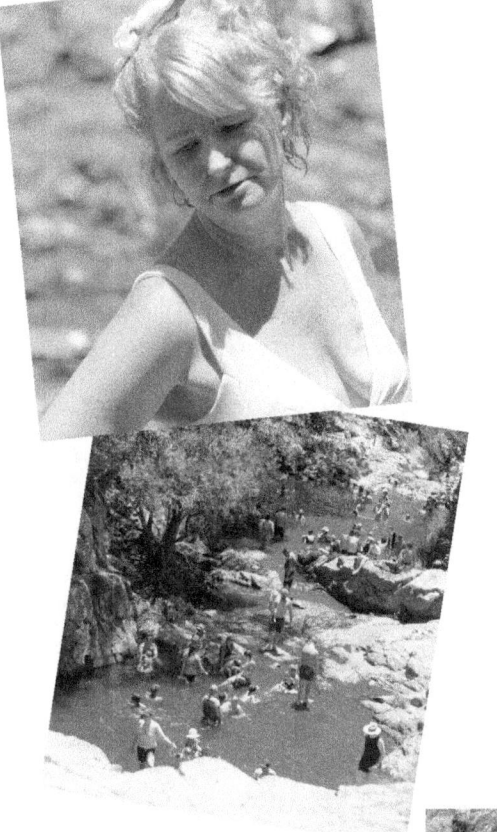

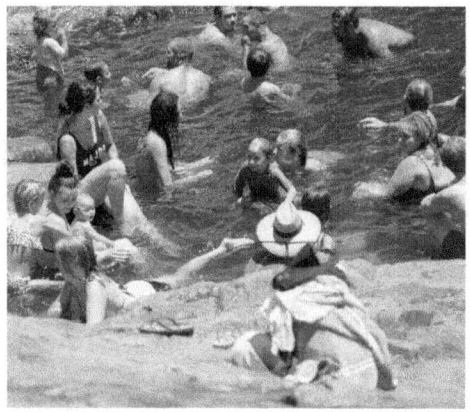

www.ingramcontent.com/pod-product-compliance
Lightning Source LLC
Chambersburg PA
CBHW080246180526
45167CB00006B/2429